Economics, Politics And Social Change In The Benue Basin, c. 1300 – 1700

A Regional Approach to Pre-Colonial West African History

By

Robert A Sargent
Associate Professor
Saint Mary's University

First Published 1999 by
Fourth Dimension Publishing Co. Ltd.
16 Fifth Avenue, City Layout, P.M.B. 01164
Enugu, Nigeria

Tel: 234-42-459969, Fax: 234-42-456904

ISBN 978-156-415-6

Illustrations by **Robin Gowen**

Fourth Dimension Publishers Co. Ltd.

Acknowledgements

I am driven to think back almost two decades to when this project was originally conceived. During those many intervening years a large number of people have been of great assistance to me and this undertaking. They all remain very special, and I hope that they are all well and looking forward to the new year with joy, health and positive anticipation.

Because this project has evolved over a long period of time it has changed and transformed numerous times. It has in the process depended on the goodwill and patience of many important people. There are, of course, individuals who provided considerable support, encouragement and intellectual, academic and personal advice. There are others who remained constant, steadfast and supportive in other ways.

These are obviously too many to thank individually. However, a few notables are worthy of special appreciation. Dr. J. B. Webster, the inspirational leader of a new generation of oral historians in Africa remains my good friend, even after I tested his considerable patience with my own unique work habits. He has provided wonderfully insightful interpretations and demanded analytical rigor while retaining his unfailing good spirits, energy and dedication. Second, I would be extremely lax if I did not thank my wife who really deserves all the credit for her good humour and outstanding example of diligence in the face of my own divergent approach to work and life. She guides me in every way.

Lastly, and perhaps of most importance I must acknowledge the contribution of the people of Nigeria, particularly those in the middle belt region. They are all very special people. I want to dedicate this project to them, and hope that somehow we can encourage more people to work with them in recording those precious memories of the past. I wish to particularly thank all those friends who gave of their time in their busy and hectic schedules to reveal their insights and knowledge of the collective memory of this quite vast and diverse community. This is their work much more than my own.

Thanks, from the bottom of my heart.

R. A. (Bob) Sargent,
Halifax,
Canada.

Table of Contents

Pages

LIST OF MAPS AND CHARTS

Chapter 1

A Regional Approach To Benue Basin History

Prior to the eighteenth century the Benue Basin was a region of considerable human diversity and natural climatic and ecological variation. Distinctions of climate, soil type, rainfall and topography were matched by an array of different social, political and economic formations. Each ethnic, linguistic, cultural, demographic, political, economic, climatic and environmental distinction added to the complexity of the region. There was, however, a sense of regional cooperation and competition that operated, not necessarily at the level of consciousness of the individual inhabitants, but certainly within their day-to-day activities in regional affairs. The ecological variations and activities of leading state and community socio-political actors thus served to operationalize regionalism in the competition for control of resources and cooperation to exploit those resources. For the historian the diversity, in all its manifestations, presents a grave challenge for the reconstruction of the past, yet an appreciation of those variations and the way they interact is vital for any construction of pre-eighteenth century regional history.

The Benue Basin included the main drainage features of the Benue, Gongola, and lower Niger river systems, covered in excess of 12,000 square kilometres, and contained three distinctive vegetation zones. To the south lay a broad forest belt with a high annual rainfall between 60 and 105 inches. The middle belt, or derived savanna, also referred to as open savanna,[1] received between 45 and 60 inches of rain per year. The northern or sudanic zone experienced as little as 20 to 45 inches of rain during two wet months.[2] These variations in climate, topography and rainfall contributed to different agricultural practices, demographics, and settlement patterns.

Crops suitable for forest zone cultivation could not be produced in the drier climate of the north, while northern crops were unsuitable for the moist soil of the south. The forest belt produced yams, cassava, kola and a variety of high moisture crops. Guinea corn and millet required dry, sunny climates and were widely grown in the derived savanna and sudanic regions. Cattle were also a prominent feature of the sudanic north and areas free from trypanosomiasis. Ecology, climate, and topography combined, therefore, to define agricultural production, carrying capacity, and demographic patterns in the three sub-regions. These agrarian distinctions provided the incentive and opportunity for regional and long distance commercial exchange of ecologically specialized goods,[3] and this trade in turn encouraged the production of agricultural surpluses. The main river and overland routes provided transportation systems which joined the diverse sub-regions in a network of regional exchange.

The Benue Basin's human population was made up of as many as 50 different ethno-linguistic populations. These different peoples were distinguished not only by language and ethnic origin, but also by religion, material culture, social organization, and political ideology. Generally speaking the forest zone contained Yoruba, Edo, Ishan, Itsekiri, Urhobo, Ijaw, Aro, and Igbo plus a number of smaller ethno-linguistic groups. The middle belt included Igbirra, Iyala, Egede, Nupe, Kede, Gwari, Afu, Goemai, Angas, Koro, Alago, Bassa, Mada, Iyala, Okpoto, Jukun, Idoma, Igbo, Etulo, Tiv, Abakwariga, Kanuri, Hausa, and Fulani. To the north there were Marghi, Kanuri, Hausa, Abakwariga, Jukun, Pabir, Bura, Tera, Shani, Chamba, Vere, Kilba, Bolewa, Birom, and Fulani.[4] The various populations in the Benue Basin were not restricted to settlement within a single zone, and northern traders settled throughout the southern forest while southern groups could be found in the middle and sudanic belts. Each ethno-linguistic population presented a variation in political culture, settlement pattern, economic activity, social organization, taste, fashion, and historical background. This variety and the interactions between different populations, coupled with the shifting economic and political conditions, ultimately defined regional affairs and regional history.

Variations in the type and size of political structures and organizations magnified the human complexity in the Benue Basin. There were acephalus societies, such as the Tiv and Igbo, which emphasized gerontocratic social and political organization.[5] Some ethnic groups were segmented in numerous small chiefdoms such as, the Idoma, Alago, Etulo, and Ishan.[6] The Angas, Jukun, Pabir and Igbirra also developed small scale chiefdoms with relatively weak central authority, but exercising power over multi-ethnic populations.[7] The Okpoto were organized in clusters of tiny chiefdoms supervised by central religious authority which shared political power with the gerontocracy of the village or lineage formation.[8] There were also city-states, such as Kano and Katsina, which had relatively large urban populations, but which controlled little territory.[9] Finally, there were larger, more powerful centralized social formations which dominated, at varying times and in varying degrees, extensive tracts of the region.

Regional history seeks, however, to transcend single state or political definitions and boundaries. In fact, Benue Basin history cannot be constructed from the examination of a single state, ethnic group, or people, no matter how detailed or comprehensive that analysis may be. Rather, regional history must be seen as a moving and often turbulent human competition for control of resources, labour, markets, and political advantage, as the various states and populations sought to establish their own relationship to the regional political and economic network. The interaction between the various states and populations created a kaleidoscope of changing regional relations, social forces, economic conditions, central place development, and shifting political authority.

By cutting across regional sub-divisions based upon ethnicity, geography, culture, language, climate or smaller state borders it is possible to develop the concept of regional history. Thus, the complexity and diversity within the region can be understood by focusing upon social formations which were central to Benue Basin regional history. Three major central-place states, Benin, Idah, and Kwararafa, reflected the sub-regional divisions, emphasized the complexity of intra-regional economic relations, and brought together the ethnically and politically divided population in the connective tissue of regional political, social and economic affairs. Commercial growth in one centre, for example, dictated production patterns in neighbouring regions, contributed to imperial expansion in support of trade, and consequently altered political and social institutions across the entire region. At another level individual ethnic groups had to choose between migration and assimilation, or perhaps between cultural emasculation and adaptation as the focal states and various other polities expanded and contracted in the shifting set of regional interactions. Central states, therefore, provided an appropriate sample of the principal social, political, and economic formations, and serve as suitable reflections of Benue Basin history between 1300 and 1700.

Yet if the focal states provide the historian with the best prism through which to view regional history, they are not in themselves the totality of that history They reflect and represent change across the region, but do not provide the only manifestation of it. They are the historian's tool, not his product. Focal states were as much affected by developments within the region as they were prime movers; indeed the two processes are frequently impossible to distinguish. It is possible, therefore, to identify a unity in the Niger-Benue past that transcends the rise and fall of an single polity, or the socio-economic and political isolation of individual groups or states. That unity is manifested in a number of different ways. At one level we can point to common political cultures, shared religious systems, ethnic intermixture as a result of migration and re-settlement, and an integrated regional commercial network, all of which down play the importance of state borders, linguistic divisions, and cultural differences. At another level unity in the Benue Basin can be seen in the vulnerability of all social formations to larger, external events, such as climatic change, and the region-wide response to those forces. Most importantly, unity existed, not as a regional consciousness, but simply because of the interdependence of the various communities in the network of social, political and economic interaction. Therefore, the Benue Basin can be viewed as a regional agglomeration of peoples, not a collection of isolated and unrelated ethnic groups, interacting across the wide spectrum of time and place in a shifting process of competition and cooperation.

Significantly, the region witnessed the growth of large imperial formations which came to dominate vast territorial acquisitions and incorporate huge multi-ethnic populations. These highly centralized polities were administered by an hereditary ruling elite, which established dynastic control over social, political and economic affairs, and, in some cases, dominated sub-regional politics for many centuries. Benin, Idah and Kwararafa were representative of this type of social formation and, at various stages in the history of the region, encompassed virtually every political, ethnic, linguistic and economic variation.[10]

Political unity across the region should not be seen as an all encompassing solidarity of political ideology and purpose. Rather the unity is evident through both the genealogically related dynasties and the association of states in a fairly coordinated administrative structure. Genealogical links existed, at one time or another, between Benin, Idah, Warri, Lagos and Nupe, while Idah was itself also related to Keana, and at different times had links to Onitsha Oturkpo, Osomari, Panda and Kwararafa. Kwararafa was related to the dynasties at Keana and Doma, Wuse and Wukari. Bui and Borno. Moreover, the states of Ondo, Akure, Owo, Ishan, Dampar and Keana, although not all directly related to Benin, adopted features of Bini political culture and thus perpetuated another level of regional political unity through adopted administrative systems, material culture and socio-economic patterns. At a different time Kwararafan political ideology spread throughout the region and was adopted and adapted in a variety of distinct social formations. Thus, a political commonality existed in the Benue

Basin based, in part, upon shared political experiences, economic interests and kinship.

The development of the informal Niger alliance perhaps best illustrates the efficacy of political association in this region: genealogical links and a common Bini heritage fostered economic interaction and commercial exchange between the trading states along the river. An interactive commercial network was thus established between Nupe, Idah, Onitsha, Aboh and Warri that sought to control riverine trade. Extensive and extended regional relations between states were thus a common, indeed a constant, feature of regional politics.

Economic organizations in the Benue Basin, therefore, contributed to regional unity, and ranged from the highly developed, commercially oriented enclaves and trading states to relatively small agrarian lineage or village formations. Agriculture was the economic base for the majority of the population, regardless of the size, type and focus of the particular social formation, and farmers not only worked for their own reproduction, but had also to service the non-agricultural populations working in commercial, semi-industrial or administrative sectors of the economy.

Agricultural labour also serviced the primary and secondary exchange cycle which occupied the commercially oriented enclaves, and provided commodities, such as yams, cattle, beans, fish, and millet, to maintain commercial exchange. Trade, therefore benefitted from agricultural specialization, regional variations, and the farmers labour. Much of the surplus labour, food, and special agricultural production was appropriated by the state, but the type of political and economic structures in a particular social formation did not necessarily preclude penetration of the commercial sphere by agriculturalists, and farmers themselves became entrepreneurs in the local, regional and long distance exchange networks.

Economic activities in the Benue Basin, in some instances at least, were organized to monopolize and exploit a single natural resource, such as salt, iron, or ivory. These monopolies called upon the resources of the agricultural sector to provide the basic food needs of the industrial complex, but derived their principal revenue from the production and distribution of the single commodity. The production of salt in Keana and Awe created commercial opportunities and provided a mechanism to expand local, regional and long distance trade. Keana and Awe thus emerged as major trading centres based upon the exploitation of salt.[11] Surplus agricultural production by neighbouring farm communities could be sold in the markets of the salt producing city-state or town, which allowed the farmer access to the regional exchange network.[12] The same principle applied to cloth and iron production specialists who manufactured and distributed their wares across the region from a fairly early period. Food could be sold to the salt, iron and cloth workers and to long distance traders attracted to the specialized markets and exchange opportunities. This suggests that craft monopolization and specialization could, in itself, promote exchange and expand the boundaries of local, regional and long distance commerce.

Other monopolies operated in the regional transportation network and service industries. Riverine transportation experts, overland porters, rest stations operators, and food and supply services formed the infrastructure of regional and long distance exchange. Through this operational net Idah ivory could be sold in Benin markets, Awe salt sold in Kano markets, and Awka iron distributed throughout the region. Certain social formations concentrated on trade for their principle source of revenue, and encouraged the organization and distribution of primary and secondary production to take advantage of existing regional demands, and trade routes. By its location, therefore, a particular state might benefit from the service to; and administration of, regional and long distance commerce. The position of Idah, at the cross roads of the Niger-Benue trading network, provided a natural advantage and contributed to the foundation of a distribution monopoly in riverine trade.[13] The administration in Idah not only provided security for local traders in the Niger-Benue system, but also taxed riverine commerce to provide state revenue. Each social formation, large or small, had a discernable economic role and could, through various mechanisms, integrate with the regional economic network. Economic advantage, however, lay with the three focal states of Benin, Idah and Kwararafa as they combined administrative skills, commercial expertise, craft and industrial production, and political power with the distribution of various ecologically specialized goods.

The exchange of primary and secondary goods established the basis of regional complement and competition. The volume of trade and profit, and the mechanisms for extracting economic returns, created friction between competing commercial enclaves. Trade set the stage for political tensions and occasional outbreaks of violence as states sought to define and redefine their relationship to the fluctuating regional economy. It also necessitated social and political interaction and complementary exchange, and could thus transcend the political and economic rivalry. Competition and complement were integral to regional relations, and commercial advantage often defined the policy and ideology of a particular social formation at a particular time.

During the 1300-1700 period the focus of the Benue Basin trade shifted from the northern desert economy to the southern forest and coastal system.[14] Prior to 1500 even Benin in the forest zone was pre-occupied with northern commerce, and expanded the boundaries of the state to take greater advantage of north-south commercial opportunities. After 1500 Benin shifted its focus to the southern coastal trade, and sought to consolidate coastal trade opportunities through the acquisition of Lagos, Mahin and Warri, and thus link northern with southern trade.[15] In the middle belt the change toward southern commerce did not occur until after 1591 and the collapse of the Songhai *pax* which had been so instrumental in developing the trans-Saharan trade network. By 1700 even Kano, Bornu and Kwararafa were turning their attention to the south and their indirect connections with Atlantic coastal trade.

The continued success of intra-regional and international trade did not depend solely on internal and external market forces: economic conditions in any one social formation relied on the ability of the state to develop its resources and to meet the challenge of changing conditions and commercial relations. The three focal states of Benin, Idah and Kwararafa were particularly effective in adapting to meet altered economic circumstances, and employed a variety of techniques to ensure their continued operation within the regional and international economy. Therefore, the economic history of the Benue Basin cannot be divorced from its political and social context. The imposition of superior might by one social formation, and the resulting acquisition of resources, labour, and territory, not only affected the stability of governments, but also altered the wealth, status, and position of the individuals and communities involved. The conquest by Benin of cotton growing territory around Akure, for example, served to consolidate the economic base of the imperial power while undermining the Akure cotton industry. Akure cotton, facilitated the development of the Benin cloth industry and fostered the expansion of cloth production for export, while the weaving and dyeing crafts in Akure were significantly reduced. Thus one of the main themes in this reconstruction of regional history is the social consequences of political and economic decisions in each of the focal states on the region as a whole.

There is within this regional analysis a sense of struggle between groups, states and populations, which connected the various polities and ethnic groups in the turmoil of commercial competition The seizure of a cotton growing area by an expanding imperial power cannot be seen as an isolated, random event operating outside regional economic and political pressures. Each such event should be seen in the context of regional forces, and must be related to the struggle between distinct populations and polities for control of commerce, resources, labour and markets.

The status of a particular state and its ability to control economic conditions depended upon the geo-political association between various competing social formations. A small state might easily succumb to a larger aggressive neighbour and thus disappear from the political geography of the region. In this sense the Benue Basin was not a static region in which states continued to reproduce and populations continued to maintain separate identities. New states and ethnic groups were created while old social formations were absorbed in the constantly shifting and changing mosaic of regional interactions. Idah, for example, could not compete with the powerful state of Benin but could carve out important commercial and political spheres of influence against weaker neighbours. The power of a state was thus defined by relations with neighbouring states, and the opportunities to exploit resources and commercial advantages. States expanded and contracted, political influences increased and decreased, trade routes shifted or closed, populations moved or were assimilated, and market forces altered or changed, in an ever shifting kaleidoscope of regional relations. In this respect the actions of complement and competition imposed change on the central place states; in their turn the states adapted policies in an effort to maximize economic resources and political authority. The relationship of an individual state to regional developments could define the ability of that social formation to reproduce as an effective social and political institution regardless of process and rate of change in its geo-political associations.

Unity in the Benue Basin can also be seen in the social relations and interactions between various segments of the diverse and highly mobile population. Enclaves of merchants and specialists settled throughout the region, regardless of political affiliations or ethnic origins. Bini trading colonies were established along the upper Benue, Idah weavers and dyers operated far beyond the confines of their homeland, Jukun entrepreneurs were settled in Pindiga, on the Jos plateau, and as far south as Calabar, and Awka iron producers travelled and settled across much of the region. This mobility provided for an increase in the social relations, and an intermixture of peoples from diverse origins. It is not surprising, therefore, that intermarriage became a common mechanism whereby an individual entrepreneur could penetrate an alien market and establish legitimacy in business relations in a distinctive population. Through the continuing process of migration, association and intermarriage many of the dispersed settlements were absorbed by the host population. It is difficult to find a single ethno-linguistic population that does not contain trace elements of other cultures and ethnic groups. It is even more difficult to find a population in the Benue Basin that has not been affected, politically, economically or socially, by other Benue Basin peoples or states.

Another regional theme in this analysis is the relationship between economic change and the adaptations in administrative ideology and social institutions. Religion, for example, was used not only as a mechanism for social control, but as a technique for the management of markets, traders and commercial transactions.[17] As conditions of trade changed the utility of a particular religious institution, such as Olokun, Ifa, Tchibiri, Islam or Christianity, could be enhanced, reduced or destroyed. The government of a particular social formation might, therefore, impose changes on the state controlled religious institutions to more effectively dominate commercial operations.

Political, social and ethnic linkages contributed to the organization of integrated trading networks which, in turn, fostered greater intra-regional connections. Thus, the entire Benue Basin became part of and dependent upon the maintenance of those economic and commercial links. Demands for ecologically specialized products provided regional commercial incentives, and trade progressed with relative ease through the set of inter-related or linked communities in the region. Productivity was maintained, market forces were translated into production incentives, and local, regional and long distance exchange became significant factors in the life of virtually every individual in the region. In some way or other every individual was directly or indirectly involved in commercial activities. Many women were actively involved in commercial production and, in some cases dominated local markets and specialized niches within the economy. Children tended crops, assisted with the harvest, and became apprentices to the region's craftsmen and artisans. Men were engaged in craft production, agriculture, and regional and long distance trade. Goods were produced, exchanged and transported throughout the region, often supported by the policies of the political leadership in the states.

Political and economic change seen through the actions of powerful state rulers who reacted to commercial opportunities and organized production and administration accordingly, represents only one aspect of change. At another level the organizations of social institutions also reflected the changing economic circumstances. The adaptation of gerontocratic organizations, such as the Otu system of Benin, was a response to economic pressures.[18] As state policy developed the impact was felt in the organizations at the village, lineage and individual level of the society. In this way we see the relationship between central place administration, non-secular authority, and the commoner population which performed the bulk of the manual labour and produced the various goods necessary for the production of society and state.

The significance of the overall regional approach to Benue Basin history is illustrated by the relations between the focal states of Benin, Idah and Kwararafa. The three focal states each fell largely within a particular, climatically defined, zone of the Benue Basin, and this geo-political separation reflected the major ecological variations in the region. Benin fell within the southern forest zone, Idah represented the derived savanna of the middle belt, and Kwararafa was a northern sudanic state. These three social formations were linked to the basic connective tissue of regional political, social, cultural, linguistic and economic relations, and as major trading formations were connected, directly or indirectly, to the economies of virtually every ethno-linguistic population in the region. Furthermore, events in Kwararafa could affect Benin or Idah, while policy decisions in the forest might influence events in the savanna or sudan. Complement and competition were, therefore, crucial to the complex series of relationships within and between the sub-regions and the three focal states of the Benue Basin.

Empires such as Benin, Idah and Kwararafa developed economic strengths to complement their political and territorial powers. They were particularly effective in the domination of markets, trade routes, and the infrastructure of regional commerce. The functional economic nexus of any state in the region was defined by its control of production, labour and distribution, and the focal states were able, through their control of commercial networks, to restrict the power of others. Also, they might export this style of government to neighbouring or even distant states, and thus seek to perpetuate regional domination through the creation or related or associated administrations. The political culture of Benin, for example was transported to Idah, Nupe, Doma, Keana, Akure, Abinsi, Lagos, Dampar, and Warri, and effectively changed the administrative ideology of a large segment of the Benue Basin.[19] In the process of imperial expansion and political consolidation Benin not only acquired important areas of primary and secondary production, but also came to dominate regional trade, markets and labour. Territorial expansion, political transformation and economic growth worked hand in hand.

The commercial nexus of the Benue Basin operated under the controlling influences of the various paramount political authorities. The entire region was divided into spheres of influence dominated by the major polities. Idah, for example, extended political and economic domination as far as Nupe, Aboh and Abinsi, and thus became one of the principal political powers in riverine trade. At the same time Idah's sphere of influence was dictated by the power of Benin and Kwararafa. But overall intra-regional competition and complement between the focal states linked the various ecological zones and political spheres in a unified trading network.

Crafts and industrial development gave certain central place social formations economic advantages in the local and regional competition for resources, labour and markets. Both Benin and Idah emerged as major cloth weaving and dyeing centres with an international reputation for quality and fashion. The success of the cotton industry provided incentives for further craft and industrial development. Bead manufacturing, iron smithing, wood carving, and brass casting all became significant craft industries, and contributed to the process of intra-regional secondary exchange. An operational nexus allowed cotton grown in one area to be woven and dyed in a second, and subsequently sold in a third. The commercial relations of the craft complex thus transcended the authority of a single social formation, and contributed to the regional network of economic associations. Craft and industrial production could set a particular state or community apart from normal regional commercial patterns. Such diversification in exchange production reduced dependence on primary production and exchange, and thus provided another avenue through which the entrepreneur could penetrate regional and long distance trade.

The turbulence and change in the Benue Basin between 1300 and 1700 can be examined through the process by which various states rose and fell in their efforts to define economic and political relationships. The process of political consolidation and centralization in one state inevitably affected others as political systems and regional controls evolved, commercial networks and economic relations were extended, and production demands and market forces increased. As one state embarked on a process of imperial expansion, and in the process imposed regional economic controls, other states were not only affected, but may have been forced to contract, move or realign their own political and socio-economic network. Imperial formations can thus subvert distinct, independent social and political groupings and remove these entities from the political geography and economic network of the region. The history of the Benue Basin is, therefore, reflected in the links between the three focal states of Benin, Idah and Kwararafa. Each polity sought to develop its organizational mechanisms, political decision-making process, and economic activities to accommodate the larger regional network. The nature of change in this region is as important to understanding regional history as the reaction to change. The often violent competition operated as a powerful force which defined relationships between state, people, and regions. This study is not necessarily an examination of success, as each of the focal states experienced decline and were forced to alter their relations to the regional political and economic system.

Vital to this construction of regional history is the regional dating framework,[20] developed from a number of independently dated chronological progression which revealed general trends in Benue Basin history between 1300 and 1700. The core of this regional dating framework provides a basic periodization through which a more detailed understanding of the past can be constructed. The details of how this regional framework was constructed have been dealt with in great detail in Chapter Two. It is important to note, however, that once a regional chronology had been established it becomes possible to analyze in more depth the impact of regional events on individual states and populations. The four hundred year period under examination here can be divided into two; the long period of wet prosperity from 1300 to 1590, and the dry, drought-ridden century from 1590 to 1700.[21]

The era of 'wet prosperity' was characterized by a period of economic growth, agricultural expansion, and relative political stability. During this period the Benue Basin witnessed the expansion of imperial social formations and a multiplication of stable polities concerned with control of local, regional and long distance trade. The forces operating in the region tended, on one hand, to assist in political consolidation and heighten competition. Stability and wealth, on the other hand, potentially enhanced regional cooperation. Resources were abundant and increased agricultural production added to primary exchange patterns, and contributed to population growth. These three factors accelerated regional economic opportunities and added impetus to the process of territorial acquisition and the consolidation of spheres of influence.

The era of 'wet prosperity' was followed by an arid century in which drought and drought-related famine affected a large portion of the Benue Basin.[22] In drought the production of food, the rendering of brine for salt, and brewing of beer, the growth of export crops, the ability to travel unmolested for long distances, and the general political stability were all adversely affected. During this century of low or non-existent rainfall and corresponding decrease in economic activity, states changed in size, population, production and influence. Normally active and prosperous trade networks were closed or lessened in scope. The struggle for survival in drought conditions meant that less agricultural production could be used for export or for the support of the non-agricultural sector. Non-farmers could face grave hardships or even death, and farmers themselves might resort to hunting and gathering. The affects of this arid period were not felt equally throughout the Benue Basin, and areas such as the moist forest zone escaped the major direct impact of low rainfall, but were not immune to the larger, regional implications.

Climatic conditions can present a powerful force which decides the course of human activity. The environment defines, for example, the progress and conduct of trade, and imposes ecological constraints upon human settlement patterns and demography.[23] Any major climatic shift must, therefore, be considered as a potentially significant determinant in the process of reconstructing the past. Africa has been susceptible to major environmental changes throughout recorded history, and these often negative shifts have presented a real barrier to sustained economic growth and stability. This is as true today as it was in the sixteenth or seventeenth century.

Only recently has research developed to the point where it is possible to begin to understand the consequences of major drought and famine and the impact of such climatic degradation upon socio-political and economic conditions.[24] The historian is now able to reconsider the evidence from the past and perhaps revise the interpretation of historical change in the light of significant ecological data. It is now possible to frame the basic periodization of African history in general, and West African history in particular, in terms of climatic trends and patterns. This development represents a major advance from current historiography.

Two primary interpretations of West African history have been presented in the conventional literature. These contributions sought to explain the pattern of socio-economic and political change through either the examination of external forces or internal political turmoil. One school of thought suggested that the economic decline of West Africa could be hinged upon the collapse of the Songhai Empire after the Moroccan invasion in 1591.[25] This interpretation does not, however, consider environmental factors and thus assumes that the political vacuum created by the disintegration of the Songhai *pax* caused the commercial collapse, social upheaval and political turmoil that followed. This argument concludes that the fall of Songhai set West Africa upon the rocky road of general economic decline. In fact, new evidence shows that the conquest of Songhai coincided with a major shift in West African climate. Also, the collapse of the *pax* was only one event in a series of geo-political changes, probably prompted by drought and famine, which subsequently altered the political and economic focus of the entire region. Thus while there is some value in the study of the Songhai Empire and the consequences of its collapse, it is not a definitive explanation for the general political or economic trend. Only if the potentially powerful forces of drought and famine are included can the real course of human activity be understood.

The second school of thought suggests rather dogmatically that it was the diversification and expansion of the Atlantic coastal trade, with the intervention of the British, French and Dutch into the Portuguese trading monopoly, that laid the groundwork for the economic degradation of West Africa.[26] The process, so these theorists argue, accelerated dramatically with the expansion of the Atlantic slave trade and the export of valuable labour from the productive economy of the region. There is no doubt that the demand for slaves exacerbated the political instability, and economic decline, but there also remains a fundamental flaw in this thesis. There is also no doubt that the extension of the Atlantic trading demand contributed to a changing commercial focus in the Benue Basin exchange network. However, that change was initially, at least, a reaction of a combination of forces and cannot be explained in simple mono-causal terms. The slavery theorist generally ignore the rational decision-making skills of the local entrepreneur and climatic conditions in Africa as a contributory, if not a decisive, factor in the widespread economic shift. Furthermore, as the environmental conditions are examined the timing of the European coastal trade thesis can be seriously questioned.

The evidence indicates that economic change, social upheaval, and political instability in West Africa pre-dates the expansion of labour demands in the West Indies and the acceleration of Atlantic slave trading in the late eighteenth century. Conventional periodization of the coastal slave trade indicates that large scale exports developed after 1750.[27] However, evidence from West Africa clearly shows that major transformations in all social, political and economic institutions, prompted by the ravages of drought and famine, had begun over one hundred years earlier.

The third argument which emerges from the study of environmental conditions suggests, therefore, a possible revision of West African historiography. This alternative perspective indicates that failing rains and crops, and spreading famine conditions persisted well into the nineteenth century in a repetitive cycle of deepening economic crises. This analysis does not claim to be all encompassing, all inclusive, or uniquely explanatory. The reconstruction of the past which includes the evidence from environmental change does, however, serve to establish a rational perspective on political and economic history between 1300 and 1700. It also establishes the foundations of a vastly different view of African social, economic and political history in the post 1700 period.

The evidence for a major shift in the climatic patterns and environmental conditions is not restricted to the Sahel or sudanic regions which were more fragile than the coastal belt or forest zone. Erratic rains on the coast also contributed to hunger and scarcity and weakened the productive capacity across the entire region. The cycle of failing rains and crops created an ecological crisis in which people ate their seed grain and thus found recovery much more difficult. Famine and drought established fundamentally unstable economic conditions which were further exacerbated by the spread of slave raiding activities in the late eighteenth century.

> The century from the 1720s to the 1840s was one of terrible turmoil...the Continental drought of the 1720s began to swell the supply of slaves and the supply curve moved up in each successive drought until the historic peak of slave exports had been reached in the Chadic Mahlatule (drought) in the 1790s.[28]

The evidence for this major climatic change comes from an extremely broad region, and indicates quite clearly that the environmental degradation began as early as the sixteenth century. Webster argues that Africa's golden age declined "during the Nyarubanga period of the 1560s and ended in the 1620s. The Nyarubanga was.an extended climatic deterioration..."[29] Bornu traditions indicate that there was "a great famine which occurred during" the reign of Mai Dunama in c. 1548-1566.[30] Algeria was hit by almost continuous famine and plague throughout the last half of the sixteenth century, and the prosperity in the Niger bend region declined rapidly toward the end of the century. This climatic shift coincided with the Moroccan invasion of Songhai and marked the real beginning of climatological deterioration that was to last into the nineteenth century.

If the sixteenth century ended on a poor note the seventeenth was a time of extreme hardship and environmentally induced turmoil. Between 1600 and 1611, eleven years of famine were reported at Kano.[31] Algeria experience "terrible drought and famine" from 1604 to 1612, conditions which persisted as "terrible famine" until 1629.[32] There was also

> very severe famine in coastal Senegambia and Guinea-Bissau"[33] between 1639 and 1642; the same time that the Niger bend experienced the great famine of the seventeenth century, with 1639 and 1643 being virtually without rain, and with low rainfall in the intervening years...The famine had begun in Djenne in February of 1639...[34]

Drought and famine conditions persisted throughout the seventeenth century and had a major impact upon the Benue Basin region. For example, in 1657-1694, during the reign of Mai Ali of Bornu "the country was afflicted with a great 'seven year' famine." During this same period the Cormantine region of the Gold Coast experienced "failure of the late (main) rains,

[and] famine [illegible] because rains had failed." In 1687, in Ardra, Dahomey, "scarcity of corn and famine" was noted. Also, in 1685 the Asben Chronicles (near Agadez) noted that "the war of famine" occurred. There is no doubt that the seventeenth century witnessed a major climatic change and resulted in lower rainfalls and drought-related famine across much of West Africa. The period c. 1681-1687 was one of drought throughout the Sahel, with the possible exception of Mauritania and western Mali, and the Guinea Coast. Conditions were drier than during most of the seventeenth centur.[35]

The environment had changed quite dramatically since the "Kitmarsontapa" or golden age between 1410 and 1580.36 It was this climatic deterioration that altered the economic conditions of Africa, particularly West Africa, and led to the declining political and economic stability throughout the region. Conditions in the eighteenth century did not improve, and drought and famine conditions were well documented in Ethopia, along the Nile, around the Niger bend, in Senegambia, Algeria, the Guinea Coast, and the Benue Basin. The prominent feature of the eighteenth century was the widespread chaos and turmoil complicated by the rising incidence of slave raiding for export from coastal ports.

> This period (1738-1756) saw a severe drought, one or two decades in duration, throughout the entire Sahel and Sudan, as well as the Guinea Coast...The last three decades of the eighteenth century seem to have been a period of climatic instability, with rapidly alternating periods of flood and drought in some regions...In the period 1770-1774 famine occurred in several regions of tropical Africa....[37]

Within the ecological framework imposed upon the Benue Basin by shifting climatological factors it is possible to establish a regional chronological progression which provides a periodization of regional history. This summary correlates evidence from climate, political events, economic forces, demographic changes, environmental factors, and the fundamental generation length dating progression, and establishes a reliable and sound progression, around which a political and economic history for the entire region can be written. Regional chronology has, therefore, become the foundation of regional history.

The synchronization of regional data depends upon the utilization and implementation of a standardized method.[38] Evidence organized outside this standard framework can be artificially isolated or insulated from comparative material elsewhere in the regional data bank. Two brief examples of this insulation are instructive. Until recently the Aro evidence from the Cross River in southeastern Nigeria could not tied into the Benue Basin reconstruction. Previously, events dated to the seventeenth or eighteenth centuries could not be related to droughts in 1720-1750 or 1780-1810. Any reference in the Aro reconstruction to an eighteenth century drought might be either of these. However, Aro history has recently been re-examined and many of the previous barriers imposed by the previously employed century-based dating system have been removed.[39] Events in Aro history can now be correlated with events - droughts, famines, wars and migrations - in the regional context.

The second example of artificially isolated regional data can be found in the construction of Yoruba history. Yoruba history, although much studied and representing a rich body of data, does not lend itself to regional correlation and comparison.Yoruba history either follows the century dating technique, or has been presented with a series of apparently arbitrary dates which bear little relation to a systematic chronological progression.[40] In this case, however, there is sufficient regnal list or genealogical information to develop partial generation dating and relate some evidence to the Benue Basin. To reduce problems of synchronization and to develop the comparative material essential to regional history it is imperative to avoid artificial isolation and adopt a standardized dating method. Wherever possible and practicable this study has restructured evidence according to the standardized dating method and has thus utilized the generation length dating technique as the basis of the regional chronology.

The three focal states in this reconstruction of Benue Basin history have been dated according to a standardized dating method. All available genealogical and regnal list information has been subjected to critical evaluation and has withstood the tests of statistical analysis and synchronization. Throughout the following chapters there are charts and schematic representations of chronological information. This data serves to reinforce and emphasize particular political, social and economic relationships through genealogical information for the individuals concerned. In this way regional history has been facilitated and clarified. Each local dating framework can be further related to the regional chronological structure and thus linked to the flow of events and interactions. Within this regional framework the events within each of the three focal states provided a basis through which evidence on a regional scale might be analyzed. The chronologies of the three focal states of Benin, Idah, and Kwararafa, therefore, became integral to the Benue Basin regional chronology.

The forest zone polity of Benin emerged as a powerful and decisive imperial state which dominated political and economic activity across a broad region. The emergence of a centralized Bini government in c. 1293-1320 established the basis for Bini hegemony which lasted until the Benin Expedition of 1897.[41] The strength of Bini political authority during this six hundred year period served to consolidate commercial management, and social control across a broad regional spectrum. The growth of Benin under the Eweka dynasty affected the middle belt through the foundation of the related dynasty of Idah in c. 1507-1537. The Bini dynasty at Idah initially represented the imperial power of Benin, but subsequently severed this connection, and became an imperial power in its own right. The Idah dynasty spread its political influence into the surrounding region, including Nupe in c.1507-1537, and continued to receive tribute from Nupe monarchs well into the nineteenth century.[42] The expansion of both Benin and Idah occurred during the era of wet prosperity.

In contrast, Kwararafa was in direct competition with Kano and Bornu during the period of prosperity, and subsequently lost the battle for direct access to trans-Saharan trade. The end of the trans-Saharan economic boom, linked to the conquest of Songhai by Morocco in 1591,[43] and the climatic decline of the

1590's, caused a corresponding political and economic decline in Kwararafa. Drought forced the powerful empire of Bornu to shift to the south of Lake Chad where it came into conflict with Kwararafa over access to the northern trade routes and markets. About 1580 Bornu destroyed the Kwararafan capital at Tagara, capturing 30,000 people and driving many refugees south towards the Benue River. As Kwararafa was driven south it rebuilt its capital and re-emerged as a middle belt social formation. The relocation in the middle belt changed regional demographic, settlement and political patterns. The settlement of Kwararafa at Biepi forced a major economic shift on the middle belt and contributed to the region-wide economic turmoil created by the shift in economic focus from the north to the south. The relocation of Kwararafa, therefore, directly affected the regional pattern and contributed to dynastic change in Idah, Etulo, Keana, Doma, and Oturkpo.

The historical unity of the Benue Basin stems, in part at least, from the interactions and relationships of the various focal states to regional affairs. As the forest zone polity of Benin expanded between before 1600 Yoruba, Ishan, Igbo, Ga, Urhobo, Itsekiri and Okpoto were affected by its imperial power. Imperial expansion also brought Benin into contact with the states of Lagos, Mahin, Ondo, Ijebu, Owo, Akure, Ekiti, Ife, Ikere, Nupe, Oyo, Udo, Agbor, Aboh, Onitsha, Warri and Idah. In the sixteenth century it has been estimated that Benin exported as much as one million pieces of cloth annually to European traders, production which involved numerous skilled and unskilled workers far beyond the confines of the kingdom.[44] Benin was, therefore, at the centre of an expansive network of regional economic, political and social relations that covered most of the forest zone and intruded into the middle belt. Thus between 1550 and 1600, the Benue peoples were being squeezed by the intrusion of Bornu from the north, the commercial expansion of Benin from the south, and the location and spread of Kwararafan influence in their midst.

Idah, located in the derived savanna, emerged as an autonomous riverine trading capital in c. 1507-1537, and established relations with a broad range of other Benue Basin social formations. Under the Bini dynasty, c. 1507-1687, Idah established links with Onitsha, Aboh, Benin, Nupe, Koton

Karifi, Panda, Keana, Doma, Abinsi, Kwararafa and a number of other Benue Basin social formations. It is possible that the influence of the Bini dynasty at Idah spread as far as the Biu plateau north of the Gongola River.[45] Through this expansion Idah developed relations with the Idoma, Igbirra, Alago, Aro, Igbo, Yoruba, Edo, Ishan, Okpoto, Jukun, and Nupe ethno-linguistic populations. In the 1680's a Kwararafa dynasty took over in Idah, at a time when the cotton industry was collapsing[46] in Benin and the kingdom's influence was shrinking. Idah thus reflected the changing power relations promoted originally by the Benin expansion south and the intrusion of Bornu in the north.

The capital of Kwararafa shifted no less than six times, and in this process relations were established through war, trade, marriage and diplomacy with Kano, Katsina, Zaria, Bornu, Keana, Doma, Wuse, Idah and a large number of other Benue Basin social formations. Its northern association brought Kwararafa into contact with the Pabir, Bura, Kanuri, Hausa, Birom, Fulani, Abakwariga, Koro and Gwari socio-linguistic groups. The move south of the River Benue in c. 1600 brought Kwararafa into contact with the Chamba, Vere, Jukun, Alago, Etulo, Tiv, Idoma and Igala. This apparently unstable capital was a reflection of the political and economic times. In many cases the movement of the Kwararafan capital reflected the varying profitability of a northern focus versus southern commerce, and thus moves were based on rational decisions to establish controls over a new or different sector of the regional economy.

While this regional reconstruction focuses upon the three central place states of Benin, Idah and Kwararafa it also examines these polities in their regional context. There is within this discussion a link to virtually every major, and for that matter minor, political, social, and ethno-linguistic division in the region. The regional history can, therefore, be seen as the study of central place states, and particularly through the concentration on the three focal states, Benin, Idah and Kwararafa which were, in fact, ideal examples of the variety and diversity within the much broader sample of Benue Basin social formations and populations. Thus, the focus has been extended more than might normally be achieved through a study of a single polity, group or region.

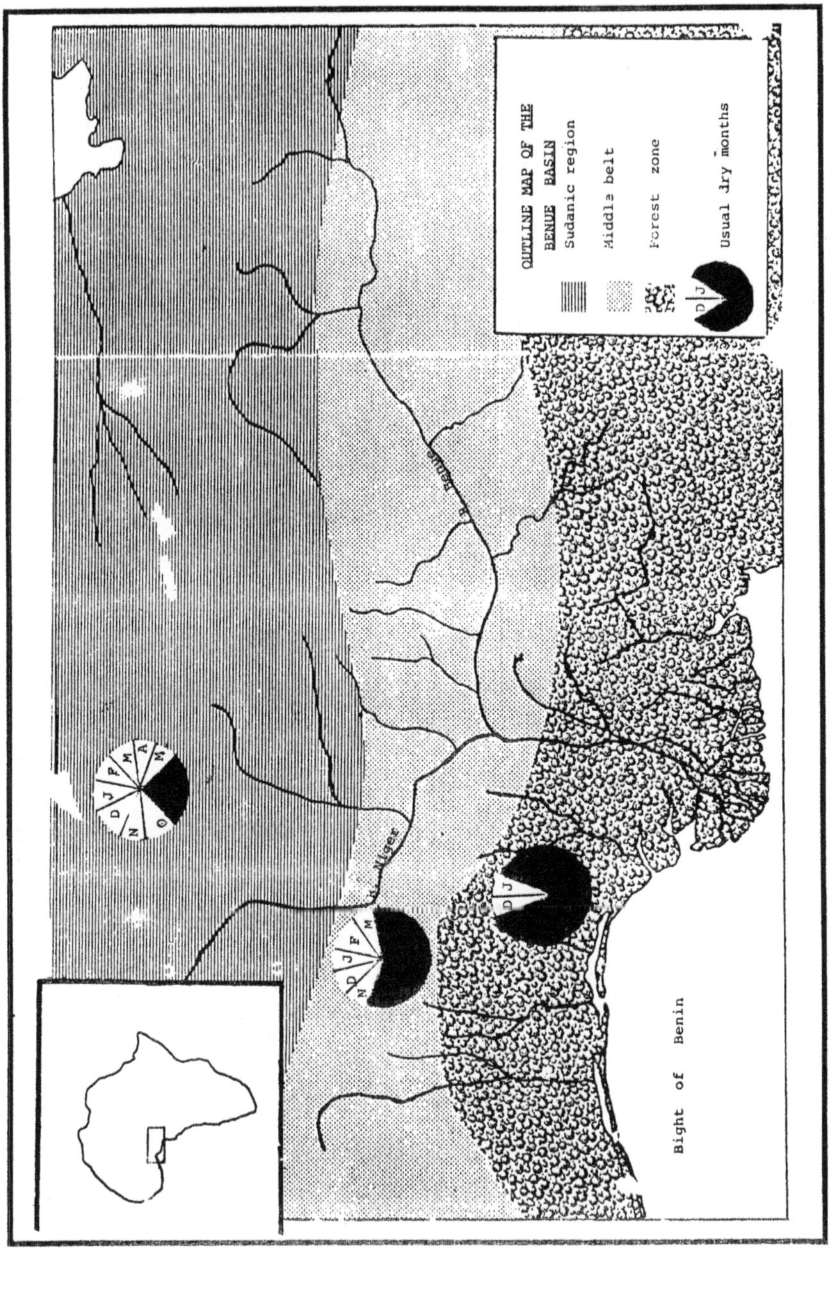

Map One: Outline Map of the Benue Basin

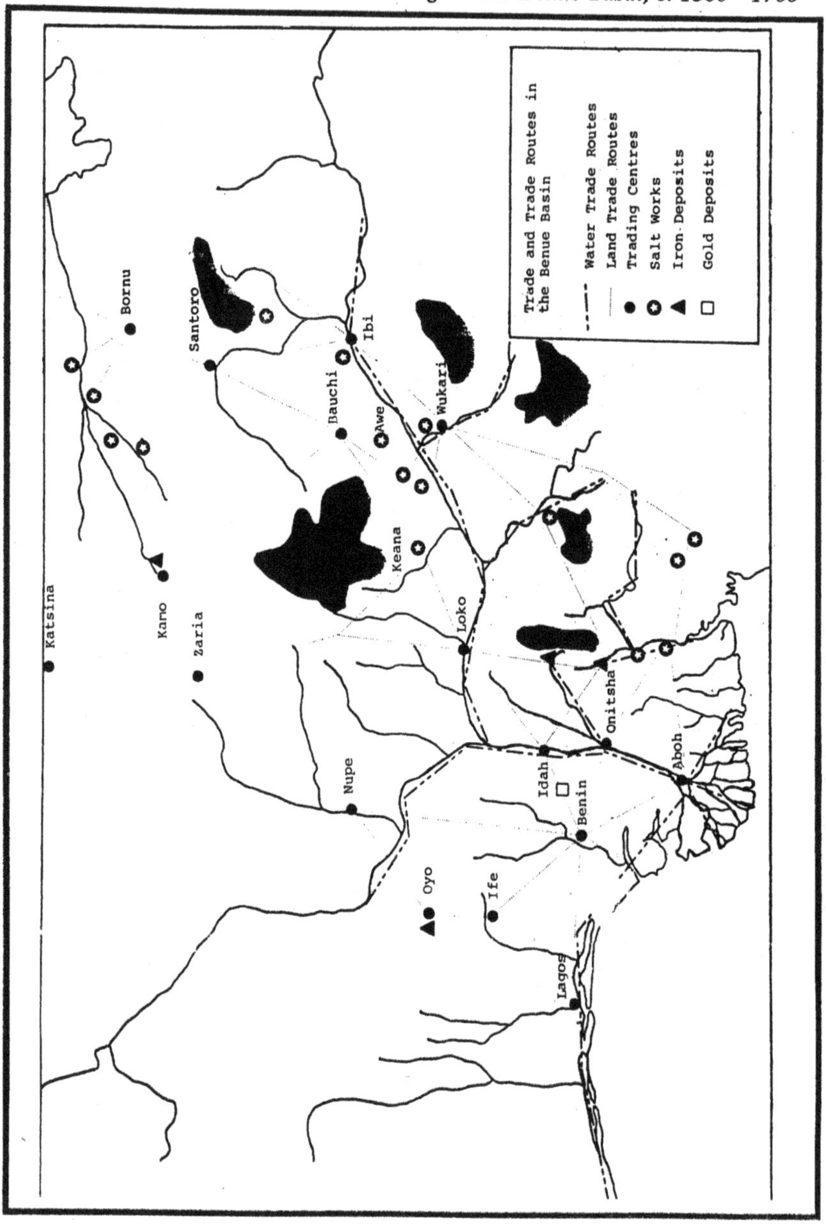

Map Two: Trade and Trade Routes in the Benue Basin

References

1. Reuben K. Udo, *Geographical Regions of Nigeria*, London, 1970, p. 118.
2. W.A. Perkins and J.H. Stembridge, *Nigeria, A Descriptive Geography*, Ibadan, 1966, p. 2.
3. R. Roberts, 'Multiplier Effects in the Ecologically Specialized Trade of Precolonial West Africa', paper presented to the African and Imperial History Seminar, Department of History, Dalhousie University, February, 1980.
4. E. Isichei, *A History of Nigeria*, London, 1983, pp. xvi-xviii provides detailed maps of Nigerian language groups. For ethnographic material refer to C.L. Temple, (ed.), *Notes on the Tribes, Provinces, Emirates and States of Northern Nigeria*, Lagos, 1922, P.A. Talbot, *The Peoples of Southern Nigeria*, 4 volumes, London, 1926, and C.K. Meek, *Tribal Studies in Northern Nigeria*, London, 1976.
5. P. Bohannen and L. Bohannen, *The Tiv of Central Nigeria*, London, 1969; J.N. Orkar, 'A Pre-Colonial History of the Tiv, Central Nigeria, c.1500-1850', Dalhousie University Phd., 1979; E. Isichei, *The Ibo People and The Europeans*, London, 1975; E. Isichei, *A History of the Igbo People*, London, 1976; and G.T. Basden, *Niger Ibos*, London, 1906.
6. E.O. Erim, *The Idoma Nationality 1600-1900: Problems of Studying the Origins and Development of Ethnicity*, Enugu, 1981; A. Adefuye, "The Alago Kingdoms: A Political History", in *Studies in the History of Plateau State, Nigeria*, edited by E. Isichei, London, 1982, pp. 108-122; J.K. Tortema, *In Search of Etulo History*, (Zaria, n.d.; J.B. Webster, 'Chiefs and Chronology: Jukun Colonies in the Benue Valley', *Benue Valley Project Papers*, microfiche, Centre for African Studies, Dalhousie University, No. 4, 1975; and C.K. Meek, *A Sudanese Kingdom*, London, 1931.
7. C. Gonyok, 'The Ngas and the Coming of Colonial Administration, 1606-1635', Ahmadu Bello University, History Essay, 1976; J.E. Miller, 'Ishan-Benin Relations, c.1455-1504', Dalhousie University, Honours Essay, 1983; G.C. Okojie, *Ishan Native Laws and Customs*, Yaba, 1960; J.E. Miller, 'A Pre Colonial History of the Babur of Biu', Dalhousie University, MA, 1984; and A.H. Groom, "Main Characteristics of the 'Inland' Igbirra of the Kabba Province, Northern Nigeria", *Journal of the African Society*, IV, 34, 1910.
8. R.A. Sargent, 'Inexplicit Data and Pre-Colonial History: Totems, Demography and Linguistics in the Igala Social Formation', paper presented to the Johns Hopkins University workshop on African History, February, 1984.
9. R. Griffeth, "The Hausa City-States From 1450 to 1804", in *The City States in Five Cultures*, edited by R. Griffeth, Santa Barbara, 1981.
10. R.A. Sargent, "The Evolution of an Imperial Social Formation, Benin, c.1293-1536", *Canadian Journal of African Studies*, Vol 1, No. 1986; R.A. Sargent, 'The Rise and Fall of the Igala Kingdom, c.1700-1900', History Seminar, Dalhousie University, March 1983; and J.B. Webster, 'Kwararafa:

A Peripatetic State', History Seminar, Dalhousie University, November, 1983.

11. A.C. Unomah, "The Lowland Salt Industry", in *Studies in The History of Plateau State*, pp. 151- 178. Also refer to P.E. Lovejoy, "The Bornu Salt Industry", *The International Journal of African History*, XI, 4, 1978.

12. R.A. Sargent, 'The Northern Tiv: Migration, War and Societal Transformation', *Benue Valley Project Paper*, microfiche, Centre for African Studies, Dalhousie University, No. 10, p. 8.

13. R.N. Henderson, *The King In Every Man*, New Haven, 1972; J.S. Boston, "Notes on Contacts Between the Igala and Ibo", *Journal of the Historical Society of Nigeria*, 2, 1962; M. Clifford, "A Nigerian Chiefdom", *Journal of the Royal Anthropological Institute*, LXVI, 1936.

14. A.A. Boahen, "The Caravan Trade in the Nineteenth Century", *Journal of African History*, 3, 2, 1962, pp. 349-350; E.W. Bovill, *Caravans of the Old Sahara*, Oxford, 1933, p. 105; A.W. Pardo, "The Songhay Empire Under Sonni Ali and Askia Muhammad: A Study in Comparison and Contrast", *Boston University Papers on Africa*, Vol. V, 1971; and G.O. Ogunremi, *Counting the Camels: The Economics of Transportation in Pre-Industrial Nigeria*, forthcoming.

15. Sargent, "Evolution of an Imperial Social Formation".

16. S.A. Akintoye, "The Southeastern Yoruba Districts and the Benin Kingdom", *Journal of the Historical Society of Nigeria*, IV, 4, 1969.

17. B.J. Belasco, *The Entrepreneur as Culture Hero*, New York, 1980.

18. H.L.M. Butcher, "Some Aspects of the Otu System of the Isa sub-tribe of the Edo Peoples of Southern Nigeria", *Africa*, 8, 1935.

19. J. Power, 'Lafia; Layers of Settlement', Dalhousie University, Honours Essay, 1984.

20. For a detailed examination of regional chronology see R.A. Sargent, "A Benue Basin Regional Chronology", *The Journal of General Studies*, (Kano), Vols. 5 & 6, No. 1, 1984, pp. 1- 38. Chapter Two also considers regional chronology and adds information appearing since 1984 that has contributed to a strengthened regional structure. A structural outline of this regional chronology appears as Chart Two and shows a generational dating progression of thirty years. Thirty years is central to the range of 65% of all dated dynasties in a global study conducted by D.P. Henige, *Chronology of Oral Tradition, Quest for a Chimera*, Oxford, 1972, p. 123.

21. J.B. Webster, "Periodization in Africa History, c.1050-1850", *The Journal of General Studies*, v. 4, No. 1, 1983.

22. S. Nicholson, "Climatic Variations in Sahel and Other African Regions During the Past Five Centuries", *Journal of Arid Environments*, Vol. 1, 1978; and S. Nicholson, 'A Climatic Chronology for Africa: Synthesis of Geological, Historical and Meteorological Information and Data', University of Misconsin-Madison, Phd., 1976.

23. J.B. Webster, (ed.), *Chronology, Migration and Drought in Interlacustine Africa*, Longman, London, 1979. Many of the chapters in this book

document the consequences of climatic deterioration on the various social formations in the interlacustine region of East Africa.

24. Nicholson, 'A Climatic Chronology for Africa', 1976 is one good example. Also see D.J. Schove, "Eclipses, Comets and the Spectrum of Time in Africa", *Journal of the British Astronomical Association*, V. 78, 1968, and D.J. Schove, "African Droughts and the Spectrum of Time", in D. Dalby and R.I.H. Church (eds.), *Drought in Africa*, London, 1973.
25. J.O. Hunwick, "Songhay, Borno and Hausaland in the Sixteenth Century", in *History of West Africa*, Vol. 1, edited by J.F.A. Ajayi and M. Crowder, Longman, London, 1971, p. 301.
26. Leading advocate of this viewpoint would be W. Rodney, *How Europe Underdeveloped Africa*, London, 1972.
27. As Hopkins points out for example, "80 per cent of all slaves landed in the New World were transported between 1701 and 1850." A.G. Hopkins, *An Economic History of West Africa*, Longmans, London, 1973, p. 102. Also see P.D. Curtis, *The Atlantic Slave Trade: A Census*, Madison, 1969. It is important to note that it was sugar production in the West Indies that accelerated labour requirements. Prior to 1650 tobacco was the main export commodity from the West Indies, J.H. Parry and P.M. Sherlock, *A Short History of the West Indies*, London, 1956, p. 66.
28. Webster, "Periodization, p. 11
29. *Ibid.*, p. 6.
30. Nicholson, 'A Climatic Chronology for Africa', p. 266.
31. J.F.A. Ajayi and I. Espie, *A Thousand Years of West African History*, New York, 1969. as cited in Nicholson, 'A Climatic Chronology for Africa', p. 275.
32. Nicholson, 'A Climatic Chronology for Africa', pp. 238-244.
33. *Ibid.*, p. 254.
34. Ibid., p. 258. The following data has been extracted from the comprehensive listings presented by Nicholson, pp. 235-299.
35. *Ibid.*, pp. 126-127.
36. Webster, "Periodization", p. 6.
37. Nicholson, 'A Climatic Chronology for Africa', pp. 133-134.
38. For a discussion on standard methods see R.A. Sargent, "A Methodology of Chronology: The Igala Core Regnal List", *History of Africa*, Vol. 11, 1984. A more detailed discussion on the practical applications of methods of oral history research is currently in production, and should shortly appear as J.B. Webster and R.A. Sargent, *Practical Oral Methods: Historical Data Collection in Africa.*
39. F.I. Ekejuiba, "The Aro System of Trade in the Nineteenth Century", *Ikenga*, Vol. 1, No. 1, 1972; and K.O. Dike and F.I. Ekejuiba, "The Aro State: A Case Study of State Formation in Southeastern Nigeria", *Journal of African Studies*, 5, 3, 1978. A more recent contribution by Apollus Nwanwab, "The Aro", Dalhousie University MA, 1990, helps define these significant links very clearly

40. R.C.C. Law, "The Dynastic Chronology of Lagos", *Lagos Notes and Records*, 11, 1, 1968; O. Johnson, The History of the Yorubas, Lagos, 1921; and R. Smith, *The Kingdoms of the Yoruba*, London, 1969.
41. A.F.C. Ryder, *Benin and the Europeans, 1485-1897*, London, 1969; and R. Home, *City of Blood Revisited: A New Look at the Benin Expedition of 1897*, London, 1982.
42. S.F. Nadel, *A Black Byzantium*, London, 1942; Sargent, "Rise and Fall of the Igala Kingdom"; and J. Abuka, 'The Decline of the Igala Kingdom, 1832- 1960', University of Jos Graduating Essay, 1982.
43. Ogbomo, Wilson, `Men and Women: Gender Relations and the History of the Owan Communities, Nigeria c. 1320-1900,' PhD thesis, Dalhousie University, 1993.
44. Boahen, "The Caravan Trade", pp. 349-350.
45. Evidence presented by J.E. Milier, 'The Pre- Colonial History of Biu', indicates Bini presence on the Biu plateau, but does not date this event or relate it to the general Bini expansion between c.1507-1657.
46. Ogbomo, *Op. cit.*

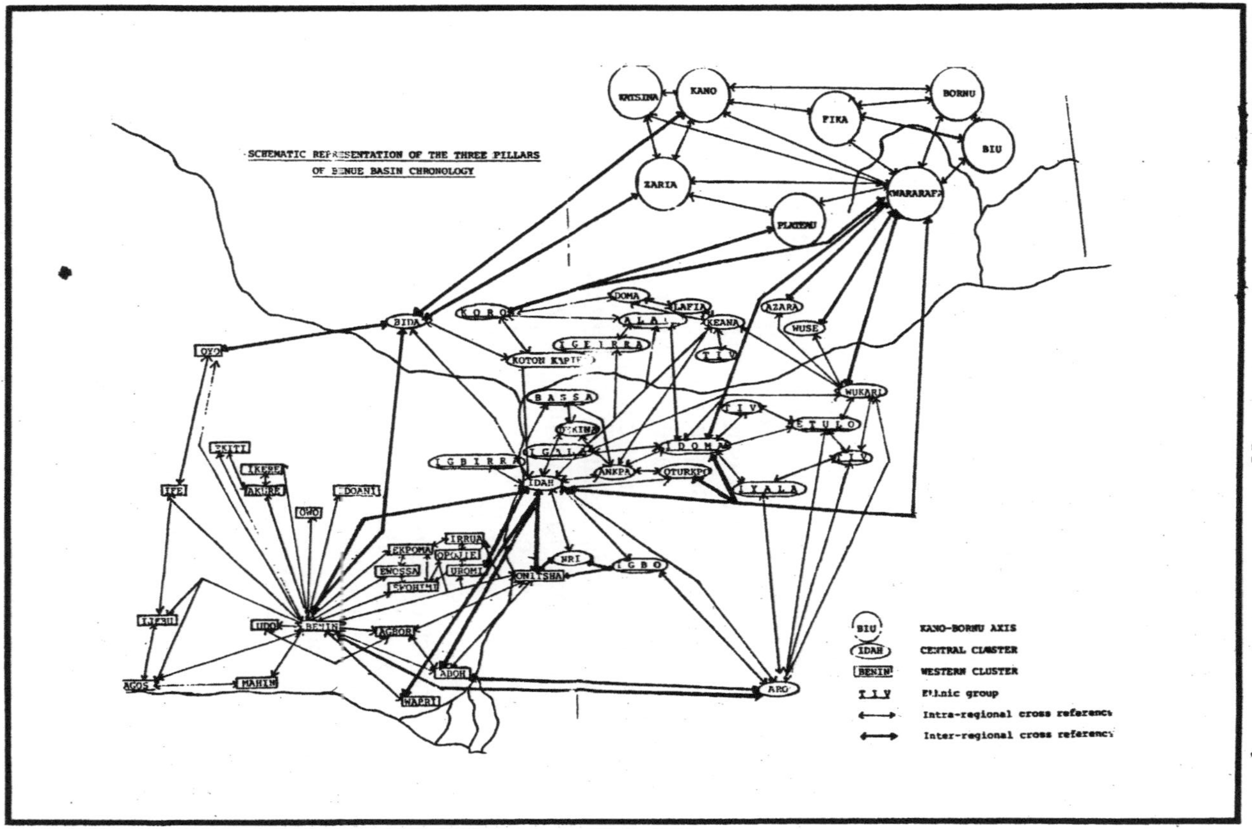

Map Three: Schematic Representation of the Three Pillars
Benue Basin Chronology

Chapter 2

A Benue Basin Regional Chronology[1]

Chronology is essentially the framework or "basis of history,"[2] and provides the structure upon which an ethno-historical reconstruction can be developed. Ethno-centric histories can, however, be relatively isolated and insulated from regional evidence, and may be compared to scattered excavations which produce a number of isolated digs without providing the basis for a regional overview. If pre-colonial African historiography[3] is to transcend ethno-centricism and the isolation associated with concentrated study of a single polity, state or ethnic group, a methodology for regional dating is required, and the developed chronology becomes the critical factor in the development of regional history. It is essential for determining which events represent regional movements or were merely local in consequence. The correlation of data from an extended (geographically defined) study area is a massive undertaking, and involves the synchronization of independently dated ethno-centric reconstructions in a regional dating progression. The following examines the evidence for a Benue Basin regional chronology,[4] correlates various forms of chronological data in the formulation of dating for regional history, and contributes to the methodology of regional dating. The discussion considers evidence from three sub-regional pillars, including the Benin cluster, the Igala nexus, and the Kano-Bornu axis.[5] It is far beyond the scope of this chapter to consider in any great detail the development of each sub-regional pillar.[6] However, the relationship between the three core dating progressions provides the basis for a viable and relatively reliable dating framework or chronological progression within which an historical reconstruction might be attempted. This discussion, therefore, establishes the basis of sub-regional dating utilizing the core chronologies of Benin, Idah and Kano-Bornu as the main pillars, and links these three sub-regional dating progressions in a unified regional chronology.

The correlation of independently dated evidence from a wide selection of regional sources establishes a unified dating structure for the Benue Basin. The conclusion offered here also suggests that a basic periodization within this regional construct is possible. This facilitates further historical analysis and reconstruction. It is important to note, however, that this discussion concentrates on relative dating in the pre-colonial African context, and advocates collection, corroboration and confirmation of dating evidence with extreme caution and care.[7] Oral evidence and genealogical data are only some of the potential sources for regional dating, and evidence from documentary and scientific sources must also be correlated in the development of regional dating. As J.B. Webster argues,

> A regional chronological framework is an essential to the achievement of precision dating, the interpretation of tradition and the dating of the history of peoples within the region who do not preserve family or clan genealogies....A regional chronological framework is achieved by a vast correlation of regnal lists and all other devices to date events such as prolonged periods of drought which are recorded in the traditions...Greater precision is a constant preoccupation. A date is suggested hesitantly and tentatively, gradually becomes strengthened or weakened as more researchers contribute to the cross-checking process and ultimately is either confirmed or rejected.[8]

In other words, it is important to establish a regional dating progression, and to expose the chronological evidence to detailed examination by other researchers.

Each sub-regional pillar in the Benue Basin framework is primarily a core regnal list with a large number of supporting genealogical cross references. The Benin and Kano-Bornu clusters form the respective southern and northern pillars in the Benue Basin dating framework while the Igala core chronology provides the middle dating structure.[9] Between these three pillars cross references are relatively few, but as information increases correlations continue to emerge. There are sufficient at present, moreover, to correlate inter-societal synchronistic evidence. Contributing to the corroboration of each sub-regional pillar, and to the regional framework as a whole, is a very substantial collection of genealogically-dated evidence. Corroborative evidence has also been incorporated from a number of diverse sources, including archaeology, eclipse data, scientifically dated drought and famine references, and an extremely large and complex network of synchronistic inter- and intra-societal cross references. This kind of data would fall into four basic categories according to D.P. Henige; including intra-societal tie-ins, tie-ins with events or personalities from neighbouring societies (inter-societal), references to astronomical or climatic phenomena, and references to events in a literate society or *vice-versa*.[10] The vast collection of data not only serves to corroborate the individual sub-regional dating progressions, but also confirms the unified regional structure identified as the Benue Basin dating progression.

As previously noted it is beyond the scope of this analysis to justify individual or even sub-regional chronological dating structures. In fact, this work has been done elsewhere.[11] It is noteworthy, however, that a number of these dating progressions in the Benue Basin have been the subject of critical evaluation for a long period. Through improvements in methodology and dating techniques relatively detailed works exist on the chronology of Benin,[12] Idah,[13], the Ishan chiefdoms,[14] the Idoma[15] and a number of other Benue Basin social formations.[16] The accumulated data and detailed analysis supersedes many earlier works by enlarging the evidence base, refining the methodology, concentrating on dating in the initial stages of historical research, and a thorough cross-checking of tentative results throughout the research phase. Therefore, rather than reiterate, repeat or duplicate existing material the following discussion adopts the most recently available information and critically assesses it in the light of evidence from the regional data bank, dated records, archaeology and other scientific evidence.[17] It is assumed that the sub-regional dating progressions have been established and only need to be checked, corroborated and correlated in a regional dating progression.

Within the Benin cluster, or south-western pillar of the Benue Basin regional chronology, there are a number of social formations which contribute corroborative data to the confirmation of the Benin core dating progression. An initial dating framework was suggested for Benin by a number of earlier writers, including Captain Roupell, N.W. Thomas, B. Struck and J.U. Egharevba.[18] Egharevba, in fact, as a "traditional" Bini historian suggested one of the first dating structures based upon a logical and detailed regnal list. The sub-regional core progression underwent further analysis by R.E. Bradbury, A.F.C. Ryder and M. Kalous.[19] Since the publications of these writers there has been a further development in the correlation of inter- and intra-societal cross references and an improvement in the general technique of pre-colonial chronology. F.B. Ataba attempted the first regional chronology which utilised Benin as the core progression and correlated evidence from Lagos, Warri, Onitsha and Aboh.[20] Subsequent research has further confirmed the Benin dating framework through the correlation of evidence from Idoani, Idah, Agbor, Oyo, Nupe, Owo, Akure, and twenty-six Ishan chiefdoms.[21] The relative reliability of the Benin core chronology has been further enhanced through the correlation of a large number of fixed date reference points from documentary evidence.[22] Chart I summarized the Benin sub-regional framework and shows the supporting thirty-nine cross references to other chronologies, plus eleven documentary dates which corroborate the genealogical dating progress based upon a twenty-seven year generation average.[23]

The correlation of the Benin dating information with the dynastic chronology of Lagos provides the opportunity to examine briefly a controverted cross reference. This example illustrates a common problem encountered when comparing regional dating information.[24] The dynastic chronology for Lagos, presented by R.C.C. Law, does not utilize the generational, reign length or parenthetical dating techniques

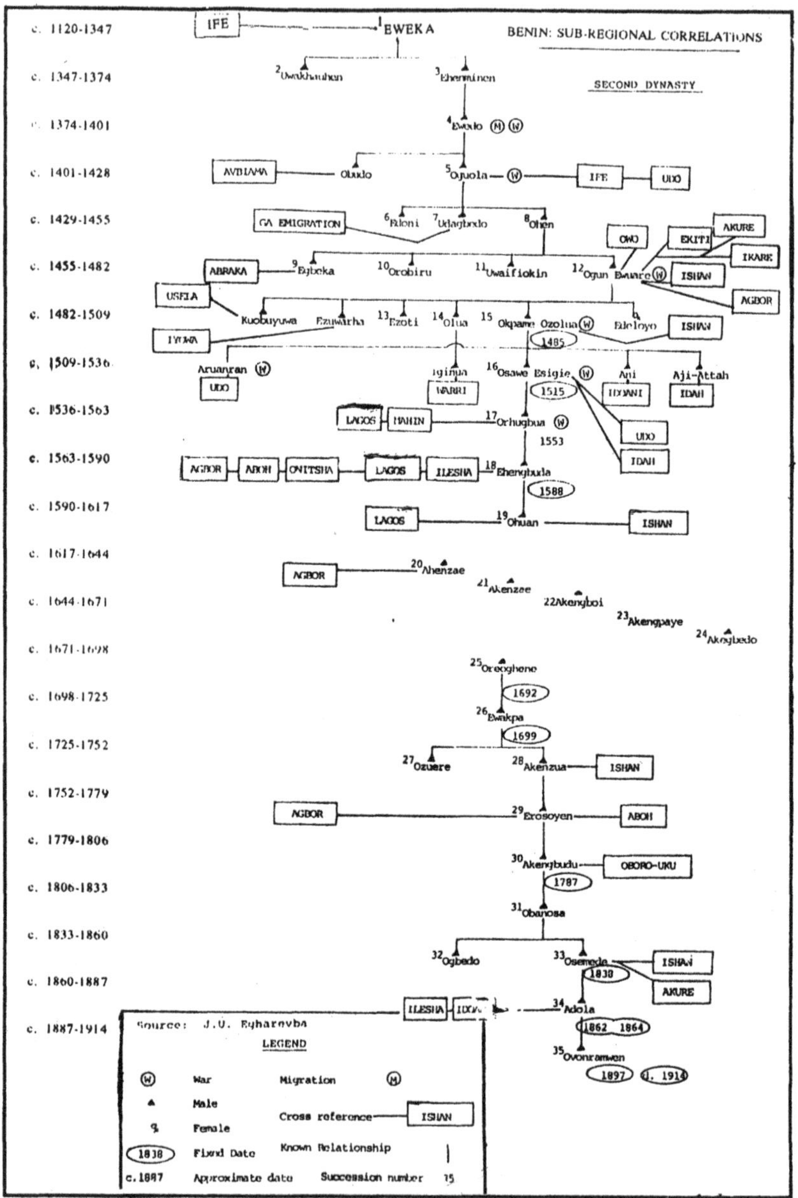

Chart I: Benin: Sub-Regional Correlations

that have become commonplace in pre-colonial history.[25] Also, Law does not seem to have collected a Lagos regnal list which would have facilitated a probe of the inconsistencies with which he has been pre-occupied. Finally, Law's analysis of the Lagos regnal list seems overly concerned with an examination of whether events occurred in 1827 or 1829; the kind of detail that generational averages, which provide a relative date, cannot expect to rectify. However, a detailed analysis of the Lagos data does provide evidence which is supportive of the dating progression for Benin, and tends to corroborate the Benin sub-regional pillar within the regional framework. For example, Law states that after the Benin conquest of Lagos by Oba Orhugbua:

> ...the Oba of Benin first reinstated the Olofin of Ido, and on his death appointed Aseru, one of the generals of the conquering army to rule the island, and after Aseru's death made Asipia Oba. This suggests some considerable interval between the conquest and the appointment of Asipia....[26]

The interval between the initial conquest of Lagos and the appointment of Asipia as the Bini ruling representative tends to imply that Egharevba was correct when he stated that Asipia was a grandson of Oba Orhugbua (c. 1536-1563).[27] This would mean, in effect, that the generation date for Asipia would be c. 1590-1617 from the Benin regnal list. From this variety of data it is possible to calculate a genealogical date for Asipia from the Lagos regnal list of c. 1622-1652, which represents a reasonable probability for the relationship between Benin dating and the Lagos evidence.[28] It would seem, therefore, that a standardized methodology and a detailed analysis of existing evidence can provide a mechanism for the comparison of apparently contradictory evidence. Clearly, the Lagos data could be re-examined and a viable dating framework established.

The central cluster of the Benue Basin regional dating structure includes a number of dated social formations which have been correlated with the Igala-Idah core progression. This sub-regional pillar includes cross references to Nupe, Wuse, Ankpa, Bassa, Keana, Doma, Tiv, Nri, Igbirra, Jukun and a large number of Idoma sources.[29]

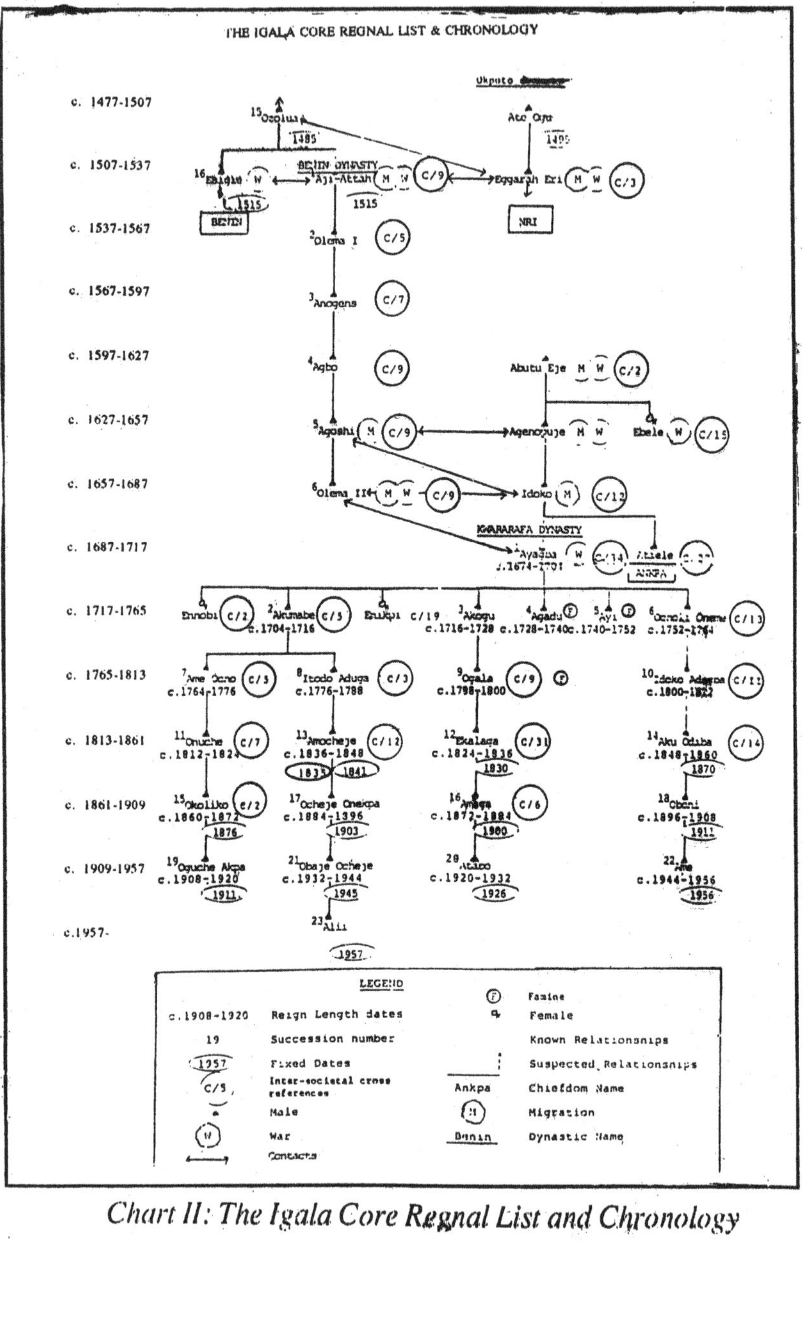

Chart II: The Igala Core Regnal List and Chronology

Chart II endeavours to summarize the Idah core chronology and shows the numerous fixed date references points, a large number of inter-societal cross references, and the generational dating progression for this sub-regional dating pillar. Identification of the Igala-Idah dating progression as a core of the Benue Basin regional chronology was based upon Idah's central place in the middle belt and the extensive collection of data available. Furthermore, the Idah chronological structure facilitated the detailed analysis of inter-regional evidence and provided a basis upon which inter-societal synchronism could be examined. The Igala-Idah dating progression, corroborated by archaeology,[30] numerous fixed date reference points,[31] and thousands of inter- and intra-societal cross references became[32] the central link in the three sub-regional pillars of the unified chronological structure.

The north-eastern pillar of the Benue Basin dating framework has been labelled the Kano-Bornu axis.[33] This cluster of interconnected dated social formations includes, among others, Kano, Bornu, Biu, Fika, Kwararafa, Zaria, Katsina and a number of plateau social formations.[34] This sub-regional pillar also provided the opportunity to examine not only genealogical dating against documentary dated evidence, but also established a correlation between eclipse data and scientifically dated famine and drought references in a sub-regional context. The famine and drought dates, for example, established fixed points for region-wide events of considerable magnitude, and of sufficient impact to impress upon the oral histories in the sudanic zone and middle belt of the Benue Basin. The correlation or region-wide drought data, therefore, provides a mechanism through which the regional chronology can be critically assessed. The supporting evidence from inter-societal synchronisms, tie-ins to fixed date reference points, eclipse data, and scientifically dated droughts establish a remarkably accurate sub-regional framework. Chart III endeavours to summarize the north-eastern pillar of the Benue Basin regional chronology, and indicates some of the internal cross references within the sub-regional dating structure.

It is important to note that while we have delineated three distinct sub-regional dating progressions in the extended regional chronology these are not mutually exclusive. In fact, the relationships documented between the three sub-regional clusters provides the basis for the development of a regional dating framework.

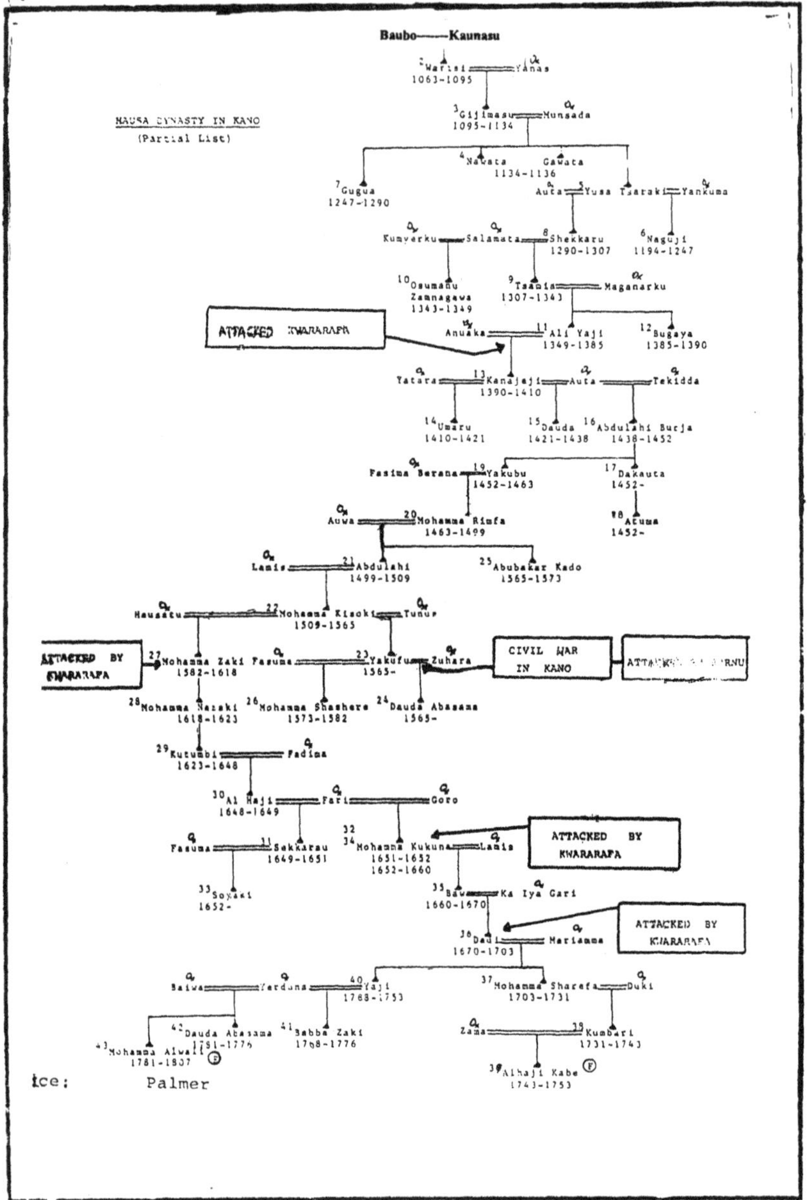
Baubo——Kaunasu
HAUSA DYNASTY IN KANO
(Partial List)
Yanas
Gijimasu
1095-1134
Munsada
Nawata
1134-1136
Gawata
Gugua
1247-1290
Auta
Yusa
Yankuma
Kumyerku
Salamata
Shekkaru
1290-1307
Naguji
1194-1247
Osumanu
Zamnagawa
1343-1349
Tsamia
1307-1343
Maganarku
ATTACKED KWARARAFA
Anuaka
Ali Yaji
1349-1385
Bugaya
1385-1390
Yatara
Kanajeji
1390-1410
Auta
Tekidda
Umaru
1410-1421
Dauda
1421-1438
Abdulahi Burja
1438-1452
Fasima Berana
Yakubu
1452-1463
Dakauta
1452-
Atuma
1452-
Auwa
Mohamma Rimfa
1463-1499
Lamis
Abdulahi
1499-1509
Abubakar Kado
1565-1573
Hausatu
Mohamma Kisoki
1509-1565
Tunur
ATTACKED BY KWARARAFA
Mohamma Zaki
1582-1618
Fasuma
Yakufu
1565-
Zuhara
CIVIL WAR IN KANO
Mohamma Nazaki
1618-1623
Mohamma Shashere
1573-1582
Dauda Abasama
1565-
Kutumbi
1623-1648
Fadima
Al Haji
1648-1649
Fari
Goro
ATTACKED BY KWARARAFA
Fasuma
Sekkarau
1649-1651
Mohamma Kukuna
1651-1652
1652-1660
Lamis
Soyaki
1652-
Bawa
1660-1670
Ka Iya Gari
ATTACKED BY KWARARAFA
Dadi
1670-1703
Mariamma
Baiwa
Yerduna
Yaji
1753-1753
Mohamma Sharefa
1703-1731
Duki
Dauda Abasama
Babba Zaki
1768-1776
Zama
Kumbari
1731-1743
Mohamma Alwali
1781-1807
Alhaji Kabe
1743-1753
Palmer

Chart III

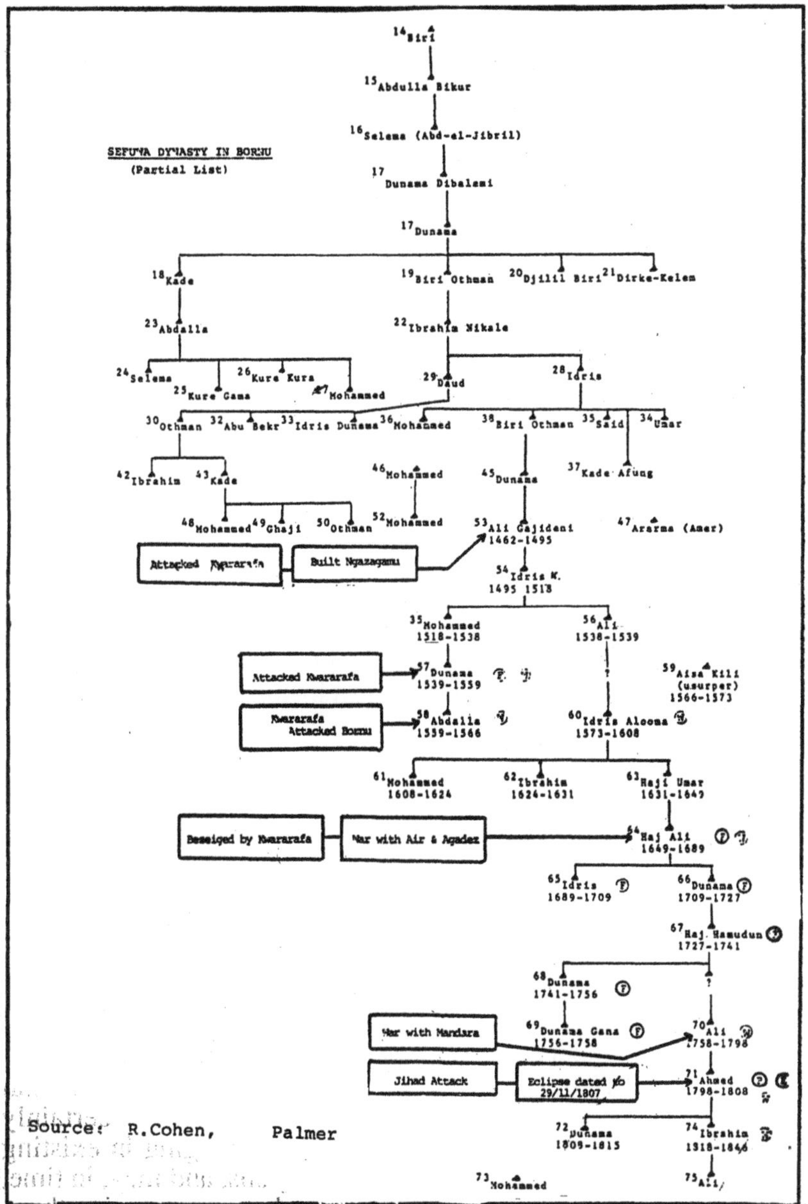

The Kano-Bornu Dating Axis

It is equally apparent, however, that this progression of dates covering the entire Benue Basin could have been extended across a much broader regional spectrum. For example, comparisons might be available between the upper Benue Valley region and the Bamenda grassfields of the Cameroons.[35] Also, evidence clearly suggests a connection between the middle Niger Valley, Benin and the Ga of modern Ghana.[36] Finally, Kano, Katsina, Zaria and Bornu extended their political and economic influence much further than the Chad depression, and relationships to Agades, Sokoto, Songhai and Air could have been considered.[37] For the purpose of this discussion, however, the correlations of regional evidence have been restricted to the three sub-regional pillars.

The methodology of dating pre-colonial regnal lists and genealogical information has been dealt with in some length elsewhere.[38] However, the on-going debate on the methodology seems, in many cases at least, to be reduced to an argument about a few years, rather than the validity of the dating exercise based upon generation averages. Clearly the techniques of genealogical, generational, reign length, and parenthetical dating,[39] coupled with synchronism and inter- and intra-societal tie-ins and fixed date reference points, establishes a viable method for dating pre-colonial African history. Furthermore, the use of approximate dates does not lead automatically to a prolonged debate about minor discrepancies of a few years or months. Regardless of the volume of data or the efficiency of the researcher, the dating progression remains a relative dating framework. However, the need still exists to provide a standardization of the methodology which will improve potential correlations in the regional data bank and avoid the problems associated with the comparison of century-dating or relative dating with the information derived from generation-dating techniques. By standardizing methodology we do not expect conformity to force fit evidence. However, the improvement in communication between sets of data will enhance understanding of the past and improve and extend the structure of regional chronology. Data which is structurally similar will certainly extend the borders of the Benue Basin by bringing in existing ethno-centric studies or under-studied regions, and may, in time, require a redefinition of the relationship between certain ethno-linguistic groups and regional events. The basic principle of standardization lies in the adoption of a viable generation length average. In the words of D.P. Henige, who has been incorrectly labelled the "high priest of scepticism",[40] adoption of a recognized generation length average between twenty-five and thirty-five years represents a viable statistical range, and that "this distribution only confirms the long standing assumption of most historians."[41] Henige went on to add that, "Sixty-five percent of the dynasties (in a global study) had generation lengths averaging between 25 and 35 years, and ninety-three percent fall in the range of 20-39 years."[42]

Let us begin the analysis of regional dating with the south-western pillar of the extended regional dating progression, and an examination of the chronological relationship of Benin to the Benue Basin. As previously noted Chart I provides a summary of the Benin dating framework and shows the evidence schematically from a number of genealogically related and inter-connected social formations. Chart IV shows the Benin core chronology in direct comparison with the regnal lists of Lagos. Chart V combines the Benin dating progression with data from a number of Idah, Agbor and Onitsha. Similar charts could be presented which correlate Benin with Idoani, Akure, Owo and a number of other Benue Basin states.[43] However, for the purpose of this discussion the correlation of a number of documentary fixed date reference points and the synchronisation of Lagos, Benin and the Idah evidence seems to establish a viable dating structure.[44] The eleven fixed date reference points shown on the charts provide a positive correlation with the Benin regnal list dated according to the twenty-seven year generation average. The total evidence, in fact, provides a 92% probability ratio for the accuracy of the Benin regnal chronology.[45]

The positive correlation of genealogical dating, regional synchronism, and the fixed date reference points clearly indicate that the Benin dating structure exceeds minimum standards established for statistical reliability. With the correlation of data from nine Ishan cross references in one generation alone,[46] coupled with evidence from Agbor, Aboh, Onitsha, Idoani, Akura, Owo, Ekiti, and Idah the Benin dating structure becomes even more reliable. Chart I reveals that the sub-regional correlations in available inter-societal evidence and inter-regional data are remarkably consistent. As further research is undertaken more and more evidence will be accumulated which will amend and/or confirm the Benin cluster chronology. At this stage, however, it is possible to conclude that this is sophisticated dating framework and that given a statistical probability in excess of 92% that the dating progression is relatively accurate.One example of the supporting evidence for the Benin chronology is worthwhile exploring further. Benin tradition records that Oba Oguola initiated the construction of the Benin city walls.[47] The generation dating structure for Benin establishes an approximate date of c. 1401-1428 for Oba Oguola's generation. G. Connah suggests that this is consistent with the fifteenth century rise of centralized government in Benin and the construction of the city walls.[48] Thurstan Shaw adds even more conclusively that "An excavation through this wall obtained charcoal from an earlier building buried beneath it; this was radio-carbon-dated to AD 1300+105, which accords well enough with the mid-fifteenth century date for the building of the wall."[49]The Igala-Idah dating progression also provides an early archaeological date for the regnal list of the Idah dynasties. B.M. Fagan summarizes the radiocarbon dates for the Ate Ogu mound in Idah - named after a monarch in the first Okpoto dynasty - as follows. This evidence seems to accord well with the generational, reign length and parenthetical dating techniques employed in the development of the Igala chronology. In fact a detailed analysis of Igala dating involved the correlation of almost 5,000 inter- and intra-societal cross references in its verification. The following radiocarbon fixed date was only one factor in the corroboration of the Igala-Idah regnal dating structure.

1-2262:	455+	95 years	-	AD 1495
1-2263:	410+	95 years	-	AD 1540

A trial excavation in a large mound said by localtradition to be a construction made by one of the early kings of Idah suggested not only that this was so, but that there might have been two periods of construction. 1-2263 was firmly in the earlier phase, and that the date is not inconsistent with what was expected as a result of analyzing local traditions. 1-2262 was in the area of the junction of the two phases and could have belonged to either.both dates can be regarded as indicating a mid-fifteenth century date.[50]

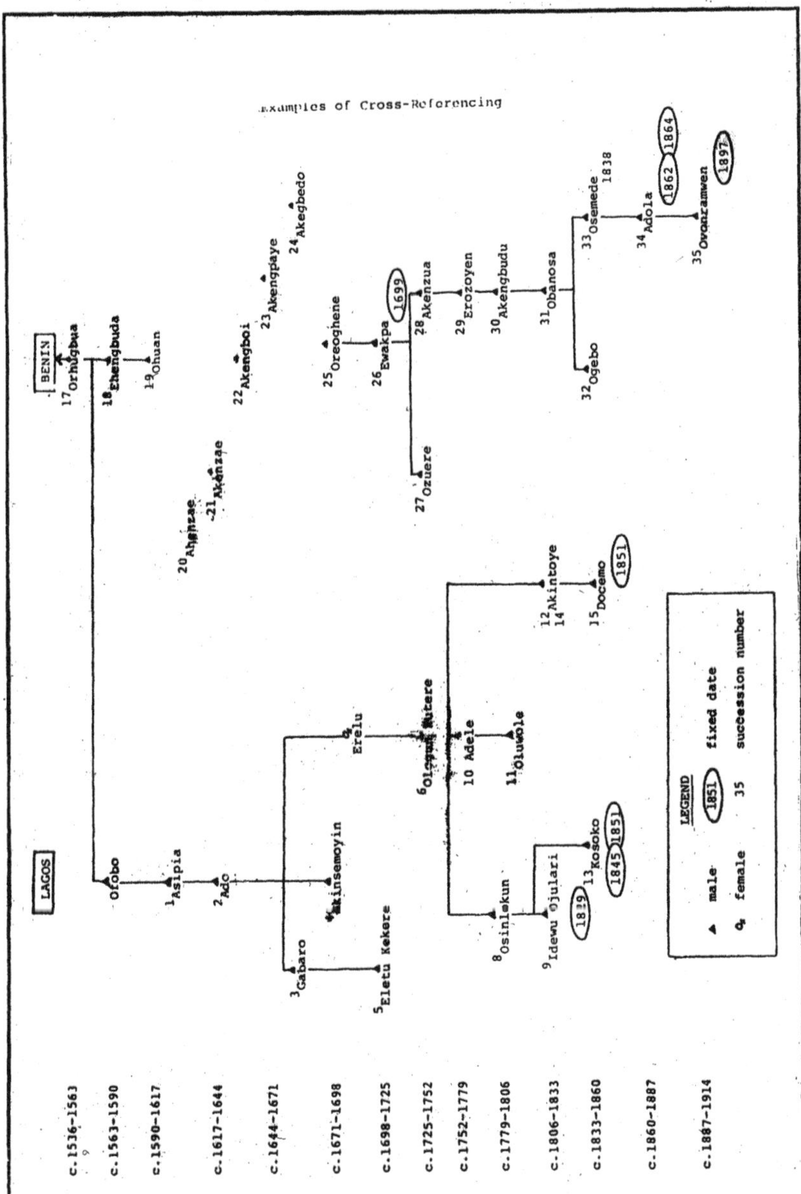

Chart IV Lagos-Benin: Examples of Cross-Referencing

Idah genealogical dating suggests that Ate Ogu reigned in c. 1477-1507, a correlation with the archaeological evidence and the "mid-fifteenth century" dated indicated by Fagan.

Chart II endeavours to summarize the Igala-Idah dating progression and schematically delineates the relationship of this core chronology to the large number of inter-societal cross references. This chart also identifies fifteen fixed date reference points which confirm the dating progression based upon genealogical and dynastic generation averages.[51] Chart VI, on the other hand, reveals some of the Idoma dating information that supports the Igala-Idah chronology. This Idoma data was collected and dated by E.O. Erim and represented only a fraction of the more than one thousand genealogies analyzed from Idoma informants.[52] The Idah chronology is, therefore, reliable and exceeds 98% probability factor for regional corroborations.

Chart III summarizes the Kano-Bornu axis, and clearly shows the correlation between generation dating and the chronological progression established from the literate Arabic traditions of these sudanic zone states. This chart also shows graphically the connections between Kano-Bornu and the now defunct state of Kwararafa. Traditions from all three polities provide a number of inter-societal cross references which can be correlated in the confirmation of the dating progression for the north-eastern pillar of the Benue Basin regional dating progression. Finally, this chronological structure, based upon evidence from sudanic zone states, located in an environment susceptible to drought and famine, provides the opportunity to correlate this information from scientifically dated events - droughts, drought related famines, and eclipses - with the genealogical dating system.

It can be argued that all three sub-regional pillars of this extended regional structure are remarkably accurate and viable dating mechanisms. The Igala-Idah framework, for example, has been correlated with a vast collection of regional synchronistic data and thousands of dated genealogies, and thus achieves a positive correlation ratio in over 98% of all references. The Benin structure, on the other hand, has been corroborated by a large number of documentary dated reference points starting in 1485 and covering over four hundred years of European contact.[53] The Kano-Bornu axis has a literate tradition and can provide correlations between genealogical dating and scientifically dated natural phenomena, such as drought and eclipses. In this respect at least, each sub-regional pillar in the regional dating framework has certain positive attributes which contribute toward the techniques

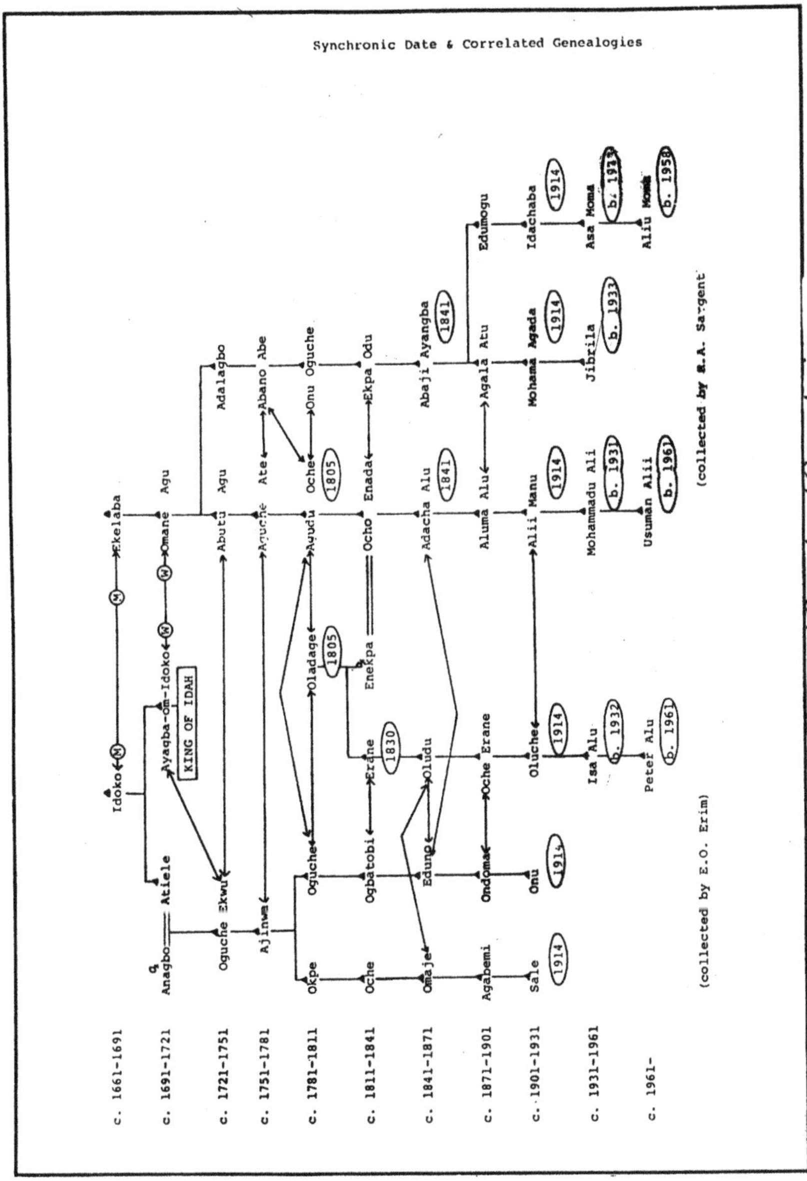

Chart V Syncronic Date and Correlated Genealogies

of dating and the verification of the methodology of chronology in the regional context.

With the delineation of the three sub-regional pillars in the Benue Basin dating structure a comparison of inter-regional cross references should provide a basis for a unified regional chronology. This mechanism also enables us to critically assess each sub-regional structure against evidence from other Benue regions. Let us begin this aspect of the analysis with an examination of data relating to the south-western pillar and the middle belt.

One of the important cross references between Benin and the Igala-Idah core chronology establishes a genealogical relationship between the Benin monarchy and the second Idah dynasty. The foundation of the second Idah dynasty in c. 1507-1537 (refer to Chart II) under Aji-Attah correlated with the reign of Oba Esigie of Benin in c. 1509-1536 (Chart I). Tradition clearly establishes Esigie and Aji-Attah as brothers and offspring of Oba Ozolua (c. 1482-1509).[54] Furthermore, Portuguese documentation corroborates the traditional accounts of the Esigie-Aji-Attah war in 1515-1516 in which Oba Esigie drove off the invading Idah army and secured the Bini throne for his son.[55] The correlation of two independent dating structures (Benin and Idah) with a fixed date reference point provides an initial cross reference between the south-west and the middle belt of the Benue Basin.

The conjunction of chronological evidence establishes not only a viable inter-relationship between Benin and Idah dating structures, but also corroborates regional dating through the evidence of documents and oral traditions. Further supporting data can be gleaned from the numerous Ishan traditions dealing with the Benin-Idah war.[56] In other words a great deal of chronological information can be marshalled to support the conclusion that the Benin-Idah war occurred in c. 1509-1536, and that the major participants were Oba Esigie of Benin and Aji-Attah, ruler of Idah.[57]

Criticism of the dating of the Benin-Idah war has generally tended to dispute the relevance of the Portuguese date and ascribe the missionary activities to another of Benin's military encounters. This suggestion seems to contradict Benin, Idah and Ishan evidence purely on the basis of speculation. It is significant, for example, that the missionaries were asked to leave Benin during the reign of Oba Ozolua (c. 1482-1509) and were only established in force when Oba Esigie mounted the throne (c.1509-1536).[58] The suggestion that the Portuguese document referred to another of Ozolua's wars cannot, therefore, be supported by any evidence, and appears to be an assumption rather than an historical reconstruction. The evidence clearly shows the relationship between dating and regional history, and effectively counters the speculation of the sceptics.

Another cross reference between the Igala-Idah chronological framework and the Benin cluster appears in the traditions relating to Idah and Onitsha.[59] For example, the marriage of Princess Ennobi of Idah, the daughter of Attah (King) Ayagba (c. 1687-1717), to the Onitsha monarch provided a dating reference point through which the two states can be compared.[60] Princess Ennobi has been dated first to the generation c. 1717-1765 - an extended dynastic generation length average based upon the succession of four collateral monarchs in a single generation - and second to c.1717-1747 by genealogical generation averages. These dates correlate with the reign of her husband, Chima Ogbuefi of Onitsha, in c. 1704-1734.[61] Further correlations between Onitsha and Idah can be found in the evidence that Eze Aroli, the offspring of Ennobi and Chima Ogbuefi, was educated in the Idah court during the reign of Attah Ocholi Oheme in c. 1752-1765 (reign length dates).[62] Eze Aroli has been dated to the generation c. 1734-1764, a perfect correlation with Attah Oheme's reign. Finally, during the reign of Obi Omozele in Onitsha, Attah Ogala of Idah provided royal regalia for the installation ceremonies of the new Onitsha monarch.[63] Omozele reigned in the generation c. 1764-1794 according to the Onitsha chronological structure, and Attah Ogala has been dated to c. 1788-1800 according to the Idah core chronology. These examples of inter-societal cross references between the Benin cluster and the Igala-Idah pillar provide a basis for the extended regional framework linking the forest zone in the south-west and the middle belt of the Benue Basin in a unified dating progression, and represent only part of the chronological data in the regional data bank.[64]

The middle belt dating structure and the Kano-Bornu axis can be correlated through a number of inter-societal cross references. For example, during the reign of Sarki Kumbari in Kano, tradition states that the Etsu (King) of Nupe was Jibrila. Genealogical dating techniques establish a dynastic generation date of c. 1717-17[65], and a reign length date of c. 1730-1743 for Etsu Jibrila.[66] The reign length date was calculated from a reign length average suggested by Robert Smith,[67] while the genealogical date was determined from the Nupe regnal list. The Kano evidence established a date for Sarki Kumbari of 1731-1743, which is a positive correlation between the dates of Nupe and Kano.[68] The inclusion of Nupe in the middle belt chronological nexus was based upon the correlation with Kano and the genealogical link between Nupe and Idah. Traditions in both Idah and Nupe indicate that the second Nupe dynasty was founded in c. 1507-1537 through the direct instigation of the Idah monarchy.

The foregoing brief analysis of corroborative synchronisms between Kano, Nupe and Idah suggest that Mason was categorically incorrect when he endeavoured to undermine Nupe dating and the Nupe regnal list.[69] In fact, Mason's efforts to dismiss Nupe chronology as mere political propaganda expose some of the weaknesses of his methodology rather than justifies his scepticism.[70] Mason's errors and omissions seriously weaken his own arguments. By attempting to repudiate the Nupe regnal lists collected by Goldsmith and Sciortino, and failing to include all the names on the Sciortino list in his analysis, Mason's calculations and subsequent analysis were seriously flawed.[71] One error, which eliminated Etsu Ali from the Nupe regnal list, would throw the calculations out by as much as a full generation. This sort of omission reflects Mason's own apparent failure to collect a Nupe regnal list, and attempt cross-referencing techniques with commoner genealogies.[72] Eventually, more detailed and comprehensive research in various central places in Nupe will eventually further solidify the dating of this important middle belt social formation.

The Nupe dynasty founded by Tsoede in c. 1537-1567 was forced out of the Nupe capital by the jihadist movement in the nineteenth century. This dynasty subsequently relocated at Pategi, and it is from there that early Nupe chronology might be best reconstructed. More current data clearly suggests that the relationship claimed in the traditions linking information gathered in Idah, for example, tends to corroborate the founding date for the Tsoede dynasty.[73] Furthermore, the cross reference to Etsu Jibrila from Kano confirms the Nupe dating structure. Even without detailed field work certain facets of Nupe dating begin to take shape, and parenthetical dating is possible.

A further correlation in the regional data bank suggests a link between Nupe and Oyo. R. Smith for example, argues that the period of turmoil in Oyo, when the Alafin went into exile, was related to the military expansion of Nupe under Etsu Tsoede.[74] The conquest of northern Oyo territory occurred in the early sixteenth century, and Tsoede has been dated to c.1537-1567. It should be noted that Tsoede was the son of Aji-Attah of Idah (c. 1507-1537) and a Nupe mother.[75] Furthermore, the foundations of the second Nupe dynasty and the relationship of this trading formation to Benue Basin regional developments have been summarized by J.S. Trimingham as follows,

> The foundation of this Nupe dynasty goes back to an immigrant, Edege or Tsoede, who lived in the fifteenth century. The 12th king, Jibril [Jibrila] (1730-1749, cf. Kano Chronicle, *Sudanese Memoirs*, iii, 124), was the first to call himself a Muslim. [76]

Another example of the correlation of the central and north-eastern pillars in the regional chronology can be found in the evidence which links eight distinct ethnic groups. Kwararafan evidence establishes that Adashu Katakpa attacked Bornu during the reign of Mai Haj Ali in 1649-1689.[77] Adashu Katakpa has been dated from the Kwararafa regnal list to the generation c.1640- 1670,[78] a perfect correlation with the Bornu dating scheme. Furthermore, Igala-Idah evidence claims that a group of Kwararafan refugees were attacked by Adashu Katakpa while they were settled in Agatu in c. 1627-1657.[79] This battle has been reported in Igala, Idoma and Alago traditions.[80] Finally, Adashu Katakpa (c.1640-1670) invaded Kano during the reign of Sarki Kakuna in 1651-1660.[81] Further correlations between Idah and Kwararafa can be found during the reign of Attah Ayagba in c. 1687-1717. In fact, Attah Ayagba fought a major war with Aku Agwabi of Kwararafa over the autonomy of Idah.[82] Adashu Katakpa, therefore, overlaps the reign of Mai Haj Ali by twenty-one years, the Igala information by seventeen, the Alago chronology by twenty, the Idoma genealogical data by fifteen and Sarki Kakuna by twenty years.

REGIONAL CHRONOLOGY IN THE BENUE BASIN

STRUCTURAL OUTLINE

PERIODIZATION	POLITICAL EVENTS	ECONOMIC FORCES	GENERATION DATES	DEMOGRAPHIC MOVEMENTS	ENVIRONMENTAL FACTORS
WET PROSPERITY	Dynastic Change Benin Foundation of Oyo		c. 1300-1330	Yoruba Diaspora	Yoruba Famine
			c. 1330-1360		
			c. 1360-1390		
		Regional Trade Expansion	c. 1390-1420		
		Coastal Trade Begins	c. 1420-1450	Ga Exodus	Songhai Drought & Famine
	Dynastic Change Idah & Nri	TRANS SAHARA TRADE BOOM	c. 1450-1480	Benin Exodus	
	Benin Expansion		c. 1480-1510	Bornu Shifts to Ngazargamu	
POOR DRY	Benin Expansion Idah Conquers Nupe		c. 1510-1540	Babur in Biu	
	Nupe Expansion		c. 1540-1570	Oyo Exiled	Bornu Drought & Famine
	Invasion of Songhai Foundations of Onitsha	Atlantic Trade Diversifies	c. 1570-1600	Benin Diaspora	Bornu Drought & Famine
	Dynastic Change Kwararafa	Trans-Saharan Trade Shifts	c. 1600-1630	Kwararafa Diaspora	Timbuctoo & Bornu Drought & Famine
	Dynastic Change Keana & Doma	Benue Salt Trade Expands	c. 1630-1660	Agatu Diapora	Bornu Drought & Famine
NORTHERN DRY / SOUTHERN MOIST	Oyo Expansion		c. 1660-1690	Jukun Expand	Bornu & Kano Drought & Famine
	Dynastic Change Idah	Atlantic Trade Expands-Slaves	c. 1690-1720		Bornu & Kano Drought & Famine
	Political Change Onitsha		c. 1720-1750		Continental Drought & Famine
		Atlantic Slave Trade Boom	c. 1750-1780		
EUROPEAN MOIST	JIHAD: Katsina, Kano, Nupe, Bornu, Zaria		c. 1780-1810	Bassa & Refuge Shift	Widespread Drought & Famine
		Atlantic Trade Turns Legitimate	c. 1810-1840	Second Jukun Expansion	
			c. 1840-1870		Kano Drought & Famine
		Royal Niger Co. Charter	c. 1870-1900		
	Creation of Northern Nigeria		c. 1900-		

Chart VI Regional Chronology: Structural Outline

Both Azara and Wuse genealogical data establish that they were founded by Agwabi's sons in c.1690-1720.[83] Since Agwabi died c.1700 this appears a perfect correlation. These multiple cross references establish regional and sub-regional links which corroborate not only the north-eastern axis of the dating progression, but also the regional basis of Benue Basin dating. A summary of this data, which includes references from Idah, Ankpa, Keana, Doma, Idoma, Azara and Wuse in the middle belt, and which was collected and analyzed by at least four independent researchers, can be structured as follows:

Inter-Regional Cross References

Adashu Katakpa of	Idah	c.1627-1657	(middle belt)
≥ Kwararafa, c.1640-1670	Ankpa	c.1627-1657	(middle belt)
	Keana	c.1630-1660	(middle belt)
	Doma	c.1630-1660	(middle belt)
	Idoma	c.1625-1655	(middle belt)
	Bornu	1649-1685	(Kano-Bornu axis
	Kano	1651-1663	(Kano-Bornu axis)
Agwabi of Kwararafa	Idah	c.1687-1717	(middle belt)
≥c. 1670-1700	Ankpa	c.1687-1717	(middle belt)
	Idoma	c.1685-1715	(middle belt)
	Kano	1670-1703	(Kano-Bornu axis)≥
	Azara	c.1690-1720	(middle belt)
	Wuse	c.1690-1720	(middle belt)

Another mechanism whereby the regional dating progression can be examined is through the comparison of drought and famine references in the various contributing social formations in the north-eastern and middle belt clusters. The south-western sub-regional pillar located primarily in the forest zone was relatively immune to the direct ravages of drought and famine, and cannot be tied-in to the regional framework through this particular technique.[84] Alago traditions, on the other hand, indicate that famine and drought effected the Obasadoma (Alago homeland) in the middle belt in c.1720-1750 and again in c.1780-1810.[85] Kwararafa traditions state that the reign of Aku Nani To in c. 1730-1760 and Aku Adi Matswen in c.1760-1790 were important periods of climatic deterioration.[86] Furthermore, Igala traditions also indicate that the reigns of Attah Agadu in c.1728-1740 and Attah Ayi in c.1740-1752 were periods when drought and famine effected areas north of the River Benue.[87] The reign of Attah Ogala in Idah, in c.1788-1800, also witnessed a large scale influx of refugees into northern Igalaland who were endeavouring to escape the massive drought and famine north of the Benue.[88] Finally, Kano and Bornu traditions establish drought and famine conditions in the periods 1743-1753 and 1734-1749 during the reigns of Sarki Alhaji Kabe and Mai Dunama respectively.[89] This impressive catalogue of famine and drought references not only confirms specific periods when climatic change affected both the middle and sudanic zones of the Benue Basin, but also illustrates the remarkable degree of consistence in the various ethno-centric and sub-regional dating progressions. It is essential to stress that the correlation of drought and famine references in a wide variety of independently dated chronological progression provided an important synchronization which confirmed the regional dating progression.

The periods of drought and drought-related famine indicated in the various traditions and dated according to a standardized methodology from the sudanic and middle belt regions can be corroborated from scientifically determined dates for climatic deterioration. Sharon Nicholson, for example, had described the mid-eighteenth century drought and famine in terms of dendrochronology, scientifically determined lake levels and weather patterns for an extended region.[90] Nicholson correlated this data with literature sources and oral evidence which established specific periods in which drought and famine were a prominent feature of this West African region. Nicholson claims that in the mid-eighteenth century:

> ...an extremely long and severe drought ravaged the entire Sahel-Soudan zone of central and West Africa from the 1730's to the 1750's, killing half the population of Tombouctoo [sic] and other parts of the Niger Bend. This period of famine and drought, perhaps the most severe one

> ever recorded, was reported in Senegambia, Mauritania, Mali, Upper Volta, Dahomey, Ghana, Nigeria and Chad.[91]

The second period of drought and famine in the late eighteenth century, and documented in Alago, Igala, Kwararafa, Kano and Bornu, has also been corroborated by Nicholson. In Kano, for example, the evidence claims that the reign of Sarki Mohamma Alwali in 1781 - 1807 was marred by severe drought and famine.[92] In Bornu the reign of Mai Ahmed in 1798-1808 witnessed widespread plague probably associated with drought and famine.[93] In Nicholson's words this was a period when

> ...a marked change began throughout tropical (northern hemisphere) Africa. In the 1790's a severe drought plagued Chad, Borun and the Kano area of Nigeria, forcing the evacuation of Agadez...and the level of Lake Chad began to fall continuously.[94]

The latter period of drought and famine in Bornu coincided with a recorded eclipse of the sun. In fact, during Mai Ahmed's reign in 1798-1808, Bornu claims that there was a total eclipse visible in the capital. Richard Gray documented an eclipse in this region near mid-day on 19 November 1807.[95] This confirmation of the Bornu dating framework, coupled with the correlations between famine and drought references throughout the Benue Basin provides a mechanism whereby regional chronology might be assessed. J.B. Webster, in fact, identified four great African droughts during the eighteenth century, three of them affecting West Africa.[96] These droughts have been listed on following table with a brief summary of the supporting evidence from West African and Benue Basin sources. The names of these drought periods were devised by Webster in order to simplify identification of each period of climatic deterioration. Following Webster's practice, the dates common to all traditions have been calculated. Only the Kwararafan date [*] fails to correlate, establishing a 92% probability ratio for the dating framework.

One of the problems with drought references is that droughts and related famines of three to five years in length are usually considered very severe, yet genealogically they are normally encapsulated in a single generation. The one drought reference in a generation, for example c.1727-1757, could refer to either the drought of the 1720's described as the Continental Drought, or the Solo-Nyamdere of the 1750's, or perhaps both. In spite of this potential confusion, however, the evidence summarized below appears to confirm that there were three eighteenth century droughts. More to the point for this discussion, it also helps confirm the regional dating progression by correlating evidence from a large number of individual genealogies and distinct social formations; data that was collected and analyzed by a number of different researchers. Furthermore, this variety of evidence helps overcome the difficulty with the specification of particular droughts within a generation. It is possible, therefore, to distinguish between periods of drought within a structure that has fairly broad parameters for dating. The Benue Basin regional chronology is just such a relative framework and facilitates the correlation of specific events to either the Continental, Solo-Nyamdere or Chadic-Mahlatule droughts. Even more significantly, the examination of droughts and related famine references suggests a possible periodization of the regional chronology based upon economic factors, and the variations in climatic conditions. This periodization provides not only a broader set of chronological parameters, but also establishes a functional framework for understanding events as part of a larger regional tapestry. Unfortunately, space precludes any further detailed examination of the inter-societal and inter-regional cross references which affirm the regional chronological structure. It would take more space than is available to summarize all evidence even when presented in chart form. This discussion has, however, provided a number of sub-regional dating progressions and provides sufficient evidence to clearly link the three pillars of regional chronology in a unified dating structure. The data, in fact, provides a relatively large number of positive correlations in inter-regional cross references, and a better than 90% statistical probability can be calculated for all inter-regional and inter-societal cross references.

Given the nature of the evidence, it is possible to state with confidence that the methodology utilized for dating pre-colonial oral tradition provides a sound basis for the development of a chronological framework for historical reconstruction.

Eighteenth Century Droughts in the Benue Basin

Webster's Terminology/ Dating	*Oral Traditions/ Chronicle*		*Common Dates≥*
Continental Drought 1720	Igala-Idah	c.1728-1740	1728-1730≥
	Bornu	1727-1741	
	Kwararafa	c.1730-1760	
	Alago	c.1720-1730	
Solo-Nyamdere 1750'S	Igala-Idah	c.1740-1752	1743-1750≥
	Bornu	1741-1756	
	Alago	c.1720-1750	
	Kano	1743-1753	
Chadic-Mahlatule 1790'S	Kano	1781-1807	1798-1800
	Igala-Idah	c.1788-1800	
	Bornu	798-1808	
	Kwararafa*	c.1760-1790	
	Alago	c.1780-1810	

That confidence is built upon the fact that correlations between various forms of ethno-centric, scientific and documentary evidence for sub-regional dating establishes a complex yet highly reliable set of dated correlations. It is only through a relatively reliable dating system for a particular social formation developed within the extended regional structure of the Benue Basin that the attempted reconstruction of regional chronology can emerge from the shadow of myth and legend.[97] An adequate chronology, however, enables the historian to relate regional events, analyze regional synchronisms, perçeive regional movements, and eventually, write regional history. Chart VII summarizes the Benue Basin regional chronology, and attempts to place political events, economic forces, demographic changes, and environmental factors within the generalized periodization of Benue Basin history. The charts utilizes a thirty year generation average to establish the core chronological progression for this regional dating framework, and thus suggest certain subdivisions within the period between c.1300 and 1900, or six centuries of Benue Basin history.

Regional chronology for the Benue Basin indicates qui clearly that the period between c.1330 and 1590 was relativel prosperous, stable, and a time of economic growtl environmental stability and imperial expansion.[98] This perio therefore, has been referred to as an age of "wet-prosperity" i the history of the Benue Basin; an age when Benin wa expanding, droughts were limited,[99] and the wide-sprea Songhai pax (1490-1591) encouraged the trans-Saharan trade t reach heights never before achieved.[100] The general prosperity o this period is revealed through the traditions of Bornu, Kano Benin, and Idah.[101] For example, between c.1455 and 153 Benin evolved into a major imperial trading formation linked t four expanding commercial exchange systems, including th north-south hinterland trade linked to the trans-Sahara commercial network, and the Atlantic overseas trade with th Europeans on the coast.[102] During this same period, (1455-1536), the Igala-Idah social formation in the middle belt developed as a major economic and commercial enclave in the expansion of Niger riverine trade, and the Bini dynasty of Idah (c.1507-1687) provided the political impetus for the organization of Igala commercial development.[103]

After the collapse of Songhai in 1591 in the face of the Moroccan invasion,[104] a number of factors contributed to end this period of prosperity. Bornu became one of the main commercial entrepots on the southern fringe of the trans-Saharan trading system, and old patterns of commercial exchange no longer provided the economic incentives that had once supported thriving dynasties in Benin, Idah, Kano, Nupe, Katsina and Kwararafa. Drought and famine, which started in Bornu during the reign of Mai Aisa Kili in 1566-1572, and which became a persistent problem after 1649,[105] seriously affected the economic environment of the entire region. A number of political events correspond with the end of the age of prosperity, including the decline of Kwararafa and a violent change in dynasty resulting in civil war.[106] The Kwararafa diaspora (c.1597-1657) also contributed to the general turmoil at the end of the golden age, and an altered political geography emerged in the middle belt with new dynasties among the Igala, Idoma, Etulo, Alago and Jukun. The politics and economics of the Benue Básin had apparently changed, and the trans-Saharan trading network no longer provided the economic mainstay of sudanic, middle belt and forest zone trading formations. After c.1630-1660 the Atlantic overseas trade diversified with the introduction of increased Dutch, English, Danish and French commercial activities to break the Portuguese monopoly. A dramatic change in environmental conditions correlated with the economic re-orientation of Benue Basin commerce.[107] The basic economic, political, environmental and demographic patterns between c.1600 and 1700 can be viewed as a manifestation of an age of turmoil and general dislocation. The major droughts of the 1720's and 1750's clearly contributed to this widespread confusion and turmoil, and it was not until the late 1750's that economic conditions in parts of the Benue Basin recovered any order or vitality.[108]

The partial recovery in the latter half of the eighteenth century was extremely short-lived. The droughts and famines returned at the end of the century to plague economic recovery and once again plunged the Benue Basin into economic and political turmoil. There was, however, a localized economic resurgence based primarily upon coastal slave trading demands, but this period did not provide any lasting economic growth. During the southern economic recovery of the nineteenth century Idah, the delta city states, and the Aro trading network experienced what might be classified as an artificial age of commercial prosperity. The main source of this economic growth was the slave trade which fed on the misery of a drought stricken age. In other areas of the Benue Basin, however, the economic, political and demographic transformation did not provide in any form of prosperity or stability, and a general economic decline pervaded Benin, Kano, Bornu and Kwararafa to name but a few of the affected states. Corresponding to the general dislocation and decline in the upper Benue Basin, and particularly in the Kano-Bornu axis, were the problems associated with the Islamic jihads combined with further environmental degradation in the major droughts and famines of c.1780-1810. It is impossible at this time to draw any major conclusions about the rapid development of the jihadist movement and the general economic depression in the sudanic zone. However, it is possible that the regional nature of the islamic revival was related to the prolonged period of economic depression, political instability and environmental deterioration.

Corresponding to the general dislocation and decline in the upper Benue Basin was a reversed situation in the southern zone. The lower Niger, the delta city states, and the Aro were relatively immune from the severe droughts and famines, and their economic prosperity and political stability were not jeopardized. These areas, therefore, did not reflect the general conditions in the Benue Basin during the nineteenth century. In fact, the southern third of this region embarked on a second golden age which fed on the declining fortunes north of the River Benue. It was a period of economic gain in the south and severe depression in the north.

Although it would seem that the southern Benue Basin experienced a second period of relative prosperity after c.1750, the decline of legitimate commerce, and the concentration on slave raiding and slave trading did not establish a sound economic basis upon which continued development and expansion of the various social formations could depend. The economic situation in Benin, for example, underwent a drastic change after the turmoil of the seventeenth century depression. The embargo against the export of male slaves was lifted in c. 1725, and Benin endeavoured to join the second golden age as an exporter of slaves rather than pepper, cloth, ivory, beads and camwood which had been the mainstay of her economic wealth in the first age of prosperity.[109] The period after c.1750, therefore, can be described as the start of economic decline as legitimate industry, crafts and commerce gave way to the temporary expediency of slave trading. In Idah, the third dynasty founded by Attah Ayagba in c.1687-1717, also turned energetically to the development of slave trading, and became a major supplier to the Niger River markets and the Aro overland system.[110] Once important indigenous industries in the middle belt, including weaving, dying, metal production and crafts, salt production and exchange, carving and brass casting all went into severe decline after c.1750 as competing products from the coast increasingly undercut local produce, and slave raiding made regional and long-distance exchange of legitimate products hazardous. In this respect at least, there is an emerging pattern to the region historiography of the Benue Basin, a pattern that can be identified and discussed because of the regional dating framework which provides a general chronological structure and places individual events in a perspective relative to others.

The basis of regional history has been the regional chronology based upon the three sub-regional pillars linked in a synchronic framework. The dating of pre-colonial history takes on new significance when the construction of the past considers the inter-actions of multi-ethnic population, various social formations, and the co-ordination of regional movements, relationships and changes. Without a regional chronology no such overview is possible. The advantage of this kind of study are obvious, and clearly lay the ground work for a major advance in the reconstruction of regional history. Benue Basin history can now begin to take on new shape and meaning, and perhaps more accurately reflect the nature of the past in this West African region.

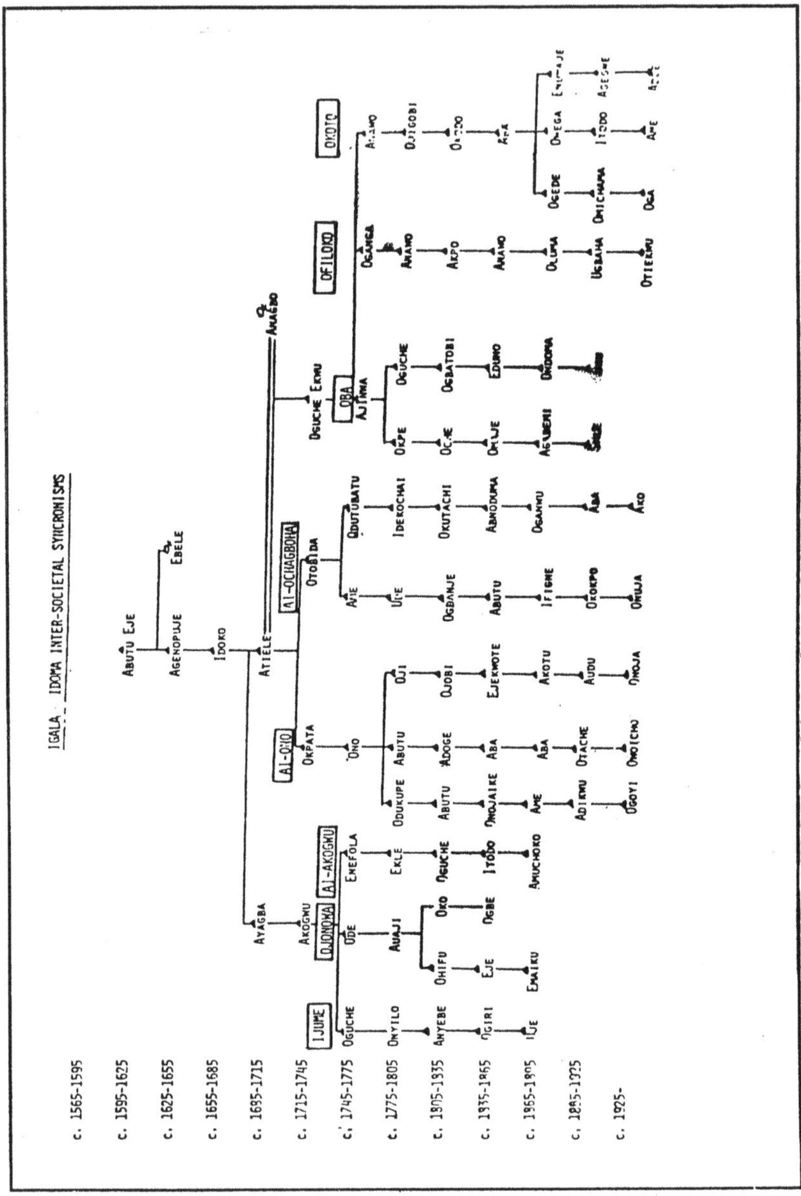

Chart VIII Igala - Idoma Inter-Societal Synchronism

References

1. The core of this chapter originally appeared as R.A. Sargent, "A Benue Basin Regional Chronology", *The Journal of General Studies*, (Kano), Vols. 5 & 6, No. 1, 1984/5, pp. 1-38. The information has been recently updated with the inclusion of number of other dated studies in the regional framework. One significant addition has been a dated framework for the foundation of Aro Chukwu. See A.O. Nwauwa, 'The Aro Chiefdom: Chronology and State Formation, c. 1690-1720', Dalhousie University M.A., 1989. Equally as important has been the work of Igbo iron manufacturing systems. Refer to O.N. Njoku, A History of Iron Technology in Igboland, c. 1542-1900',Dalhousie University Ph.D, 1986.

   This new information also extended the known boundaries of the Benue Basin and enabled this reconstruction to include more detailed evidence about hinterland commercial relations with the coast. Links to the Rio del Rey - 1500 to 1660 - and with Calabar - 1660 onward - affected developments in the interior. Thus the economic and political events within the Benue Basin can now be seen in a clearer light of events on the periphery of the region.

   It is interesting to note, however, that the original structure was not critically or negatively affected by the subsequent studies. Rather the principles of dating in a regional context, and the framework of a sound regional chronology has been reinforced by the addition of the new dating information.

2. J.B. Webster, 'Chiefs and Chronology: Jukun Colonies in the Benue Valley', Benue Valley Project Paper No. 4, 1975. The Benue Valley History Project collection can be obtained on microfilm through the Killam Library, Dalhousie University, (Special Collections Branch), Halifax, Nova Scotia, Canada. For further perspectives on chronology refer to D.F. MacCall, *Africa in Time Perspective*, New York, 1969; Y. Person, "Tradition Orale et Chronologie", *Cahiers d'Etudes Africaines*, II, 7, 1962; N. Dyson-Hudson, *Karimojong Politics*, Oxford, 1966; J. Lamphear, *The Traditional History of the Jie of Uganda*, London, 1976; M.I. Finley, "Myth, Memory and History", *History and Theory*, IV, 1965; D.W. Cohen, "Survey of Interlacustrine Chronology", *Journal of African History*, XI, x, 1970; J.B. Webster, (ed.), *Chronology, Migration and Drought in Interlacustrine Africa*, New York, 1979; E.J. Alagoa, "Dating Oral Tradition", *African Notes*, 4, 1, 1966/67; D.H. Jones, "Problems of African Chronology", *Journal of African History*, XI, 2, 1979; D.P. Henige, "Oral Traditionsand Chronology", *Journal of African History*, XII, 3, 1971; and D.P. Henige, *The Chronology of Oral Tradition: A Quest for a Chimera*, Oxford, 1972, among others.

3. In the words of D.P. Henige it is certainly encouraging that "more serious attention has been paid to efforts to establish a reliable, if necessarily inexact, framework for pre- colonial Africa", Henige, "Oral Tradition and Chronology", p. 371.

4. Regional history based upon a growing regional chronology seems to be one of the most positive and rewarding developments in pre-colonial

African historiography. As more evidence comes in this network of interconnections across a broad expanse of West Africa the better we begin to understand the complexity and vitality of regional economics, social relations and political development.

5. The schematic representation of the three pillars of regional dating in the Benue Basin and shows graphically some of the inter-societal and inter-regional cross references. One Chart shows the Benin sub-regional pillar in a dated regnal list which utilizes Benin as the core chronology for this south-western cluster. Another graphically represents the Igala-Idah dating nexus, with indications for the numerous cross references which substantiate this dating framework for the middle belt. Further, another shows the Kano-Bornu axis. A `pillar' of regional chronology is a core regnal list or chronological structure that can be tested against a large body of data from the whole region in various sub-regional correlations. As a pillar of regional chronology these structures are major supports for the reconstruction of the past.

6. In fact, the examination of ethno-centric dating has been dealt with elsewhere, and provides a detailed mechanism for ethno-centric and sub-regional dating for the specific societies utilized in the development of this regional chronology. Refer, for example, to R.A. Sargent, "A Methodology of Chronology: The Igala Core Dating Progression", *History in Africa*, Vol. II, 1984; E.O. Erim, *The Idoma Nationality, 1600-1900: Problems in Studying the Origins in Ethnicity*, Enugu, 1981; F.B. Ataba, 'Some Recent Developments in the Use of Non-Documentary Evidence, with Special Reference to Totemism and Regional Chronology', Dalhousie University, M.A., 1976; J.E. Miller, 'Ishan-Benin Relations, c.1455-1509', Dalhousie University Honours Thesis, 1983; and R.A. Sargent, `Benin. Chronology: Statistical Probability Ratios and Regional Synchronism', Dalhousie University, History Seminar, January 1984.

7. This is clearly a perspective advocated by J.B. Webster, H.F.C. Smith, D.P. Henige and many others concerned with both the fragile nature of oral evidence and the validity of pre-colonial dating techniques. Refer for example to J.B. Webster, "Through the Palace Gates, Chiefs and Chronology: Developing Reliable Dating Structures", History in Africa, Vol. II, 1984.

8. Webster, *Chronology, Migration and Drought*, p. xiv.

9. The Igala core dating progression was developed during an extensive period of field work in which over 1,000 genealogies were collected from a variety of Igala informants. This body of data was compared with an equally large collection of dated genealogies compiled by E.O. Erim, and an extensive collection of regional synchronisms. The Igala-Idah dating progression has been examined in detail in Sargent, "A Methodology of Chronology".

10. Henige, *The Chronology of Oral Tradition*, p. 18. Contrary to a popular misconception Henige does not discount pre-colonial chronology, but argues on the side of continued caution and extreme care when faced with dating solely from oral evidence. When utilizing documentary data, archaeology, eclipse references, and regional synchronism Henige argues

for a statistical probability for a relative reliable dating progression that critically examines all available evidence. Any dating progression based upon orally preserved data, no matter how comprehensive the corroborative information, must be considered a relative structure and not a year by year chronicle of events.

11. Ataba, 'Some Recent Developments', and Sargent, "A Methodology of Chronology".
12. Sargent, 'Benin Chronology', also refer to M. Kalous, "A Contribution to Some Problems of Benin Chronology", *Archiv Orientalni*, 38, 1970, and J.U. Egharevba, *A Short Story of Benin*, Ibadan, 1968. Other works which contribute to Benin chronology include R.E. Bradbury, *Benin Studies*, edited by P. Morton-Williams, Oxford, 1973, and A.F.C. Ryder, *Benin and the Europeans, 1485-1897*, Ibadan, 1969.
13. Sargent, "A Methodology of Chronology", and also R.A. Sargent, 'Dating Collateral Succession: The Igala Kingdom in the Middle Belt", Benue Valley Project Paper No. 15, 1976.
14. Chronological development among the Ishan chiefdoms was based upon a detailed analysis of Ishan traditions collected by C.G. Okojie for all twenty-six polities in Ishan Division. J.E. Miller based his work on this collection. Refer to C.G. Okojie, *Ishan Native Law and Customs*, Yaba, 1960. Miller, in fact, correlated nine Ishan chiefdoms with the Benin regnal list. Miller also provided five genealogical correlations between Ishan and Benin, and number of dated cross references.
15. Erim, *Idoma Nationality*, pp. 1-35. Erim examined sixteen Idoma chiefdoms which claimed genealogical relationship to the Igala monarchy. Each chiefdom provided a number of individual genealogical cross references dated by Erim which confirmed the Igala-Idah dating progression. An example of this correlation between Idah and the Idoma dating structures can be found in Chart VII.
16. For example, refer to J.N. Orkar, 'A Pre-Colonial History of the Tiv of Central Nigeria, c.1500-1850', Dalhousie University, Ph.D., 1979; J.B. Webster, 'Periodization in African History', Benue Valley Project Paper No. 34, 1983; and J.H. Morrison, 'Jos Plateau Societies: Internal Change and External Influences, 1800-1935'. University of Ibadan, Ph.D., 1976.
17. Eclipse data and scientifically dated droughts are two good examples of important tools for pre-colonial dating.
18. Captain Roupell's Benin regnal list was published in H. Ling-Roth, *Great Benin, Its Customs, Art and Horrors*, Halifax, 1903. N.W. Thomas who collected a Benin regnal list in the 1920's has not published this information, but it is repeated in B. Struck, "Chronologie der Benin-Altertumer", *Zeitschrift fur Ethnologie*, LV, 1923; and Egharevba, *A Short History of Benin*.
19. Bradbury, *Benin Studies*, pp. 17-43, and also R.E. Bradbury, "Chronological Problems in the Study of Benin History"; *Journal of the Historical Society of Nigeria*, 1, No. 4, 1959; Ryder, Benin and the Europeans, and Kalous, "Contribution to Some Problems"

Ataba, 'Some Recent Developments'.

21. Miller, 'Ishan-Benin Relations', and Sargent, Benin Chronology'.
22. Sargent, 'Benin Chronology'.
23. Fixed date reference points for all charts have been displayed in a uniform manner. It would be virtually impossible, however, to cite, discuss and analysis every fixed date reference point relevant to this regional discussion. This is especially true given the large number of regnal lists and genealogies which have been correlated to formulate this regional dating progression. Examples of these sources would range from archaeology, to a letter from a Portuguese missionary in Benin to the King of Portugal in 1515-1516. In fact, the letter from Duarte Pires to King Dom Manual in Lisbon dispatched in 1516 has been cited in Egharevba, *A Short History of Benin*, p. 29, and E. Sanceau, *The Reign of the Fortunate King*, New York, 1969. Also relevant for the establishment of fixed date reference points are sources such as T.J. Hutchinson, *Narrative of the Niger, Tshadda, and Benue Exploration*, London, 1855, to name only a few. A complete bibliography for the Benue Basin region can be found in R.A. Sargent, 'Politics and Economics in the Benue Basin, c.1300-1700', Dalhousie University, Ph.D., 1984.
24 Without a standardized methodology the synchronism of regional correlations becomes a complex and time consuming task. In fact, when one researcher adopts a century-based dating technique it serves to isolate that ethno-centric reconstruction from neighbouring societies and regional events.
25. R.C.C. Law, "The Dynastic Chronology of Lagos", *Lagos Notes and Records*, Vol. 11, No. II, December 1968, pp. 46-54.
26. *Ibid.*, p. 52.
27. Egharevba, *A Short History of Benin*, p. 29.
28. Refer to the chart which schematically shows this relationship.
29. Sargent, "A Methodology of Chronology". The study of Igala history and chronology followed in the wake of efforts by M. Clifford, "A Nigerian Chiefdom", *Journal of the Royal Anthropological Institute*, LXVI, 1936, and J.S. Boston, The Igala Kingdom, Ibadan, 1968 which attempted to provide reasonable dates for the Igala core chronology. Unfortunately both writer seemed convinced that there was only one Igala dynasty which led to some confusion. Also, Boston and Clifford published their work prior to the development of chronological methodology and were apparently unable to reconstruct a viable dating progression for the Igala regnal list. Neither researcher seems to have collected individual genealogies. The main works contributing to the development of dating and oral research methodologies were published after 1965. The first major contribution was J. Vansina, *Oral Tradition*, London, 1965, and the pioneering efforts to date oral evidence were undertaken by R. Oliver, "The Ancient Capital Sites of Ankole", *Uganda Journal*, 23, 1956, followed by B.A. Ogot, *History of the Southern Luo*, Nairobi, 1967. The majority of work and development on pre-colonial dating, however, has been published in the 1970s and 1980s (refer to footnote 1). Unfortunately, Boston's analysis of Igala history has been accepted in some quarters as dogma. His perspective does

not allow for the development of Igala historical reconstruction past the label of 'myth'. Recent detailed field work, however, has exposed some of the problems of conducting research only via the present ruling dynasty in the Igala capital, and provided the opportunity to uncover and examine variant traditions which established not one Igala monarchy, but three distinct dynastic periods between 1500 and the present.

30. B.M. Fagan, "Radiocarbon Dates for Sub-Saharan Africa", *Journal of African History*, VIII, 3, 1967.

31 For example, J.C. Monkton, "Burial Ceremonies of the Attah of Idah", *Journal of the African Society*, XXVI, 1922-1923; C. Partridge, "The Burial of the Ata of Igara and the Coronation of His Successor", Blackwoods Magazine, 1904; and R.S. Seton, "Installation of the Attah of Idah", *Journal of the Royal Anthropological Institute*, LVIII, 1928 provide first-hand observations on the Igala monarchy.

32. The large number of inter- and intra-societal cross references to the Igala-Idah core chronology have been discussed in Sargent, "A Methodology of Chronology".

33. The core dating progression for this sub-regional pillar has been established from both the Kano and Bornu regnal lists. This basic information can be obtained in H.R. Palmer, *Sudanese Memoirs*, London, 1928; H.R. Palmer, *Gazetteer of Bornu Province*, Lagos, 1929; H.R. Palmer, *The Bornu, Sahara, and Sudan*, London, 1936; R. Cohen, "The Bornu Kinglist", *Boston University Papers on Africa*, XI, 2, 1970; J.A. Burdon, *Northern Nigeria*, London, 1909; A. Schultze, *The Sultanate of Bornu*, (translated by P.A. Benton), London, 1972; Also refer to S.J. Hogben, *The Muhammadan Emirates of Northern Nigeria*, London, 1966; W.P. Gowers, *Gazetteer of Kano Province*, London, 1921; and Y. Urvoy, "Histoire de l'Empire de Bornou", *Memoires de l'Institute Francais d'Afrique Noire*, No. 7, Paris, 1949 among others.

34. For information on the chronological relationship between the plateau states and Kwararafa refer to Morrison, 'Jos Plateau Societies'. Where he states that Kwararafa "ascended the plateau at Pankshin and followed a route through Angas' country", p. 39. Also refer to J.G. Davies, "Gyel Farm Society in Jos Division", *Farm and Forest*, 7, 2, June/December, 1946.

35. E.M. Chilvers, "Nineteenth Century Trade in the Bamenda Grassfields, Southern Cameroons", *Afrika und Ubersee*, 45, 1961, pp. 233-258.

36. Eva L.R. Meyerowitz, *The Early History of the Akan States of Ghana*, London, 1974, p. 74, and M. Manoukian, *Akan and Ga- Adangme Peoples*, Part I, Ethnographic Survey of Africa, edited by D. Forde, London, 1950, p. 67.

37. For example, refer to Burdon, *Northern Nigeria*, p. 35 where the *Kano Chronicle* documents a war with Katsina and Kwararafa during the reign of Sarki Mohamma Saki. Also refer to Palmer, *The Bornu, Saharan and Sudan*, which he refers to a war between Mai Haj Ali of Bornu and Air, Agadez and Kwararafa. (p. 246). Finally, refer to E.W. Bovill, *The Golden Trade of the Moors*, London, 1953, pp. 106-110 where he refers to Songhai's conquest of the Hausa states.

38. J.B. Webster and R.A. Sargent, *Practical Oral Methods: Historical Data Collection of Africa*, forthcoming.
39. Parenthetical dating requires at least two fixed date reference points. One at a relatively early date and one in the eighteenth or nineteenth century. These fixed date reference points should correlate with the generational dating framework, and thus corroborate the chronological progression.
40. Erim, *Idoma Nationality*, p. 154.
41. Henige, *Chronology of Oral Tradition*, p. 123.
42. *Ibid.*
43. A large number of charts relevant to the Benue Basin regional chronology have been reproduced in R.A. Sargent, 'Benin to Bornu: Regional Chronology, Regnal Lists and Genealogies', Benue Valley Project Paper No. 31, May 1983.
44. This kind of methodology can be adopted as a standardized technique for pre-colonial dating. The significance of a standard methodology lies in the potential to develop inter-societal cross references, and the possible development of regional correlations which lead to regional dating. When an ethno-centric reconstruction is dated by century-based dating techniques and another by regnal lists and genealogical dating it is difficult, and sometimes impossible, to compare and contrast the data. It is equally difficult to correlate the information effectively and efficiently. For example, K.O. Dike and F.I. Ekejuiba, "The Aro State: A Case Study of State Formation in Southeastern Nigeria", *Journal of African Studies*, 5, 3, 1978, endeavours to discuss the development of the Aro state in terms of a seventeenth century evolution. This century-based date does not allow enough chronological comparison with neighbouring or regional evidence dated according to the generation principles. The problem lies in the imprecise nature of Aro dating and the century-based reconstruction. The problems of regional relationships, therefore, reinforce the argument for a standardized chronological methodology
45. Sargent, 'Benin Chronology'.
46. Okojie, *Ishan*, provided a large number of Ishan regnal lists and for the correlations between the twenty-six Ishan chiefdoms and Benin, Miller, Ishan-Benin Relations', critically assessed the Ishan data and correlated this large collection of inter-societal evidence with the Benin chronology.
47. Egharevba, *A Short History of Benin*, p. 11. The Benin chronology establishes a generation date of c.1401-1428 for Oba Oguola.
48. Refer to G. Connah, "Benin", in *Lectures on Nigerian Pre-history and Archaeology*, edited by T. Shaw, Ibadan, 1969, and G. Connah, *The Archaeology of Benin*, Oxford, 1975, pp. 98- 106.
49. T. Shaw, Nigeria, London, 1978, p. 170. Also refer to G. Connah, "New Light on the Benin City Walls", *Journal of the Historical Society of Nigeria*, 3, 1967, pp. 593-609.
50. Fagan, "Radiocarbon Dates", pp. 517-518.
51. The fixed date reference points for the Igala-Idah regnal list are primarily in the nineteenth century. However, two early fixed dates provided the

opportunity to examine the Idah chronology by the parenthetical dating technique. Refer to Sargent, "A Methodology of Chronology"

52. More of the Idoma genealogies have been reproduced in Erim, *Idoma Nationality*, and Sargent, 'Benin to Bornu'.
53. Sargent, 'Benin Chronology'.
54. Igala Historical Text (hereafter cited as I.H.T.) No. 19, group interview in the Attah's palace, February 5, 1977. The I.H.T. were collected in an extensive field work period between 1976 and 1978.
55. A Portuguese missionary accompanied Oba Esigie in his defense of the capital, and documented their relationship in a letter to King Dom Manual of Portugal in 1516. Refer to Sanceau, *The Reign of the Fortunate King*, p. 73, and Egharavba, *A Short History of Benin*, p. 29. For a full discussion on the Benin-Idah war, its causes and consequences, refer to Sargent, 'Politics and Economics in the Benue Basin'.
56. Okojie, *Ishan*, p. 325. Also refer to Shaw, *Nigeria*, p. 172, Bradbury, *Benin Studies*, p. 36, and J.U. Egharevba, *The Murder of Imaguero and Tragedy of the Idah War*, Benin, 1948 (also in a Kraus Reprint, Nendeln, 1973, pp. 23-24):
57. Clearly Igala traditions support this conclusion, refer to I.H.T. No. 19, and I.H.T. No. 106, Otakpa village, July 20, 1977.
58. Bradbury, *Benin Studies*, pp. 36-40.
59. Onitsha evidence has been collected and analyzed by R.N. Henderson, *The King in Every Man*, New Haven, 1972. Although Henderson does not provide a chronology he does provide a detailed regnal list for the Onitsha monarchy, and establishes cross references to neighbouring and even distantly related social formation. This has enabled the writer to date Onitsha by the generation method.
60 Schematic examples provide a graphic illustration of the relationship between Idah and Onitsha and documents the cross references between these two riverine capitals.
61. Refer to the Onitsha chronology on Chart VIII.
62. Henderson, *The King in Every Man*, p. 86, and I.H.T. No. 89, in Dekina, July 4, 1977. Reign length dates have been utilized in the development of the Igala-Idah dating progression as a technique to double check the genealogical and dynastic dating framework. A considerable amount of data was compiled to establish a twelve year reign length during periods of collateral succession. Similar calculations, by Jones, "Problems in African Chronology", *op. cit.*, and R. Smith, "The Alafin in Exile: A Study of the Igboho Period in Oyo History", *Journal of African History*, VI, I, 1965, concluded that a range of 12 to 14 years was most probable for all dynasties with more than two rulers per generation. The correlation of a twelve year reign length average in the Idah example with fixed date reference points provided a consistent corroboration of this dating progression and suggested a statistical probability in excess of 70%.
63. Henderson, *The King in Every Man*, p. 88.

64. Refer to Sargent, `Benin to Bornu', for a graphic illustration of the multitude of inter-societal and cross- references.

65. *Kano Chronicle,* (as reproduced in Burdon, *Northern Nigeria*, p. 40.

66. In Chapter Six the relationship between Nupe and Idah and has been discussed more fully, and reveals the details of the cross reference to Etsu Jibrila.

67. Smith, "The Alafin in Exile", p. 73.

68. Positive correlations are those that provide an overlap in the suggested range of years. In this example, the positive correlation is represented by eleven years utilizing the reign length dates for Etsu Jibrila.

69. M. Mason, "The Tsoede Myth and the Nupe Kinglist: More Political Propaganda", *History in Africa*, 2, 1975.

70. Mason's dependence upon regnal lists collected by others, for example, suggests that he did not collect his own during his field work. Furthermore, Mason does not even attempt to correlate regional, inter- and intra-societal cross references to confirm his negative opinion. If all the cross references fell out of a recognized range for statistical probability then perhaps Mason's conclusion would gain credence. In fact, a detailed analysis of the same evidence reveals a remarkable consistence in the regional cross references.

71. Refer to Goldsmith in Burdon, *Northern Nigeria*, p. 51, and A. Sciortino, in Burdon, *Northern Nigeria*, pp. 17-19. Also refer to S.F. Nadel, *A Black Byzantium*. London, 1942.

72. Mason did not deal effectively with the Kano cross reference, and does not consider the Igala-Idah evidence which clearly substantiates the Nupe data. Refer for example to I.H.T. No. 82, Shintaku, Ahiemogbo clan, June, 1977; and Nadel, *A Black Byzantium*, pp. 76-79. Finally, refer to M. Mason, 'The Nupe Kingdom in the Nineteenth Century: A Political History', University of Birmingham, Ph.D., 1970.

73. Sargent, 'Politics and Economics'. As others work and research within the same parameters, the dating structure continues to expand. In c. 1505 Songhay defeated Borgu and establishd a barracks of soldiers there. In the generation of Tsoede (c. 1537-1567), two Nupe dynasties were created in northern and central Borgu and were not overthrown until the late eighteenth century. See Julius Adekunle, `Nigerian Borgu c. 1500 - 1900: An Analysis of a Segmentary Society', PhD thesis, Dalhousie University, 1993.

74. Smith, 'The Alafin in Exile", p. 61.

75. I.H.T. No. 86, and Nadel, *A Black Byzantium*, p. 73. The reference to Oyo conquering Nupe, for example, does not relate to the central Nupe kingdom but to the Nupe sub-chiefodm in Borgu, Adekunle, *op. cit.*

76. J.S. Trimingham, *A History of Islam in West Africa*, Oxford, p. 201, fn. 1.

77. Refer to the Bornu regnal list (Chart IV), and also see Palmer, *The Bornu Sahara and Sudan*, p. 240.

78. Chapter Seven shows the regnal list of Kwararafa and places Adashu Katakpa in the generation c.1640-1670.

79. I.H.T. No. 10, Idah, January 12, 1977 and I.H.T. No. 18, Idah, February 5, 1977.
80. Erim, *Idoma Nationality*, pp. 52-77, and Keana Historical Text No. 100, June 24, 1974, Alhaji Audu, Alhaji Adamu and Egwu of Keana, collected by E.O. Erim as part of the Benue Valley History Project. Also refer to Agwatashi Historical Text No. 101, June 27, 1974, Osoho's palace, in Agwatashi, collected by E.O. Erim. Finally, refer to Idoma Historical Text, Agatu No. 6, and Idoma Historical Text No. 42, collected by E.O. Erim during an extensive period of field work in 1976.
81. *Kano Chronicle*, p. 38.
82. I.H.T. No. 103, Adeny, July 18, 1977, I.H.T. No. 26, Ejule, February 17, 1977 and Boston, *The Igala Kingdom*, pp. 95-96.
83. J.B. Webster, 'Chief and Chronology', Benue Valley Project Paper No. 4, 1975; Webster, "To the Palace Gates, Chiefs and Chronology". Information concerning Kwararafa, and the Kwararafa regnal list can also be found in Meek, *Sudanese Kingdom*, and 'The Official and Traditional Installation Pamphlet', a programme produced for the coronation of Aku M. Abe Ali in 1970.
84. Drought reference correlation was suggested as a technique in Webster, *Chronology, Migration and Drought*, pp.1-37, and has been developed and expanded by S. Nicholson, 'A Climatic Chronology for Africa" Synthesis of Geological, Historical and Meteorological Information and Data', University of Wisconsin-Madison, Ph.D., 1976, and D.J. Schove, "Eclipse, Comets and the Spectrum of Time in Africa", *Journal of the British Astronomical Association*, 78, 1968.
85. Refer to the Keana and Doma regnal charts in Sargent, 'Benin to Bornu'.
86. Drought references appear in Meek, *Sudanese Kingdom*, pp. 51- 55. Also refer to Webster, 'Periodization', *op. cit.*, and Nicholson, 'A Climatic Chronology', pp. 236-300, which is an extensive collection of data covering the African continent and the whole period under discussion here.
87. I.H.T. No. 199, Aku, September 30, 1977.
88. *Ibid.*, and I.H.T. No. 198, group interview in Lakai village, Unana clan, September 19, 1977.
89. Palmer, *Sudanese Memoirs*, p. 125.
90. Nicholson, 'A Climatic Chronology', pp.1-31, and pp.113-120.
91. S. Nicholson, "Climatic Variations in the Sahel and Other African Regions During the Past Five Centuries", *Journal of Arid Environment*, 1, 1978, pp. 3-24.
92. Palmer, *Sudanese Memoirs*, p. 127.
93. Refer to the Kano-Bornu dating schematic.
94. Nicholson, "Climatic Variations", pp. 3-24.
95. R. Gray, "Eclipse Maps", *Journal of African History*, IX, 1, 1969., p. 260.
96. Webster, 'Periodization'. *op. cit.*
97. P. Muntz, "History and Myth", *Philosophical Quarterly*, 6, 1956, p. 2, where he argues that "myth...differs qualitatively from historical accounts,

in that it is vague in its specification of time and space". Boston, *The Igala Kingdom*, p. 16, utilized the specification of "myth" at least three times, and concludes that "In all probability the historical events alluded to in this myth are compressed in time." (p. 17), but since he never calculated time, this statement may be dismissed.

98. The chonological chart and regnal list both note the relative absence of environmental factors, population movements or political instability.

99. Sargent, 'Politics and Economics'.

100. A.A. Boahen, "The Caravan Trade in the Nineteenth Century", *Journal of African History*, III, 2, 1962, pp. 349-350, andA.W. Pardo, "The Songhay Empire under Sonni Ali and Askia Muhammad: A Study in Comparisons and Contrasts", *Boston University Paper on Africa*, Vol. V, 1971, p. 55.

101. The traditions of these West African states and a number of other pre-colonial polities have been examined in Sargent, 'Politics and Economics'.

102. For a more detailed analysis of Benin and the connections between the evolution of central administrative institutions, political authority and commercial activities refer to R.A. Sargent, 'The Evolution of an Empire: From a Redistributive to an Imperial Social Formation, Benin. c.1293-1536', paper originally presented to the Canadian Association of African Studies Conference, Universite Laval, Laval, May 1983.

103. Sargent, 'Politics and Economics'.

104. The invasion by Judur Pasha in 1591 effectively destroyed Songhai hegemony over the southern trans-Saharan trade network. Refer to Boahan, "The Caravan Trade", pp. 349-350, and Pardo, "The Songhay Empire", p. 55. Also refer to A.A. Boahan, *Britain, The Sahara and the Western Sudan. 1788-1861*, Oxford, 1964, and E.W. Bovill, *The Golden Trade of the Moors*.

105. Refer to the Bornu regnal list--Chart IV.

106. J.B. Webster, 'Animals of the Kingdom: Crocodiles and Hippos, Manatees and Fishes', Benue Valley Project Paper No. 6, 1975, and Webster, "Three Phases of Kwararafa", Benue Valley Project Paper No. 9, 1976.

107. The dramatic shift noted here was also evident in the Gold Coast region during the same period. Refer to R. Kea, *Settlement, Trade and Polities in the Seventeenth Century Gold Coast*, Baltimore, 1982, pp. 11-12.

108. Refer to the regional chronological chart, which reveals schematically the basic periodization for the Benue Basin.

109. Sargent, 'Politics and Economics', also refer to Ryder, *Benin and the Europeans*, pp. 5-93, and Bradbury, *Benin Studies*, p. 49.

110. I.H.T. No. 86.

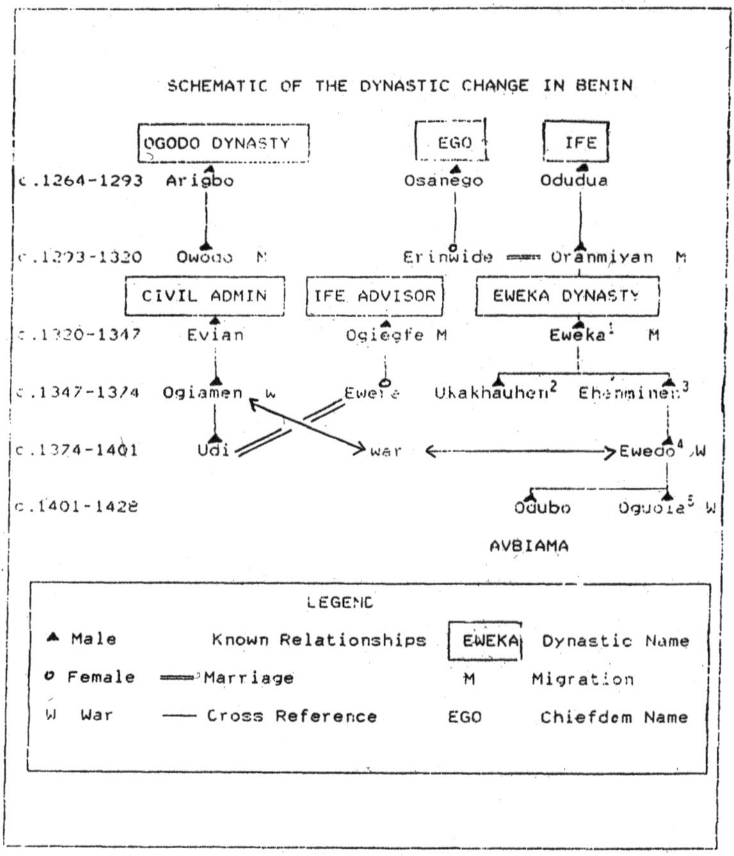

Chart VIII Schematic of Dynastic Change in Benin

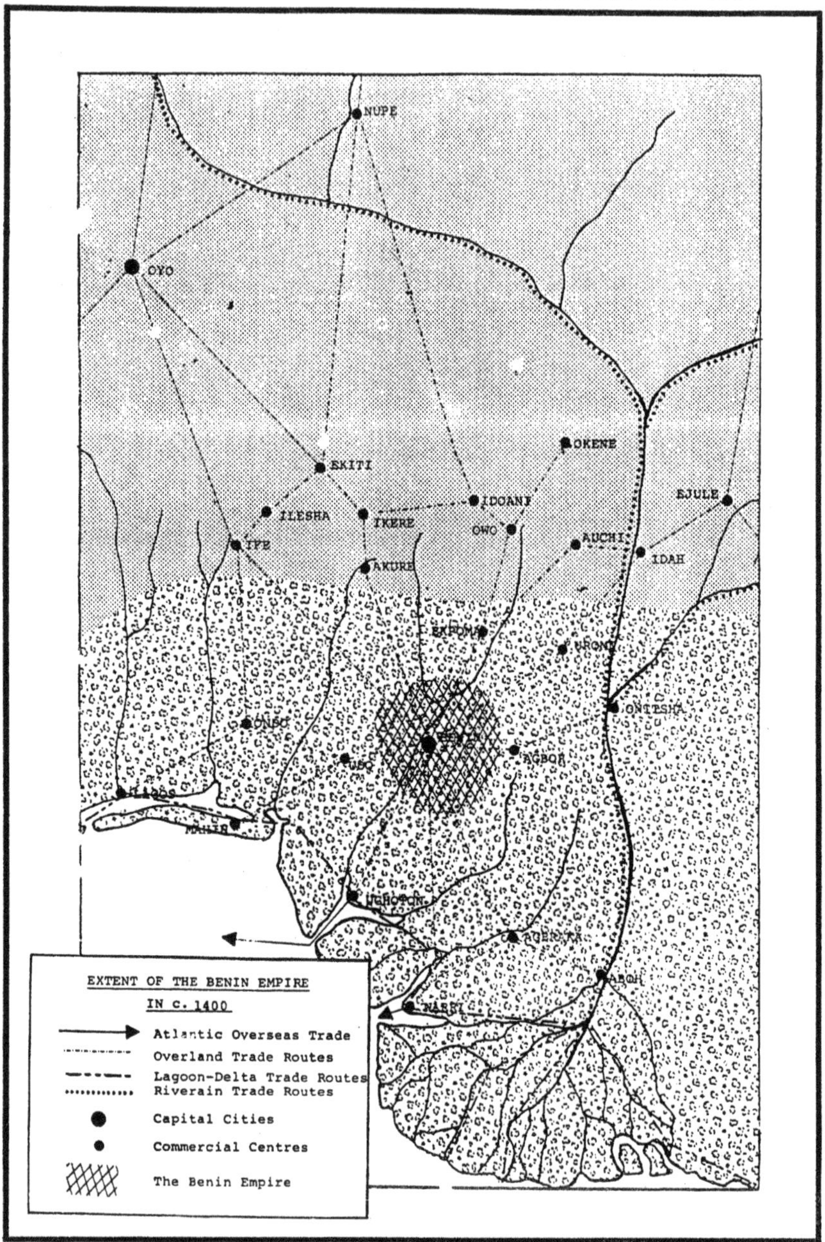

Map Four: Extent of the Benin Empire in c. 1400

Chapter 3

The Golden Age Of Prosperity: Dynastic Change And Political Consolidation, Benin, c. 1300-1455

A detailed historical reconstruction in the southern sector of the Benue Basin becomes possible only for the period after 1300. Prior to that the evidence is intriguing but not sufficiently rich or detailed enough to support a thorough reconstruction. The data base and circumstances are improving, however, and eventually a detailed examination of the period prior to 1300 may be possible. Certainly extensions of the work by P.J. Darling[1] and others will enable some informed speculation about earlier Benin history to take place. It is interesting to note, moreover that the greater detail and richness of the oral evidence for the post-1300 period coincides with an age of increasing regional prosperity, characterized by competitive although relatively stable politics, expanding trade, dependable climate and demographic growth. As the fourteenth century progressed the stability, economic expansion and wealth generation spread across a broader segment of the population. It was apparently a time of cooperation to exploit the resources and opportunities of a golden age. It was also a time of competition to ensure that the various sectors, factions and social formations had access to a reasonable proportion of this potential wealth. To fully understand this combination of cooperation and competition it is necessary to analyze the political transformations in the major southern sector state of Benin.

The dynastic history of Benin can be divided into two periods. The Igodo dynasty ruled from c. 996 to 1320, and following a period of transition c. 1320- 1347,[2] was succeeded by the Eweka monarchy. Under the Eweka rulers the process of political centralization and consolidation, coupled with the development of social differentiation and increased economic exploitation, contributed to the emergence of an expansive, commercially oriented empire. This polity eventually came to dominate the forest zone of the Benue Basin through economic, political and social controls imposed on the subordinate population, and eventually an imperial outlook on regional and long distance commerce emerged. The roots of Benin's imperial development can be found in the struggle for political pre-eminence between the Igodo and Eweka dynasties. The success of the Eweka monarch in this constitutional turmoil changed the process and style of administration, and effectively restructured Benin society to limit opposition and consolidate imperial authority. There was much to gain through the control of political power and authority, and the competition was intensified by the increasing sense of potential for wealth.

The emergence of Benin as the major forest zone social formation occurred in three phases. The initial phase was dominated by the takeover in the capital enclave by the Eweka monarchy, and the reduction of Igodo influence in state decision-making. The second phase accounted for the consolidation of political power through association with the Uzama Nihinron (Kingmakers Council), and the development of economic controls through expansion of regional and long distance trade. The third and final phase in the transformation of Benin involved the complete reduction of regional opposition, and the acquisition of new territory, market opportunities, resources, and subordinate populations. By c. 1455 the Eweka monarchs had laid the foundations of an imperial administrative system, and had established political and economic controls across a broad area of the forest zone. This transformed administration, different in scope and policy from the former Igodo regime, could effectively govern a diverse population and dominate a number of subordinate states.

Prior to expanding on Eweka dynastic history it is necessary to understand, as far as that may be possible, the situation in the region under the Igodo rulers. The era of the Igodo dynasty was characterized by a relatively undifferentiated society, and by an intercursive power relationship between the chief and various local authorities. Intercursive power relations, marked by a "balance of power and a division of scopes between the parties,"[3] were most clearly reflected in the relations established between the Ogoso (chief) and the Council of State, Kingmakers Council, and Enejie (village chiefs). State officials, each supported by their own tribute network, co-operated in the central decision-making process, and thus shared political power and authority. Succession to the highest office was determined through the decisions of the Kingmakers Council, ratified by the Council of State and Enejie. The unsuccessful candidates for the Ogoso office became Enejie, and thus retained status as part of the state nobility. The Enejie also gained clearly defined areas of political responsibility, and had economic support through the allocation of rural fiefs within the state. Order was maintained through regular council meetings, and decisions were implemented through the Enejie. The most powerful voice in the council was that of the Ogodo, but intercursive relations served to limit his authority. The Enejie were not simply instruments of state domination, but could exercise an extremely effective voice in state policy formulation.

The relatively small number of state officials lessened the tribute exacted from the subordinate village populations. The Igodo administration apparently did not possess sufficient authority, skill or influence to increase tribute demands or appropriate village production for the advance of centrally controlled commerce. The Ogoso were able to accumulate sufficient tribute to support partially a small retinue of craftsmen known as the Onwina and Igbeseamwan[4] - carpenters and wood carvers. Also, the limited volume of regional trade, as the preserve of both the Ogoso and Enejie, added to elite revenues, and served to minimize appropriations on the tribute-paying social sector.

The political and economic system under the Igodo dynasty reflected the segmentary nature of the formation, and the intercursive relationships between the various state factions. The tribute-paying sector represented the majority of the population, and provided economic support for the maintenance of the Ogodo and Enejie, and thus had a slight economic edge over the central hierarchy. Withholding tribute could be construed as an intercursive power relationship, and the option to disassociate from a coercive state government suggests that there were potentially fragile links holding this multi-ethnic population together. The population consisted of Yoruba,[5] and a mixed Edo- and Igbo-speaking people[6] in a constellation of over 130 relatively undifferentiated secondary chiefdoms.[7] The rural population was agricultural and paid its tribute for the support of the Enejie and Ogodo in the products of farm and forest.

It is likely that the early (probably immigrant) population in the southern savanna and forest region west of the River Niger was also responsible for building the vast network of earthworks (iya) which cover much of Benin and Ishan.8 The iya network clearly pre-dates the emergence of the Eweka dynastic period, and seems to develop from about 900 onwards in a progressively more complex and detailed enclosure system which defined village and petty chiefdom boundaries. These well defined and protected villages and chiefdoms characterize the Igodo dynastic period, and suggest that the political culture and economy were not only based upon local forces but were, in part at least, conditioned by regional events as well.

Village authority was based upon the principles of gerontocratic social, economic and political control. Village and lineage elders retained, at least symbolically, control of land, land usage, and productive and reproductive mechanisms in the local organizations. This control over the land was probably facilitated by the iya earthworks which served to enclose and define village areas. The structural basis of gerontocratic authority was the Otu (age grade system) which defined relations within the various village and lineage groupings, and which divided the population into functional social and economic units. The Otu, therefore, became an

> organized system of public opinion, a complete guide for the activities of each individual and the method whereby every man was enabled to take his proper place in society with the maximum of usefulness. If a man did not comply with the requirements of custom he was a nobody.[9]

The various grades of the Otu system were organized to contribute to village production, and thus became part of the economic, social and political structures of every group, village, or state

> Those in the lowest Otu...are called *Egbonughele* sweepers of the street. Under this name are classified all the youths of the clan. They perform all the ordinary communal tasks, they hew wood and carry water, mix mud for house building, and clear the farm paths. The actual tasks are usually apportioned among themselves, the elder boys assisting the younger. Next come the Igele, the adults in the prime of their strength, most of them with homes and families. They were called out to work when it was beyond the power of the youths. The senior Igele only went to war in a major conflict, leaving minor raids to the younger men. Though individually they had no legal right to speak in the full village council, yet their preponderance of numbers and the fact that they were the Elders of the future lent considerable weight to their ideas. They formed the main body of public opinion. Above them come in some groups a rank called Igbama which are 'Junior Elders' - if they may be so described. These are the heads of families, seniors in the small divisions of the villages, who have in some cases performed a promotion ceremony to free themselves from the obligations of communal labour, but who are not yet admitted to the full clan councils.
>
> Finally come the *Edion*, the Elders, the grave and reverend seniors of the village, the repositories of custom, the village tribunal of justice, at the head of whom is the Odionwere or senior elder...In most groups he is the administrative as well as the religious head of the village, just as the Onojie is the head of the whole group.[10]

Surplus production was collected by the Edion and Odionwere and funnelled to the Enejie or Ogoso. The Edion also had considerable influence with the Enejie, which tended to ensure that the Council of State would consider the wishes of the gerontocracy of village society.

The Igodo dynasty therefore presided over a decentralized and fairly fragmentary political culture in which the representatives of local social institutions played a key role in the organization of production and state decision-making. Yet in the late thirteenth and early fourteenth centuries relations within this system began to undergo profound change. The demographic balances were altering and economic forces on regional and long distance exchange were increasing in both volume and scope. The response seems to have been a shift in political relations toward a more centralized process particularly at the village level, but also in terms of relationships between villages and chiefdoms.

> Increasingly hierarchical village structures, therefore, may have been a response to the needs of short-distance migrants for territorial legitimacy and mutual defence in the pre-14th [century] period.'[11]

The last monarch in the Igodo dynasty apparently attempted to govern without the advice and consent of the State Council. Ogoso Owodo (c.1293-1320) "never convened a meeting except in times of trouble or crises."[12] Owodo was eventually banished from the throne by the combined Enejie, Uzama Nihinron, and village Odionwere. The behaviour of Ogoso Owodo suggested that economic changes had begun which challenged the intercursive relations upon which the political structures had been built. The economic pressures of the emerging golden age were apparently having an impact within the political structures. These changes included the expansion of local, regional and long distance commercial exchange, and an increased need to develop the economic resources of the central administration to participate in and control this trade.[13] The egalitarian agrarian society of an earlier age was changing, throwing up a class of traders who were becoming an important political force within the social fabric of the state. Control of commercial activity thus demanded an expansion of central authority.

After the removal of the increasingly unpopular Owodo a commoner, Evian, apparently became civil administrator of the state government. He had risen to prominence (probably through commerce) during Owodo's reign and as civil administrator was considered both a temporary and a non-partisan ruler. The struggle for access to the rewards from trade and commerce apparently demanded recognizably fair arbitration by the central administration. Evian, however, endeavoured to legitimize the rule of his family by appointing his son, Ogiamwen, as successor. This move destroyed his non-partisan appeal, and mobilized the Uzama Nihinron, titled nobility, state bureaucracy, village gerontocracy, and "the people" to reject Ogiamwen, arguing that he was not a legitimate contender for the Ogoso title.[14] "While this was still in dispute" representatives of the Uzama Nihinron "sent an ambassador to the Oni Odudua, the greatest and wisest ruler of Ife, asking him to send one of his sons to be their ruler."[15] It was apparently unacceptable for one of the commoner, subordinate segments, represented by the Evian lineage, to replace the Igodo dynasty as paramount in the decentralized although hereditary office of Ogodo, and thus the invitation to Ife.

The approach of another candidate for the throne, Eweka from Ife, apparently represented a political compromise in the potentially violent competition for paramount authority. The fact that Eweka was the son of a marriage between the Ife ambassador (Oranmiyan) and a daughter of a powerful local Enejie provided at least a rudimentary claim to political legitimacy. In fact, intermarriage has been one of the more important vehicles for establishing at least some semblance of political acceptability.[16] Many political disputes and rivalries have been either settled or exacerbated by the question of legitimacy, and to be able to claim marital connections with a powerful lineage in the existing political hierarchy often serves as a mediating factor.

The Enejie of the vassal village of Ego had been founded by an unsuccessful royal prince of the Igodo dynasty, and therefore the daughter represented the female-side linkage with the previous royal house. Furthermore, Oba Eweka (chief Eweka) aligned his new administration with the Uzama Nihinron by making the positions hereditary and thus establishing a permanent Uzama (Kingmakers) Council. This alliance was cemented through the marriage of two of Oba Eweka's daughters to the leading representatives of the Uzama council and the foundation of a female-side relationship between the two central administrative organization.[17] Previously the Uzama Nihinron had been appointed bureaucrats in the Igodo administration, [18] and their elevation to hereditary nobility created major alliance between the old government and the new monarchy. The foundation of an hereditary Uzama council, moreover, enhanced the power, authority and prestige of the councillors, and established an intercursive relationship between the Eweka monarchy and the Uzama Nihinron. The principle of hereditary Uzama succession removed a democratic element from the system of administration, and shifted political power from the villages to the central government. The new dynasty did not immediately alter other aspects of the intercursive relationships within the state, but it had already set the stage for future conflict between the related parties of the state government, specifically between the Eweka monarchy and the new state nobility.

The political transformation of the Benin government did not initially involve any major changes in the style of administration, in relations with the village gerontocracy, or in tribute demands. However, during the four generations between c. 1347 and 1455, Benin developed as a centralized monarchy which made increased demands on its subjects, and was perhaps better able to exercise authority in the expanding regional economy. This transformation was not sudden, but it was dramatic and involved a fundamental reorganization of political relations to respond effectively to economic forces. The first phase ended with the coronation of Oba Ewedo (c. 1374-1401) and represented the period of political and economic con olidation. The second phase was marked by an increase in the integral power of the Oba, and a reorganization of the central administration. Relations between the capital and the village governments were substantially altered, and a national Otu structure developed which organized the entire population into one cohesive social and political system.[19] The third phase opened with the installation of Oba Oguola and the systematic reduction of internal opposition by various segments of the subordinate population. In this subjugation of vassal administrations, Benin embarked on a process of territorial acquisition and regional consolidation which laid the foundations of imperial occupation of the forest zone political economy. Coupled with this process of adaption and change in the style of central government was the expansion of regional trade and commerce which provided further incentive for political reorganization and the development of integral powers.

The first phase of political consolidation by the new dynasty began during the reign of Oba Eweka (c. 1320-1347) who institute policies designed to enhance the legitimacy and acceptability of the new rulers. Tribute payments, for example, were apparently not increased. Also, commoner relations with the state bureaucracy and nobility were reinforced through marriage. The introduction of the title 'Oba' to replace the 'Ogoso' title of the former dynasty seems to have partially divorced the new monarchy from the discredited Igodo rulers.[20] The only other substantive change accompanying the accession of the Eweka dynasty was the increase in the power of the Uzama Nihinron at the expense of the rising trader or commercial class. The Uzama council, including the titled officials Oliha, Edohen, Ero, Ezomo, Eholo n'Ire, and Oloton, provided goodwill and economic support to the new monarchy. The dynasty had no independent, recognized residence of their own and was thus dependent upon the economic and political support of the Uzama. The Oba lived in the Uzama palace and exercised whatever measure of authority they were permitted by the Uzama.

Eweka I was succeeded by one of his older sons, Uwakuahen, who in turn was succeeded by his brother Ehenminen, another of Eweka's sons

> There were no events of importance during their reigns but tradition says that there was peace, concord and contentment throughout the kingdom. The chiefs [Uzama and Enejie] wielded much influence during these reigns. Uwakhuahen and Ehenminen reigned and ended their days in the Usama [Uzama] palace. [21]

Although their real authority was clearly much circumscribed, the new dynasty had established a legitimate base, and was recognized and accepted as the official rulers of the kingdom.[22]

Fundamental changes in political relations began during the reign of the fourth king, Oba Ewedo (c.1374-1401), when the Oba freed the monarchy from the influence of the Uzama Nihinron by moving his palace from Usama to Benin. The Uzama Nihinron, Enejie and local authorities violently objected to the move, looking upon the establishment of an autonomous capital by Ewedo as a threat to their political power. While it resided in the Usama palace the monarchy was relatively easy to control; tribute payments channelled through the Uzama network of clients only secondarily arrived in the hands of the Oba. Establishment of an autonomous palace would necessitate a redefinition of the tribute system, and would thus allow the monarch to generate support through an independent network of clients and subordinate officials. The relocation of the royal palace, therefore, was an important step in the reorganization of the central government, and reflected an emerging power in the office of the Oba. This development has been recorded in Benin traditions, and reveals the nature of the internal political struggle between the Oba, Uzama and various factions in the central government. "Prior to his (Oba Ewedo's) coronation he was much concerned because of the power and aggrandizement of the Uzama Nihinron (Kingmakers) which equalled that of the Oba, and decided to remove the seat of his government from Usama which was in their midst, to the present palace. He made all the necessary arrangements for his removal. without informing the Uzama Nihinron... So Ewedo left Usama about an hour after his coronation... Ewedo had to undergo similar troubles to those which his great-grandfather Prince Oranmiyan had from the ferryman at the Ovia River. Itsekherhe refused to allow him to over his ground, so a bridge was made... As the Oba landed from this bridge Ogiamwen took up arms to prevent his entry into the city... but through the aid of royal troops the Oba was able to take up his residency on the site of the present palace.

A period of seven days was fixed at the end of which they (Ewedo and Ogiamwen) should meet for a fair fight. In this the leader of Ogiamwen's forces, Oliha-Ogiamwen, was killed and Ogiamwen was pursued and defeated.he surrendered and made peace with the Oba. By the treaty of Ekiopagah he was made a chief, retaining the nickname Ogiamwen as his title ... Ever since, every Oba has to cross a bridge at Itsekherhe quarter on his coronation day and, on the seventh day fight with Ogiamwen in memory of the victory ..."[23]

This event was a significant development in the political history of Benin. Darling states that "the entry of the new dynasty into the Benin City area, as re-enacted annually and at every coronation ceremony, was accompanied by a sharp break between the Oba and the Uzama". [24] It would seem that political change in the structure of centralized government may have been prompted by economic circumstances. The period of Oba Ewedo's rule corresponded with the era of great prosperity in which increasing volumes of commercial exchange prompted entrepreneur and monarch alike to focus on the economics of regional and long distance trade. The relocation of the royal palace, and the freedom associated with the extension of integral power relations established in the civil war, enabled the monarchy to organize its authority independent of other state institutions. That autonomy enabled Ewedo to exercise some control over the existing east-west trading system which connected the Niger delta to the Lagos lagoon.[25]

Ewedo's relocation of his capital, therefore, not only strengthened his political power but also established dynastic control over an important commercial network. Furthermore, the foundation of Oyo to the northwest of Benin under a related dynasty suggests that the growth of hinterland commerce was affecting political developments on a regional scale.[26] Trade between Oyo, in the savanna, and Benin, in the forest belt, eventually became one of the economic mainstays of the Eweka dynasty. The establishment of a more centralized Bini monarchy in c. 1374-1401 was apparently connected to regional trade expansion and the desire to participate as an active force in the development of east-west and north-south commerce. Quantitative economic evidence is poor for this period. However, the causal relationship between economics and political change were stronger during subsequent generations of the Eweka dynasty, and indicate that a direct correlation could exist between political action and commercial development. Possibly the monarchy was seeking monopolies over important items of trade to prevent the growth of an independent and powerful trader class.

The founding of an independent palace by Oba Ewedo was an important step in the organization of central government controls over regional commercial opportunities, and represented only the initial phase in the consolidation of political and economic power and the total reorganization of Benin. The Oba expanded his authority through the appointment of a number of minor titled officials,[27] and significantly altered the investiture procedures for all appointed and hereditary officials. Previously, the Uzama Nihinron had been able to appoint secondary officials on their own prerogative. These appointed bureaucrats would have owed their allegiance to the Uzama, who would benefit from any fees or tribute attached to the title. Ewedo abolished this privilege and established all patronage within the Oba's authority. To administer the new patron-client system he created the Iyase (town chief) who was responsible for appointing and investing all secondary titled officials, including the Uzama councillors.[28] The only exceptions to this new policy was the Oliha, who received his office directly from the Oba. Oba Ewedo took one other significant step to reduce the influence of the Uzama, forbidding them the right to carry "swords of state."[29] Ewedo reserved this privilege exclusively for the monarch, and the sword of state became symbolic of the growing authority of the

Eweka monarchy. The fact that Oba Ewedo could "confirm titles on commoners in order to enlist their support against the nobles"[30] from the relative security of his own palace, protected by his own loyal and tested troops, and tour the streets of the capital displaying the sword of state indicates a substantial change in the balance of power.

One of the effects of the reorganization of the administration instituted by Oba Ewedo was an increase in tribute requirements from the vassal village producers. The expansion of the state bureaucracy, through the addition of a number of new titled officials in the Oba's client network, placed an additional burden on the redistributive capacity of the monarch. This in turn translated into a demand for larger non-commercial tribute payments from the village Otu system. Tribute was henceforth demanded from the rural areas more frequently:

> ...twice yearly, every village in the Benin kingdom was required to send tribute to the Oba in the form of yams, palm-oil, and other foodstuffs...The more remote vassal chiefs beyond the suburban area of the capital sent slaves and livestock. [31]

The imposition of increased tribute demands apparently caused changes in the village Otu system. In some villages the Igbama age organization was abolished, and it was no longer possible to purchase exemptions from communal labour, indicating that the productive capacity of the Otu was stretched to the limit. In other villages the Igele age grade was forced to integrate back into the communal labour pool to augment productive capacity and thereby meet the increased central demands. Further impositions on village productive capacity were made by the expansion of centralized commercial activity, and the organization of the Oba's direct involvement in regional and long distance trade. As trade developed so did the exploitative nature of the administration, and tribute demands were altered to include commercial requirements of the state controlled entrepreneur. Therefore, the reign of Oba Ewedo imposed a two-fold increase in tribute demands, one to provide the necessary non-commercial, food, tribute for redistribution to clients, and the second to facilitate expansion of the Oba's participation in commerce. Ewedo converted the redistributive chiefdom, based upon decentralized forms of administration, into a centralized state that demanded increased volumes of tribute to foster the control and penetration of regional and long distance trade.[32] Commerce was, therefore, a crucial motivating force in the political and economic transformation of Benin under Oba Ewedo.

The reorganized administration of Oba Ewedo, while centralizing power, nevertheless retained a reasonably effective system of checks and balances. Previously such checks had been established through the relationship of the monarchy to the Council of State, and excesses were in some measure mitigated by the effective voice of the Enejie and Odionwere. The new system of government provided for an initial restriction on the monarch by requiring him to be nominated and installed by the Uzama Nihinron. The actions of the Uzama were checked by the Iyase who was responsible for their installation. The Oba controlled the appointment of the Iyase and Oliha. This tripartite system of checks and balances, although recognizing the hereditary nature of the royal and noble factions, created at least nominal control over excessive power concentration by any one element of the central administration. Internal competition between members of the same family or faction for an appointment brought into play the restrictions and checks on any particular individual. The changes in the central government had reduced the effective voice of the Enejie and Odionwere, and limited their power to village administration. Relations in the central hierarchy were between the monarchy, Uzama Nihinron, and Iyase, and did not involve the Enejie in the intercursive structures. Thus, the Enejie and Odionwere found their status and authority set between the central government and the vassal population and fulfilled the role of municipal or local administration.

The appointment of commoners to even relatively minor positions served, on one hand, to minimize internal discord and opposition to state policy and the increasingly exploitative economy. On the other hand, the establishment of an enlarged state bureaucracy enhanced the potential for upward social mobility. Thus, the ability of the monarchy to align commoners with the central authority and against the Uzama established a solid base of support for the new constitutional arrangement, consolidated the Eweka dynasty's hold over the state, and opened horizons for territorial expansion to control larger segments of the regional economy.

The emergence of Benin as a central-place state with imperial ambitions and exercising regional powers occurred in the face of three potentially aggressive pockets of resistance - Udo, Agbor and Ekpoma. In reality only the opposition from Udo materialized as a serious threat to the territorial ambitions and regional authority of the Oba. In the other areas of potential resistance the opposition of Agbor was undermined by the slow process of political acculturation, whereas Ekpoma became an economic dependency and was forcibly co-opted into the Benin sphere of political and economic influence.

Ekpoma, located approximately eighty miles north-east of Benin represented the weakest potential opponent of the emerging regional domination by the Bini administration. Ekpoma seemed unable or unwilling to resist the expansion of Bini influences, perhaps a result of its dependency on Benin for distribution of the gold produced in the Ekpoma mines.[33] Certainly the location of Ekpoma prevented access to the regional and long distance commercial network unless it was through Benin controlled markets and trade routes.

A second potential competing polity was Agbor, located approximately sixty miles east of Benin. Agbor was founded in a migration of Igbo-speakers from Udo in c. 1401-1428 under the leadership of Dein.[34] Dein forced various disparate groups around Agbor to recognize, at least nominally, his authority and thereafter enabled his son, Igbudu, to establish a reasonably influential chiefdom. It is significant that the migration from Udo occurred as Oba Ewedo was instituting a more coercive and exploitative relationship with the vassal villages. Perhaps the exodus of Igbo-speakers represented an effort to escape the growing control of the Oba and thus total Bini domination. Agbor was eventually subordinated through diplomacy to tribute-paying status within the Benin sphere. This incorporation proceeded slowly and was not totally complete until c. 1509-1536, when Bini paramount authority was firmly entrenched throughout the sub-region.

Agbor's political structures were copied from the Benin of an earlier period, and resembled those evident under Oba Ewedo (c. 1374-1401) and Oba Oguola (c. 1401-1428).[35] The political acculturation of Agbor, therefore, suggests that although the potential for competition existed there was also an important political interaction between the Yoruba-speaking dynasty in Benin and the Igbo-speaking leadership in Agbor. Part of this interaction may have been fostered by the marriage of Igbudu to a Yoruba-speaking woman called Ufo. The successor to the Agbor throne was sent by his mother (Ufo) to "learn human relations and art of government"[36] in her own country. This is apparently still a typical function of the maternal home in Benin political culture. "It is still a practice of Bini women to return to their mother for the birth of their first and even subsequent children..." [37] In this way Bini political culture was imported into Agbor, and the system of central administration came to resemble the Bini style established by the Eweka dynasty.

The Onojie of Udo, a semi-autonomous, Yoruba-speaking enclave, harbouring political and economic ambitions beyond the status of a vassal village within the Benin administrative sphere, and backed by a relatively influential group of ritual specialists continued to express opposition to the exploitations of the capital. The major conflict was over political status, but economic resources and access to commercial relations were also significant factors in this dispute. As a vassal tributary chiefdom. Udo was expected to provide for the needs of the capital, but had previously been an influential chiefdom in its own right. Three factors thus combined to encouraged Udo ambitions. Religion, economics and politics were the major forces leading to the violent confrontation.

Udo has been described as a significant political centre, perhaps as the "maternal homes of the first Ogiso." [38]

> Udo reputedly held sway over all the settlements west of this (the Ovia) river and east of the Siluku River... If Udo was one of a number of Yoruba mini-states between Benin and Ife ... then their sharing of such cultural traits and chieftaincy titles and structures..., would not be unexpected ... If Udo and Benin were powerful borderland centres of the opposing Yoruba and Edo cultures, and if the rapid introduction of Yoruba orientation at the head of the Benin polity does imply political violence, then it seems likely that Udo played a most crucial role in the proceedings. [39]

Udo was an important religious centre within the Benin state, and represented a traditional religious enclave with political ties to Igbo local administration. Oba Ewedo had been placed under the care of "the priests of Ugbo" centered in Udo prior to his coronation.[40] These ritual specialists created an important indigenous' religious centre which had been increasingly ignored by the state complex of religious institutions and the succession of Eweka monarchs. In political terms Udo had been also ignored in the development of regional government, and thus religion and politics combined to enhance the resentment in Udo.

In economic terms the establishment of Ewedo's palace and the reorganization of the central administration created a capital enclave which expected obedience and support from the tributary chiefdoms. The Oba apparently wanted to exercise economic control across the Ovia River, and thus competed directly with Udo. The efforts to control regional commerce, therefore, brought the capital enclave into direct competition and conflict with peripheral centres such as Udo. Udo was located astride the same east-west trade route as Benin, and given the opportunity for independent decision-making could have exploited this commercial network. However, as an ancillary part of the Benin kingdom Udo was denied the opportunity to exploit regional or long distance trade, for it could not operate within the commercial infrastructure in competition with the capital without incurring the wrath of the

Oba. Based upon the aspirations of the central administration and the conflicting goals of the vassal chief at Udo, serious opposition and confrontation developed.

Upon the death of Oba Ewedo, Prince Oguola succeeded to the Benin throne. Oba Oguola reinforced the status of the capital as the administrative and economic centre of the state, and took steps to provide for the security and defense of the palace and government headquarters. The ability of the Oba to mobilize a labour force capable of the large-scale community construction envisaged to extended the iya or defensive walls that encircled the capital suggests a substantial population within the capital. Furthermore, the extent of the city walls indicates that urbanization was becoming a major factor in the development of the capital, and also that the city may have faced a real threat from external aggression or hostile neighbours. The struggle with Udo, in part at least, prompted the Oba to embark on the massive improvement and construction exercise, and Oguola "set men to the task of digging trenches right around the city to keep out enemies, especially his greatest and most powerful enemy, Akpanigiakon of Udo."[41] The construction took over three years to complete,[42] and once safely established behind this protective wall Oguola embarked on a campaign of peace and diplomacy offering one of his daughters to Akpanigiakon in marriage.

Marriage diplomacy did not improve relations between Udo and Benin, and Akpanigiakon eventually declared war against the capital. The Bini defense rallied under the command of Ogiobo (the Iyase),[43] and Akpanigiakon was driven off and eventually killed. The Udo elders were brought to Benin and executed in an effort to prevent any renewal of opposition, and Ogiobo was appointed administrator of Udo as a reward for his military service. Ogiobo became the first appointed vassal administrator in the expansion of Benin under the Eweka monarchs.

The subjugation of Udo paved the way for the development of Benin as the most significant forest zone administrative and commercial centre. Udo seems to have been the last major competitor for forest zone domination. In fact, the development of a centralized government, capable of meeting military contingencies, coupled with state control of commercial opportunities forced the Yoruba, Edo and Igbo population to accept the political culture of Benin as tribute-paying members of the social formation.[44] Political stability enabled further development of economic potential, including an expansion of both art and craft production in and around the capital enclave.

The development of the artistic community contributed to commercial expansion and commercial connections were necessary to maintain the supplies of copper, hides and other raw materials for this cultural growth. For the maintenance and continued expansion of the artistic community, particularly those craftsmen with casting skills, it was necessary to ensure supplies of copper and tin. Thurstan Shaw has argued that copper supplies were available through the trans-Saharan trade system; continuing research is endeavouring to identify the actual source of this copper.[45] Tin was available on the Jos plateau in the northern regions of the Benue Basin,[46] but supplies and supply routes depended upon the ability of the state to develop intra-regional commerce. The volume of north-south trade reaching Benin apparently met the needs of the Benin metal workers which meant, in effect, that copper and tin trading networks were functioning well and accessible to Benin traders.

One of the important developments in the consolidation of the Eweka monarchy during the first century of its rule was the reduction of the dependence upon east-west trade. Benin had previously been involved in the exchange of camwood, cloth, salt, canoes, beads and specialized agricultural products through the east-west trading network.[47] The expansion of the north-south system evident by c. 1401-1428, primarily for the importation of copper, tin, horses, livestock, cotton, and iron (probably from Oyo), contributed to an increased production of export produce, including camwood, pepper, salt, dried and/or smoked fish, cloth, oils, kola, beads and a limited amount of gold.[48]

General peace and security enabled successive monarchs to encourage further development of the craft industries and focus upon the expansion of hinterland production for the consumption of the urban population and commercial system. Oba Udagbedo (c.1428-1455), for example, has been remembered in Benin traditions as a kind and industrious ruler who "much encouraged" farming.[49] The expansion of agriculture was necessary to provide for the growing urban and specialized population, and was required to ensure the reproductive capacity of the state. Tribute to the Oba was funnelled through the Iweguae (Palace Otu)[50] and consisted of both commercial and non-commercial goods. The non-commercial accumulation was used for the support of the palace, and was redistributed by the Iwequae to the artistic, craft, and other specialized workers in the capital. Thus the Oba, as the paramount authority, established a pattern of inter-dependency and inter-relationship between his own ritual and political position, the agrarian producers, and the specialized services in the state.

This complex set of relationships was organized through the extension of the village Otu system into the palace hierarchy and state bureaucracy. The development of a national Otu structure effectively linked every individual in the capital enclave and hinterland region within the palace-centred Otu organization. With the expansion of the craft and artisan community under the auspices of Oba Oguola,[51] there was an increase in the demand for food tribute. Artisans were producers of non-commercial luxury goods for the consumption of the palace, and in order to provide their subsistence needs the Oba demanded greater amounts of tribute. The national Otu system provided the mechanism through which increased central demands could be imposed on the vassal village producer, and established the infrastructure to channel this support to the palace and supported workers. Apart from regular, twice yearly tribute payments, the Oba apparently added "ad hoc levies."[52] Thus if the Oba needed pepper for export, taxes were introduced on pepper production, or should accumulated redistributive food supplies fall short, levies were placed on agricultural surplus and were collected by the palace representatives of the national Otu system.

The relationship of individuals in the urban centres to the rural, agrarian producer was determined through the collection and distribution of centrally controlled tribute. The Oba and state elite - including the Iyase, Oliha, Uzama councillors, regional representatives, Enejie, and Iweguae - established the central basis of the state administration. This elite segment of the urban population was supported by the tribute-paying social sector who performed the bulk of the labour and provided the material support. Tribute thus became the mechanism of rural exploitation, and imposed production demands on the organization structures in the tribute-paying social sector. As trade and commerce increased the subordinate population was required to provide additional support for the state elite to develop centrally controlled commercial opportunities. Thus commerce added to the tribute demands. Despite these burdens, which had been increasing steadily since c. 1374-1401, the gerontocratic village Otu remained functional although it experienced some minor adaptations to service the growing demands of the state.

The three sons of Oba Oguola - Edoni, Udagbedo, and Ohen - ruled in succession in c. 1428-1455, as the paramount in a consolidated and stable regime. Apparently the exploitation by the state prompted some reaction during this period from segments of the subordinate population. The emigration of groups which became part of the C[illegible] during the reign of Oba Udagbedo, for example, was probably related to the growing exploitation and increased central domination of political and economic affairs, as was the exodus of groups who became absorbed into the Urhobo and Ishan [53] in the following generation. Opposition to the increased state requirements for commercial, non-commercial, and ad hoc levies were also reflected in the civilian upheavals of c. 1455-1482. Possibly as a reaction to the coercive nature of the Eweka administration, the Uzama Nihinron attempted to reassert its authority before

Oba Ohen's eldest son, Egbeka, succeeded to the throne. Egbeka endured several "civil wars with the Uzama",[54] but managed to retain control of the throne and actually expand the state's capacity for regional and long distance commercial exchange.

Coupled with the commercial reorganization was the development of Bini controls over both east-west and north-south commerce. The expansion of commercial domination was an integral part of the Eweka dynasty's administrative system, and one of Oba Ewedo's sons spent a great deal of time and energy leading an "expedition to Ibo-land where he remained for many years fighting."[55] This campaign was apparently organized to increase Bini domination of eastern commerce and undermine local authority -possibly that of Agbor - over significant commercial networks.

The stability of the government was further enhanced through commoner support. It was "in the interest of traders to uphold the integrity of the Benin polity in order to ensure a state of security in which trade would flourish."[56] By c. 1455-1482 trans-Saharan trade was increasing dramatically and north-south exchange was entering one of its most productive periods. The relationships between the state government and entrepreneurs in this expanding economy became even more significant, and reinforced the stability, power and authority of the Eweka monarchy. The repeated subjugation of the Uzama Nihinron by Oba Egbeka indicated the efficiency of the coercive powers of the state, and suggests that the political and economic policies of the monarchy had been accepted by certain segments of the commoner population. Uzama opposition did not prompt general rebellion. Rather the support of the entrepreneurs and tribute-paying social sector dictated the survival of the Eweka dynasty and prevented a return to the Uzama form of administration. The subjugation of the Uzama effectively altered the status of the Kingmakers, and limited their ability to compete for hegemonic powers, while enhancing the integral authority of the Oba. The process of political, economic and social consolidation apparently led to differentiation in the various segments of the population. The ability to identify various strata and factions in Benin society suggests that the formerly undifferentiated social formation had changed dramatically.

Through the decline of Uzama political fortunes and the corresponding increase in the authority of the Oba it has been possible to analyze the growth of integral power in the central government. Clearly the Oba had developed strong centralized control over state functions, and could withstand violent opposition from any competing sector. The monarchy had increased economic support through an expanded tribute base, and withstood the protests (through exodus) of the Ga, Urhobo and Ishan groups without any apparent deleterious affects. Furthermore, it had survived the violent opposition of Udo, whose reduction served to enhance rather than undermine the stature of the Oba. This process of consolidation and political growth set the stage for an era of aggressive leadership and concerted administrative change which would further entrench the Eweka dynasty as the paramount authority in the state.

While Benin was undergoing a period of consolidation and reorganization, other states in the Benue Basin were undertaking similar social, economic and political transformations to expand their relations within the regional economy. Benin developed commercial links with the regional economy and expanded trade relations with Oyo and Nupe; two important social formations in the middle belt which had consolidated middleman positions in regional and long distance trade.[57] The Okpoto and Igbo populations near the confluence of the Niger-Benue also contributed to the increase of regional commerce, and developed commercial relations with Awka iron producers to the south and livestock traders to the north. Further north in the sudanic region Zaria had embarked on an active process of territorial acquisition and imperial expansion.[58] Kano and Katsina had emerged as major trading city-states along the southern edge of the trans-Saharan commercial enterprise.[59] Bornu was in the process of shifting its capital west of Lake Chad and would more directly affect the process of regional and long distance trade from Ngazargamu.[60] The relocation of Bornu and the expansion of Kano translated into a reduction and decline of Kwararafa based in its capital at Santolo.[61] Kwararafa was subsequently defeated by Kano and forced to shift its capital southward to Tagara. Therefore, while Benin expanded in the forest zone and became the main southern trading formation in the Benue Basin political and economic growth also occurred in the middle belt and northern regions.

In general terms, therefore, the fourteenth and fifteenth centuries saw dramatic changes in regional politics and economics. The focus of the main Benue Basin social formations was toward the north where the expansion of trans-Saharan trade contributed to economic growth, regional geo-political adaptations, and the development of a set of regional relationships between diverse peoples and states. The main beneficiaries during this period of relative prosperity were Benin, Nupe, Zaria, Kano, Katsina and Bornu. The greatest negative impact was felt in Kwararafa.

This initial period of the Eweka dynastic era in Benin can be schematically represented to summarize the rule of the various monarchs. The consolidation of Eweka rule took three generations, and by c. 1347-1401 the monarchy was firmly entrenched. Between c. 1401 and 1482 the rulers of Benin launched an effective campaign to eliminate restrictions on their central authority, and expand state control of social institutions. The founding generations of the Eweka monarchy, between c. 1320 and 1482, provided the basis of imperial regional government ,and a further growth of regional domination under subsequent rulers.

Between c. 1320 and 1482 Benin passed through a number of stages in its social, political and economic development. Under its first dynasty (before c. 1320) it was a gerontocratic lineage formation organized around the Otu system. The Igodo dynasty established a chief over the Otu and created a redistributive chiefdom with loose intercursive central powers. The second dynasty strengthened the power of the ruling monarchs at the expense of the state nobility and the gerontocracy of the village Otu. Substantial political and economic change came under Ewedo and Oguola who forged an even more centralized administration which demanded and received tribute from the subordinate social sector. These latter changes were prompted, in part, by the growing importance of trade along both the lagoon route and the overland route to the north. By c. 1455-1482 Benin was developing into a major regional power, and had emerged as a prominent sub-regional or forest zone social formation.

The development of integral power relations forced an expansion in the productive capacity of the subordinate gerontocratic village Otu system, but did not impose any substantive changes in the function and organization of this basic social structure. In the early stages of the second dynasty relationships between the Eweka dynasty and the productive segment had remained relatively stable; labour and productivity were provided at fundamentally the same rates as under the Igodo dynasty. After c. 1374-1401, however, Oba Ewedo dramatically altered the economic, social and political balance, and expanded commercial, non-commercial and ad hoc levies from the tribute - paying sector. The exploitative nature of the internal relations was continued by Oba Oguola and demands apparently surpassed the tolerance of some groups in the subordinate segment who opted to migrate from Benin. The increase in royal powers, coupled with the decline in effective checks previously exercised by the Uzama and Enejie, reflected the development of highly coercive and exploitative state authority. Benin, therefore, conformed to Catherine Coquery-Vidrovitch's description of a developing social formation on the verge of territorial consolidation and expansion. She has argued that:

> ... as the state organization became more centralized it began to use the concept of territorial power ... but the prestige of the sovereign never completely effaced tribopatriarchal authority. At most, the kingship took the form of a superimposed bureaucracy which nevertheless respected the structure of rural life. [62]

Clearly the Eweka dynasty "respected" the Otu organization in the vassal villages, but through the development of integral central power relations was able to utilize this institution as part of the state administrative and economic nexus.

The foundations of the Eweka monarch in c. 1320 - 1347 established the basis of political and economic transformation, and resulted in the emergence of a powerful forest zone trading formation. This transformation occurred through three distinct phases, starting initially with the emergence of the dynasty and the forging of legitimate political power. The second phase involved the reduction of the former politically powerful office holders and institutions, and the limitation of the bureaucracy and nobility as patron-clients under the Oba's control. The third and final phase involved the military confrontation with opponents of state policy and the forcible limitations of internal rivalry and opposition. The third phase also launched the territorial period in Benin history, where the Oba embarked on a policy of regional domination and the direct control of regional labour, resources, markets and administration.

References

1. P.J. Darling, *Archaeology and History in Southern Nigeria: The Ancient Linear Earthworks of Benin and Ishan*, Cambridge Monographs in African Archaeology, II, Cambridge, 1984. Also, refer to P.J. Darling, "A Change of Territory: Attempts to Trace More than a Thousand Years of Population Movements by the Benin and Ishan Peoples of Southern Nigeria," in C. Fyfe and M. McMaster (Eds.), *African Historical Demography*, Vol. II, Edinburgh, 1981.

2. The chronology of Benin has been correlated with data from a large number of independently dated sources. One of the first detailed reconstructions was by F.B. Ataba, `Recent Developments in the Use of Non-Documentary Evidence, With Special Reference to Totemism and Regional Chronology', (Dalhousie University MA., 1976). Later work included J.E. Miller, 'Ishan- Benin Relations, 1455-1509', (Dalhousie University, Honours Essay, 1983), and R.A. Sargent, "A Benue Basin Regional Chronology", Benue Valley Project Paper, No. 27, 1984.

3. D.H. Wrong, "Some Problems in Defining Social Power", in *Recent Sociology, on the Social Basis of Politics*, (edited by H.Dreitzel, London, 1969), pp. 46-60. Opposing intercursive power was "integral power in which decision making and initiatives to action are centralized and monopolized by one party alone."

4. J.U. Egharevba, *A Short History of Benin*, (third edition, Ibadan, 1960), p. 3. This volume has undergone some substantial changes from edition to edition.

The majority of references in this work are to the fourth edition of 1968. Only where specifically noted will the citation come from any of the other three editions. The third edition contains extensive and informative appendices, unfortunately absent from the fourth.

5. Darling, *Archaeology and History*, p. 158.
6. R.E. Bradbury, *Benin Studies*, (London, 1973), pp. 6-16.
7. Egharevba, *A Short History of Benin*, (third edition), p. 4, identifies a large number of villages in "Benin division (that) have hereditary chiefs (Enegie) who are descended from sons of the different Ogosos".
8. P.J. Darling, 'Emerging Towns in Benin and Ishan (Nigeria), 500-1500 A.D.,' paper presented to the 11th World Archaeology Congress, Southampton and London, 1986 and P.J. Darling, *Archaeology and History*, pp. 1-54.
9. H.L.M. Butcher, "Some Aspects of the Otu System of the Isa Sub-tribe of the Edo Peoples of Southern Nigeria", *Africa*, (Vol. 8, 1935), p. 150.
10. *Ibid.*, pp. 151-152.
11. Darling, 'Emerging Towns in Benin and Ishan,' p. 2.
12. Egharevba, *A Short History of Benin*, (third edition), p. 2.
13. J.D. Fage, "Some Remarks on Beads and Trade in Lower Guinea in the Sixteenth and Seventeenth Centuries", *Journal of African History*, (III, 2, 1962), pp. 343-344. Fage suggests that there was an early east-west trading system connecting the Niger delta with the Lagos lagoon. This suggestion was supported by E.J. Alagoa, "Long Distance Trade and States in the Niger Delta", *Journal of African History*, (XI, 3, 1970), p. 319.
14. Egharevba, A Short History of Benin, p. 5.
15. Egharevba, *A Short History of Benin*, (third edition) p. 6. A.F.C. Ryder, "A Reconsideration of the Ife-Benin Relationships", *Journal of African History*, (VI, 1, 1965), p. 25, states that "after banishing the last ruler of the first dynasty the people tried to establish a non-monarchical form of government, but when dispute arose they sent to Ife asking Odudua to give them one of his sons as their ruler."
16. R.A. Sargent, "Women, Power and Authority in Pre-Colonial Africa", *History in Africa*, 1991.
17. Refer to the schematic chart of the dynastic change in Benin, (Chart I) which clearly shows the relationship of Erinwide to the Chief of Ego and her marriage to Oranmiyan.
18. Egharevba, *A Short History of Benin*, (third edition), p. 9.
19. Bradbury, *Benin Studies*, p. 60.
20. When Benin became the capital of an empire, 'Oba' could be translated to mean emperor'. However, while in the Yoruba system, Oba meant a ruler subordinate to Ife, and initially at least the Eweka dynasty might be seen in this way.
21. Egharevba, *A Short History of Benin*, p. 9.
22. Egharevba, *A Short History of Benin*, (third edition), p. 8. The location of the palace was Usama while the title of the Kingmakers Council has been differentiated by utilizing 'Uzama'

23. Egharevba, *A Short History of Benin*, pp. 9-10. It is interesting to note that there is a distinct similarity between the pronunciation of `Itsekherhe' and the 'Itsekiri' ethnic group in the Niger Delta region.
24. Darling, *Archaeology and History*, p. 39.
26. The connections between political developments (stability) and economic growth and trade are significantly reinforced throughout the history of this region.
25. The Eweka dynasty and the dynasty in Oyo claim similar origins in Ife. For more details refer to R. Law, *The Oyo Empire, 1600-1836*, (Oxford, 1977); S. Johnson, *The History of the Yorubas*, (Lagos, 1922); Ryder, "A Reconsideration of the Ife-Benin Relationship"; and also G.A. Akinola, 'The Origins of the Eweka Dynasty of Benin: A Study in the Use and Abuse of Oral Tradition', (paper presented to the Joint Seminar, University of Ibadan, 1976). Also refer to P. Morton- Williams, "The Influence of Habitat on Trade in Oyo and Ashanti", in *Man in Africa*, (edited by M. Douglas and P.M. Kayberry, London, 1969), pp. 79-98.
27. Egharevba, *A Short History of Benin*, p. 10. Oba Ewedo "created various minor titles including the *Uwange*, the Master of the Oba's Wardrobe; Esekurhe, the Recorder of Deaths, etc., of each Oba; the Osodin and Uso, the Keepers of the Oba's harem." He also established a prison known as `Ewedo' after his name, and appointed a prison warden called Erigbo.
28. Bradbury, *Benin Studies*, p. 138.
29. Egharevba, *A Short History of Benin*, p. 10.
30. Bradbury, *Benin Studies*, p. 136.
31. *Ibid.*, p. 53.
32. J.B. Webster, 'A Typology of Pre-Colonial Social Form[illegible]ns', (paper presented to the Canadian Association of African Studies Confer[illegible]e, Universite Laval, 1983).
33. C.G. Okojie, *Ishan Native Laws and Customs*, (Yaba, 1960).
34. J.O. Ijomah, `The Evolution of Kingship Among the West Niger Igbo Chiefdoms, With Particular Reference to Benin Influences', (unpublished manuscript, 1981).
35. *Ibid.*
36. J.B. Webster, J. Bucher, et. al., 'A Critical Analysis of the Royal Chronicle of Agbor', Benue Valley Project Paper, Microfiche, Centre for African Studies, Dalhousie University, No. 13), p. 5.
37. Darling, *Archaeology and History*, p. 148.
38. *Ibid.*, p. 154.
39. *Ibid.*, pp. 157-158.
40. Egharevba, *A Short History of Benin*, p. 9.
41. *Ibid.*, p. 11.A map of the Benin City walls has been included to show the extent of the construction. In fact, the overall construction, occurring during the reign of Oba Oguola (c. 1401- 1428) and improved during the reign of Oba Ewuare (c. 1455-1482) resulted in more than ninety miles of walls and ditches. For more details refer to G. Connah, "New Light on the Benin City Walls", *Journal*

of the Historical Society of Nigeria, (III, 4, 1967), pp. 593-609. Also refer to P.J. Darling, *Archaeology and History*, 1984.

42. Darling assumed that one cubic metre of earth per man per day could be used to calculate the time and labour required to construct the iya systems. ".the total quantity of earth moved at Udo (c. 532,000 cubic metres) is only about 40% of that estimated to have been shifted at Benin (c. 1,345,000)." Darling, *Archaeology and History*, p. 149. For the Benin City walls, therefore, assuming a work force of 10,000 it would still require approximately 134 days to complete the work. It is unlikely at this early period that a work force of that magnitude could have been assembled and maintained for that considerable length of time.
43. J.U. Egharevba, *Concise Lives of the Famous Iyase*, (Lagos, 1946/47), p. 12.
44. In a compilation of language data C. Hoffman, 'The Languages of Nigeria by Language Families' (Department of Linguistics Paper, University of Ibadan, 1972), placed Edo (1.A.4.3) of the Kwa (1.A.4) sub-group in the Niger-Congo (1.A) language family. Edo includes Bini, Esan (Ishan), Emai, Ososo, Okpe, Uham, Ghotuo, Epie, Degema, Urhobo, and Iyekhee among others.
45. T. Shaw, *Igbo Ukwu*, (two volumes, London, 1972). Also refer to R. Mauny, "A Possible Source of Copper for the Oldest Brass Heads of Ife", *Journal of the Historical Society of Nigeria*, (II, 3, 1962), pp. 393-395.
46. J.J. Grace, "Tin Mining on the Plateau Before 1920", in *Studies in the History of Plateau State, Nigeria*, (edited by E. Isichei, London, 1982), pp. 179-190, and also refer to O. Davies, *West Africa Before the Europeans*, (London, 1967), Note 1, p. 31.
47. Specialized agricultural products, based in part on ecological variations, can encourage commercial exchange between different ecological zones and diverse populations. Beans, for example, produced in one zone may be highly prized as a luxury food item in another.
48 M.D.W. Jeffries, "Arab Knowledge of the Niger's Course", *Africa*, (Vol. 25, 1955), p. 86 identifies fish oil as a trade commodity from the coast far up the River Niger from a relatively early period.
49. Egharevba, *A Short History of Benin*, p. 11.
50. Bradbury, *Benin Studies*, pp. 66-67.
51. G. Connah, "Benin", in *Lectures on Nigerian Pre- History and Archaeology*, (edited by T. Shaw, Ibadan, 1969), p. 54. Connah indicated that Benin "iron working...and *cire perdue* casting techniques were to become second to none."
52. Bradbury, *Benin Studies*, p. 53.
53. M. Manoukian, *Akan and Ga-Adangme People*, (Part I, Ethnographic Survey of Africa, edited by D. Forde, London, 1950), p. 67; Egharevba, *A Short History of Benin*, p. 12. For the Urhobo refer to J.W. Hubbard, *The Sobo of the Niger Delta*, (Zaria, 1948), p. 198, and O. Ikime, *The Isoko People, A Historical Survey*, (Ibadan, 1972). The Ishan are discussed in Okojie, *Ishan Native Laws and Customs*, and Miller, 'Ishan-Benin Relations'.
54. Egharevba, *A Short History of Benin*, p. 13.
55. Bradbury, *Benin Studies*, p. 49.
56. Law, *The Oyo Empire*, and S.F. Nadel, *A Black Byzantium*, (London, 1942).

57. D. Sweetman, "Amina of Hausaland", in *Women Leaders in African History*, (London, 1984), pp. 22-27.
58. R. Griffeth, "The Hausa City-States from 1450- 1804", in *The City State in Five Cultures*, (edited by R. Griffeth, Santa Barbara, 1981), and E.M. Hiskett, "City of History: The Story of Kano", *West African Review*, (28, 1957).
59. Y. Urvouy, "Chronologie du Bornou", *Journal de la Societie des Africanistes*, (XI, 1941, and VII, 1942); H.R. Palmer, *The Bornu, Sahara and Sudan*, (London, 1936).
60. J.B. Webster, "The Three Phases of Kwararafa: A Peripatetic State", Benue Valley Project Paper No. 7, 1984.
61. C. Coquery-Vidrovitch, "The Political Economy of the African Peasantry and Mode of Production", in *Political Economy of Contemporary Africa*, (edited by P.C.W. Gutkind and I. Wallerstein, Beverly Hills, 1976), p. 92.

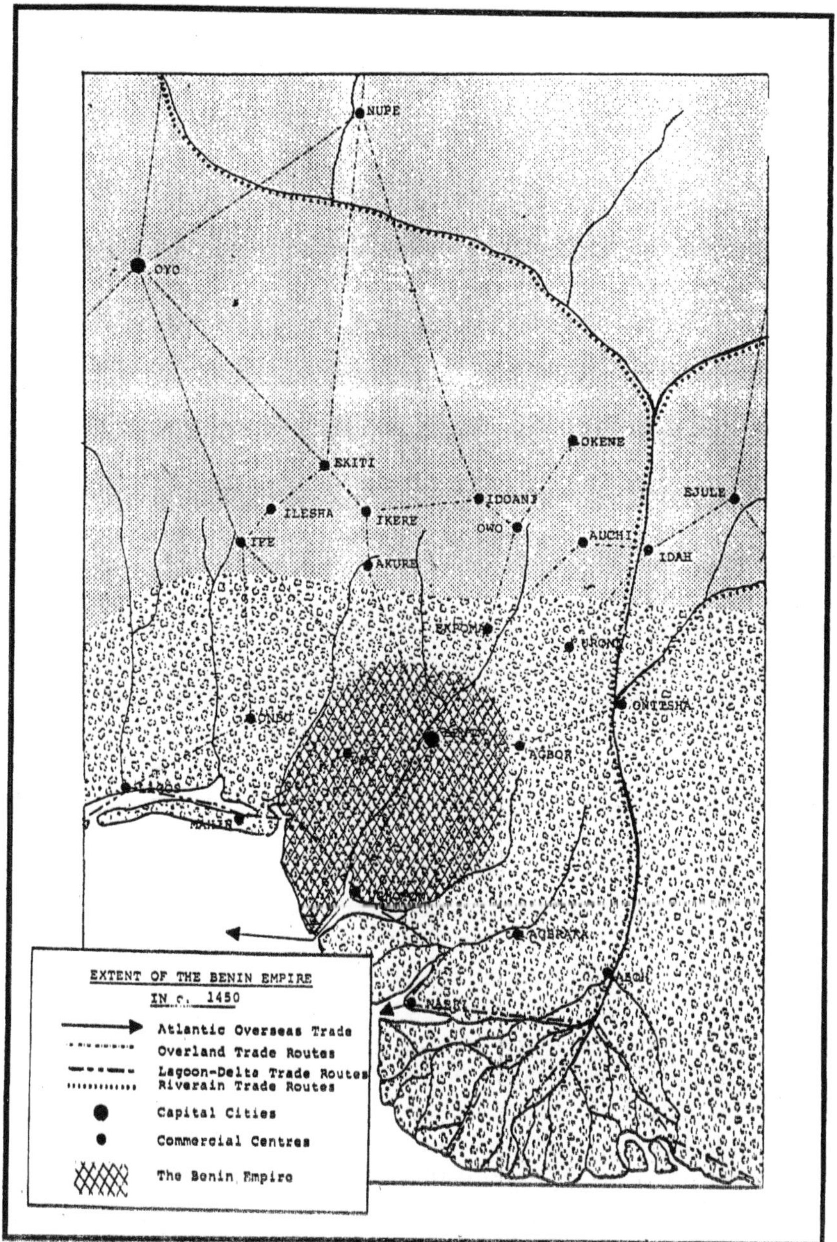

Map Five: Extent of the Benin Empire in c. 1450

Chapter 4

Commercial Imperialism in an Age of Economic Expansion Benin, c. 1455-1509

With the foundation of a reasonably sound and stable political infrastructure in the previous four generations succeeding monarchs in Benin were able to utilize this base to extend regional ambitions. The basis of state wealth had been established through levies on delta and lagoon commerce, and the opportunity of increased commercial exchange through expansion into two other trading systems provided the impetus for the formation of a conquest state - a state that sought regional authority through violent confrontation (conquest) as part of political policy. Oba Ewuare, c. 1455-1482, consolidated his authority in order to augment Bini control of trade and trade routes. The reign of Ozolua, c. 1482-1509, marked the period of greatest territorial expansion, the organization of state commercial monopolies, and the commercial domination of an expanding trading nexus that stretched from the coast to the confluence region. This territorial and economic growth established Benin as the major forest zone trading formation at the centre of four inter-connected exchange networks: the east-west lagoon trade; the Igbo interior trade through the delta to the east; the north-south hinterland trade linked to the trans-Saharan system; and the European overseas trade at the coast.

Each of Benin's main trading networks was linked to a distinct religious institution which controlled the commercial operations and entrepreneurs operating in that system. The waterborne lagoon trade was dominated by the Olokun cult, the eastern interior system functioned under Igbo ritual authority, the north-south trade was the preserve of Ifa, and the European coastal trade was represented on the Benin side by Olokun which was combined with Christianity to cope effectively with the alien ideals and norms of the European merchants. Thus the central administration was able to utilize a variety of religious institutions to dominate commercial relations effectively, and to employ force when necessary to back up this economic hegemony.

The monarchs who followed Oba Egbeka to the Benin throne were aggressive leaders who actively sought nomination to the paramount position. The often violent competition for the throne was probably as much a reflection of the disarray within the Uzama Nihinron, after their losses in the civil war, as it was a desire on the part of each potential heir to attain the throne in this increasingly wealthy state. Normal succession would have been acquired through Uzama nomination and investiture by the Oliha. However, after the death of Oba Orobiru, two surviving brothers vigorously contested the nomination. One brother was eventually assassinated after an extremely short tenure, and his assassin, Oba Ogun Ewuare, an extremely ambitious and powerful ruler was installed.[1] Not only did Ewuare kill his closest rival, but he also "had the innermost and greatest walls and ditches made around the city,"[2] and embarked on the reorganization of the military to foster regional power and solidify territorial domination.

The main thrust of Ewuare's conquests corresponded with the state's interest in greater control over the interior trade routes and the northward links to the Niger. Ekiti and Ikere were two prominent commercial enclaves on the main trade route to Nupe and Oyo. The conquest of these towns and the subjugation of Kukuruku provided the Oba with control of the north-south hinterland routes which connected Benin with the trans-Saharan network. Through this military exercise Oba Ewuare also expanded the tribute-paying population, and thus received increased revenues for the maintenance of his armies and the payment of his administrators. "He fought against and captured two hundred and one towns and villages... He took their petty rulers captive and caused the people to pay tribute to him..."[3]

The growth of Benin under Oba Ewuare occurred as the trans-Saharan trade system was on the verge of the greatest boom in its history. Increased commercial activity in the northern reaches of the Benue Basin impacted on Benin in the forest zone to the south. A wide variety of goods moved fairly rapidly through the interconnected exchange network. The peak of this commercial enterprise has been described by A.A. Boahen as "the period 1490-1590 when the Songhai Empire under the Askias and the Bornu Empire under the Sefuwas dominated the Sahara and Sudan, and maintained such political stability and order as have probably not been known in those areas since that time".[4] The Askias of Songhai did a great deal to foster the golden age of Sudanic trade:

> Commerce flourished under Askia. He instituted the Muslim practice of market inspectors to enforce honesty and justice, as well as standardization. The trading cities of Timbuktu and Jenne prospered, especially since the traders were free from conscription into the army and could devote themselves to trade. Large amounts of European merchandise found its way south to these markets, in exchange for gold, slaves, kola nuts and ivory.[5]

Further evidence which describes this period of prosperity is provided by the *Kano Chronicle*.[6] The reign of Sarkin Yakuba in 1451-1463 is described as a period of increasing involvement in the trans-Saharan trade, and of relative peace and prosperity in which commerce could flourish.

> ...salt became common in Hausaland. In the following year merchants from Gwanju began coming to Katsina; Beriberi came in large numbers, and a colony of Arabs arrived. Some of the Arabs settled in Kano and some in Katsina. There was no war in Hausaland in Yakubu's time.[7]

As the trans-Saharan trade entered this prosperous period events in a number of states, including Kano, Songhai, Katsina, Bornu, Zaria, Nupe, Oyo, Kwararafa and Benin, reflected the development of commerce and the general economic growth. In 1421-1438, during the reign of Sarki Dauda of Kano, for example, "Zaria, under Queen Amina, conquered all the towns as far as Kwararafa and Nupe."[8] The economic boom also contributed to tension and commercial rivalry between Kano and Katsina, Kano and Bornu, Bornu and Kwararafa, and Benin and

Oyo. Inter-state relations within the forest zone were no less competitive and while Benin emerged as the dominant polity and major commercial enclave this position was gained only after a prolonged and often bitter struggle between the leaders of the conquest state and the conquered polities.

During the era of Benin expansion, c. 1455-1536, the commercially significant Yoruba region between Benin and Ekiti, which included Uwo, Owo, Akure and Ikere, was annexed by Oba Ewuare. Owo, located approximately fifty miles north of Benin, sat astride the main north-south trade route, and represented an important strategic gain for Benin. The conquest state thus almost systematieally confronted and ultimately co-opted many of the major commercial enclaves, trading networks and regional adminstrative centres in the southern region. Conquest and co-option into the imperial sphere additionally meant that the political culture and social organization of Benin would be adopted in these perhipheral centres, such as Owo.

> Owo appears to have been very closely controlled from Benin. This was probably due partly to Owo's comparative nearness to Benin and her location along the main routes. The Olowo sent tributes to Benin annually through a resident official and the Owo had to pay to the Oba of Benin obeisance customarily due to an Oba. For instance, in most parts of Yoruba country any hunter who killed a tiger or leopard had to give it up to the Iba. In Owo, any hunter who killed either of these animals was made to carry it to the Oba of Benin. Moreover, Owo was made to surrender its princes as hostages in the Benin court. Many Owo rulers therefore had Benin education and were responsible for introducing Benin culture to Owo.[9]

When Owo rebelled against the authority of the Oba, Ewuare "swallowed his dislike and made friends with" Chief Iken of Usela,[10] and dispatched Iken to quell the rebellion. During Iken's absence on the campaign, Oba Ewuare placed his son, Kuoboyuwa, in Usela to act as temporary administrator. Iken was killed shortly after he had suppressed Owo, and with no legitimate successor in Usela to inherit Iken's crown, Kuoboyuwa became Enejie.[11] Oba Ewuare also established an alliance with the chief of Umela, and utilized this ally to bring the "rebellious people of Akure to their minds."[12] The rebellion was violently suppressed and strong Bini controls were re-established over Ekiti, Ikere, Owo and Akure.

> Akure, where there was already a sizeable Edo trading community, became a sort of Benin military outpost, from where the Benin armies led out expeditions into the Ekiti interior..A secondary post seems to have grown up at Ikare [Ikere] .As military ventures the Benin invasion appear to have been remarkably successful...the evidence would seem to justify our regarding Owo and many Ekiti and Akoko towns as part of the Benin empire in the sixteenth and seventeenth centuries...In Ekiti, Benin control was firmest over Akure and Ikere kingdoms...Akure and Ikere had Benin military outposts, while a large Benin trading community lived at Akure and Igbara-Oke in the Akure kingdom. According to Akure chiefs...Akure 'used to send him [Oba of Benin] yearly presents. Whenever our king is dead and we want to enthrone another we used to obtain the sanction of the king of Benin before doing so; and have to send the following presents namely three slaves, ivory and corals to the king...and give one slave to the resident from Benin.'[13]

The fact that Akure, Ekiti, Ikere and Owo were important commercial enclaves, strategically located astride the main north-south trade routes, controlled directly by an appointed Bini resident, indicates the degree of Bini influence in regional commercial affairs. The trans-Saharan trade boom,[14] provides an explanation for the expansion of the conquest state and the encroachment of the imperial trading formation into the northern hinterland. Region-wide commercial prosperity was reflected in the political transformation of the region - the imperial expansion of Benin under Oba Ewuare, and the similar expansion of Oyo, Zaria, Nupe, Kano, Katsina, Bornu and Kwararafa.

A fairly standardized system of administering newly conquered territory was implemented by Oba Ewuare. Military conquest followed by the appointment of an administrator over an indigenous chief, or the establishment of a vassal-tributary relationship with the indigenous ruler recognized as the Bini representative, became the mechanism whereby Oba Ewuare and his sucessors in Benin expanded regional authority. Conquest, and the establishment of governments subordinate to Benin through appointed governors and vassal chiefs, enabled Benin to create and manage a large empire. The conquest of Ikere, Ekiti, Akure, Owo and Kukuruku, for example, established the state's paramount authority in areas vital to the economy, security and political stability. The dominion engineered by Oba Ewuare, and controlled by a succession of powerful rulers in Benin, dominated north-south trade, regional politics, and social affairs across a broad stretch of territory from the Niger to the Ogun River,[15] and from the coast to the confluence. Apparently the same sense of order and stability had been created in Benin as that which fostered the economic boom in the trans-Saharan system and the sudanic region under the Askias of Songhai and the Sefuwas of Bornu.

One significant feature of the imposed sense of order in the Benin regional administration was the development of links between religion, commerce and the state. Religion had been a powerful mechanism for the control of both regional and long distance trade since the inception of the Olokun cult under Oba Ohen [c. 1428-14820].[16] The Olokun cult, dedicated to god of wealth and commerce,[17] was apparently introduced to expand the monarch's direct domination of trade and commerce, not only through the north-south network but also in the east-west waterborne system. Furthermore, the development of the Olokun cult as a major ritual specialization facilitated entrepreneurial activity under the control of the Oba.[18] Oba Ohen was aware that royal control over trade and trade routes could be implemented and reinforced through control of related religious institutions and fostered Olokun as the medium of state domination.

> The beginnings of Olokun devotion is attributed to Benin's Oba Ohen...The Olokun cult, at that early date [c. 1428-1455], had a political dimension rooted in the Benin state's perception of the significance of overseas trade. It has been stated that Olokun worship was established prior to European landings. This would be consistent with the suggestion of an early east-west lagoon [trade] among various Guinean littoral peoples.[19]

Olokun devotion and administration of trade were initially centred at the cult shrine at Ughoton. However, direct responsibility for the cult priesthood was provided through the palace in Benin, and the appointment of a royal relative as the Olokun priest. The cult, representing wealth, trade, and commerce, became a significant commercial institution through which the pursuit of trade was sanctioned and blessed. The fact that Olokun was associated with the sea, and yet appears as an important commercial cult in states far removed from the ocean, suggests that the development of hinterland commerce was also facilitated through common Olokun worship, for example, the development of Benin iron industries was initially dependent upon iron supplies from the mines of Oyo. Oyo adopted the Olokun cult as part of the state religious institution which encouraged trade between two related Olokun states, and thus Olokun became an organizational mechanism which prompted, facilitated, and controlled trade across a broad regional base. The founding of the Olokun cult, therefore, indicates that Benin had finally established control of the east-west lagoon trade and replaced the Igbo ritual and commercial agents with Bini priests and entrepreneurs.

The power of religion in commerce depended upon the belief systems of the various merchant and commercial classes who looked to their religious authorities for divine sanction of trade. The chief priest thus had the power to directly influence commercial decisions and could bless or condemn trading enterprises through his interpretation of ritual symbols. Religious sanctions became a necessary obligation for all commercial ventures in the three trading systems operating within Benin, and the merchants paid handsome fees for the approval of trade and commercial activities. It was virtually impossible for any merchant operating in the waterborne system to achieve any measure of commercial success unless they had the approval of the Olokun priesthood. Not only could the religious authorities call upon the power of the gods to rid the trading network of undesirable commercial interlopers, but as the links between religion and the state were developed the priests could also call upon the power of the state. Thus a mutually beneficial system of inter-related support emerged which gave the palace controlled religious institutions total command of state-sanctioned commerce.[20]

Religious domination represented much more than a simple control of non-secular matters. Religion was an important mechanism for the control of markets, behaviour, actions, and economic or social activity, and could be used to ensure peaceful passage of traders through potentially hostile regions. Ritual specialists and cult priests, therefore, became overt agents of economic expansion, social domination, and political paramountcy.

Oba Ewuare incorporated the Olokun cult even more directly under palace control by appointing a close relative as the chief priest. Ewuare thus indirectly exercised control of all waterborne and most inland trading systems, and defined the close interconnection between religion, commerce and the state. Paramount in this administrative structure was the Oba, who could appoint and dismiss the chief priest, but direct control remained with the religious leaders who were recognized as state officials. In this way

> Olokun worship was elevated to the level of state devotion and became a formidable political weapon wielded through the agency of the Olokun chief priest, who were either of the royal lineage or were the Kings offspring.[21]

To utilize the Igbo ritual system, Oba Ewuare extended palace controls by appointing two recently arrived Igbo, Osa and Osuan, as priests of the royal gods of Ora and Uwen.[22] The incorporation of these ritual specialists was in itself not surprising for Igbo ritual authority had been influential in Benin for some time. Although the appointment of outsiders as agents of royal deities might affront indigenous Igbo religious institutions, which had become aligned with Udo's political and economic ambitions, it better served the Oba's purpose. Osa and Osuan presumably had commercial links to the eastern interior trade, and as newcomers to the state would have been easier for the Oba to control because they would have exhibited less kinship or "descent-group based" concepts of authority.[23] The palace, therefore, adopted a simple expedient to expand direct control over an important religious institution with economic ramifications beyond the confines of the state.

The introduction of Ifa from Nupe during the reign of Oba Ewuare established palace controls over the third commercially important religious institution in the state. The fact that Ifa was adopted by a large number of diverse political, cultural and ethnic entities demonstrates its pervasive qualities and suggests that it was an efficient mechanism in the promulgation of long distance commercial exchange.

> ...the whole system was invented by...Setilu, who was born blind in Nupe...He had many pupils and admirers who were spreading his teachings...Setilu crossed the Niger and reached Benin, then Ife, where he settled down for good...it was carried from Ife to the far distant places of the Gulf of Guinea only during the sixteenth and seventeenth centuries. This would also explain the close similarities of the Ifa terminology, preserved up to this day, over a relatively very extended area...[24]

Ifa represented much more than a simple religious institution from a northern trading partner designed to exercise social controls. Implications of Ifa divination intruded upon state decision-making processes, for example, where Ifa priests were consulted as to a particular course of action. Also, Ifa was an important mechanism for market control and the organization of commercial activities. Domination of such a pervasive system, in which virtually every day to day decision could be decided by the Ifa priest, was therefore not solely a religious concern, but directly involved secular authority as well. Ifa divination in the hands of a priesthood not fully integrated into the state government or administrative hierarchy, or perhaps one supporting a political or economic rival rather than the ruling monarch, could seriously affect the balance of power and the ability of the monarch to exercise effective economic, social and political control. The Ifa system, although alien to Benin, was attractive to the administration as a mechanism of social control, and because it could extend domination over commerce and hinterland commercial relations. Ifa divination could overcome "barriers to the smooth conduct of the market," and encouraged the state's domination of those central commercial institutions.[25]

The development of Ifa facilitated the expansion of trade between diverse socio-linguistic groups which held common Ifa traditions. It therefore contributed to the expansion of Benin as an imperial trading formation and, concurrently, strengthened palace controls over long distance trade. Ifa spread along with the expansion of Benin which explains why its terminology is almost identical among the Igala, Idoma, Igbo and Edo. In particular, the adoption of Ifa solidified commercial relations with Nupe and Oyo which had similar Ifa systems. Oba Ewuare was particularly effective in the organization of direct palace controls over Ifa, the Olokun cult, and the Igbo ritual system. By dominating these religious institutions the Oba established paramount authority in every major commercial network in the sub-region.

Another of Oba Ewuare's major accomplishments, as the founder of the conquest state,. was the extension of Bini influence over a number of the Ishan chiefdoms. Some of these chiefdoms had been founded in migrations away from the exploitation and domination of the Eweka monarchy, but the freedoms gained by the migrants were short-lived. Ewuare exercised diplomacy rather than force, and brought the Ishan chiefdoms back into the empire after convening a conference of the Ishan leaders in Benin. Ewuare appointed those that attended as Enejie of their respective Ishan communities and thus incorporated no less than nine chiefdoms into the imperial sphere, including Ubiaja, Ugboha, Uromi, Ewohimi, Ohordia, Ekpoma and Ugbegun.[26] C.G. Okojie, in his collection of Ishan traditions, describes the Ewuare conference in the following terms.

> Ewuare the Selfish invited all the War Leaders in Ishan to Benin City... There... Ewuare played his master stroke; working on the human love for power, he created those that attended Ojie [King] of their people and made it abundantly clear that the honour was not transferrable. The title

> made each invested person the unquestioned ruler and master of his people responsible only to his good self -*Ewure*! [27]

In addition to extending Bini domination into conquered and annexed territory for the purpose of establishing political and economic controls, Ewuare also embarked on a process of further centralization in the internal administration of the capital. He created the Eghaebho n'Ogbe [palace chiefs] and the Eghaebho n'Ore [town chiefs] who performed almost all state administrative functions, excluding only the military command.[28] He also appointed ten new titled officials - the Eson, Osuma, Edogun, Ihaza, Ehioba, Eriyo, Osia, Ogua, Utomwen and Osogua.[29] Oba Ewuare thus made all titles "apart from Ologbose which was hereditary" part of the "Oba's gift, and any of his freeborn subjects...could aspire to them."[30]

The organization of patronage and clientage as part of the Oba's gift system created a dependent network of officials and bureaucrats, and a number of subordinate title holders. The Oba could utilize titles as rewards for faithful or outstanding service to the state, palace or monarchy, and thus establish a relatively large and devoted group of state supporters. The fact that every "freeborn man in the Benin kingdom considers himself a member of the palace Otu" organizations,[31] suggests that social and political relations between individuals, lineages, and villages, on the one hand, and the palace on the other, were clearly defined and understood. Upward social mobility could be achieved through the village Otu system, and ultimate elevation into the Edion ranks.[32] However, even more prestige and social, political and economic benefit could be attained through access to the palace Otu organization. This meant that:

> ...each individual had a sense of personal identification with the central institutions of the state, and thus they helped maintain popular support for a highly exploitative political system. In its relations to the capital, the village had the quality of a peasant culture...the ultimate pinnacles of ambition lay outside the village. Relatively few managed to transpose themselves...yet virtually everyone had a kinsman or neighbour who had succeeded in doing so. When a man was made an elder...of his palace [organization]... he automatically became an elder of his village and, to this

extent there was a measure of integration of village and palace hierarchies.[33]

Oba Ewuare also organized the capital into "corporate wards, each characterized by (a) particular craft or ritual service."[34] The corporate wards developed Otu organizations similar to those in the villages, and each ward paid allegiance tribute through its own Otu hierarchy. Each ward was also tied to the palace dominated Otu structure through the ward chief and his association with the Eghaebho n'Ore (town chiefs) further strengthened the bonds with the central institutions. In this way the Oba created a centralized authority which dominated the administration of the rural and urban population and connected various components in the state administration to the organization of the palace.

To extend further palace controls over virtually every aspect of social, political and economic life, Oba Ewuare initiated policies designed to augment the power of the ruler and define each individual in the social structures of the society. For example, "he is said to have been the first Oba to persuade his freeborn subjects to let their sons take up retainer service in the palace." Ewuare also "decreed that all his freeborn... subjects should be marked with the common pattern of scarification which distinguished *evien-Oba* from royals, slaves, and foreigners, all of whom were excluded from the palace."[35] Thereafter only suitably marked individuals could aspire to palace appointments in the national Otu system. Oba Ewuare can be credited with founding a common ideology which linked freeborn commoners to the palace and thereby to the Benin social formation.

It is significant that the Ishan adopted Bini markings during the reign of Oba Ewuare, and thus joined the growing number of commoners who owed allegiance to the state and central government. Ishan traditions suggest that they adopted Bini scarification because they were proud of their Bini heritage, but it would seem that they did so as a political expedient and thus became integrated with the palace and central administration of the state in order not to remain political, economic and social outcasts.[36]

The last major change instituted by Oba Ewuare was the creation of the Ediaken title (heir apparent), who was appointed to sit as the seventh member of the Uzama Nihinron.[37] The role of the Uzama as the Kingmaker's Council was substantially altered and its influence greatly reduced because nominations would have become almost automatic. Clearly through the appointment of the Ediaken, Oba Ewuare had restricted the authority of the Uzama Nihinron, and increased the integral power of the monarchy.

Oba Ewuare nominated his son, Ezoti, as the first Ediaken and he eventually became Oba in c. 1482-1509. The organization of Benin had, it would seem, become highly codified and rigid, with every sector of the population expected to integrate and associate with state policy or remain recognized as "slaves, and foreigners." The various policies implemented by Oba Ewuare contributed to the development of social norms whereby rights of access to the palace hierarchy were clearly defined, and the status of each individual clearly understood. Oba Ezoti died shortly after his installation, and his son, Prince Owere, the Ediaken, was nominated to inherit the crown.[38] Prince Okpame Ozolua, Oba Ezoti's younger brother, assassinated Owere and his mother while they were on their way to accept the nomination. The Uzama Nihinron, apparently sitting without an Ediaken, called upon Prince Olua, Oba Ezoti's other brother, to take the crown. Olua refused the nomination, fearful perhaps of violent reprisals from Ozolua. The Uzama then turned to Princess Edeloyo, Ezoti's sister, in a desperate attempt to avoid nominating Prince Ozolua. Edeloyo accepted the nomination but was deemed ineligible when she came down with "a female complaint."[39] It is possible, however, that Edeloyo was deterred by her aggressive brother rather than by some infirmity. The Uzama Nihinron finally convinced Prince Olua to accept the crown, and the heir ordered his youngest son to guard the approaches to Benin and prevent intervention from Ozolua. This son established himself at Eho, and prevented any encroachment upon the capital by the rejected candidate. Olua mounted the throne with some trepidation, but the coronation proceeded in relative peace, and Oba Olua eventually ruled Benin with a degree of harmony and security, but ever watchful for a renewal of violence from his ambitious brother. Ozolua remained in exile awaiting an opportunity to revive his candidacy for the throne.

Was there a religious connection within this contested succession? Unfortunately the present state of research makes it difficult to relate the three competing male candidates - Owere, Olua and Okpame Ozolua - to the three dominant reigious factions operating in Benin. However, the fact that there were three distinct religions and three potential candidates suggests certain intriguing possibilities and a possible explanation for the chain of events which transpired during this struggle for political power. Given the pattern of succession in normal circumstances certain relationships between the various legitimate heirs and the competing religious institutions are implied. For example, Ezoti and Owere were probably fairly conservative candidates, and therefore would have opposed the development of Olokun and Ifa. Owere probably best represented Uzama political and religious preferences. But Uzama political ambitions were thwarted by the assassination of Owere, and they presumably turned to Olua as a compromise candidate in this highly contested succession. The selection of Olua also avoided the nomination of Prince Okpame Ozolua who had exhibited violent tendencies and was the least acceptable candidate in the minds of the Uzama. Opposition to Ozolua may have been based upon his violent approach to politics, his assassination of Owere, but may also have considered his affinity with Ifa which would have been the least acceptable religious option to the Uzama Nihinron.With Prince Okpame Ozolua banished to Ora for the murder of Owere, Iginua, son of Oba Olua, held the Ediaken title and acted as advisor to his father.[40] Iginua also appears to have been a supporter of Ifa, and based his advice upon the counsel of Ifa priests. In doing so he managed to offend or alienate a large number of people, particularly the Uzama Nihinron who had apparently opposed the succession of an Ifa supporter in the previous contested nomination.

Olua's Contested Succession

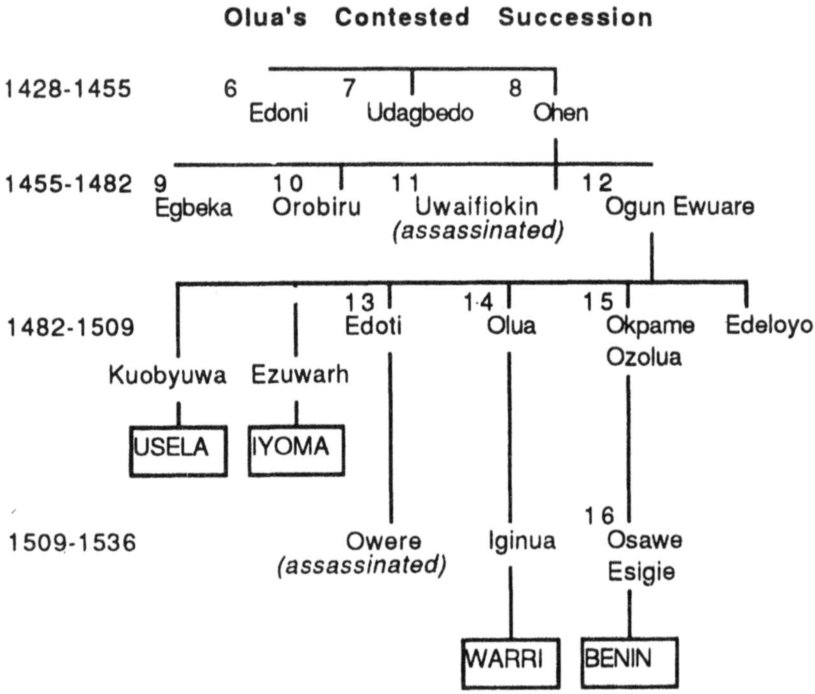

The following tradition recalls how Iginua was called upon for advice, and reveals that Iginua's rule, should he have inherited the throne, would certainly have been despotic. The tradition also indicates how Ifa divination would have generated opposition in the society, and why Iginua, as the most prominent proponent of this religion, was eventually forced to fee.

> Once Olua sent to the royal wine maker for some wine, who replied that there was no wine, and why did Olua send to him for it instead of preparing it for himself? The Oba then sent to Omare who was in charge of the royal dogs...asking him to send him a dog for sacrifice...The reply sent back that there were only three dogs and that he had sent one to the Oliha, one to the Edohen, and he had sacrificed the third to the god of his own medicine.... The Oba... called his son, Iginua, to ask his advice...Iginua advised his father to sacrifice the old

> woman [who had insulted the Oba] at the beginning of the new year, in order that the sun might be less scorching and to avert epidemics...He also advised that the lame man [who also insulted the Oba] should be nailed to a stool by a long nail from his head through the length of his body...Also, that a present of a woman should be sent to the wine makers and, when he came to the palace to return thanks, his hands and feet should be bound together and tied to a cow's leg so that he could be dragged about the streets until he died. Lastly, that he should send presents of a coral necklace and anklet to the Omare, and when he came to give thanks to the Oba, he should be sacrificed to the gods of medicine instead of the dog. Olua did so to all four. But because of the bad advice which Iginua had given to his father, the people said they would not have him [Iginua] for their Oba.[41]

This tradition is instructive in a number of other important ways. For example, the fact that a minor official, Omare, had given one royal dog to the Oliha and another to the Edohen, both important members of the Uzama Nihinron, suggests that the Uzama had partially recovered from the civil war with Oba Egbeka and were exercising a considerable degree of political influence in the capital. Given the fact that rival candidates had been squabbling over the throne, it would seem reasonable that the Uzama might have developed increased authority, and thus gained the support of some minor officials. The mounting opposition to Prince Iginua among the Uzama was probably an expression of their antagonism toward Ifa, and their failure to penetrate the northern commerce dominated by Yoruba merchants, and their newly augmented status in the social and political decisions of the state.

Resistance to the prince increased to the point where Oba Olua feared for the life of his son, which prompted the monarch to suggest that Iginua should leave Benin and "found a kingdom by the sea."[42] Iginua accepted the proposal even though it meant relinquishing his Ediaken title and his opportunity to inherit the throne, and quietly crept out of Benin in c. 1509-1536.

> Ginua [Iginua]...was smuggled out of Benin in a wooden box, but was escorted by seventy Benin chiefs. When clear of the Benin kingdom Ginua emerged from the box clad in his regalia and led the astonished escort to new settlements as their king [Olu, after the name of his father

> Oba Olua]...Ginua's son. Ijijen succeeded him and led his people to Opotomo. Here they met Itsekiri who acknowledged the king and gave him land near his own settlement, where he [Ijijen] built his town and the capital of the kingdom of Warri.[43]

The large number of Bini chiefs and supporters who accompanied Iginua suggests that he had acted as spokesman for a significant faction in Benin. He became the leader of an Ifa chiefdom in Warri outside the Benin empire, but with relations to the Bini monarchy.

The foundation of Warri represented one of the first royal emigrations from Benin; other royal princes had been appointed administrators of vassal villages within the empire, but none had ventured beyond the confines of the state to establish related, but autonomous polities. The Bini monarchy of Warri developed as an important peripheral authority, adjacent to but outside the imperial sphere. Warri's economic base was firmly rooted, from the outset, in lagoon-delta trade, Niger commerce, and the overseas Atlantic trade with the Europeans. This was a period when Portuguese traders were visiting the Guinea coast, and Warri established very close relations with them.

> By the year A.D. 1588 they [the Portuguese] had become so friendly with Itsekiri, that they had established trading stations at Warri and Gborodo. Their export was principally slaves, and spices, and pepper from Benin, and occasionally elephant tusks. Among the Portuguese was one magnate named Mingo, who took one of the Olu's daughters, Princess Magheghoeye, for a wife, and by her had a son, whom he named Anthonio. Anthonio went to Angola for education, and when he returned to Warri, he struggled for, and gained the position of Olu, although he was a mulatto, and, coming from the female side of the royal tree, had no right to the throne.[44]

Upon the death of Oba Olua in Benin the successors to the throne, for the most part, had been either killed or banished, and this created an opportunity for the Uzama Nihinron to to increase their political authority. The Uzama Nihinron sought to initiate a system of government which enhanced their own authority and stature while reducing the power of the Oba. In this power play they endeavoured to govern Benin under a "republican form of government," with the Oliha as President.[45] This short period of Uzama rule was really a thinly disguised return of their authority, as it had been during the first Igodo dynasty. This experiment may also have revealed a general reluctance to nominate Prince Okpama Ozolua who had so violently disrupted the two previous successions. The experiment in republicanism failed leaving disorder and general confusion, and the Uzama finally invited Ozolua to return from Ora and become the next Oba of Benin. Ozolua, the fifteenth monarch in the Eweka dynasty, became widely known as Oba Okpame Ozolua (The Conqueror).[46] The reign of Oba Ozolua re-established the monarchy as the dominant political power and authority in the capital, and launched his career in conquest, territorial acquisition and imperial expansion.

The reign of Ozolua (c. 1482-1509) may be the most significant in Benin history. During this period European overseas trade increased to the point where it could rival northern hinterland commerce in the economy of Benin, and thus prompted the monarchy to reconsider the religious controls of the palace-dominated commerce. The introduction of Christianity would, potentially it seems, allow the palace to penetrate and dominate coastal trade as the major trading partner in Portuguese commerce. Oba Ozolua also took advantage of his position as paramount to finally reduce the status of the Uzama Nihinron and entrench the power of the dynasty once and for all. With the development of integral power, and the expansion of the fourth trading network, Benin embarked upon the most active period of regional domination, and Oba Ozolua "fought and won no less than two hundred battles" to expand Bini regional control.[47]

One of Oba Ozolua's first steps was to limit the political status of the Uzama Nihinron and clearly define the relationship between it and the monarchy. Ozolua followed a precedent established by the Uzama Nihinron when they had rejected normal collateral succession to nominate Prince Owere as a primogenitary candidate. He established primogeniture as the rule rather than the exception. This policy may have received support from the Christian segment of the society; a growing group which was developing greater political and economic interests in the administration of the state. Also, primogeniture would have received the support of the Ifa adherents who had backed Prince Ozolua from the outset. The constitutional change would not have been popular with the Uzama Nihinron, however, as it eroded any remaining authority vested in the Oliha and Uzama. The appointment of Ozolua's eldest son, Prince Esigie, as the Ediaken was the final step in the implementation of primogeniture, and served to remove any potential checks on the integral power of the Oba that may have been exercised by the Uzama. This constitutional change and new succession policy effectively relegated the members of the Uzama Nihinron to purely symbolic functionaries and eliminated their voice from decisions of state. As Bradbury observed:

> ... the Uzama had not always been set apart from the management of the state... Up to the reign of the sixteenth Oba, Esigie, the Oliha is portrayed as the Oba's main antagonist...Ritual expression is still given to the ancient opposition between the Oba and Uzama in...the form of pantomimic battles This rite, and myth's relating how various kings got the better of the Uzama, have a continuing social meaning in that they reassert the Oba's unchallengeable supremacy...But it is likely that they refer, also, to an historical decline in the power of the Uzama correlated...with the rise of the Eghaebho [Town and Palace chiefs]...; and with the shift towards a doctrine of automatic primogenitary succession to the kingship... They continued to receive the new kings installation fees and to inaugurate his reign, but they had no more effective voice in determining his identity.[48]

Oba Ozolua was also famous in Benin traditions as the first monarch actively to foster Christian missions in the capital.[49] This policy served to exacerbate the conflict between the competing religious systems already seeking hegemony in the palace controlled set of ritual institutions. Although Ozolua personally did not develop close personal ties with the missionaries, he encouraged his son and heir to do so. Esigie learned to speak and read Portuguese and his apparent commitment to Christianity alienated the traditional religious authorities, and eventually offended the Oba. Esigie was suspected of "intriguing with the Portuguese" against the throne, and to placate his father, Esigie advised "them [the missionaries] to go away and return after he had himself become Oba."[50] It would appear that Oba Ozolua was not so easily satisfied, and despite Esigie's position as Ediaken, came to favour his second son, Prince Aruanran. The Oba established Aruanran as the Bini administrator in Udo, and thereby created, inadvertently one must assume, the circumstances that would eventually lead to civil war between Esigie and Aruanran; a war between the Christian-Ifa elements represented by Esigie, and the Olokun-Igbo religious orders represented by Aruanran.

The growing importance of Atlantic overseas trade provided an economic advantage to Prince Esigie, and contributed to his success as the central political figure in the administration of the state. Aruanran, although favoured by his father, represented the weaker political and economic institutions, and thus did not hold a strong hand in the impending struggle. This conflict would be among the various competing commercial factions, each linked to a different religious ideology which allowed them access to a particular component in Benin's extensive commercial relations. European contacts and the advent of Christianity became, therefore, an exacerbating factor in the internal conflicts which would develop upon the death of Oba Ozolua.

Ozolua is perhaps most famous in Benin traditions as a military leader who actively pursued imperial policies which served to establish Benin as one of the most important long distance trading states on the Guinea coast. His systematic destruction and incorporation of states on the periphery of the empire appears to reflect the importance of hinterland distribution routes, natural resources, labour supplies, markets and production centres. The defeated territories included Ijebu-Ode, Owo, Oromi, Uzea, Ejide, Umagba, Ewiagkagbu, Ogbe, Oka, Utekon, Iwu and Iguisi, to name but a few.[51] Perhaps the most significant military success came at the expense of Ijebu-Ode, which controlled access to the vast interior markets of the Oyo empire, and dominated an important commercial crossroads.[52]

Oba Olua had inaugurated the policy of establishing royal administrators on the periphery of the empire by encouraging

Iginua to settle at Warri, and Oba Ozolua followed with the appointment of Aruanran at Udo. Oba Ozolua also sent royal governors to Idoani, Okpe, Owo, Ijebu-Ode and Ora, and thus expanded the authority of the imperial formation through related dynasties in a large number of associated social formations. Idoani traditions document the process of imperial expansion and the establishment of the Bini dynasty:

> Some time in the middle of the sixteenth century, the first Oba of Idoani in the person of Ani, was reported to have entered the town...there is the imperialist account which states that the Oba of Benin...had commissioned a number of his children to found new kingdoms and that Ani was one of the Princes commissioned by the Oba of Benin...considering the circumstances of the entry of Ani to Ido, it is reasonable to assume that he came in a conquering mood, but like other imperialists of his age, he soon recognized the fact that while he might succeed for a brief period in subduing the native population, he could not hope to retain their loyalty and keep the peace unless he enjoyed their confidence.[53]

Oba Ozolua's imperial expansion, therefore, utilized the military to conquer and annex territory, and also employed royal governors to establish related although autonomous political regimes. The latter seems to have been mainly used for areas on the periphery of the empire where strong allies could protect the core of the empire, and bear the brunt of opposition to Bini regional domination. This policy allowed Ozolua to concentrate on his own military conquests without concern for the general security of the border regions controlled by his sons.

Oba Ozolua's final military campaign was prompted by a rebellion of Agba, the Enejie of Uromi, who apparently felt exploited under the paramount authority of Benin. Agba aspired to sever the vassal-tributary relationship between Uromi and Benin and set himself up as an independent ruler. He believed that Benin domination had been accomplished by a "trick...which had brought his father, Ichesan,...under the suzerainty of Benin."[54] Agba succeeded in forging a secret alliance with Ekpoma, but failed in his efforts to secure either widespread Ishan support, or the support of the Idah monarchy for his rebellion.

> Agba, the Ogie or Onojie of Uromi, rebelled and demonstrated a hostile attitude against his overlord, Ozolua, and urged all the people in Ishan to join him to make war on Benin...Ozolua was ultimately compelled to declare war on Uromi and organized a sharp operation against the Onojie. At first Agba... went to Idah to seek the help of the Attah but he was treated with every indignity and discourtesy. He therefore returned home to face whatever might be the consequences.[55]

The King of Idah, Eggarah Eri, refused to assist Agba for fear that Oba Ozolua might turn the Bini army against the Okpoto capital. Although the most influential and prestigious Okpoto sovereign on the eastern bank of the River Niger, the Idah monarch was no match militarily for the more numerous forces of Benin. Furthermore, a number of recent refugees from the military campaigns on the west bank of the Niger had migrated to Idah to seek sanctuary under the paternal wing of the Okpoto monarchy. Their message had been to avoid conflict with Benin because "Ozolua is a fierce and violent warrior who conquers better equipped and more able enemies."[56] This message did not go unheeded in the Okpoto court at Idah, and Agba was turned away without the help he sought.

Ozolua was apparently informed of Agba's mission to Idah, and the position and stature of the Okpoto polity was brought to his attention as a potential threat to the peace, security and trade of the empire. He therefore dispatched his son, Aji-Attah, toward the Okpoto capital on the Niger. Aji-Attah was supported in his campaign by a number of settlers, a substantial segment of the Bini army, and the moral support of his father. The bulk of the Bini army, however, remained under Ozolua and prepared for the final assault on the rebel stronghold of Uromi.

Oba Ozolua defeated Agba in a prolonged conflict, and the Uromi forces eventually scattered before the victorious army of Benin. In the aftermath of battle both Agba and Ozolua were killed. Ozolua the Conqueror had led his last military expedition, and according to Benin traditions was poisoned "by his own soldiers for ungratefulness and selfishness."[57] With victory in hand, and released from military service by the death of the Oba of Benin, the soldiers returned home. In the capital Prince Esigie prepared for his coronation as the successor to Oba Ozolua, and the next monarch in the Eweka dynasty.

The Benin-Uromi war represented one of the last major military campaigns of the conquest state, and therefore the Benin Empire. Oba Ewuare had instituted the policy of regional administration through appointed vassals, and his successor, Oba Ozolua, had expanded on his administrative policy to utilize more royal princes in regional government. Ewuare had not utilized royal administrators, as each royal son in that period had a legitimate claim to contest royal succession, and he therefore tended to appoint loyal retainers. With the introduction of primogenitary succession, however, a considerable pool of administrative talent had become available, and royal princes who could not compete for the crown perhaps preferred the option of regional governorships. Oba Ozolua utilized his talent to expand and develop the process of regional administration and domination, and established a number of sons as governors in peripheral states. With the first sign of imperial weakness, these royal administrators sought total independence, thereby creating an internal and inherent weakness in the imperial formation.

The state inherited by Oba Esigie in c. 1509-1536 was vastly different from the Benin established by Eweka. It was also substantially different from the Benin ruled by Oba Ewedo in c. 1374-1401. One of the major affects of this transformation of Benin had been in the village society of the empire. The development of commercial exchange under the auspices of the imperial government generated demands for tribute from the village producers. The increasingly heavy burden of tribute and appropriation of surplus agricultural production from the gerontocratic Otu system may have been somewhat eased by the incorporation of an expanded slave labour force. The conquest state provided a means for the acquisition and incorporation of slaves, and thus facilitated the development of a domestic slave-labour system. It is difficult to gauge the effects of slave labour on the production capacity of the state, but the scarcity of evidence suggests that it was not employed to any great extent, and probably remained a royal monopoly utilized as direct support of the paramount and not as a generalized production force. Slaves seem to have been part of the Oba's tribute demand, and were dispatched to the capital from peripheral areas of the empire. Slaves were also redistributed by the Oba as one of the monarch's gifts within the patron-client system. Thus the gerontocratic village organization was coerced into increasing its own productivity to meet the rising demands of the dominant segment in the society, and to facilitate the development of primary and secondary commercial exchange networks forged and maintained by the conquest state.

Imperial expansion also affected the commoner population by requiring vassals to contribute labour and military service to the state. Military service became part of the required obligation of the Igele age rank in the village Otu system, and demands generated by the almost constant state of war under Ozolua the Conquerer must have placed increasing pressures on the Igele grade men. The eventual assassination of Oba Ozolua by his own soldiers seems, therefore, to reflect the growing dissatisfaction in the subordinate segment of the population. The productive capacity of the social formation, required to meet demands for increased commercial, non-commercial, and ad-hoc levies, as well as provide months of military service every year, was probably stretched to the limit. Military service not only limited agricultural production for the state but reduced the farmer's capacity to reproduce enough for his own needs. Although Oba Ozolua had managed to expand the tribute paying social sector by including a large number of new vassal villages, this apparently was not enough to meet the excessive demands of the conquest state and its army which was kept in active service for many years.

The transformation of Benin had enlarged the capacity of the state to dominate regional markets and market forces through various religious institutions. Ifa and Christianity had been grafted on to the complex of palace controlled religious institutions and allowed the Oba to direct commerce from the capital of the empire. Ifa and Christianity were used, therefore, to augment Olokun and the Igbo-Aro ritual system in the co-ordination of regional commerce, and eventually surpassed these existing ritual practices in economic importance. The integral power of the Oba, coupled with the state domination of two expanding trade networks - north-south and Atlantic overseas - through the commercially oriented religious institutions established clearly defined patterns of trade, markets and production focused on the capital of the empire.

> The organizational ensemble of political and economic controls built into the Benin division of labour, buttressed by a statist cult structure, enabled the palace to siphon off the surplus labour of several social sectors: non-food producing, luxury goods, artisans, producers of external trade goods...., and other producers of goods which supported the various strata of Benin society.[58]

Benin in this half century had become a stratified social formation with clear distinctions between the tribute-paying social sector and the dominant or ruling stratum. The Oba sat at the apex of this social pyramid, and looked down upon various lower categories in the politically, economically and socially stratified society. The top level was represented by the titled nobility who retained some semblance of political and economic power. The middle level contained the bureaucrats and local administrators, or Enejie in village society, who were generally absolved from communal labour and were recognized as localized political agents. At the lower levels the commoner population performed the bulk of the labour and provided the majority of material support for the Oba, nobility and bureaucrats. Finally, the slaves operated at the bottom of the social scale and presumably received the smallest return for their investment in the state. This socially divided population lived very different lives from the basically undifferentiated population under the Igodo dynasty and the first monarchs in the Eweka administration. Since the reign of Oba Ewedo (c. 1455-1509) Benin had become a stratified society with social, political and economic relations defined by the individual's rank in the organization of the social formation and rigidly maintained by the national Otu and the policy of the Oba in demanding tribute to reproduce the Eweka dynasty as the paramount in the state.

The establishment of the conquest state under the successive administration of Ewuare and Ozolua served to define clearly the regional parameters of the Benin Empire. Powerful and ambitious leadership in the capital had transformed Benin from a relatively circumscribed polity, which nevertheless had significant commercial ties to an expanded regional and long distance trading network, and to an enlarged imperial state with regional, political and economic powers. This transformation resulted in the incorporation of a number of significant peripheral states under Bini paramount authority. The territorial expansion, coupled with the development of hegemonic and integral powers, established the Oba of Benin as the dominant figure in an increasingly wealthy imperial social formation. The influence of the Oba was felt as far north as the confluence region, as far west as the Ogun River, down to the coast in the south, and as far east as Idah and the related dynasty established by Aji-Attah. Indirect influences stretched much further afield, and probably reached Kano in the north. By c. 1482-1509, Benin had emerged as the dominant political and economic force in the forest zone of the Benue Basin, and had established a sophisticated centralized administration, features of which were exported to and adopted by a number of distant polities.

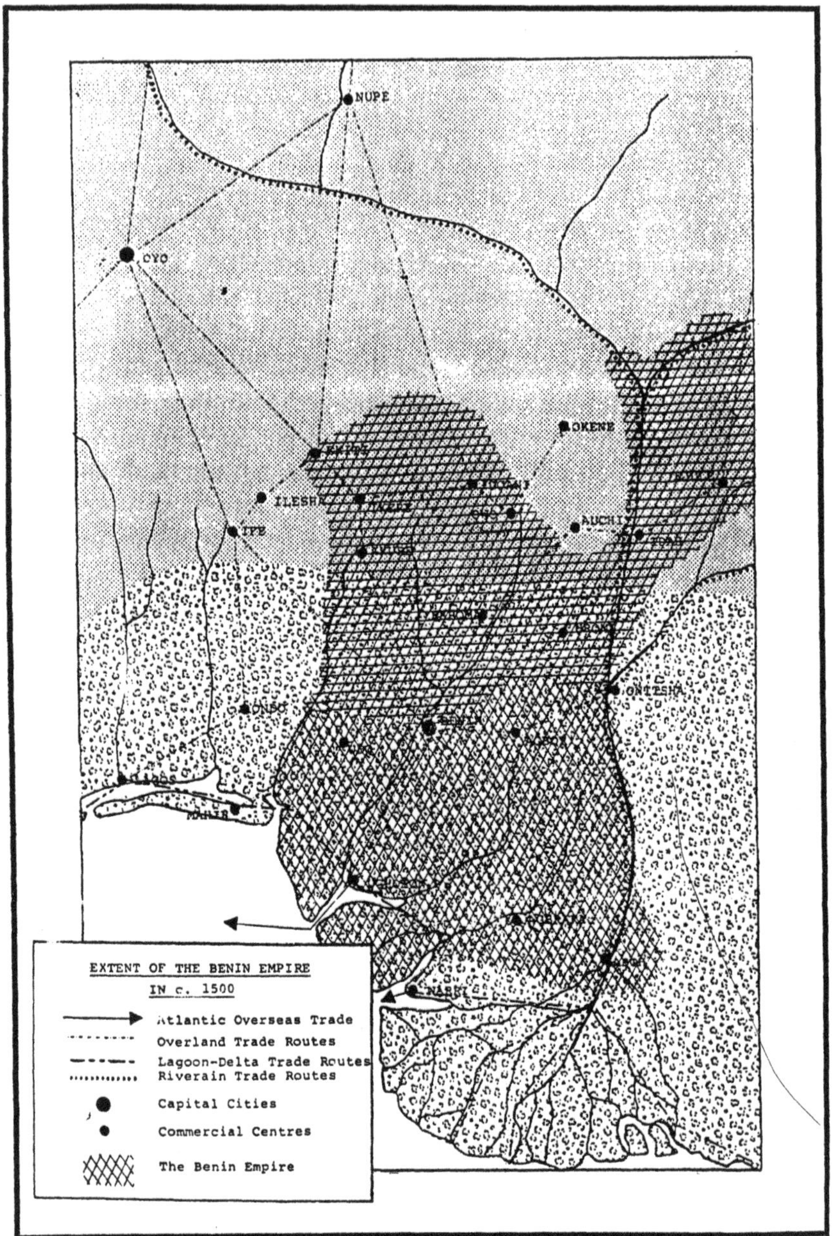

Map Six: Extent of the Benin Empire in c. 1500

References

1. Egharevba, *A Short History of Benin*, p. 13.
2. *Ibid.*, p. 13-14.
3. *Ibid.*, p. 14. See also G. Connah, "New Light on the Benin City Walls", *Journal of the Historical Society of Nigeria*, III, 4, 1967, pp. 563-609. Connah estimated that construction would have occupied 5,000 men working full time for at least one year, and this innermost construction represents approximately 10% of the total.
4. A.A. Boahen, "The Caravan Trade in the Nineteenth Century", *Journal of African History*, III, 2, 1962, pp. 349-350.
5. Anne W. Pardo, "The Songhay Empire Under Sonni Ali and Askia Muhammad: A Study in Comparisons and Contrasts", *Boston University Papers on Africa*, Vol. V, 1971, p. 55.
6. H.R. Palmer, "The Kano Chronicle", *Journal of the Royal Anthropological Institute*, 38, 1908, also repeated in J.A. Burdon, *Northern Nigeria*, London, 1909.
7. Burdon, *Northern Nigeria*, p. 32.
8. *Ibid* p. 31.
9. S.A. Akintoye, "The North-eastern Yoruba District and the Benin Kingdom", *Journal of the Historical Society of Nigeria*, IV, 4, 1969, p. 550.
10. Egharevba, *A Short History of Benin*, p. 14.
11. *Ibid.*, p. 14. At a later date Oba Esigie (c. 1509-1536) established Usela as the home of the Queen Mother, and all subsequent monarchs sent the Queen Mother to Usela with the title Iyoba. Chief Iken was probably a descendant of the Igodo dynasty whose great great grandfather had been an unsuccessful candidate for the Igodo crown. The establishment of a Bini prince, Kuoboyuwa, as the hereditary chief of Iken, represented, in effect, a change in dynasty in Usela. Kuoboyuwa is an unusual name, perhaps indicating that his mother was a representative of the indigenous population. More detailed research may, in fact, uncover that Kuoboyuwa's mother came from Usela, and that the prince was at least a semi-legitimate successor as an Usela chief. This possible interpretation would have made Kuoboyuwa a female side candidate for the Usela title, and could have thereby contributed to his acceptability as the new administrator after Iken's untimely death.
12. *Ibid.*, p. 15.
13. Akintoye, "The North-eastern Yoruba Districts", pp. 348-350.
14. Evidence about the trans-Saharan economic boom has been relatively well documented by Pardo, "The Songhay Empire", and E.W. Bovill, *Caravans of the Old Sahara*, London, 1933, pp. 82-113. Bovill stated, for example, that the "rise of Songhai power on the Niger had brought political stability to a vast area and this had naturally stimulated the caravan trade", (p.105).
15. P. Morton-Williams, "The Oyo Yoruba and the Atlantic Trade, 1670-1830", *Journal of the Historical Society of Nigeria*, (III, I, 1964), p. 30.

16. B.I. Belasco, *The Entrepreneur as Culture Hero*, (New York, 1980), pp. 77-78.
17. R.E. Bradbury, *Benin Studiesa*, (London, 1973), p. 34.
18. R. Law, *The Oyo Empire*, 1600-1836, (Oxford, 1977), pp. 217-218, and Belasco, The Entrepreneur, p.130 where he states that "the Edo [Benin] Olokun was assimilated as a Yoruba god."
19. Belasco, *The Entrepreneur*, pp. 77- 78.
20. For a more detailed discussion on the role of religion in West African commerce refer to J.F. Stevenson, *Population and Political Systems in Tropical Africa*, (New York, 1968), pp. 188-277, and S. Ottenberg, "Ibo Oracles and Intergroup Relations", *Southwestern Journal of Anthropology*, (14, 1958), p. 312.
21. Belasco, *The Entrepreneur*, p. 79.
22. Egharevba, *A Short History of Benin*, pp. 15-16.
23. C.G. Okokie, *Ishan Native Laws and Customs*, (Yaba, 1960), p. 181.
24. M. Kalous, "Ifa Divination", *New Orient* (6, 4, 1967), p. 123. Kalous states that Ifa terminology is almost identical among the Idoma, Bini, Ibo, Igala and very similar among the Nupe, Tiv and Jukun.
25. Belasco, *The Entrepreneur*, pp. 56-57.
26. J.E. Miller, 'Ishan-Benin Relations, c. 1455- 1509', (Dalhousie University Honours Essay, April 1983).
27. Okojie, *Ishan*, pp. 209-229. The emphasis was added by Dr. Okojie.
28. Bradbury, *Benin Studies*, p. 133.
29. Egharevba, *A Short History of Benin*, (third edition), p. 79.
30. Bradbury, *Benin Studies*, p. 67.
31. *Ibid.*, p. 62
32. Butcher, "Some Aspects of the Otu System", p. 151.
33. Bradbury, *Benin Studies*, p. 62.
34. *Ibid.*, p. 139.
35. *Ibid.*
36. Miller, 'Ishan-Benin Relations'.
37. Bradbury, *Benin Studies*, p. 139.
38. Egharevba, *A Short History of Benin*, p. 19. Much of the following has been reconstructed from Egharevba's extensive account.
39. *Ibid.*, p. 20.
40. *Ibid.*, p. 21.
41. *Ibid.*
42. *Ibid.*
43. P.C. Lloyd, "The Itsekiri", in *The Benin Kingdom*, (edited by D. Forde, as part of the *Ethnographic Survey of Africa*, Part XIII, London, 1957), p. 179.
44. W.A. Moore, *History of the Itsekiri*, (London, 1936), p. 88.
45. Egharevba, *A Short History of Benin*, p. 22.

46. *Ibid.*, p. 23.
47. *Ibid.*
48. Bradbury, *Benin Studies*, p. 58.
49. A.F.C. Ryder, *Benin and the Europeans, 1485-1897*, (Ibadan, 1969), p. 67.
50. Egharevba, *A Short History of Benin*, p. 27.
51. *Ibid.*, p. 25.
52. The relationship between Benin and Ijebu has been explored superficially by Belasco, *The Entrepreneur*, p. 19.
53. D.O. Asabia and J.O. Adegbesan, *Idoani Past and Present*, (Ibadan, 1970), pp. 10-11.
54. Okojie, *Ishan*, p. 323.
55. *Ibid.*, p. 227.
56. Igala Historical Text (hereafter cited as I.H.T.), No. 5, group interview collected by R.A. Sargent, in Idah, January 9, 1977, and I.H.T. No. 120, group interview with the Igala Mela clans, in Ochijenu, July 18, 1977.
57. Egharevba, *A Short History of Benin*, p. 25, and Okojie, Ishan, p. 225.
58. Belasco, *The Entrepreneur*, p. 81.

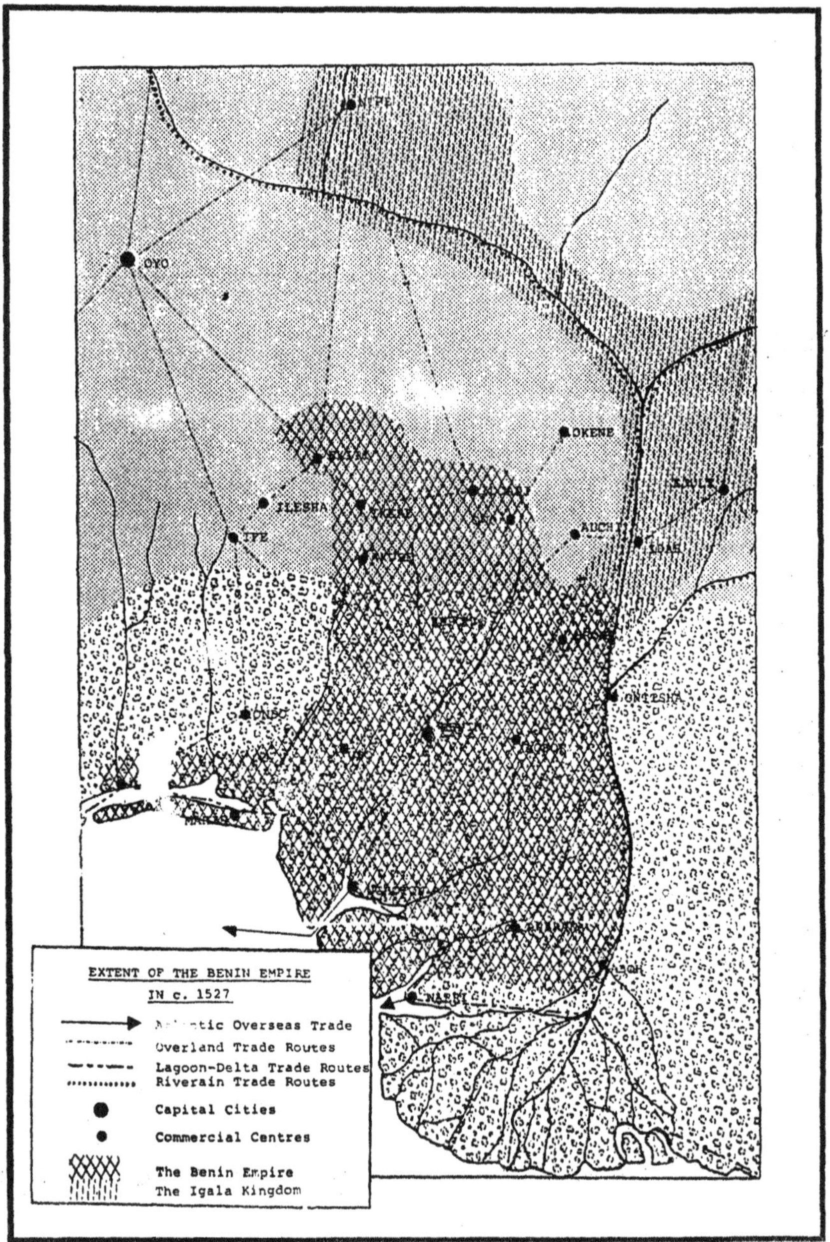

Map Seven: Extent of the Benin Empire in c. 1527

Chapter 5

Recombinant Political Geography In The Benue Basin c. 1509–1536

The reign of Oba Esawe Esigie marked the beginning of a substantially different economic age in Benin and the Benue Basin. Benin had been associated with a variety of prosperous commercial ventures, including north-south commerce linked to the trans-Saharan trade and east-west waterborne trade. Also, in the previous generation a significant link had been established with the Portuguese at the coast which started the Atlantic trade connection. This latter development launched the new age in which production for export, monetization of the economy, and centralized commercial management combined to push the state further to the forefront of regional political and economic affairs. In c. 1509-1536, it can be argued that a dramatic shift occurred in regional and long distance trade relations, based primarily on the interactions with Portuguese merchants on the coast, but also linked to the booming trans-Saharan trade system. At the same time the peripheral administrative centres within the imperial structure, which were organized to assist in the development of production, and establish an orderly flow of goods into the capital economy, acquired political and economic ambitions which threatened the unity, peace and security of the state. Their restricted access to direct commercial links and their limited market opportunities in an expanding economy provided the motivation for rebellion against paramount Bini authority. The new economic age combined, therefore, with a mounting pressure to reorganize imperial relations, and the impetus by peripheral governments to develop a new political geography that would establish them as regional powers in their own right. The rebellion of Idah, a Bini royalist enclave on the River Niger established by Aji-

Attah in the expansion of the conquest state under Oba Ozolua, was prompted in part by the desire to redefine political and economic relations in the forest zone and middle belt, and thus release Idah from vassal ties to Benin. Aji-Attah also had ambitions to become Oba of the imperial formation,[1] and his efforts to realize these ambitions provides the opportunity to examine relations between the capital of the imperial formation and a rebellious peripheral administrative and commercial centre.

The rise of Oba Osawe Esigie (c.1509-1536) in Benin was violently opposed by Enegie Aruanran of Udo. This struggle was based, in part, upon political and religious rivalry, but also reflected the need to control economic resources and commercial opportunities. Benin dominated the booming north-south and coastal trade, while Udo was limited to ancillary relations within the empire and had restricted links to only the less active and profitable east-west waterborne commercial network. Opposition from Udo was seen, therefore, as a threat, not only to the succession of Oba Esigie, but to his authority and the maintenance of coastal trade. Oba Esigie decided to attack and silence Udo to ensure the continued domination of Benin controlled commerce, and protect the distribution of imports beyond the restricted confines of the capital. One of Esigie's motivations, therefore, must have been to establish the peace and security essential for commercial growth and expansion.

In the battle between Udo and Benin, Prince Aruanran's only son, Oni Oni, was killed, and Aruanran himself committed suicide to avoid capture.[2] There was a subsequent period of peace, but the confrontation politics of Udo continued and forced another major military encounter, necessitated by the political competition for economic access and opportunity: "Osemwughe, the Iyase of Udo, to avenge the defeat and death of his master, challenged the Oba to fight. So troops were sent against Udo once more. In this campaign a series of battles were fought and the town of Udo destroyed. Osemwughe and the other rebels fled ... after a short time Osemwughe had to pay a yearly tribute to the Oba as his overlord .... Shortly after his return from the war, Esigie made a law that no prince should be made ruler of Udo any more. "[3]

The battle for political and economic supremacy consolidated Oba Esigie, killed one of his main rivals, and scattered the rebellious population throughout the region. The destruction of Udo removed the last internal pocket of resistance in the empire, and paved the way for the development of unopposed Bini authority in the forest zone.

Once securely entrenched Oba Esigie extended Benin contacts into the international (Atlantic) trading system by sending an ambassador to Lisbon, an unprecedented move that indicated the degree of sophistication and international awareness in the Bini government.[4]

> Esigie therefore sent Ohen-Okun, the Olokun priest at Ughoton with him (John Affonso d'Aveiro) as an ambassador to the King of Portugal, asking him to send priests who would teach him and his people the faith. In reply the King of Portugal also sent some Portuguese traders who established trading factories at Ughoton, the old port of Benin. They traded in ivory, Benin cloths, pepper and other commodities.[5]

Ohen-Oken was probably chosen as the Benin ambassador because Olokun had been originally organized as the state cult which controlled the delta-lagoon waterborne trade, and the initial coastal trade of the Portuguese had been placed under the religious control of the Olokun Priests. The Portuguese were thus seen as carriers in the Guinea coast trade, perhaps as a refinement and extension of waterborne-lagoon commerce. The addition of the Atlantic trade fostered the export of Benin production, including camwood and cloth, all along the coast. Thus when it was time to select an ambassador the Oba chose a representative who spoke Portuguese, had connections with the Portuguese trading community, and was an integral part of the state religious authority.

Esigie extended his close personal relations with the Portuguese and once the missionaries and traders returned to the capital he exercised direct control over their actions and related commercial opportunities. Missionaries, for example, were not allowed to organize outside the capital, and traders were forced to deal only with palace controlled commercial agents.[6] Economically Benin was securely entrenched as the main trading partner on the Guinea coast, and the Oba would tolerate little interference with the peaceful conduct of trade and commerce. The main rival coastal base in c. 1509-1536 was at the Rio del Rey, providing ample opportunity for Benin-state entrepreneurs to exploit commercial ventures at Ughoton. The primacy of north-south and coastal trade in the capital forced a major functional change on the east-west waterborne and interior eastern trading systems. They were reduced, in fact, to feeder networks and distribution routes for Benin commerce rather than operating as independent regional and long distance exchange systems. Trade was routed through the capital, controlled by the palace, and organized to benefit the centre, much to the consternation of peripheral administrative and commercial centres like Udo.

All major commercial transactions, during this new economic age, whether routed into the north-south hinterland trading system or into the Atlantic overseas trade at the coast, were of the luxury commodity variety. It has been argued, in some quarters at least, that luxury exchange did not necessarily affect the basic productive and reproductive capacity of the population,[7] and represented an export of surplus luxury goods and an import of luxury commodities designed for consumption by the palace and wealthy individuals in the state. Trade in these circumstances, therefore, benefitted the Oba, nobility and entrepreneurs, but did not penetrate the lower social and economic divisions in the state. It thus contributed to the wealth, power, status and prestige of the dominant elite, and had little impact on the bulk of the population. The export of beads, cloth, pepper, camwood, ivory and female slaves through the coastal ports in exchange for copper, iron, special forms of cloth, cowries, manillas and some European manufactured goods represented a cycle of commercial relations in which surplus could be siphoned off for the benefit of the Oba, and the development of wealth concentrated in the hands of the dominant social sector. Just because the volume of trade was increasing it did not necessarily imply a general economic benefit, since most overseas and north-south commerce was strictly controlled by the palace.

The introduction of cowries as an import item during the reign of Oba Esigie, and the subsequent monetization of the Benin economy, based upon cowrie currency, represented a dramatic shift in economic policy and a transformation of economic relations. A monetized economy, with rates of exchange and all major business transactions organized by the palace, tightened economic domination by the government. It also meant that the former luxury commodity exchange through barter became a restricted yet orderly commercial exchange in which Bini exports had a related currency value and could be purchased by the Portuguese. The money supply was controlled by the palace an thus heightened exploitation of the region's main agricultural producers to feed and support the palace and state nobility. Increased commercial demands, palace controlled monetary circulation, centrally dictated rates of exchange, and increased tribute demands all added to the exploitative pressures on the tribute-paying social sector. The transformation of economic policy and the coercive exploitation of the vassal sector suggests that a major change had occurred during the new age of commerce in the reign of Oba Esigie.

The relations with the Portuguese reinforced state control of commerce as the European link was organized through the Eweka dynasty's monopoly on external trade, and in turn reinforced the status of the capital as a wealthy and powerful political, social and economic centre. The state-dominated infrastructure, which controlled the production, distribution, transportation, and price of commercial goods, provided the mechanism to integrate with coastal commercial demands. The expansion of coastal trade, therefore, served to reinforce the dominant position of the Oba and contributed to an economic shift in the Bini commercial nexus. East-west and eastern interior commercial links had already declined in importance.

and by c. 1550 it would appear that the north-south overland route linked to the trans-Saharan trade system was reduced to second place in Benin commercial priorities.

In the eight years between 1498 and 1506 Benin became a major supplier of pepper to European markets. A shortfall in pepper supplies from India invigorated Bini production and export. In this period the "Portuguese factor at Antwerp received 75 quintals (7500 pounds) of Benin pepper annually."[8] However, when Indian production returned to the Venice market, the most important spice market in Europe, after 1506 the Benin trade declined.[9] It would seem that Bini exports were affected by European market conditions, but European fluctuations in a particular commodity, while imposing unstable demands on Benin commerce, did not permanently affect Bini production. The productive forces were organised to provide cloth, which was sold along the Guinea coast, pepper, camwood, ivory, beads and a variety of other products which could be stored for future exchange transactions.

The production, exchange and distribution of beads had been a significant part of Bini commercial activity long before the advent of European commerce on the coast.[10] Beads continued as an important export, and presumably increased in value as European demands developed. For example, in 1522-23,

> ...stone beads available in Benin ... could be exchanged for gold (on the Gold Coast). so they (the Portuguese) began to buy them in large quantities in 20 months.at Ughoton ... (the Portuguese factor) bought 33,382 coris [blue stones veined with red], 900 yellow beads and 162 of the grey.[11]

During a 1526 trading voyage a Portuguese merchant bought 9,200 coris in the Benin market.[12] Of this total 3,200 beads were purchased at the "price of five for one manilla", while the remaining 6,000 beads cost four for one.[13] This would mean that during this single voyage 2,140 manillas were imported into Benin. It is interesting that an equivalent number of manillas could have purchased, at the 1526 rate, approximately 38 female slaves, but apparently the Portuguese saw greater benefit in acquiring beads which they could exchange for slaves or gold elsewhere on the Guinea coast. This suggests that Bini exports were considered valuable trade commodities in the international markets in both Europe and Africa.[14]

European trade demands at the coast fostered an expansion of existing productive forces in Benin, and prompted an increase in bead production. The expansion of the bead industry, in which stone had to be found, shaped, polished and drilled, suggests that Benin was able to generate sufficient artisan production to meet overseas demands. Therefore, by 1526 the bead industry had developed considerably as Portuguese traders sought greater quantities of bead exports.

The Benin cloth industry met similar success, indeed it emerged as the economic mainstay of Benin's export production, and thereby contributed to an expansion of cotton production, weaving and dyeing skills. These multiplier effects in the cloth trade provided additional incentive for the expansion of the cloth industry, and Benin cotton demands encroached upon Akure and Owan cotton growers. As previously noted Ogbomo suggested that exports of cloth might have reached one million strips annually. This greatly increased production can be linked to the exodus of people from Benin to Owan. People moved from Benin to Owan, and possibly Ishan to exploit economic opportunities in cotton production and trade. Cotton thus became a major exchange commodity as Owan exported raw cotton and finished cloth to Benin. Towards the end of the sixteenth century Benin had emerged as the major West African supplier of European cloth needs. The expansion of Dutch shipping in particular contributed to the economic boom in the Bini cloth industry, and eventually established Benin as the major supplier to Portuguese, Dutch, French and English merchants. "Dutch ships began to appear in West African waters in the last decade of the sixteenth century ...they made more than 2,000 voyages in the years between 1593 and 1607, and later maintained an average of at least twenty voyages a year."[15]

In one year, at one coastal port, the Dutch factor, in competition with other European trader's accumulated 16,000 Benin cloths for export.[16] The expansion of the cloth industry to attain this level of production represented a major development in the Benin economy. In fact, cloth became the major export after c. 1563, and reflected the general enlargement of scale, productive capacity, and efficient regional intra-relationships between producers of raw materials, weavers, dyers, and the administration of commerce.

The development of the Bini cloth industry and export market represents another example where European trade demands were grafted on to an existing production and exchange system. Cloth exports provided an opportunity for European merchants to exchange Bini cloth along the Guinea coast, in markets where it was prized for its quality and fashion, and acquire slaves and gold. R. Kea noted in his study of the seventeenth century Gold Coast, for example, that Bini cloth could be exchanged quite easily for local gold,[17] and thus contributed to the further expansion of the Bini cloth industry.

The consolidation of political and economic domination by Oba Esigie, coupled with the expansion of European overseas commerce, and the ability of the Benin producers to develop export production, provided the incentive for the Oba to extend royal monopolies over specific export items. The strict control of European trade had encouraged the production of pepper, ivory and camwood which became exclusive preserves of the monarchy. A.F.C. Ryder has also suggested that "elephant hunters constituted a special class in Benin with an organization resembling that of other trades and skills devoted to the service of the Oba."[18] These special service and craft organizations were part of the supported segment of the population, provided for by the redistribution of accumulated surplus tribute. It is also possible, in the case of the ivory hunters, that the by-product of their main activity (meat) became the property of the hunters and, therefore, provided further incentive for their participation in commercial production of ivory for the Oba. More importantly, however, the development of royal monopolies provided the opportunity for the elite to avail themselves of imported luxury items, and develop their economic base at the expense of agrarian and hinterland producers. The distinctions between the capital enclave and urban elite, and hinterland producers, would appear to have been widening during this new age of commerce.

The introduction of European firearms under Oba Esigie also contributed to this widening gap. These new and potentially devasting weapons encouraged Oba Esigie to establish a special service ward in the capital charged with the care and maintenance of the Oba's arsenal.

> ...at Benin city there is a ward, Iwoki, dated to Esigie's reign, which is charged with the care of the Oba's guns and cannon. Some Iwoki members even claim European descent.... Further, when European iron became a critical commodity, this added to the importance of the European connection, signified by the 'shrine of the gods of iron' at which the Iwoki worship (which is called Ogun-Esigie).[19]

Under Oba Esigie the dominant mode of production in the empire - the means of production through which the majority of the population derived their income - was still organized through the gerontocracy of the village Otu system[20] However, as state monopolies and increasing revenues from commercial taxation provided more and more income, the primary mode of production, from which the rulers and elite derived their principal income and revenues, became trade.[21] With this increase in wealth and the concentration on commercial revenues, demands on subordinate populations of the society were not diminished. Rather, as trade increased appropriation of agrarian production in the village Otu system increased. Thus the rapid expansion of overseas trade, the necessity of expanded support for the central administrative, entrepreneurial sectors, and the royal monopolies of the Oba, imposed demands on the tribute-paying social sector, and relations between capital and hinterland became more coercive and exploitative.

The distinction between dominant and primary modes of production is significant because it served to separate further the capital from the hinterland economy, as did the development of European overseas trade, and the domination of hinterland trading routes, production centres, and distribution points. The relative isolation of the hinterland economy from the benefits of coastal commerce contributed to the underdevelopment of the hinterland regions. The only possible source of an expanded hinterland relationship to the commercial system evident in Benin was along the major trading arteries, and even this limited potential was restricted by Bini administrators in enclaves like Akure, Owo and Ekiti.[22] Royal administrators in Idah, Idoani, Warri and Ijebu established another component in the regional administrative infrastructure, but were no more likely to foster hinterland penetration of the regional and long distance exchange network, and thus by-pass their own opportunities to generate revenue, than either the appointed governors or the Oba. While this basic administrative structure provided efficient political and economic management, and provided for the mobilization of resources from up to "three hundred of miles inland."[23] it did not close the gap between the agricultural and trade sectors of the imperial economy.

The embargo on the export of male slaves imposed by Oba Esigie provides an example of the centralized control of regional and long distance trade.[24] Slave exports might have generated revenue for the population involved, but state policy closed this potential avenue for export of surplus labour and captives. Apparently the requirements of internal production, as perceived by the Oba, to meet commercial, non-commercial and ad hoc levies absorbed most available males in the production system. Esigie imposed the ban because relatively low benefits could be derived from the sale of slaves, whereas they could be profitably employed in the imperial economy. The embargo remained in effect until the early eighteenth century when a combination of economic factors forced the Eweka monarchy to rescind it.[25]

The utilization of slave labour, particularly in the non-commercial production process, served to depress the prices of food products and limit their commercial value, thus also further retarding the hinterland economy. Since non-commercial tribute could only be extracted efficiently from the core or suburban regions of the capital the supported segment of the differentiated population required low cost food, and employed slave labour to produce it. The non-producing population in the capital enclave grew steadily as various craft and service industries were established. Eventually the consuming population surpassed the capacity or willingness of the suburban population to supply support. Instead of developing food production as a commercial venture, as was the case in the seventeenth century Gold Coast,[26] state policy was designed to employ slave labour in non-commercial production, and use profits from trade to buy commercial goods Slave labour, therefore, prevented the commercialization of food produced in the hinterland regions, which in turn emphasized the distinction between capital or urban and rural economies.

The formal adoption of cowries as a specific currency form, controlled by Oba Esigie's palace,[27] enabled the state to establish stringent supervision of all standards of exchange and consolidated the dominance of the urban sector. As Marion Johnson has noted, cowries were in "no sense a 'primitive' money, but a sophisticated form of currency capable of adaptation to the particular needs of West African trade."[28] A typical Portuguese trading voyage to Benin in the early part of the sixteenth century introduced large numbers of manillas and cowries to the capital enclave economy. An account of 1526 reveals certain details about the exchange system and provides clear evidence of the commercialization, or monetization, of the Benin economy.

> Porters brought up [from Ughoton] 110 loads of manillas (each load contained 100 manillas) (or 11,000 manillas), 70 loads of cowries weighing altogether 20 quintals (2,000 pounds), and 10 loads of linen and red cloth. The head loads thus amounted to approximately 30 pounds (each) ... (this cargo) was expended on 170 female slaves... 80 of these slaves were bought with manillas ... cowries were used to pay for another 60 slaves ... the remaining 30 slaves were bought from the Oba in exchange for all the cloth in the cargo... the pilot bought yams to the value of 1,600 manillas, as against 828 in 1522 when there were

> only half the number of slaves [to feed] but the yams paid for with cowries cost 89,000 cowries compared with the 8,000 expended (in 1522) Another 55,000 had to be given for yams, wood and water.[29]

The substantial importation of currency during the early part of the sixteenth century set an exchange pattern that was to persist for the next two hundred years. The single voyage of 1526, for example, introduced 11,000 manillas and approximately 800,000 cowries,[30] and indicated that significant changes had occurred in the relative values of these currencies between 1522 and 1526. In 1522 one female slave had cost 50 manillas; by 1526 the price had risen to 57, a 14% increase. In the same period the exchange of manillas for yams had remained constant, but the differential on cowries for yams was remarkable. In 1522, 8,000 cowries purchased sufficient yams to feed 80 slaves, and rate that worked out to 100 cowries per yam/slave.[31] By 1526 it cost 89,000 cowries to provide subsistence for 170 female slaves, at a unit price of 523 cowries per yam/slave. This represents an apparent massive devaluation of the cowrie, and a corresponding increase in the number in circulation. Such an increase demanded a centralized control mechanism through which the state could organize circulation, maintain standards of value, and control distribution, and this was achieved through development of a strung-cowrie currency form controlled directly by the palace.

The increase in cowrie importation established a monetized economy, and fostered the development of region-wide currency as a medium of exchange. Cowries emerged in Nupe, for example, by the mid-sixteenth century,[32] and were adopted in Idah during the reign of Aji-Attah in c. 1507-1537.[33] In contrast Kano tradition indicates that cowries were not introduced as a currency form until the reign of Mohamman Sarefa in c. 1703- 1731.[34] The introduction of cowries through the coastal ports would not necessarily provide an immediate value attachment to this currency in hinterland or interior markets. Trading patterns in the middle belt or sudanic region could not automatically be expected to transform their own economic structures and abandon existing currency forms to integrate with the commercial system of the forest zone trading states.

The introduction of the cowrie system of currency in Benin, and in the Benin sphere of influence, controlled by the senior palace Otu, represented an important development in the economy of the imperial trading formation. The formal stringing of cowries established a new monetary standard which greatly improved state commercial controls. Previously cloth had probably been the medium of exchange by which business transactions were measured, and the introduction of an 'artificial' medium - an item without intrinsic value of its own - not only allowed for improved circulation within the commercial network, but also altered the economic basis of the cloth industry which had been so significant in the development of the empire. Cloth subsequently became valued as an export item, but lost its role as a measurement of exchange values. Belasco has summarized the significance of palace dominated cowries, and described it as a state instituted mechanism of commercial control and "institutionalized exploitation."

> Especially evident within this exploitative nexus was... care of the Oba's reserves of cowrie shells, beads, cloth and other trade goods... The Iwebo was in charge of stringing the royal coral beads bought by the Europeans. And it should be stressed that the Iwebo was the senior palace society; its leading chiefs were in charge of European trade, and the interpreters in that trade also belonged to the Iwebo ... Furthermore, all European traders were counted as Iwebo members... The close ties and shared interests of the Iwebo and Portuguese suggest the probability that at this time, the late fifteenth and early sixteenth centuries, there emerged a reinterpretation of cowries as a standard of exchange superimposed on, and concurrent with, the continued use of cowries as a petty barter, or nonmonetary, medium in the local marketplace. The Portuguese desire for the economic integration of the West African trade and the Benin state's need for political consolidation of a dynasty scarcely 200 years old found a common focus in monetizing the loose cowries in the form of a palace-controlled stringing system...formalization of strung cowries served as a state instituted mechanism (a) for trade good standardization and thereby a means of channelling production to state-defined ends, (b) for administering exchange rates and terms of trade, (c) for draining wealth out of the

> social and ritual cycle, (d) for enabling trade transactions of ever increasing volume and variety, and (e) by its circulation, for introduction of local, autonomous markets to translocal, state run trade channels.[35]

Paul Einzig, in his analysis of currency forms, suggests that the formal institutionalization of any currency could have a "role in the evolution of civilization."[36] In Benin the development of palace controlled cowrie currency meant that the Oba could establish a unified value system and exercise direct authority over rates and process of exchange. The Oba's role in the development of commerce and the expansion of state-run trade was restricted, by design, to the capital enclave, but the impact of monetization was felt in the rural areas of the empire. The demonetization of cloth, therefore, would also contribute to the centralization of currency control as all imported cowries ended up at the palace, while cloth could be produced by hinterland petty merchants, weavers and craftswomen. The reduction of cloth as a recognized medium of exchange therefore restricted access to the economy. The 'social theory of money' as expressed by Einzig, would have contributed to the development of the capital and the enclave economy and, to a much lesser extent, the expansion of hinterland production and monetization of the peripheral economy.

> ...a social theory of money, endeavouring to present money as a social institution which in primitive as well as modern communities provides the incentive to produce goods beyond the immediate requirements.in ... the final results primitive money as modern money had been the driving force making for better utilization of economic resources and producing capacity.[37]

In a situation where more than 18% of an imported cargo was expended on yams, lodgings, wood and water it is relatively easy to see the contribution to the monetization of the capital economy. This 'money' was expended in areas outside the normal bounds of palace control, and thus contributed to the circulation of currency in local and regional markets. Also, when 83% of an imported cargo consisted of currency forms the incentives to produce goods beyond the immediate requirements of the society seems clearly evident.[38] In Benin this would presumably have meant higher tribute demands imposed upon the subordinate segment of the population, and an increase in commercial production to meet trade demands. The disadvantage of reduced control over currency production and supply, by allowing Portuguese traders to become the main suppliers of currency, was apparently offset by the advantages gained in palace control of all money forms. As cowries developed as the standard of exchange palace control over strung-cowries enabled the state to augment its domination of the commercial sphere and develop commercial management to meet the demands of a new economic age.

The reign of Oba Esigie marked the completion of the prolonged process during which the regional economy was brought under the authority of the Oba. Egharevba referred to the era as the "golden age" of Benin.[39] The monarchy had emerged as the paramount authority in a highly coercive, exploitative, and efficient social, political and economic system. The empire had been organized to reflect the dominant concern of regional and long distance trade, and the development of the capital enclave. Elite wealth, based upon accumulated tribute, exploited slave labour, and revenues derived from commercial taxation, confirmed the position and status of the central political hierarchy.

The capital enclave was the centre of political authority, commercial management, and social control, but peripheral centres also performed significant functions in the administration of regional production, commerce and distribution. These peripheral centres were of two types, ruled either by royal administrators or by appointed governors. The former included Warri, Idoani, Ijebu, Lagos,[40] and Idah, while the latter included the Ishan chiefdoms, Ondo, Akure, Ekiti, Ikere, and Agbor. Imperial administration worked through a relatively large and complex bureaucracy and nobility, which was organized to foster the development of commerce and protect imperial trade. However, this golden age was not entirely a period of peaceful growth, cooperation, and unopposed expansion and consolidation. The rebellion of Udo early in Esigie's reign had been an expression of open hostility to the policies of the central administration, and represented the last attempt by that centre to seize a portion of the commercial wealth. The rebellion of Idah in 1515-1516[41] indicated that a shift in the balance of power within the empire had occurred, and that the organization of an imperial administration based, in part, on the loyalty of peripheral governments had not prevented the emergence of political and economic aspirations which opposed the policy of the imperial authorities. The preference of the central authority for the European overseas trade, a commercial system that they were in a better position to control and influence directly, allowed northern peripheral centres a certain measure of freedom to enjoy the fruits of north-south commercial transactions. While coastal trade had become paramount in Benin's commercial organization, the trans-Saharan trading system had entered the peak period of that commercial enterprise, and north-south commerce was still an important economic consideration in much of the Benue Basin.

The Idah rebellion threatened to disrupt the economic and political status quo in the empire, and could have led to a fundamental reorganization of it. The Bini dynasty in Idah, established by Aji-Attah, a son of Oba Ozolua, when he conquered the Okpoto monarchy, resembled the imperial government in most major characteristics. However, Aji-Attah had not appointed a kingmakers council in Idah,[42] as primogenitary succession defined the process of accession to the throne, and did not require nomination or confirmation by an independent agency. Furthermore, Aji-Attah had not legitimized Bini administration with the existing population on the eastern bank of the Niger, had not integrated the Bini conquerors with the Okpoto and Igbo, but had established integral power and authority in this peripheral enclave.

The multi-ethnic population on both sides of the River Niger above the confluence with the Anambra River contained two major segments - the Okpoto and the Igbo.[43] The population also included a number of smaller ethnic groups, including the proto-Aro,[44] Kede, Awka, and some Bini refugees. The political organization of this multi-ethnic mix in the confluence region, before its incorporation into the empire, fell to a number of small segmentary chiefdoms under Okpoto ritual authority. Idah represented the largest chiefdom at the centre of a cluster of Okpoto polities, but contained a relatively small population. Other ethnic groups in the Niger valley did not contribute much numerically to the overall population, but there was a functional integration of specialized economic services, which allowed proto-Aro and Kede riverine traders to interact with Igbo farmers and overland merchants, and Awka iron workers with Okpoto weavers and ritual specialists. It was this complex socio-economic structure which Aji-Attah came to rule, and his authority at Idah focused economic activities on the Benin trading network. Thus Okpoto, Igbo, proto-Aro and Bini settlers became part of the imperial formation, albeit under the peripheral authority of the colonial government of the Bini/Idah monarchy.

The conquest of Idah by Aji-Attah was accomplished through an alliance of the Bini invaders with an important, although numerically small, riverine community. The conquest of Idah was delayed while the Bini army endeavoured to find a way across the Niger barrier, and only the assistance of the riverine people made the invasion possible. Note how in the following tradition, informants refer to the riverine people and their totem, as if they were one and the same.

> When the Bini invaded Idah a long time ago they could not cross the Niger because they had no canoes. Aji-Attah offered prayers and consulted the Ifa priests who were with him to find an answer to his problems. And luckily his prayers were answered by the manatee. Out of respect and gratitude, and in memory of their assistance the manatee have been remembered in Idah. The manatee cannot be eaten by some, and their canoes are always welcome in the river markets.[45]

The manatee population referred to in this tradition had been operating along the Niger for some time. The common totemic symbol of this riverine community, which occupied the Niger from the delta to Raba, and the Benue as far as Ibi, is one of the few remaining indications of common origins for this extensive, although numerically small population.[46] Totems are a symbol of kinship and thus are relatively immune to change even over long periods of time. The fact that the Banu on the Benue, the Kede near Nupe, and the proto-Aro on the lower Niger below the confluence maintain the manatee totem suggests a closer ethnic or kinship affiliation in the past. As these riverine people integrated, and presumably inter-married with the larger populations on the river bank there was a slow process of ethnic differentiation, language shift in favour of the majority, and a disintegration of the unique cultural features of the riverine specialists. The Banu became Jukun, the Kede became Nupe, and the proto-Aro became Igbo-ized. To simplify understanding of the earlier demographic structure we have adopted the use of their totemic symbol to distinguish them from other groups in the region. The Manatee aligned with the Bini invaders and thereby materially contributed to the overthrow of the Okpoto monarchy in Idah. This direct and overt involvement may have been brought about by economic considerations, as the lack of Bini waterborne skills - i.e. canoe making, paddling, swimming, and navigation - provided an opportunity for the Manatee to increase their direct involvement in regional commerce. The riverine specialists were already involved in widespread commercial activity, some of it local in nature but some destined for the up-river markets. Any expansion of trade on the Niger under a Bini administration would have positive effects on their commerce, security and profits. The Manatee, therefore, aligned with the Bini invaders in the hope that they would benefit from increased commercial activity.[47] Only a generation later, the same Manatee people would ally with Tsoede, a son of Aji Attah, when he began his conquests north and south of the River Niger in the Nupe area.

This alliance between the Manatee and Bini proved overpowering for the Okpoto monarchy under Eggarah Eri. Eggarah Eri migrated inland away from the Niger, and eventually resettled south of the Benue Valley. Tradition recalls that the Okpoto monarch fled before a powerful Bini military force.

> Followers of Eggarah left Idah because Aji-Attah had more influence and could command the support of an important part of the population, and was more powerful. Aji-Attah was a great military-minded and determined conqueror like his father Ozolua of Benin, and he was determined to conquer Idah and establish his authority like his father had ordered. He possessed great regalia which was superior to anything owned by Eggarah Eri. This regalia and his military might forced the people to recognize his right to rule.[48]

The conquest of the Okpoto also appeared in a tradition collected by T.J. Hutchinson during a Niger expedition in 1854. This account has been repeated here not only because it confirms the Bini conquest of the Okpoto, but also because it reveals just how little some orally preserved records can change over long intervals.

> Eggarah was the name of the King who was regnant over the Appoto (Akpoto or Okpoto) people - the aborigines of the country - before their subjugation to the first Attah. The latter ... impelled perhaps by ambitions or urged by some imaginary insult, and strengthened by the accession of more of the natives of Adoh (Benin) he attacked the Appoto and drove them away ... and constituted himself the Attah or 'father' of Eggarah. From him twenty Attah's have descended.[49]

Eggarah Eri and his followers relocated at Nri and founded a relatively influential religious and political dynasty in northern Igboland. His own fairly impressive array of royal regalia, coupled with his connections to the Awka cult and iron manufacturing centre on the Udi plateau,[50] contributed to the success of Nri as a ritual, commercial and political centre. M.D.W. Jeffries has pointed out in his study of Nri that "all their traditions and culture point to Igala origins."[51] Elizabeth Isichei has also stated that when Eri came down the Anambra River he set out to unify the surrounding country, indicating that Eggarah originated in the Idah area.[52] The Bini conquest of Idah resulted not only in the foundation of a powerful Benin royalist administration in the former Okpoto ritual centre, but also in the creation of another significant ritual and political centre in the Anambra River Valley.

The Bini victory in Idah was not achieved through military superiority alone, and nor was the imposition of Bini authority an automatic and easy process. Without the co-operation of the riverine traders along the Niger the conquest of Idah might never have taken place. In addition, Aji-Attah utilized the impressive royal regalia of Benin as a symbol of royal legitimacy which made the monarch at least recognizable in the eyes of his own subjects. The royal mask called Ejube- `auilo (the eye which brings fear to all other eyes) became symbolic of Bini political and military domination.[53] This most impressive pectoral mask, perhaps the "most sensational of all" the items in the royal regalia of Idah,[54] was described by K.C. Murray as "the most sacred of the regalia of the Atah [Attah]... a very beautiful example of Benin work of a fairly early period."[55]

The description of the mask as the "eye which brings fear to all other eyes" is perhaps an accurate account of how the Okpoto population viewed the Bini invaders. Clearly the Bini dynasty, army and settler population imposed a new and unwelcome political, economic and social order upon the Idah area. This Bini royal outpost, administered the Niger-Benue waterways for the imperial powers in Benin, and initiated a new era in the organization of the middle belt and confluence region. The domination or riverine commerce was completed with the establishment of outposts at Abinsi, Itobe and Agodo on the Benue and, of course, the related and tributary Nupe kingdom on the Niger. Thus the Bini invaders not only occupied Okpoto territory but cooperated with the Manatee to establish a commercial presence on the main regional riverine trade routes, the Benue, Niger and Anambra.

To commemorate the alliance with the Manatee which had been so instrumental in the conquest of Idah, Aji-Attah introduced a royal headdress called Onunu Ehre (tail of the manatee) to the Bini royal regalia. This headdress has also subsequently become an important part of the symbolic representation of the relationship between Benin and Idah, while serving to identify the association of the Bini and the riverine community. Significantly, ivory and cowries appear in Onunu Ehre, the former became one of the important exports from Benin and a monopoly of the Oba in the Atlantic overseas trade. Some of the Benin ivory exports probably came from Idah. Cowries were a royal monopoly in Benin and were slowly being distributed throughout the imperial outposts as currency. Red cloth, also part of the headdress, was another royal prerogative in Benin and had become symbolic of members of the ruling aristocracy.[56] Thus the symbolism in the Onunu Ehre clearly connects Idah with Benin, with their with their Manatee totem allies, and with the major commercial articles of the age, ivory, cloth and beads.

> ...it is formed in two parts, first a chaplet made of small red feathers of the loloki bird ... which is worn low down on the forehead, and next - which covers it - a red cap which is covered with cowries and has a flap or tail (hence the name) at the back which hangs down on the neck. On the front of the cap is a small ivory disk which is surrounded by rows of amber beads to suggest the moon's rays.[57]

In the first few years of Bini rule at Idah Aji-Attah was concerned primarily with the consolidation of imperial political and economic controls along the Niger. This river trading network was the major natural transportation system in the entire region, and represented a significant economic link between north and south, and east and west. Aji-Attah was, in some respects, a colonial administrator serving the needs of the empire from his subordinate position on the periphery of the imperial formation. He was also an ambitious governor and aspired to extend his authority through further conquests in the confluence region and middle belt. Indeed the foundation of the new centralized polity at Idah invited the return to previous practices of the imperial state: Aji-Attah had ambitions to build the kind of conquest state at the periphery of the empire that his father, Oba Ozolua, had constructed in Benin. He pursued his territorial ambitions, presumably with the official sanction of the Oba, by marching northward against the Niger valley states beyond the confluence.

During an expedition against Nku (Nupe) - clearly an impossible undertaking without the support of the Manatee - Aji-Attah is said to have fathered a child, Tsoede, by the daughter of the Nku chief. Before his return to Idah he left a special ring and charm for this offspring. Nupe traditions indicate that some years later, after the death of the vassal chief of Nku, the male child was sent to Idah as part of the annual tribute payments. The successor to the Nku throne probably objected to his inheritance of vassal status, and utilized Tsoede as a political pawn to express his opposition to Idah's imperial authority.

> At the time the Nupe people were tributary to the Attah (king) of Gara, at Eda (Idah) far down the Niger. The tribute was paid in slaves, and every family head had annually to contribute one male member of his house. These slaves, as tradition has it, were always sisters sons... The Atta Gara ... fell in love and lived with her (a daughter of the old chief of Nku) for some time... He left her a charm and a ring to give to their child when it was born. This child was Tsoede. Then the old chief of Nku died, his son became chief and... sent him (Tsoede) as his sister's son, as a slave to Eda. The Atta Gara recognized his son...by the charm and ring.and kept him near his person, treating him almost like his legitimate sons.[58]

Although this Nupe tradition may appear fanciful - according to Idah tradition - Aji-Attah eventually dispatched "an illegitimate son by a Nku woman to avenge himself on the Nku chief."[59] Tsoede was equipped with significant Bini-style royal regalia, an adequate military force, his father's support and blessing, and ordered to return to Nku and kill his uncle who had sent him into slavery.

Tsoede conquered Nku and established a powerful state on the Niger which owed allegiance and paid tribute to Idah. Tsoede eventually attacked and defeated Oyo, and started a period in Oyo history that Robert Smith referred to as "the Alafin [King of Oyo] in exile."[60] The Nupe hero-founder also spread his influence down the banks of the Niger towards Idah, conquering Yagba, Kakanda, Ebe, Kambiri and Kanuku, and other smaller communities. As the power and influence of Nupe grew, partially through the military success of the Tsoede dynasty, and partly because of its location as a prominent middle belt trading formation linking the commerce of Songhay to that of Idah and Benin, the connection with Idah weakened. However, Nupe remained a tribute-paying associate of Idah until well into the nineteenth century when the link was broken by a Fulani dynasty which replaced the descendants of Tsoede.[61]

As Aji-Attah extended his political power and consolidated his authority along the Niger he was also creating a potent power-base for the realization of his ultimate ambition, to become the Oba of Benin. He had ensured by conquest and subordination a regional power base and established himself as the paramount in the confluence region - and far up the Niger and Benue river systems - a position which gave him the capability to question his subordinate status within the Benin Empire. However, as long as Idah remained a vassal administrative centre within the imperial formation the net results of his military exploits and commercial management skills would accrue to the Oba and not the colonial administrator. From his base at Idah, Aji-Attah maintained his subordinate status by providing regular tribute payments to the Oba, but he also nurtured his ambitions for supreme political authority.

The foundation of a powerful peripheral enclave within the empire, supported by a vast tribute network which provided independent revenues for the colonial government, established an unusual balance of power in the imperial structure. It was an unequal relationship that favoured the Idah administration, and fostered Aji-Attah's hankering for political and economic autonomy. His aspirations, based in part on the legitimate claim to the Benin throne, and in part upon his success as a colonial governor, were facilitated by the economic status gained from the management of the lucrative riverine trade, and access to overland routes to the north and south. Thus the importance of riverine commerce and the political aspirations of the Idah monarch ultimately led to a struggle for paramount authority in the empire. The invasion of Benin in 1515-1516 was not, therefore, intended to break-up the empire, but was initiated with the idea of replacing Oba Esigie as ruler of the imperial formation. If Aji- Attah could not "rule Benin as the Oba, then he would at least rule Idah as if he were."[62]

Aji-Attah continued to send his regular tribute, but also recruited mercenaries and plotted the removal of Oba Esigie.[63] He was apparently convinced that he would have popular support in Benin, and fully expected a fairly general uprising against the exploitation of the Oba. Aji-Attah apparently expected, at the very least, that the Oliha, who had approached him in support of his candidacy for the Bini throne would join the rebellion. When Aji-Attah finally marched on Benin he "planned to go in the grandest style befitting an Oba",[64] and was apparently confident of both support and ultimate success.

Unfortunately it is difficult to assess precisely what role the Oliha and Uzama Nihinron played in the rebellion by Idah. It would seem that they did not rush to Aji-Attah's cause, and might have been manipulating the Idah monarch to further their own political agenda. The following Benin tradition provides the imperial explanation for the outbreak of the Benin-Idah war in 1515-1516, and should not be considered a balanced account. It is also presented in a clever allegorical framework which dresses up the political context and disguises other factors. It does reveal, however, the complicated nature of internal politics in the imperial capital and the possible machinations of the competing factions in the royal court.

> This war was caused by the then Oliha who had a beautiful wife named Imaguero. The Oliha one day said to the Oba and other people that his wife was the most beautiful and faithful woman in the whole world.(the Oba set out to test Imaguero and prove the Oliha wrong) At length the Oba summoned a meeting, and asked the Oliha to again repeat what he had said about his wife. Oliha again said without the slightest suspicion that his wife Imaguero was the most faithful woman in the whole kingdom. The porter [who had tempted Imagureo] was presented... and told to confess what had transpired... He related how he had been able

to win her with only a few beads. Imaguero was then called and she confessed ... This annoyed the Oliha so much that he instantly ordered her strangled. The Oliha did not stop there; in order to bring disaster on the Oba for the trick he had played, he sent his servant named Aigbonuleghe to tell the Attah of Idah that the Oba of Benin was preparing to invade his country, and that he should prepare to defend himself... Aigbonuleghe also said that the Oliha would assist the Idah troops as far as possible. The Attah mobilized his troops without delay and marched against the Binis. [65]

Most historians have interpreted the Benin-Idah war as an economic conflict. A.F.C. Ryder related the confrontation to possible trouble on the middle Niger, and therefore implies a stronger economic motive in a battle for domination of the major north-south commercial artery in the entire region. He also saw the outcome as a major victory for Benin.

Esigie is remembered for his defeat of the invading forces of Idah - a victory of great significance for Idah was a powerful state with a system of kingship which in many ways resembled that of Benin. Furthermore, since both Benin and Idah acknowledge relationships between their ruling dynasties it is possible that the war had a deeper significance than is common in Benin traditions. It may, for example, have arisen from a general disturbance of the pattern of power along the middle Niger. [66]

Thurstan Shaw referred to the relationship between war and commercial opportunities, maintaining that the "conflict with Idah [occurred] for control of the Niger waterway."[67] For J.U. Egharevba this war represented a rebellion against Bini authority, and an attempt to overthrow an unpopular regime.

At first, the Binis refused to take part in the fight, because the then Oba, Esigie, was very selfish. But when news of the marching of the Idah troops was echoing in the City of Benin daily, an aged man from the Avbiogbe the Commissioners of Land took a belt, and began to ring the same around the city, in the streets, squares and market places, an in the gates of the higher ranked titled chiefs saying...Edo, Udo, Usela and Uzebu you must rise to defend your father's land and not listen to the saying of the selfish party [Esigie]. With these expressions. the Binis rallied together. Each man began by saying, "Truly this is my father's land and it does not belong to the Oba alone; then I must do my utmost to defend my father's land." [68]

Aji-Attah went to war against his brother, the Oba of Benin, for a number of reasons. He was certainly jealous of Esigie's paramount authority in the empire, and thus sought to replace him as the Oba. He was also anxious to develop autonomous political and economic powers in Idah should he fail in his attempted coup.[69] The commercial prominence of Idah - Aji Attah had, after all, almost doubled the size of the Benin Empire - thus provided an economic incentive to the military option. These two factors combined to promote the rebellion, and the Idah rebels virtually breached the gates of Benin. They were repulsed by the defensive city walls, the rallying cry of the Avbiogbe, and the efforts of Oba Esigie to marshall his imperial forces. "Like the son of Oba Ozolua he was, he led his armies personally and chased the Idah warriors" back across the Niger.[70] Aji-Attah, therefore failed in his bid to become the Oba, but did achieve the autonomy of Idah.

The outcome of the war was paradoxical; a military victory for Benin and a political and economic victory for Idah. Exploitation and commercial development of the Niger would hereafter proceed under the direct control of the independent Bini monarchy at Idah. The vassal tributary link to the Benin empire had been severed, and Aji-Attah and his successors became the dominant merchant princes in an expanding complex of regional and long distance trade. The Bini-Idah elite, concerned with movements on the Niger, and trade along overland routes, established a highly centralized administration devoted to the control of local, regional and long distance trade. The transformation of Idah from the segmentary political structures of the Okpoto to the highly organized tributary structure of the second Idah dynasty had started with the invasion of Idah and was fundamentally complete before the death of Aji-Attah. Although Idah lost the war with Benin, its demonstrated desire for independence, and the inability of Oba Esigie to reimpose central control, resulted in the foundation of a new economic and political power in the confluence region.

The reign of Oba Esigie and Aji-Attah saw a transformation of political authority and commercial patterns in the Benin

Empire. Esigie consolidated the monarchy, removed the opposition of Udo, and directed the expansion of European overseas trade as it grew to become the prominent commercial activity in the capital enclave. Despite this political and economic consolidation the peripheral royal administrative centre at Idah gained autonomy. The Benin-Idah war of 1515-1516 substantially altered political geography, with Idah at the centre of an expansive middle belt imperial trading formation which dominated the territory along the Niger from Borgu to Onitsha. The northern boundaries of the Benin empire were thus redefined to exclude the Idah sphere in the middle belt, while Benin was limited to the forest zone. In economic terms Idah dominated the Niger commercial traffic, while the Eweka regime in Benin retained control over interior overland routes into Nupe and the middle belt. Although the imperial formation was reduced in size and scope by the loss of an important peripheral enclave on the north-east frontier, Benin was more than compensated by the seizure of Lagos and Mahin in c. 1536-1563.[71] This subsequent expansion along the coastal belt suggests that the economic priorities of imperial Benin were redirected toward the south and European coastal trading contacts. However, the north-south routes connecting Benin with the trans-Saharan commercial network were not completely ignored, and commercial relations with Oyo, Nupe and Idah were maintained. Nevertheless, Idah not Benin became the major beneficiary of the northern and Songhay commercial link. Idah faced north and west, Benin looked south.

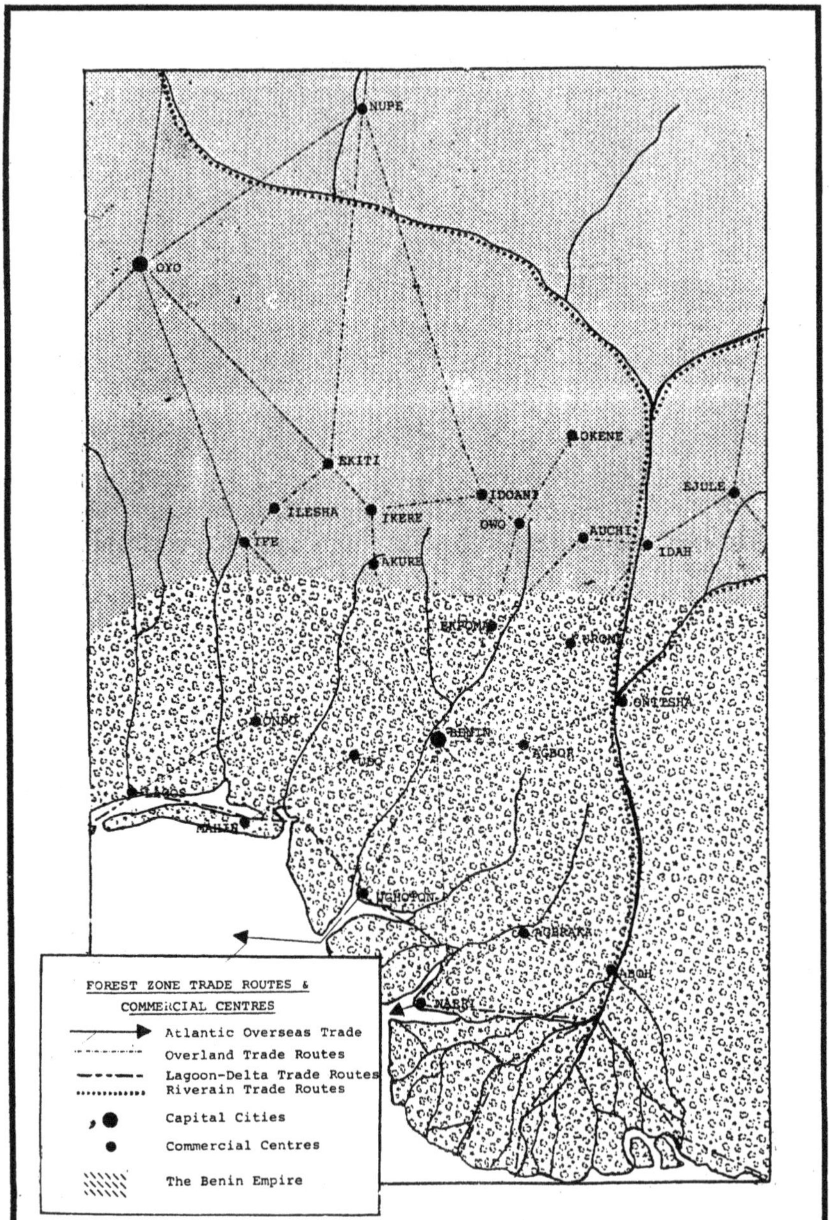

Map Eight: Forest Zone Trade Routes and Commercial Centres

References

1. Igala Historical Text (hereafter cited as I.H.T.) No. 117, Igala Mela Clan Heads, group interview, July 22, 1977.
2. Egharevba, *A Short History of Benin*, p. 27, and Bradbury, *Benin Studies*, p. 35.
3. *Ibid.* It is interesting to note that the rebels who fled from Udo were called the Emwa n'Udo. According to N.W. Thomas this could be translated as "suiting or fitting peace", *Anthropological Report on the Ibo-Speaking Peoples of Nigeria*, (Part II, London 1913). Also, the law established by Oba Esigie prohibiting princely succession in Udo suggests a royal link to aruanran. There is, however, no evidence to either confirm or deny this implication.
4. Ryder, *Benin and the Europeans, 1485-1897*, and E. Sanceau, *The Reign of the Fortunate King, 1495- 1521*, (New York, 1969), p. 72.
5. Egharevba, *A Short History of Benin*, p. 27.
6. *Ibid.*, p. 26.
7. I. Wallerstein, "Three Stages of African Involvement in the World Economy", in The Political Economy of Contemporary Africa, (edited by P.C.W. Gutkind and I. Wallerstein, Beverly Hills, 1976).
8. Ryder, *Benin and the Europeans*, p. 38.
9. India provided black pepper, and Benin alligator or red pepper was possibly only a temporary substitute to cover the shortfalls in the Venice market.
10. Fage, "Some Remarks on Beads and Trade", pp. 343-344.
11. Ryder, *Benin and the Europeans*, p. 37.
12. Milan Kalous, "Akorite", *Journal of African History*, (2, 1979), pp. 203-217 suggests that 'akori beads' were "made of silicate glass slag from local iron smelting."
13. Ryder, *Benin and the Europeans*, p. 63.
14. Fage, "Some Remarks on Beads and Trade", pp. 343- 344.
15. A.F.C. Ryder, "Portuguese and Dutch in West Africa Before 1800", in *A Thousand Years of West AFrican History*, (edited by J.F.A. Ajayi, I. Espie, Ibadan, 1965), p. 227.
16. A.F.C. Ryder, "Dutch Trade on the Nigerian Coast During the Seventeenth Century", *Journal of the Historical Society of Nigeria*, (3, 2, 1965), p. 203. Ryder also points out that the English were at the same time buying as many.
17. R. Kea, *Settlement, Trade and Polities in the Seventeenth Century Gold Coast*, (Baltimore, 1982), pp. 2-25.
18. Ryder, *Benin and the Europeans*, p. 53.
19. Belasco, *The Entrepreneur*, p. 83. See also J.U. Egharevba, *Concise Lives of the Famous Iyase of Benin*, (Benin, 1956), p. 13, where it states that Iyase Odia "was the first Iyase to use guns in warfare".
20. Webster, "A Typology", p. 2.
21. *Ibid.*
22. Akintoye, "The North-eastern Yoruba Districts", pp. 548-550.
23. Ryder, *Benin and the Europeans*, p. 94, and Belasco, *The Entrepreneur*, p. 62.
24. Ryder, *Benin and the Europeans*, p. 45. "The restrictions on the export of male slaves developed within a few years into a total embargo.striking evidence of Benin's general indifference to the demands and opportunities of the European slave trade."

25. The removal of the ban signified economic problems in the imperial formation, as legitimate commerce was undermined by European competing products, particularly Dutch cloth, and the expansion of demands for slaves over other exports. The removal of the embargo against the export of slaves in c. 1725 did not, however, solve the mounting problems in Benin's commercial development. Europeans had been trading in slaves from other West African ports and adequate collaborators elsewhere apparently provided sufficient exports to satisfy European demands. Ryder, *Benin and the Europeans*, pp. 196-238.
26. Kea, *Settlement, Trade and Polities*, p. 25.
27. Belasco, *The Entrepreneur*, pp. 81-82.
28. Marion Johnson, "The Cowrie Currency in West Africa", *Journal of African History*, (XI, 1, 1970), p. 17.
29. Ryder, *Benin and the Europeans*, p. 63.
30. According to Johnson, "Cowrie Currency", cowries can be calculated from anywhere between 166 and 400 per pound, but 400 per pound provides a reasonable basis for the calculations for 1526.
31. The concept of 'yam/slave' represents the number of cowries that it costs sufficient to buy yams to feed one slave.
32 Johnson, "Cowrie Currency", (part I), p. 27, and M. Hiskett, "Materials Relating to the Cowry Currency of the Western Sudan", *Bulletin of the School of Oriental and African Studies*, (XXIX, Part 2, 1966), p. 355.
33. The dating framework for Idah was discussed extensively in R.A. Sargent, "The Methodology of Chronology: The Igala Core Dating Progression," *History in Africa*, Vol 11, 1984.
34. Burdon, *Northern Nigeria*, p. 41.
35. Belasco, *The Entrepreneur*, pp. 81-82.
36. Paul Einzig, *Primitive Money*, (Oxford, 1946), 125.
37. *Ibid.*, p. 139.
38. Ryder, *Benin and the Europeans*, p. 63 provides the details on the 1526 Portuguese trading voyage. The remaining 17% of this cargo consisted of linen and red cloth. Red cloth was, in fact, one of the Oba's monopolies and became symbolic of elevated status in the Benin social and political hierarchy.
39. Egharevba, *A Short History of Benin*, p. 29.
40. Lagos was added as a royalist outpost by Oba Orhugbua in c. 1536-1563. See Egharevba, *A Short History of Benin*, p. 29, Sargent, "A Regional Chronology", and R.C.C. Law, "A Dynastic Chronology of Lagos", *Lagos Notes and Records*, (II, 1, 1968).
41. The fixed date of the Benin-Idah war was provided by a letter from a Portuguese missionary in the Benin court reporting back to King Dom Manual (the fortunate King) in Lisbon. This letter from Duarte Pires was dated in 1516 after he returned from the war. Sanceau, *The Reign of the Fortunate King*, p. 72, Egharevba, *A Short History of Benin*, p. 28 provides a translation of this letter dated 20 October, 1516.
42. I.H.T., No. 122, Igala Mela group interview, July 30, 1977. The Igala Mela clans are descendants of the Okpoto.
43. I.H.T. No. 129, Okaku group interview, August 5, 1977.
44. The term proto-Aro has been employed here because according to the most recent evidence a distinct population centred on the Aro Chukwu shrine and Aro

state cannot be identified prior to c. 1690-1720. Refer to the excellent reconstruction and analysis of Aro history by A.O. Nwauwa, 'The Aro Chiefdom: Chronolgy and State Formation, c. 1690-1720', Dalhousie University MA., 1989.

45. I.H.T. No. 36, group interview in Ayagba, February 18, 1977.
46. For more on the theory of totemism see R.A. Sargent and J.B. Webster, Practical Oral Methods: a *Practical Guide to Historic Data Collection in Africa*, Dalhousie African Studies Series, forthcoming.
47. The Aro have only recently been the subject for a detailed historical reconstruction. A.O Nwauwa, 'The Aro' has examined a variety of evidence, including genealogies in order to date the founding of Aro Chukwu. On the other hand, certain features of Aro History including the political power of the state and its commercial activities in the nineteenth century have been relatively well documented. Attention to their past has seriously affected the ability of other historians to place them in a proper regional perspective. Hopefully this situation has been be rectified. K.O. Dike and F.I.Ekejuiba, "The Aro State: A Case Study of State Formation in Southeastern Nigeria", *Journal of African Studies*, (Vol. 5, No. 3, 1978). See also A.E. Afigbo, "Trade and Trade Routes in Nineteenth Century Nsukka", *Journal of the Historical Society of Nigeria*, (VII, 3, 1973); D. Northrup, *Trade Without Rulers*, (London, 1980); D. Northrup, "The Growth of Trade Among the Igbo Before 1800", *Journal of African History*, (2, 1973); R.F. Stevenson, *Population and Political Systems in Tropical Africa*, (New York, 1968), pp. 188-225; S. Ottenberg, "Ibo Oracles and Intergroup Relations", *Southwestern Journal of Anthropology*, (14, 1958), pp. 205-217.
48. I.H.T. No. 117, Igala Mela clan heads, group interview, July 22, 1977.
49. T.J. Hutchinson, *Narrative of the Niger, Tshadda and Benue Explorations*, (London, 1855), pp. 54-55.
50. Afigbo, "Trade and Trade Routes", p. 79. Afigbo states that "Aro and Nri ritual specialists and diviners were said to have played a great part in the distribution of these metals."
51. M.D.W. Jeffries, "The Divine Umundri Kings", *Africa*, (Vol. 9, 1935), see also M.D.W. Jeffries, "The Umundri Traditions of Origin", *African Studies*, (III, 3, 1956), and 'The Divine Umundri Kings of Iboland', (University of London Ph.D., 1934).
52. E. Isichei, *The Ibo People and the Europeans*, (London, 1973), p. 30, see also M.A. Omwuejeogwu, 'The Political Organization of Nri, Southeastern Nigeria', (University of London, M.Phil., 1974), and *An Igbo Civilization: Nri Kingdom and Hegemony*, (London, 1981).
53. I.H.T. No. 7, interview in Idah, January 9, 1977 and I.H.T. No. 15, interview in Ejule, January 16, 1977.
54. M. Clifford, "A Nigerian Chiefdom", *Journal of the Royal Anthropological Institute*, (LXVI, 1936), p. 421.
55. K.C. Murray, "Idah Masks", *Nigerian Field*, (No. 86, 1948), pp. 85-92. See also W.B. Fagg, "The Seligma Mask From Benin", *Man*, (No. 144, 1957).
56. Ryder, Benin and the Europeans, p. 63. See also J. Voight, "Notes on the Portuguese Cloth Trade in West Africa, 1480-1540", *International Journal of African Historical Studies*, (VII, 4, 1975), p. 648.
57. Clifford, "A Nigerian Chiefdom", p. 421.

58. S.F. Nadel, *A Black Byzantium*, (London, 1942), p. 73. Also repeated in a very similar form in I.H.T. No. 204, group interview in Abata, October 2, 1977. The Nupe tradition has been attacked by M. Mason, "The Tsoede Myth and the Nupe Kinglist: More Political Propaganda", *History in Africa*, (Vol. 2, 1975), but his arguments are flawed and unconvincing. He used, for example, a kinglist recorded by Scortino, but has ignored at least two monarchs named in this regnal list.
59. I.H.T. No. 230, interview in Adoru, January 8, 1977.
60. R. Smith, "The Alafin in Exile: A Study of the Igboho Period in Oyo History", *Journal of African History*, (VI, I, 1965). See also Nadel, *A Black Byzantium*, p. 74 where he states that "Tsoede carried out big and victorious wars against many tribes and kingdoms, conquering in the south the countries of Yagba and Bunu (two sections of the Yoruba), Kakanda, as far as Akoko, and in the north the countries of Ebe, Kamberi and Kamuku."
61. J. Abuka, 'The Decline of the Igala Kingdom, 1832- 1960', (University of Jos Graduating Essay, July 1982).
62. I.H.T. No. 203, group interview in Idah, October 2, 1977.
63. I.H.T. No. 232, interview in Anaga, January 10, 1978, and I.H.T. No. 233, group interview, Idah, January 11, 1978.
64. I.H.T. No. 106, interview, Otakpa, July 20, 1977.
65. Egharevba, *A Short History of Benin*, pp. 27-28, and Bradbury, *Benin Studies*, p. 36.
66. Ryder, *Benin and the Europeans*, pp. 13-14.
67. T. Shaw, *Nigeria*, (Ibadan, 1973), p. 172.
68. Egharevba, *The Murder of Imaguero*, pp. 23-24.
69. I.H.T. No. 117.
70. Okojie, *Ishan*, p. 325, and Bradbury, *Benin Studies*, p. 36.
71. Egharevba, *A Short History of Benin*, pp. 29-30.

Chapter 6

Commercial Cooperation And Political Hegemony In The Middle Belt, c. 1507-1687

The hard-won autonomy of the Bini dynasty at Idah established a powerful, independent polity near the confluence of the Niger and Benue rivers, which contributed to, and became the hub of the development of middle belt political and economic relations within the Benue Basin regional system. Through the one hundred and eighty years of its domination in Idah the Bini monarchy pursued an economic policy designed to extend control over both hinterland and riverine commerce. Other policies were implemented to consolidate middle belt political hegemony and extend Idah's authority beyond the restricted confines of the riverine enclave on the Niger. The consolidation and expansion of Idah power was predicated upon three sets of regional relationship First, the monarchy operated through an informal commercial alliance on the Niger to extend riverine trade in an organized framework of economic exchange. Second, it embarked on a process of imperial expansion through the conquest of neighbouring communities and the subordination of those populations. Third, the new monarchy sought to control overland long distance and regional trade, including routes that tapped the commercial exchange of the coast and sudanic regions. These developments substantially altered the middle belt, and affected Idah's relationship with both forest zone and sudanic region states as the Idah dynasty emerged as politically powerful and economically dominant Benue Basin trading formation.

In the sixteenth century a number of riverine states organized commercial exchange to facilitate the orderly flow of goods and services in the regional trading system. The Niger commercial alliance linked Songhay, Borgu, Nupe, Idah, Onitsha, Aboh and

Warri in a complimentary and cooperative pattern of transportation and trade along the north-south axis. Idah eventually emerged as the major trading partner in this riverine commercial system, and extended political authority, economic controls and diplomatic preeminence to the other riverine trading communities. Relations with the riverine states were based, in part, upon previous connections in the Benin imperial government, but were also deliberately fostered by the Bini dynasty at Idah in order to control regional commercial exchange.

Trade on the Niger was organized to reflect the paramount position of Idah, and merchants and commercial agents representing the Bini dynasty could move relatively freely from Songhay to Aboh along the Niger and from Idah to Abinsi along the Benue. Although Idah-based canoes dominated these rivers, they were in some respects dependent upon the good will of the various riverine polities through which the trade passed. Trade canoes moving south of Idah were under the protection of the monarchy, but traversed territory controlled more directly by Onitsha and Aboh.[1] The influence of the state thus transcended national boundaries in the interest of commercial exchange. On the other hand, but in the spirit of cooperative trade Aboh merchants were allowed up river as far as Idah where they had to transfer their north-bound cargoes to Idah-based canoes. They in turn moved up the Benue and up the Niger to Rabba where they met the canoes and exchanged products coming from Songhay. In most cases these canoes were operated by Manatee traders who benefitted from their relations with the political leadership primarily at Idah, and secondarily at Aboh, Abinsi and Rabba.

The ecologically specialized products of the various sub-regions of the Benue Basin moved up and down the River Niger in an organized pattern of profitable commercial exchange. Delta salt and fish were carried to Aboh by Warri merchants. The markets of Aboh became the meeting point for Warri, Aboh and Idah traders, and goods exchanged in this central place at the apex of the delta were transported north by both Aboh and Idah merchants. At Idah goods were exchanged and the delta products continued northward in Idah canoes, the Aboh merchants returning down river with northern sudanic products toward the forest zone and delta markets.[2] This organization of commerce, centred on the principal economic depots of Aboh and Idah, reflected the relative importance of these two trading enclaves.

This economic enterprise on the Niger was fostered by the connections between the various states. Commercial transportation links were facilitated by a common relationship with the riverine population in all the major states. In fact, three of the trading states on the Niger - Aboh, Onitsha, and Idah - had been founded with the help of the Manatee population, and this common link contributed to the organization of the informal trading alliance. Moreover, profit contributed to the regional cooperation, and as goods moved further from their source of production or point of entry into the regional economy they gained considerable value. Iron, for example, entering at the coast in the form of iron bars, gained value as it was crafted by local artisans into viable commercial products and moved progressively further inland. Horses moving southward increased dramatically in exchange value and thus created profit for the long distance trader.

Relations within the Niger alliance were also forged through political contact, conquest, and most significantly, the common origins of the ruling groups in the allied states.[3] Aji-Attah of Idah and Iginua of Warri, for example, were cousins, and had emigrated from Benin as political leaders in the Benin diaspora of the early sixteenth century. Aji-Attah's son was the ruler of Nupe and thus extended Idah's influence northwest of the confluence. The close genealogical connections between Warri, Idah and Nupe established a linguistic and cultural association in which commercial relations could develop between states that were both related and similar. Connections between Idah, Aboh and Onitsha were also based upon more than simple economic self-interest. They were strengthened by the ties to the Manatee population on the Niger, a common heritage in the Benin Empire, and subsequently cemented by inter-marriage of the three royal houses. The informal alliance was thus based upon very formal links, and established a strong basis for the organization, management and development of regional commerce.

The informal Niger alliance originated in the desire for profit, and was forged by the genealogical association between the Idah and Warri monarchies. The roots of both Iginua and Aji-Attah lay in the Yoruba-speaking dynasty of Benin, and they were descendants of former Bini monarchs. These similar origins can be seen in the Yoruba language classification, which includes Yoruba, Igala and Itsekiri in a single sub-group of the Kwa language family in the Niger Kordofan segment of Nigerian languages.[4] The Eweka dynasty of Benin remained Yoruba-speaking until after the sixteenth century diaspora, and did not adopt the Edo language until after Iginua and Aji-Attah had established Warri and Idah respectively. Although one linguist has suggested that Itsekiri and Igala are divided by as much as nineteen centuries, the historical evidence seems to refute that argument.[5] The Igala and Itsekiri languages were both altered from the sixteenth century onward by interactions with various other, distinct language groups.[6] However, the common basis of language contributed to the development of social, political and economic connections, and allowed Niger merchants to operate within a single cultural system.

The links between the confluence and the delta can be further emphasized by examining the religious institutions common to both cultures. Religion, as an organizational mechanism in the commercial system, provided a positive connection between Idah and Warri. The Yoruba-speaking dynasty in Benin had adopted Ifa as the state ritual system prior to the emigration of Aji-Attah and Iginua in c. 1509-1536, and Ifa was introduced into the delta and confluence regions during the Benin diaspora.[7] Ifa was also prevalent in Nupe, indeed some seem to have been created there. Genealogy, language and culture therefore contributed to the Niger commercial alliance and economic cooperation between Warri, Idah and Nupe.

The linguistic, cultural and genealogical relationships between Idah and the ruling houses in Onitsha and Aboh are less obvious. Both Onitsha and Aboh emerged from the Benin empire in c. 1563-1590, at a time when Benin was at the peak of its power. As the Yoruba-speaking dynasty in the capital forcibly extended its influence, Igbo aspirations were suppressed. By c. 1617- 1644, in fact, Igbo authority in Agbor had been completely subordinated by the Eweka dynasty.[8] The emigration of Igbo, beginning in c. 1536-1563, and continuing after the subjugation of Agbor, was a reaction against this extension of Eweka power. Esumai Ukwa led a substantial Igbo-speaking group away from Benin's imperialism and founded new dynasties in Onitsha and Aboh. As an expression of resistance to, and disassociation from, increasing imperial authority the foundation of Onitsha and Aboh represented another phase in the Benin diaspora. This Igbo phase contained groups which had not adopted the Ifa ritual system, and were not genealogically related to the Benin royal family. Nevertheless their re-settlement along the Niger brought them firmly into the riverine commercial alliance through diplomatic, political and economic links with both Idah and Warri.

The emigration to Aboh has been described as an exodus of Aro leaving Benin.[9] More recent evidence suggests, however, that to call this group Aro may have been a misnomer. They may have been proto-Aro, a group related to developments within the Aro-sphere at a later date but not necessarily distinctly Aro in c. 1563-1590. A.O. Nwauwa suggests, in fact, that the origins of the Aro chiefdom can be dated to c. 1690-1720.[10] These religious specialists and commercial agents, defined as proto-Aro, had their economic focus on the extensive eastern overland trade system which had been part of Benin's commercial sphere. The development of imperial authority by the Eweka monarchy, and the consolidation of Ifa in the hands of the Yoruba-speaking dynasty, effectively undermined proto-Aro economic and religious power. The process of disenfranchisement contributed to the decision to disassociate and thus prompted the move to Aboh along the Niger.

Onitsha was also founded in an emigration from Benin in c. 1563-1590,[11] and was based upon the growing links between the Yoruba-speaking monarchy and the Edo population in the empire. The Igbo, who had been centred in Udo and Agbor found their status and position increasingly untenable, and opted for emigration and total disassociation from Benin's authority. This decision was not necessarily welcomed by the Eweka monarchy, and the Igbo dissidents were forced to fight their way clear of imperial domination.

The exodus of Igbo from Benin occurred in two distinct stages: firstly, the movement out of Udo into Agbor after Oba Esigie's destruction of the former, and, secondly, the emigration from Agbor to the Niger River almost one hundred years later. All accounts of this emigration refer to the eastward migration of Igbo throughout the period c. 1509-1617. The sixteenth century in Benin's history was marked by an energetic imperial expansion with a significant increase in the power and authority of the Eweka dynasty. The reorganization of the central administrative structures, development of royal monopolies on trade, and the introduction of Ifa as one aspect of the state religion, all contributed to the declining fortunes of both Igbo and proto-Aro in the Benin empire. Trade and religion had been the areas in which these groups excelled, and their active participation had contributed to the growth of the empire. However, changing patterns of relationships within the imperial government, bureaucracy and state institutions reduced their role and may have forced their disassociation response.

Disassociation meant a reallocation of resources and a reluctance to pay tribute to the Benin monarchy. It is not coincidental, therefore, that Benin traditions recall a military expedition against Eka (Agbor) in c. 1563-1590 when both the Igbo and proto-Aro attempted to remove Bini imperial impositions. When Oba Ohengbuda discovered that they "had neglected to pay their usual tribute" he dispatched the army to re-establish order.[12] The emigration, and the subsequent foundations of both Aboh and Onitsha occurred, therefore, in the face of this aggression and in spite of the Oba's efforts to force them to recognize his paramount authority.

The location of the two new states reflected the Igbo and proto-Aro concerns for both security and trade. Aboh, for example, is located at the apex of the Niger Delta, which established the disenfranchised leaders in an advantageous geographical position from which to control the delta and eastern overland trade routes. It is important to note, moreover, that the focal point for commercial opportunities in the eastern routes may have been established in response to economic opportunities as much as to political pressure. Because "by c. 1500 the Atlantic trade had begun to flourish in Rio del Rey." [13] The Igbo contingent re-located in a secure area across the River Niger at the confluence of the Anambra and Niger rivers, and found their opportunity to influence both hinterland and riverine commerce.

Totemic theory and the use of totems as a source for historical reconstruction suggests a method whereby it is possible to come to some understanding of events and socio - political interactions which have been presented in more inexplicit terms. For example, the Manatee totemic population which appears extensively along the Niger-Benue river system can be identified as the progenitor of the modern Aro, Kede and Banu. The common kinship totem provides at least one clue to a common ancestry. This hypothesis is corroborated by the similar political and social artifacts maintained by these three sub-groups. It would appear, however, that their unique heritage has been subverted or altered according to relations developed with the larger populations occupying the banks of the Niger and Benue. Thus the Manatee-proto-Aro have become Igbo-speakers, the Manatee-Banu have become Jukunized, and the Manatee-Kede are identified as part of the larger Nupe population.

This process of differentiation was probably not well developed in the fifteenth or sixteenth century, but clearly proceeded more rapidly through the seventeenth and eighteenth. In the fifteenth century the most lucrative carrying trade for the Manatee canoemen involved the transport of southern forest and coastal products to the markets of Songhay. There were few if any political units along the river systems strong enough to impose any constaints upon that trade. In the sixteenth century authority was imposed by powers such as Nupe, Idah and Aboh. From long distance commerce, stretching from the delta to Songhay, the Manatee were forced to engage in shorter distance transport, which induced them to settle closer to the riverine region they monopolized. Once Songhay fell in c. 1591 the inducement for the long distance trade option declined substantially. Settling down and assimilating into the cultures which held political power, at least provided another option. Thus, their commerce could continue but within the political framework that had emerged to dominate the riverine systems. By the nineteenth century the extended and unified Manatee ethnicity had almost been forgotten. For the purpose of this study we have endeavoured to maintain the modern ethnic labels. That is, where connections along the lower Niger below the confluence were between the Manatee-proto-Aro we have tried to identify that group appropriately. Where the reference is general, that is to the larger extended, or undifferentiated community, they have simply been referred to as Manatee.

Relations between Onitsha, Aboh, and the Bini monarchy in Idah developed initially through the common alliance with the riverine Manatee totemic community along the Niger. The Manatee population had become influential allies and agents of the Bini dynasty at Idah, fostering both political and economic links with other trading formations. Both Aboh and Onitsha emphasized the significance of the Manatee in their political foundations, and perpetuated the Manatee connection through various institutionalized symbols and rituals. Also, the common manatee link facilitated commercial interaction, and thus contributed to the integration of both Onitsha and Aboh in the Nupe-Idah-Warri riverine alliance, thereby adding two more trading enclaves to this extensive network of commercial exchange.

The co-operation between Aboh leadership under Esumai Ukwu and the Manatee community along the Niger was not unusual. Both groups had similar economic, cultural, linguistic and political interests, and perpetuated the association through the maintenance of common ritual prohibitions and taboos.[14] Just as the Bini monarchy in Idah had implemented similar ritual prohibitions and adopted the royal headdress Onunu Ehre (tail of the manatee), the leaders of Aboh sought to preserve the memory of Manatee assistance during their flight from Benin when another riverine people sought to halt their advance. The following tradition provides a number of significant parallels with those from Idah and Onitsha.

> The Aboh king journeyed with his people to the bank of a certain creek, where they had no chance to cross over. Standing there the king saw Ewelie people, who knew how to pull canoe, so he begged them to cross him and his people... The king started to send his people...but contrary to this the people [Ewelie] pulled to a corner of the creek and capsized the king's people o death [sic.] ... The people repeated this cruel deed several times ... He again sent into the canoe very powerful warriors... Through this they were safely crossed to the land, in which they saw no one, and they entered the canoe, and crossed to tell the king what had happened. So the king with those that remained with him were helpless. Thinking what to do, a certain man took a pole to measure the depth of the creek. Then he found the creek shallow, so they started to wade across the creek. After they all had gone on land, they saw a number of manatees emerging from the very line they waded across... the manatees, which merely formed a bridge-like line for them to pass over. The king having seen the kindness of the animals showed to them ... passed a decree to all his people that no one should either kill or eat manatee. [15]

The adoption of the manatee totemic symbol demonstrates the existence of a linked riverine alliance which utilized the Manatee population as the agents of the Niger commercial network. The traditions associated with the Manatee served to maintain within these communities an explicit form of remembrance, and thus reinforce the significance of Manatee assistance in the foundations of these three states. The common relations between the various riverine enclaves, including the Bini at Idah, the Igbo at Onitsha, and the proto-Aro at Aboh, were forged through the group of Manatee who had "miraculously...formed themselves together into a mass" and ferried the various groups across the Niger.[16]

The common Manatee relationship is illustrated in other ways. In Onitsha the Igbo are forbidden to "kill or eat the manatee."[17] In Aboh the manatee cannot be referred to by its name, *amei*, and such terms as *anunso umudee* (animal that is taboo to the princess), or *di wenyi* (he who shows us) must be used instead.[18] In Idah the taboo against killing or eating manatee was applied, and the royal headdress called Onunu Ehre served as permanent reminder of the gratitude owed the Manatee population on the Niger.[19] It would seem, therefore, that the Manatee were instrumental in not only changing the demographic patterns along the Niger, but in effectively altering the political administration of the river valley areas through their contribution to the development of the riverine states and the emergence of the Niger trading alliance. Any expansion of population and commercial activity in a peaceful process of commercial cooperation would have enhanced Manatee economic prospects. In fact, as riverine trade grew, and Manatee merchants and transportation specialists became welcome in virtually every riverine market, the Manatee population grew to be one of the significant trading groups on the Niger and reaped substantial economic rewards.

The problem still remains to set the Manatee population on the Niger in a proper regional perspective. It would appear, for example, that this community was not particularly large in any one settlement or region, and also that it stretched from the delta beyond the confluence to Songhay on the middle Niger, and along the River Benue, perhaps as far as Ibi. This riverine population were certainly experts at waterborne trade and transport, and concentrated their activities along these rivers and river valleys. Two reasons might account for the apparent small size of the Manatee population scattered as it was along the waterways. Estimates are difficult for a population which lived most of their lives on the water as transient commerical agents. They might have been more numerous than they seemed from their small settlements. In addition, as the political geography of the Benue Basin changed, and as the Manatee assimilated into the dominant political cultures, they may have given up their connections to the Manatee. For example, the riverine Kede became associated with Nupe, and among the Jukun there were numerous Banu clans.[20]

The Manatee-Banu were particularly influential along the middle and upper Benue river, and the manatee totem was a recognized part of the Kwararafa clan identification structure.[21] In fact, the Manatee influence spread along both the lower Niger and upper Benue; Manatee assistance was important in the political success of Aji-Attah (c. 1507-1537); the foundations of Onitsha and Aboh (c. 1563-1590); and a Manatee- Banu king emerged in Kwararafa (c. 1610-1640). This spreading influence of the Manatee therefore affected not only the organization of the Niger alliance and the development of riverine commercial traffic, but eventually encroached into the political sphere and the direct management of an important trading state on t' ᴗ upper Benue.

The political transformation of Kwararafa from a sudanic zone state into the middle belt with a Jukun-speaking Manatee monarch clearly represented a major alteration in the balance of power in the Benue Basin. J.B. Webster points out that Adi Agba Kenjo of Kwararafa was a Jukun-speaking manatee ruler who came to power in Beipi in c. 1610-1640.[22] This realignment of Kwararafan politics suggests that the Manatee population had expanded its sphere of influence, and extended its concerns into the political arena. T.M. Macleod also argues for a territorial expansion of Manatee influence and suggests that the Aro in the Cross River Basin were originally Jukun-speaking, but subsequently became Igbo-speakers,[23] and were probably of the Manatee totemic group. The evidence from totems, migrations, and linguistics suggests that there was a connection between the Jukun who originated in the Cross River Basin, the development of the Aro state, and the expansion of Manatee economic and political influences throughout the riverine zones of the Benue Basin.

> ...the Ibo stand for the aborigine...extending down both sides of the Niger; that the old Ibo...is cognate with the Dama of the upper river;...150 years ago [c. 1775] the semi-Bantu Munshi [Tiv] came over

> Sonkwala range, attacked Wukari [Chika was renamed Wukari in c. 1830, therefore read Beipi or Kwararafa] the influence of which extended to the Cross River. The result was that the Jukun of Msimbila went south and became Ibo-speaking under the name of Aro Chuku; they became the dominant caste among the Ibo and the Ibo religion is the Aro (Jukun). [24]

While Macleod's dating is inaccurate, his reconstruction provides possible insights into the relationships between the Manatee, Jukun and Aro, and assists in placing the Manatee in the proper regional perspective by making clear their relationship with the Cross River and Aro Chukwu. K.O. Dike and F.I. Ekejuiba claim that "the Akpa, who were acknowledged founders of the Aro state, also claim that they are derived from a rather shadowy kingdom in the region of Ekoi to the east of the Cross River."[25] This would place the Akpa in the same approximate location as the Jukun who moved northward from the Cross River Basin into the Benue Valley in the early sixteenth century.[26] It would also establish a geographic relationship with the Okpoto-language group, a language which has been also referred to as Oring and has been classified in the Cross River language family (1.a.5.3).[27] There was, therefore, a relatively close relationship between the Akpa (Jukun), Okpoto, and Aro, for the Manatee totemic symbol appeared in many of the groups originating from this cluster.

The totemic evidence supports the contention that the Manatee population along the Niger were related to Benue Valley Jukun, and Cross River Aro, Okpoto, and Akpa. The manatee totem appears as a secondary totem among a number of populations, including the Alago, the Ijaw, and the people of Calabar.[28] The available data, therefore, indicates a fairly widespread network of Manatee groups, with each being closely related to the others through the use of the totemic symbol.

The relationship of the various riverine trading states with the Manatee populations established a complementary interaction of politically powerful administrators with experienced riverine traders. The Bini dynasty in Idah, for example, was politically and economically powerful, but lacked the necessary skills to exploit waterborne commercial opportunities, and thus utilized the Manatee merchants and traders as part of the Idah-based commercial organization. Although Idah was only one state among the various riverine trading communities which exploited this link to Manatee merchants, it was the largest and most influential of the states in this informal alliance.

The foundation of the second Idah dynasty by Aji-Attah in c. 1507-1537 introduced major changes in the political and economic relations between the three zones of the Benue Basin. Idah emerged as a dominant middle belt political power and commercial enclave, and the foundations of the Bini, Yoruba-speaking dynasty imposed dramatic changes on intra-regional relations. There was an alteration in the ethno-linguistic balance of power, with the Bini population coming to dominate both politics and economics. The new state also affected the Niger alliance and hinterland trade through the overland routes centred on Idah. The monarchy, through successive generations, tightened regional controls, expanded territorial interests, and imposed Bini domination across a broad stretch of the middle belt. This transformation under various Bini rulers between c. 1507 and 1687 introduced a new set of regional economic, political and social relations with Idah at the centre of an expanding network of regional commerce, a network that was oriented toward the north and access to, and control of, north-south exchange. The location at Idah was ideal for exploring the economic opportunities and commercial advantages not only of riverine trade but in the overland system as well.

> It is certain...that the Igala (formerly Akpoto) country historically was the gateway in the transmission of ideas, trade commodities and technology southwards into Igboland and northwards from Igboland. The Igbo-Ukwu artifacts suggest trade links with the savanna region and even beyond the Sahara desert.[29]

In c. 1507-1537, prior to the Yoruba-speaking conquests of Idah, the confluence region of the Benue Basin contained at least two major ethno-linguistic components. The population included a substantial number of Okpoto and Igbo, but there were also a number of smaller ethno-linguistic groups, including the Awka,

Manatee, and some Bini refugees who had fled the violence of the Benin empire. The introduction and eventual domination of the third major population caused considerable social, political and economic transformation. The imposition of Bini rule at Idah coincided with a regional economic boom, generally associated with the expansion of the trans-Saharan trade, but also with an increase in Atlantic coastal commerce based at the Rio del Rey, and the organization of regional trade from central-place trading states like Benin, Warri, Idah, Nupe, Kano and Kwararafa to exploit such commercial opportunities.[30] The growth of Idah as a major central-place trading formation, and the consolidation of Bini political authority in the confluence region, meant that various non-Bini populations were forcibly coerced under the imperial designs of the Bini monarchy.

As the political power and economic base of the Bini dynasty in Idah increased and expanded, interest in both riverine and hinterland trade became a crucial issue in the administration of this imperial formation. Initially Aji-Attah had been concerned with the Manatee association and the development of the Niger informal commercial alliance. The Bini dynasty paid little attention to Okpoto chiefdoms in the hinterland, and viewed the Igbo-dominated overland trade as a minor commercial endeavour.[31] However, when the Igbo trade continued to flourish and regional commercial demands enlarged production needs, the Bini administration began to view the interior as a fertile place for both political and economic exploitation. King Olema I (c. 1537-1567) endeavoured to extend Idah's influence into the interior, and brought increasing numbers of Okpoto and Igbo into tributary, vassal relations with the Bini monarchy.

The political institutions and style of government in Idah under the Bini monarchs resembled the structures inherited from Benin. The monarch was considered by the Bini settlers as a paramount authority. There was a strong central government based upon the recognized authority of the king, and run by a number of appointed Bini officials. The Idah system, unlike its parent organization in Benin, did not provide many avenues for social, political and cultural integration, and established a distinctive split between the central ruling hierarchy and the commoner, non-Bini, population.

There were no apparent efforts by the Idah administration to foster a sense of nationalism or patriotism in the colonial state. The Bini population clearly enjoyed preferred status, and were thus distinguished from the Okpoto and Igbo commoners as citizens of the empire and peripheral state. This policy differentiated Idah from Benin, where the monarchy had sought legitimacy, and perpetuated a national ideology even in conquered and annexed territory. In Idah the Bini monarchy adopted a policy of social isolation, and remained aloof and withdrawn from both the Okpoto and Igbo. The national Otu structure that had been such an important feature of Benin economic and political organization was not employed in Idah. Thus, judicial, military, social, religious, cultural, economic and political affairs were totally dominated by Bini settlers to the exclusion of the non-Bini vassal population.[32]

This highly centralized administrative structure suffered internal tension manifested in the restrictions imposed on the Bini military commanders which prohibited their entry into the capital except at the direct behest of the king. The bulk of the Bini army was settled south of the capital at Ibaji. This specialized settlement pattern was designed to protect Idah from a possible military encroachment from Benin, and to safeguard the monarchy from the political involvement of the army. Aji-Attah's father. Oba Ozolua, had been assassinated in a military revolt during the Benin-Uromi war, and while the Idah monarchs were dependent upon the army for support they also feared its intercursive power.33 The monarchy, therefore, decided to keep the political centre and military headquarters physically separate, and thus inaugurated another of the institutional changes which distinguished the Idah government from that of Benin.

Representatives of the Bini settler community were appointed to the state bureaucracy as non-hereditary military officers, commercial agents, officials and administrators.[34] These appointees, appointed with red cap titles, established a connection between the commoner Bini population and the central government, but not the other ethnic groups. The Okpoto and Igbo peoples thus provided most of the material support but derived little of the political or economic benefits. The Okpoto and Igbo, as the agricultural community and the principal overland traders respectively, were coerced into providing tribute in order to maintain the Bini administration. Some Bini settlers did join the agricultural sector of the economy, but derived additional benefits from their close association with the Bini monarchy and the opportunity to earn political and economic patronage. The Bini settlers were able to claim lower tribute rates, and were expected to provide less labour.

Under Bini rule the tribute demands on the Okpoto and Igbo populations established usufructuary rights but did not confirm possession or ownership of the land.[35] This policy left the agriculturally productive stratum without guaranteed rights over the basic means of production; land which they had previously owned and worked under the Okpoto dynasty. In the new, imposed system ownership was vested in the Bini monarchy and was dispensed to Bini supporters as patronage for loyalty and service.[36] Fundamental ownership rights, therefore, were violated by the superior might of the Bini conquerors, and Okpoto and Igbo either had to accept vassal status or disassociate from the exploitative social formation founded by Aji-Attah. The prospect of dispossession, at the whim of an alien monarchy, and the possibility of co-option into occupations removed from the land as slaves, or in commercial services as porters, hunters, paddlers or labourers, established a clear distinction between the Bini and the Okpoto-Igbo subordinate population, and introduced a degree of instability in vassal, tributary life that had not been experienced under the previous Okpoto rulers.[37]

As a result the lower stratum in the Idah social formation opposed the Bini administration, and by c. 1537-1567 were expressing their opposition through emigration or open hostility. The Okpoto and Igbo political, social and economic structures had, for the most part, been swept away and replaced with a highly exploitative and coercive central authority to which they had little or no attachment or loyalty. They clearly had no effective voice in the government of the state, and were not encouraged to integrate with Bini social, political and economic structures. Even Okpoto chiefs, who remained in the Idah enclave, exercised little influence with the Bini administration, and were used as agents to collect the royal appropriation or impose the royal will without deriving any of the normal benefits associated with such administrative practices. Opposition to this system of rule manifested itself in both subtle and overt ways, and some Okpoto and Igbo migrated beyond the Idah enclave to escape the impositions of the Bini monarchy, while others tried to withhold tribute to express their dissatisfaction.[38] Such opposition was quickly crushed, and segments of the Bini military were kept busy maintaining order.

King Olema I consolidated the coercive power of the Idah government, and expanded the Bini bureaucracy to control the flow of accumulated tribute and force the vassal Okpoto chiefs to maintain order in areas of the state under their indirect control. The Bini administrators, and some Okpoto chiefs, replaced the Enejie of the Benin administrative system, with two major exceptions. Firstly, the localized bureaucracy was unable to prevent any increased exploitation imposed by the central government, and had little intercursive power with the monarchy. Secondly, the Eweka dynasty in Benin, having been invited into the state, had aligned with the indigenous nobility (Uzama Nihinron) and appointed them as hereditary kingmakers. The Bini dynasty in Idah, having imposed itself by force, was under no such obligation, and retained integral power and authority rather than devolving any power to a kingmakers council, or integrate Okpoto and Igbo in the administration. In fact, the connections between King Olema and the indigenous populations were characterized by clear-cut paramount-vassal relations. The various populations in Idah were separated not only by political relations, but were stratified along ethnic lines, and the social structure represented a hierarchy of ethnicities with the Bini at the top, their allies and associates in the middle, and the Okpoto and Igbo at the bottom.

With the consolidation of political power, organization of the Niger alliance, and the establishment of dominant administrative relations, King Anogens (c. 1567-1597) embarked on a process of territorial expansion. Okpoto and Igbo communities beyond the borders of the Idah enclave were forced into vassal relations with the Idah monarchy. Okpoto leaders in Dekina and Ankpa, who had retained their political and economic autonomy during the initial conquest and consolidation of Idah, were subjugated and obliged to provide tribute to Idah.[39] Although these peripheral Okpoto chiefdoms succumbed to the superior might of the Bini government, they were able to retain some of the existing social and political organization which distinguished them from the chiefdoms in the Idah heartland. Exploitation of the Okpoto and Igbo beyond the borders of the enclave, therefore, was less oppressive, but tribute nevertheless remained a tremendous economic burden. The Idah enclave was ruled directly, and serviced the needs of Anogens and successive Bini rulers, while the hinterland was governed indirectly through recognized vassal Okpoto chiefs who owed their legitimacy to their non-Bini subjects but paid high tribute payments to the Bini government.[40]

Relations with the hinterland were affected by other policies of the Bini government. In c. 1567-1597 King Anogens utilized the strong base established in Idah to develop an external slave trade as part of the commercial nexus of the state. The organization of a slave exchange system brought a drastic change to the commercial patterns of the middle belt. In Benin an embargo on the export of male slaves was imposed by Oba Esigie in c. 1509-1536 and remained in effect until c. 1725.[41] While slaves had been demanded as tribute from distant vassal regions they provided labour for the central elite, and worked in cloth production and agriculture, and were not exported. In Idah the connections to the northern trading system provided an outlet for slave exports, and the administration organized slave exchanges, and demanded slaves as tribute in order to penetrate this long distance trade. The distinctions between Benin and Idah, on the slave trading issue, were based, in part, on the productive capacity of each state. Benin produced and sold ivory, beads, cloth, pepper, camwood and a variety of other forest zone products. In Idah internal production was limited to an infant cloth industry, and a flourishing ivory and metal working. The external demands for slaves, therefore, meant an expansion of the commercial opportunities, and encouraged the Idah monarchy to develop slave exports to the north.

Slaves were either captives of the Idah military or obtained as tribute payments from vassal chiefdoms. In either case there was an important new variable in the relations between the Bini administration and the subordinate strata. The conquest of Nupe and the foundation of a related, but subordinate administration, resulted in the imposition of tributary relations and the payment of slaves to Idah. Peripheral areas in the middle belt not directly incorporated into the imperial sphere centred on Idah became regions where supplies of slaves could be acquired, and a large number of captives were funnelled into the Idah economy. Through both mechanisms Idah emerged as a major entrepot for the northern slave trade.[42] Relations between the state and people who might expect future enslavement were tense, and the easterly exodus of Okpoto and Igbo to escape the impositions of the Idah monarchy increased dramatically. The administration therefore contributed directly to the turmoil of a new political age, and provided little in the way of policy which might establish secure and stable conditions in neighbouring regions. Rather Bini policy cultivated turmoil and encouraged violence as a source for slave exports.

Despite the violence and turmoil on the periphery of the state, associated with the growth of the slave trade, the Bini/Idah dynasty managed to develop the craft industries and foster a general expansion of the regional economy. The Bini settler community had imported weaving and dyeing skills reminiscent of those used in the Benin cloth industry, and established a vibrant industrial base in the Idah enclave. Idah emerged in c. 1567-1597 as an important cloth producing centre, and exported production into the middle belt and northern exchange systems. Some cloth markets directly south or west were generally closed or difficult to penetrate because of competition from Benin. However, by c. 1597-1627 Idah cloth was entering Igbo markets to the southeast, and contributed to the growing importance of the north-south overland trade routes. In this respect the Bini dynastic era fostered an expansion of craft production and provided the impetus for the organization of commercial production of cloth, metal products, and specialized agricultural goods. Eventually, Bini craftsmen began to explore the profitability of exporting not only the production but the technology itself, and weavers and dyers began to settle in the main market areas of the Benue Basin. Just as Benin had become famous in the forest zone as a centre for crafts production, with a wide reputation for quality cloth, Idah emerged with a similar reputation in the middle belt.[43] By c. 1627-1657 Idah weavers and dyers were settled far beyond the capital enclave and followed closely in the wake of the expanding political influence exerted by the government. Idah cloth production, and the weaving and dyeing industries, developed with the regional economy, and contributed to the commercial reputation of the imperial formation.[45] Bini weavers and dyers were prominent in the northern Igbo areas for their skill and quality products. In Nupe the cloth industry expanded, and commercial cloth opened up new markets well to the east of Idah. This economic development had ramifications throughout the confluence region and the middle belt in general, as more and more farmers turned to cotton production. Thus craft development complemented commercial exchange and promoted Idah as a central-place in both regional and long distance trade.

Idah's control of the Niger, at least in the earlier generations of the Bini dynastic period (c.1507-1627), provided one major avenue through which trade expanded. Political and personal links with Nupe during these four generations emphasized the importance of north-south trade, as Nupe emerged as an important central place commercial and administrative point with well defined links to Idah and northern markets. Furthermore, the demands of coastal trade from the Europeans, an important factor in the southern forest zone and delta ports, was only now becoming a significant factor in the middle belt. However, while Warri or Benin could respond directly to the Atlantic overseas trade demands, any commercial opportunities that entered the Niger commercial alliance were filtered through Aboh and only provided secondary exchange opportunities for Idah. The prices were obviously higher than on the coast but the profits were not insignificant. On the other hand, the trans-Saharan trade was highly developed and long distance commerce from the northern sudanic region directly affected the orientation of Idah's trade, and commercial organization. Idah was the paramount Niger trading formation, and could benefit from the various commercial links, including the infant Atlantic trade and the booming trans-Saharan network.

The Bini administration in Idah viewed the Niger as the main trade network, but began to see the commercial benefits in the hinterland regions of the middle belt, and sought to control directly overland routes between the forest zone and sudanic region. In c. 1597-1627 King Agbo managed to wrestle control of the overland routes through the Loko cross-river point on the Benue from the Igbo traders, and thus imposed Bini management on an important commercial link.[45] To consolidate commercial management the Bini dynasty established military outposts at strategic points along the overland routes, particularly at Loko and Ejule. King Anogens and Agbo both sought to expand the Ejule and Adoru markets and develop these hinterland commercial entrepots, mainly to control the horse trade. Horses were thereafter "brought overland from Loko in greater numbers and sold in the Ejule market."[46] The army ensured that threats to regional and long distance traders were minimized.

While riverine commerce on the Niger and Benue remained critical to Idah's prosperity, overland trade was rapidly rising in importance and involved Bini commercial management at the expense of both Okpoto and Igbo entrepreneurs. The expansion into, and the success of, overland trade was contingent upon a number of policy decisions by the Bini monarchs. The overland trading system had been operating under Igbo control long before the advent of the Idah enclave economy. The expansion of the Ejule market ensured that trade in the international market place remained in Bini hands, and salt, horses, cloth, cattle, metal products, and various other goods were imported and exported on a increasing scale. The overland routes flourished and profits accumulated in Bini hands. Markets were secured and established as legitimate places where business transactions could proceed according to clearly defined and acceptable rules. The military ensured peace, and Ejule and Adoru were free from the disruptions of slave raiders.[47] Policy decisions and the implementation of specific actions to ensure commercial development thrust Idah to the forefront of regional and long distance trade.

Anogens and Agbo were the main patrons of commercial development, and fostered the expansion of riverine and overland trade. Anogens, for example, encouraged Bini efforts to extend commerce in the sudanic zone, and an expansion of the salt trade with Keana and Awe resulted. Salt became a major item in Idah controlled markets.[48] Reduced duties were established for the importation of horses which encouraged the horse traders to increase imports. Iron products also moved quite freely within the system, and in c. 1571-1601 the iron producing network expanded, apparently in response to the available commercial opportunities.[49] Finally, special market taxes provided revenue for the central treasury and established stability in the various international markets. Traders had no worries about arbitrary commercial levies at Ejule or Adoru because they were "free of fear, and knew how the market operated."[50] All these state enterprises and expanded commercial activities along the main overland routes can be attributed to the policies of Anogens and Agbo in c. 1567-1627.

The development of trading centres and the organization of central management brought a dramatic change in the economy of Idah and its relations with the rest of the middle belt and Benue Basin. Traders based at Idah, Ejule or Adoru transported goods northward along the main overland routes to Loko on the Benue, or along the river network to Nupe, and purchased cloth, iron products, slaves, salt, cattle, hides, horses and various agricultural products for the return journey. The exchange rates on horses were particularly high, and although the total volume of livestock was probably not very large, operating at the level of luxury commodity exchange, there was a persistent demand for horses throughout the northern Igbo region. Various northern commodities were brought into the international markets and exchanged for slaves, kola nuts, ivory, cloth, metal products, and an increasing variety and volume of European goods penetrating inland from the coast. These goods were taken north to repeat the cycle. Each exchange brought increased profits and benefitted the elite of Idah. By c. 1597-1627 Idah had developed into a relatively wealthy imperial trading capital with commercial links into a flourishing overland and riverine exchange networks.

The establishment of the Bini-dominated state with imperial designs on the confluence region and dominating an expansive commercial network, also provided the impetus for the foundation of a number of trading outposts. In its early years Idah utilized the military outpost at Loko. and the trading stations at Abinsi Itode and Agodo. By c. 1597-1627, however, other commercial settlements were founded further up the River Benue in an effort to exploit and control that aspect of middle belt commerce. The expansion of Bini royal representatives, bearing the royal leopard totem, as far east as Ibi on the Benue suggests that Bini merchants could exploit this riverine system through a network of Bini colonies and administrative centres. As subsequent developments reveal, the expansion of Bini settlement and mercantile outposts along the Benue ultimately faced intense and often violent competition from other imperial trading formations, particularly the sudanic zone state of Kwararafa. However, in the sixteenth century, when trans-Saharan trade flourished, and before Kwararafa became entrenched in the middle belt, Bini merchants and entrepreneurs from Idah found the Benue system fertile ground for their commercial activities.

The decline of the trans-Saharan trade. after the conquest of Songhai by Morocco in 1591, had a dramatic impact in the middle belt. During the reign of King Agbo in Idah (c. 1597-1627), the organized northern commerce through the riverine and overland routes experienced a sharp decline. The negative impact was somewhat mitigated by increasing revenues from southern trade into the Atlantic overseas system and the distribution of European goods imported from the coast. The collapse of the Portuguese monopoly in the coastal trade expanded commercial exchange and increased the volume and variety of goods entering the coastal trading ports. The changing coastal commercial links did not totally compensate for lost trans-Saharan trade, and Idah experienced a hiatus in commercial exchange which undermined the basis of Bini wealth and forced the administration to adopt specific fiscal policies designed to nurture new export markets. The decline of trans-Saharan trade forced a redefinition of Idah's commercial activity; a slow process that contributed to the drastic change in the administration of the confluence region and a realignment of commercial patterns.

Certain activities associated with northern trade patterns were not seriously affected by the conquest of Songhai and the alteration of Benue Basin trade routes. For example, the horse trade remained a relatively profitable concern throughout the depression, and salt retained its market value and continued to be a principal component of overland and riverine traffic. However, the northern market for slaves dwindled, and other commodities were demanded instead. King Agoshi (c. 1627-1657) endeavoured to reinforce the northern trade links from Idah, and encouraged the export of cowries, European cloth, and various metal products.[51] In the face of changing regional economic patterns throughout the Benue Basin, Agoshi sought to protect the flow of wealth, based primarily upon the northern exchange patterns, and maintained the importation of horses, salt and other northern products. This struggle to maintain northern commerce was, however, doomed to failure, particularly in the light of the regional shift in commercial exchange patterns.

Commercial activity on the Niger, and the expansion of down river trade, introduced a new phase in Idah's commercial development. The reign of King Agoshi witnessed a slight increase in the demands for slave exports to the south; canoes loaded with slaves moved progressively down river and utilized the Niger alliance to exchange their goods for European imports. The organization of Niger commercial traffic became, therefore, increasingly important and relations with Warri, Aboh, and Onitsha were instrumental in the expansion of riverine exports to the south. The volume of this southern trade eventually surpassed that of the northern system, thus emphasizing the importance of the Niger alliance in Idah's regional economic relations.

One of the major distinctions which set Idah apart from Benin was that the former was much more of a commercial middleman in regional and long distance trade, whereas Benin was directly involved in commercial production of beads, clotn, camwood, metal products, ivory and pepper. Idah was in the middle, buying and selling products from widely separated societies and exchanging these goods for the ecologically specialized production of the various zones of the Benue Basin. In this respect Idah was more susceptible to the variations in exchange patterns, environmental conditions, and external influences which affected the organization and development of commerce. Idah could experience economic hardship if routes were closed, trading partners revolted, or drought prevented trade.

After 1650, the European commercial demands on the coast shifted more toward the slave trade and away from legitimate' commerce. More significantly, Atlantic coastal trade shifted from the Rio del Rey to Calabar in approximately 1660.[52]

> In about the 1660's the Efik, who had settled at Creek Town, persuaded European traders to visitthe estuary of the Cross River, a customary traderoute to the tar north of the hinterland. Shortly,Rio del Rey collapsed as a leading commercial centre of the Bight of Biafra.[53]

In Idah, however, much of the commercial organization had been geared toward legitimate commerce, and had been oriented toward the north. Under the Bini dynasty, the slave traders did not directly benefit from the shift to the coast, as the coastal trading states could supply slave demands without calling upon the interior states. The Bini monarchy was less able, therefore, to exploit changing exchange relations, and turned to the army to coerce increased tribute payments to supplement declining revenues, and enforce production demands on the subordinate population. The Idah soldiers organized slave raiding parties, but often faced increasing opposition, particularly after c. 1627-1657 when a shift in the political balance of power altered relations with the vassal population in the middle belt. The military solution to the economic problems of the seventeenth century had a reverse effect, and the Okpoto and Igbo tribute-paying population violently opposed Bini policy and military intrusions. The economic and political balance of power in the confluence region was clearly shifting, and with it the Bini dynasty suffered a further economic decline.

The economic developments coupled with growing opposition to Bini rule brought about a change in the balance of power in the confluence region. The era of Bini rule in Idah had wrought a dramatic change to the economy of the middle belt through the development of trading centres and the organization of commercial production. The commoner population near Idah, Ejule, Adoru and Loko had turned more and more toward supplying support services for long distance traders, and accommodating the demands of the central, Bini management of trade. Transportation networks, rest stations, food production, and ancillary services all increased between c. 1507 and 1657.[54] Profits increased dramatically as efficient support services developed and facilitated the exchange of horses iron, cloth, yams, kola nuts, fish, oils and slaves. A number of wealthy families emerged at the centre of regional and long distance exchange, with the wealth derived from commercial exchange concentrated in Bini hands. Bini administrators and traders were thus often economically differentiated from the Okpoto and Igbo population. Tribute as an appropriation of agrarian products, or a demand on labour services to the state, seriously affected the productive capacity of this lower stratum. Time spent in service to the state, for example, reduced the effective capacity of an Okpoto farmer to provide subsistence and tribute. The coercive power of the state ensured compliance with exploitative demands. One response to the impositions of the government was a slow but steady drift away from the Idah enclave.[55] The area currently recognized as Idomaland became a major Okpoto re-settlement area as this segment of the dissatisfied population protested with its feet and moved further and further away from Bini coercive pressure. The administration, particularly under Agbo and Agoshi, responded to this emigration through increased use of the military to force compliance with state policy, which in effect quickened the pace of emigration.

The exodus of Okpoto and Igbo did not initially jeopardize the productive capacity of the imperial trading formation. Additional support for state controlled production and trade could be derived from an expansion of the slave labour input, an extension of the tribute base, or an increase in tribute demands. The risk of enslavement once the emigrants were outside the state apparently was not enough to keep the Okpoto and Igbo within its confines. Furthermore, as commerce developed, the monarchy derived additional revenue from commercial levies, which could replace lost income from the reduced population in the tribute paying social section.

Despite the importance of trade to the Bini elite and entrepreneurs, the mainstay of the economy for the bulk of the population in the Idah imperial formation remained the agrarian activities of the subordinate Okpoto and Igbo. Few Bini became involved in agriculture, and the food requirements of the non-agricultural population had to be met by Okpoto and Igbo farmers, or more rarely by the exploitation of slave labour. Slaves were more profitable as exports than as coerced agricultural labour, and profits from the sale of slaves attracted the Bini more than their ability to produce either commercial or non-commercial goods. Therefore, unlike Benin where the village-lineage production articulated with slave labour, Idah's economy rested on the subordinate Okpoto and Igbo lineage productivity and depended upon this agricultural output for both commercial and non-commercial support. The exploitation and coercive appropriation of the Bini administration depended upon military power to maintain order and retain the flow of tribute, commercial production for export, and non-commercial food supplies for Bini consumption.

Neither the military power nor the economic development of Idah could prevent the mounting opposition of the subordinate population. In fact, military force and economic policy had widened the gap between the Bini rulers and the Okpoto and Igbo commoner population. As commerce continued to be the mainstay of the Bini monarchy and Bini entrepreneurs, the vassal Okpoto and Igbo became economically depressed and increasingly hostile.[56] The opposition of the majority of the population developed and contributed to the polarization of the society. On one side the Bini elite and Bini entrepreneurs supported by the Bini military sought to maintain the trading formation; on the other side, the Okpoto and Igbo sought to topple it.

Idah's principal pattern of trade was in luxury goods, which represented no real "transfer of surplus"[57] out of the state, and only benefitted a few. This exchange system reflected the ability of these few to develop mechanisms whereby they could participate effectively in state affairs as either rulers, administrators or entrepreneurs. In both Benin and Idah the government had been able to devise and implement sophisticated policy and develop sufficient management skills not only to participate in, but also dominate commercial exchange across a broad regional base. Prior to c. 1627-1657 Idah reflected the organized system of commercial administration which utilized coercive force to encourage' production and foster exchange. Both the Okpoto and Igbo in Idah were exposed to the despotic and often rapacious demands of the Bini monarchy, and were compelled to provide increasing supplies of basic commodities to support the growing administrative and entrepreneurial segment of the society. The retention of usufructuary rights depended upon the whim of an unsympathetic monarch, and the prospect of disassociation from the basic means of production remained an ominous spectre. In this situation the Bini government and commercial entrepreneurs probably viewed slave exports as an exchange of a social surplus, but for the Okpoto and Igbo the expanded slave trade represented a real threat to their lives and security. With the striking decline of the northern trade, the Bini ruling elite placed greater burdens on the commoner population. The Bini government repeatedly undermined the economic, political and social structures of the subordinate population and thus reinforced the polarity between Bini and Okpoto-Igbo.

Increasing economic deprivation under successive Bini monarchs added fuel to the mounting opposition of the subordinate sector. Increasing tribute demands represented a major hardship for the agrarian population and would not endear them to a government that was perceived as illegitimate in the first instance. Therefore the vassal population declined in political, social and economic terms. Polarization of the society reflected the distinctions of ethnic origins, class structures, economic differentiation, and Bini policy. According to Okpoto and Igbo subordinate sectors of the population it was a condition that could not persist, and emigration and violent opposition mounted as the regional patterns of politics and commerce changed in the latter half of the seventeenth century.

By c. 1627-1657 an immigrant group from Kwararafa had settled in Agatu, north-east of Idah, and had come to dominate a major north-south overland trade route through competition with the Bini merchants.[58] This immigrant group attracted a number of Okpoto and Igbo followers through its policies of integration, inter-marriage and co-operation. The option to disassociate from Idah and associate with Kwararafan political institutions in Agatu contributed further to the process of polarization in the Bini dominated enclave. Okpoto and Igbo aligned with Kwararafans against the Bini government, and actively sought ways in which to weaken its stranglehold on riverine commerce and overland trade. This struggle for power contributed to the decline in the fortunes of the Bini government, and administrators, entrepreneurs and royalty suffered with every Agatu success.

The influx of the Kwararafans, therefore, not only altered local demography, but substantially changed the political balance of power and the economic focus of the entire middle belt.

In the regional struggle for trade, markets, and political domination in the wake of the trans-Saharan commercial depression of the seventeenth century the Bini government in Idah found its policies ineffective. Up to c. 1650, the state had ruthlessly suppressed opposition and utilized benefits from windfall commercial profits to consolidate their stranglehold on the subordinate population. Therefore, changes in peripheral relations with the Okpoto and Igbo, and the violent appropriation of surplus production contributed to the potential for opposition in the tribute paying social sector. The option to disassociate and align with an alternative state became, therefore, an attractive proposition The Okpoto and Igbo found that they were able to enter the exchange economy of Agatu, and discovered avenues for upward economic, social and political mobility in that Kwararafan state. The government of Agatu had not been imposed by force, and did not, therefore, impose a coercive and exploitative relationship with those that they wished to attract. Politics in the confluence region had become competitive, with the coercive Bini dynasty in Idah losing ground to a more amenable and attractive political system operated by the Kwararafans in Agatu.

As the competition for regional economic and political domination between Agatu and Idah escalated, the Bini dynasty sought to increase its economic prospects through the expansion of southern riverine slave trading. This expansion of the slave trade demanded even more coercive efforts to accumulate slave exports, and the decision by King Agoshi to seize a number of riverine Manatee proved fatal for his administration.[59] The alienation of the riverine Manatee in c. 1627-657, exposed the inherent weakness in the highly centralized political structures of the Bini government, and forced them to align with the Okpoto and Igbo. From that moment onward, the political, economic and social relations in Idah became increasingly divisive, and Okpoto, Igbo, Kwararafans and riverine Manatee began to express their opposition openly. For an administration that had not sought to develop any sense of legitimacy for its rule in the subordinate population, or even provide a rudimentary excuse for the subordinates to provide tribute, the alienation of the one remaining ally was a critical error. Dependence upon the Manatee community on the Niger had been a major factor in the development of regional commerce and Idah's economic domination. Oppression of the Manatee severed the political and economic association and virtually closed the Niger to Idah's commercial traffic.[60] Presumably, the decision to sever old ties meant that the government felt secure in their international relations and the efficiency of the Niger alliance to operate without Manatee good will. It was a tragic error in judgement. The alienation of the Manatee population undermined any legitimacy and weakened the Bini hold on riverine commerce and regional affairs.

The embattled Bini administration in Idah found that its declining fortunes and the increase in overt opposition was partially a result of a reduction in the coercive capacity of the centralized government. During the two generations between c. 1597-1657, the military forces had been slowly disbanded and ex-soldiers were incorporated into the economic infrastructure as traders and transportation specialists. The inability to exercise and maintain coercive pressure, and thus protect trade, trade routes, and markets, provided a measure of political and economic freedom for the Igbo, Okpoto and Manatee communities in and around Idah. By c. 1657-1687, Okpoto chiefs to the east were refusing to make tribute payments on a regular basis, and felt reasonably secure that there would be no violent retribution.[61] Igbo traders preferred the Agatu controlled markets, where they were free of Bini coercive domination and thus undermined Idah's commercial paramountcy in regional economics. Overland traders and the riverine Manatee community therefore turned to the Kwararafan government in Agatu and actively sought to expand mercantile relations along the Benue. The power of Bini imperial domination was clearly waning, and the Bini dynasty was unable to maintain the central controls previously enjoyed.

The rule of the Bini dynasty between c. 1507 and 1687 can be seen as a dramatic and traumatic period in the history of the middle belt, confluence region and the entire Benue Basin. The six generations of coercive Bini government witnessed drastic changes in the political structure, economic focus, social organization, and administrative policy of one of the main trading formations in the region. There were also significant changes in the linguistic patterns, demography, and ethnic composition of the confluence region. Crucial to this period of transformation, was the development of international relations and the emergence of the Niger alliance as a principal trading network. As the power and authority of the Bini dynasty in Idah weakened between c. 1627 and 1687, its role in the Niger alliance also weakened.

The period also witnessed the growth of an increasingly polarized society in Idah. Polarization began with the foundations of the conquest state in c.1507-1537, and accelerated during the period of decline. The political, ethnic, linguistic, social, cultural, economic and religious rift contributed to the failure of the Bini monarchy to retain regional domination. The idea that a distinct ethno-class consciousness emerged from this polarization may be difficult to prove, but it seems likely given the opposition of one segment of the population to the actions of another in the growing relationship of dominance and subordinance which characterized the Bini administration. The Okpoto and Igbo endeavoured to remove or avoid the impositions of the Bini state. Those not inclined to move were forced to accept Bini demands, but when an alternative political option emerged, in the form of the Kwararafan polity at Agatu, both emigration and opposition accelerated. The rapid development of the Okpoto, Igbo, Manatee, and Kwararafa alliance, cemented through co-operation, interaction, and intermarriage, was indicative of the level of alienation and dissatisfaction with the Bini administration.[62] In this respect the Okpoto and Igbo seemed to have had a basic awareness of their oppressed status, and were willing to seek alternatives through political association with the Kwararafans in Agatu.

The success or failure of the Bini dynasty should not be solely measured by its political or social policies. If these criteria were used, the Bini administration would appear to have been a resounding failure. The dynasty was successful, however, in the development of limited commercial production, establishment of long distance trade links, and the opening of major markets for international exchange. The economic success and the expansion of commercial enterprise did not mitigate the opposition of the subordinate, tribute paying social sector because that stratum did not participate in it. In fact, as the Bini elite increased in size and as commercial and non-commercial production was appropriated on an extended scale, opposition mounted. The continuity of the state was apparently dependent upon the ability of the government to expand and maintain coercive, integral power relations. The demobilization of the army reduced the coercive capacity and the administration was no longer able to force tribute payments, raid for slaves, protect territorial integrity, or ensure revenues from commercial transactions. In some respects, therefore, the Bini dynastic era established a viable mercantile structure, but failed to provide general access to this commercial economy. It also failed to establish any sense of political legitimacy, and polarized the society to such an extent that vassal subjects actively sought alternatives to Bini rule. Therefore, while various Bini monarchs endeavoured to restructure the commercial operations of the state to meet the new demands of the seventeenth century, they faced an increasingly hostile local population. King Agoshi, for example, sought to rebuild trade links with the north, but found that access through the Loko cross river point had been cut off by Agatu. As the pressures mounted Agoshi and eventually his son King Olema fled Idah and left the capital of a once powerful trading formation to the opposition.[63]

Thus by c. 1687-1717, the middle belt was on the verge of another major political, economic and social transformation, a change which would, in fact, reunite the segmentary society left by King Olema, and launch a new age of economic prosperity and political unity in Idah. The emergence of the Kwararafan, Okpoto and Igbo alliance as the dominant power in the middle belt provided the basis for a reformed imperial social formation centred at Idah, and established the economic foundations of a rejuvenated international long distance trading network.

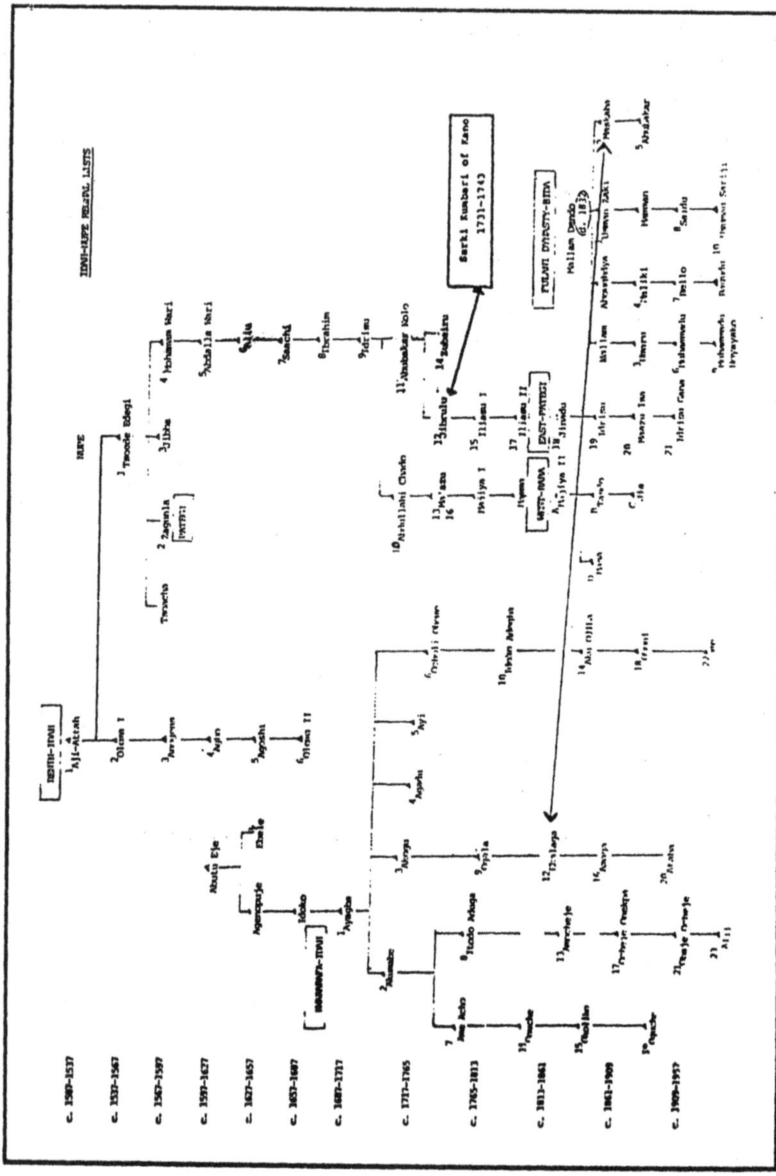

Chart IX: Idah, Nupe and the Kano Cross-Reference

References

1. R.N. Henderson, *The King in Every Man*, New Haven, 1972, pp.65-68.

2. I.H.T. No. 117, Igala Mela group interview, Achanyuwo clan principal informant, July 22, 1977.

3. The Benin regnal list shows that Aji-Attah was the son of Oba Ozolua, and Iginua was the son of Oba Olua. Ozolua and Olua were brothers.

4. C. Hoffman, "The Languages of Nigeria by Language Families", in *Studies in Nigerian Language*, 5, 1976, Zaria Institute of Linguistics. The language chart adopted from Hoffman represents only a small portion of all Nigerian language families.

Nigerian Languages by Language Family

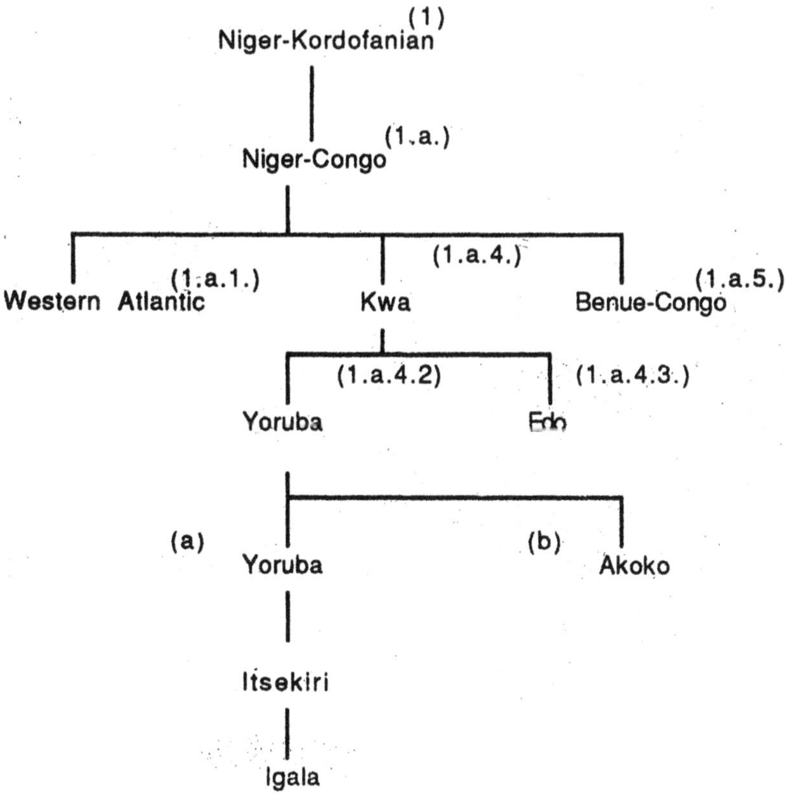

For more information on linguistics see K. Williamson, 'Lexicostatistica Comparison of Itsekiri, Standard Yoruba, and Igala', Department o Linguistics, University of Ibadan, 1972; R. Armstrong "Glottochronology and African Linguistics", *Journal of African History*, III, 2, 1962; R. Armstrong, "Comparative Word List of Two Dialects of Yoruba with Igala", *Journal of West African Languages*, 2, 2, 1965; and R. Silverstein, 'Igala Historical Phonology', University of California, Ph.D., 1973.

5. Williamson, 'Lexicostatistical Comparison'. The length of separation was postulated from the relative glotto- chronological data and the distance between each of these language groups. The evidence, however, shows that each group developed interactive relations with other language clusters, and presumably experienced a different rate of linguistic shift according to the time and rate of these interrelationships. The Bini, Yoruba-speaking group of Idah, for example, interacted with Okpoto (Delta-Cross River language - 1.a.5.3.), Igbo (Lower Niger language - 1.a.4.7.), and Idoma (Idoma language - 1.a.4.6.). By the time of Williamson's study the Igala language had experienced a considerable shift toward Idoma. The Bini, Yoruba-speaking group in Warri developed interactive relations with the Ijo (Ijo language - 1.a.4.8), and Urhobo (Urhobo language - 1.a.4.3.). These different associations contributed to the process of linguistic change and separation, and would have accelerated this process in different directions. The numbering system utilized here to define specific languages and language clusters and can reveal both vertical and horizontal affinities between various clusters. Vertical links supersede associations on the horizontal plane, and thus reflect the internal coherence in a particular language family.

6. E.J. Alagoa, *History of the Niger Delta*, Ibadan, 1972, p. 10. Also see R. Armstrong, "The Igala", in *Peoples of the Niger-Benue Confluence*, in the Ethnographic Survey of Africa, edited by D. Forde, London, 1955.

7. J.S. Boston, "Ida Divination in Igala", *Africa*, XVIV, 4, 1974, and M. Kalous, "Ifa Divination", *New Orient*, VI, 4, 1967. See also B.I. Belasco, *The Entrepreneur as Culture Hero*, New York, 1980, and W. Bascom, *Ifa Divination*, Bloomington, 1969.

8. J. Ijomah, 'The Evolution of Kingship Among the West Niger Igbo Chiefdoms',, unpublished paper included in the Benue Valley History Collection, Dalhousie University, 1983. Also see J. Ijomah, 'A Pre-Colonial History of Agbor', University of Birmingham, M.A., 1976, and J.B. Webster, J. Bucher, *et. al.*, 'A Critical Analysis of the Royal Chronical of Agbor', Benue Valley Project Paper No. 13, 1972.

9. J.W. Hubbard, *The Sobo of the Niger Delta*, Zaria, 1948, p. 198.

10. A.O. Nwauwa, 'The Aro Chiefdom: Chronology and State Formation, c. 1690-1720," Dalhousie University MA., 1989, p. 66

11. Henderson, *The King in Every Man*, p. 68; C.K. Meek, *Law and Authority in a Nigerian Tribe*, London, 1937, p. 11, and Webster, 'Critical Analysis'. Also see E. Isichei, *The Ibo People and the Europeans*, London, 1973, pp. 39-40, E. Isichei, *A History of Nigeria*, London, 1983, p. 137.

12. J.U. Egharevba, *A Short History of Benin*, Ibadan, 1968, p. 32.

13. Nwauwa, 'The Aro State'; p. 78.

14. Ritual prohibitions act somewhat like secondary totems and can be adopted for political reasons to establish a link between a non-aligned population and the central political power in the state. For more details on totems, totemism and ritual prohibitions refer to F.B. Ataba, 'Recent Development in the Use of Non-Documentary Evidence, With Special Reference to Totemism and Regional Chronology', Dalhousie University, M.A., 1976, and J.B. Webster and R.A. Sargent, *Practical Oral Methods: Historical Data Collection in Africa*, Dalhousie Series in African Studies, forthcoming.

15. K.O. Ogendengbe, 'The Aboh Kingdom of the Lower Niger, c. 1650-1900', University of Wisconsin, Ph.D., 1971.

16. Henderson, *The King in Every Man*, p. 47.

17. *Ibid*., p. 32, and also see I. Nzimiro, *Studies in Igbo Political Systems*, London, 1972.

18. Ogendengbe, 'The Aboh Kingdom'.

19. I.H.T. No. 117.

20. S.F. Nadel. 'The Kede: A Riverine State in Northern Nigeria", in *African Political Systems*, edited by M. Fortes and E.E. Evans-Pritchard, London, 1940, pp. 165-166. Also see T.M. MacLeod, 'Ethnological Report on the Okpoto, Egedde of Idomaland', KNA, K2003, 1925.

21. J.B. Webster, 'Animals of the Kingdom', Benue Valley Project Paper No. 6, 1975.

22. J.B. Webster, "The Three Phases of Kwararafa: A Peripatetic State", Benue Valley Project Paper No. 7, 1983.

23. MacLeod, 'Ethnological Report'. Also see A.E. Afigbo, "The Aro of Southern Nigeria: A Socio-History Analysis of Legends of Their Origin", Part I, *African Notes*, VI, 2, 1971, pp. 31-46.

24. MacLeod, 'Ethnological Report'.

25. K.O. Dike and F.I. Ekejuiba, "The Aro State: A Case Study of State Formation in Southeastern Nigeria", *Journal of African Studies*, 5, 3, 1978, p. 269.

26. Webster, "The Three Phases of Kwararafa", where he notes that 'Akpa' may refer to Abakwariga specifically, or more generally to all the people of Kwararafa.

27. Hoffman, "The Languages of Nigeria", p. 177.

28. P.A. Talbot, *The Peoples of Southern Nigeria*, (4 volumes), London, 1926, Vol. 2, p. 257.

29. O.N. Njoku, "A History of Iron Technology in Igboland, c. 1541-1900,' Dalhousie University PhD, 1986, p. 65.

30. A.A. Boahen, "The Caravan Trade in the Nineteenth Century", *Journal of AFrican History*, III, 2, 1962, pp. 349-350.

31. I.H.T. No. 112, Igala Mela group interview, July 27, 1977.

32. *Ibid.*

33. *Ibid.*, and also see G.C. Okojie, *Ishan Native Laws and Customs*, Yaba, 1960; Egharevba, *A Short History of Benin*, p. 28;and J.E. Miller, `Ishan-Benin Relations, c. 1455-1509', Dalhousie University, Honours Essay, 1983.

34. I.H.T. No. 115, Igala Mela group interview,Unana clan principal informants, July 27, 1977.

35. *Ibid.*

36. I.H.T. No. 117, Igala Mela clan heads, group interview, July 22, 1977.

37. I.H.T. No. 119, Igala Mela group interview, July 28, 1977.

38. *Ibid.*

39. I.H.T. No.117.

40. I.H.T. No. 119.

41. A.F.C. Ryder, *Benin and the Europeans, 1485-1897*, London, 1969.

42. I.H.T. No. 119, and I.H.T. No. 78, Okpuchu, in Dekina, June 27, 1977.

43. I.H.T. No. 78.

44. I.H.T. No. 177, Akpa Ali, Arwa, September 15, 1977. Also refer to A.E. Afigbo, "Trade and Trade Routes in Nineteenth Century Nsukka", *Journal of the Historical Society of Nigeria*, VII, 1, 1973.

45. I.H.T. No. 115.

46. I.H.T. No. 26, Aluta of Ejule, February 17, 1977.

47. I.H.T. No. 15, Aradu Odu, Atem and Orgunu, Ejule, January 16, 1977.

48. I.H.T. No. 26.

49. Njoku, `A History of Iron Technology in Igboland', p. 88.

50. *Ibid.*, and I.H.T. No. 78.

51. I.H.T. No. 61, Okwoli, Idah, June 3, 1977.

52. Nwauwa, `The Aro Chiefdom', p. 77

53. Ibid., pp.79-80.

54. Ancillary services might include the production of fodder for the horses, making of bridles and ropes, providing food for the traders, and baskets for the transportation of salt. I.H.T. No. 249, Idah, January 16, 1978.

55. I.H.T. No. 115.

56. I.H.T. No. 112.

57. I. Wallerstein, "The Three Stages of African Involvement in The World Economy", in *The Political Economy of Contemporary Africa*, edited by P.C.W. Gutkind and I. Wallerstein, Beverly Hills, 1976, pp. 30-32.

58. This immigration into Agatu and the confluence area has been more fully discussed in a subsequent chapter. However, the penetration of the confluence region by the Kwararafan refugees clearly overlaps in time with the Bini period, and directly contributed to the declining fortunes of the Bini dynasty in Idah.

59. I.H.T. No. 118, Igala Mela group interview, Obajadaka clan principal informants, July 28, 1977.

60. I.H.T. No. 117.

61. I.H.T. No. 117.

62. R.A. Sargent, "Igala Masks: Dynasty History and the Face of the Nation", in Tricksters, *Transvestites and Warriors: African Masks and Cultural Systems*, edited by S.L. Kasfir, African Terurven, Brussels, 1989.

63. I.H.T. No. 112, and I.H.T. No. 115. Agoshi left Idah and settled north of the River Benue where he established a short lived Bini dynasty in Keana. Bini influences in the Alago Obasadoma (homeland) were quickly undermined by changing political fortunes and the rise of Kwararafan emigrant power. One of the few remaining indications of direct Bini settlement north of the Benue is in the persistence of the leopard totem. Refer to J. Power, `Lafia: Layers of Settlement', paper presented to The Johns Hopkins Workshop on African History, Baltimore, 1984.

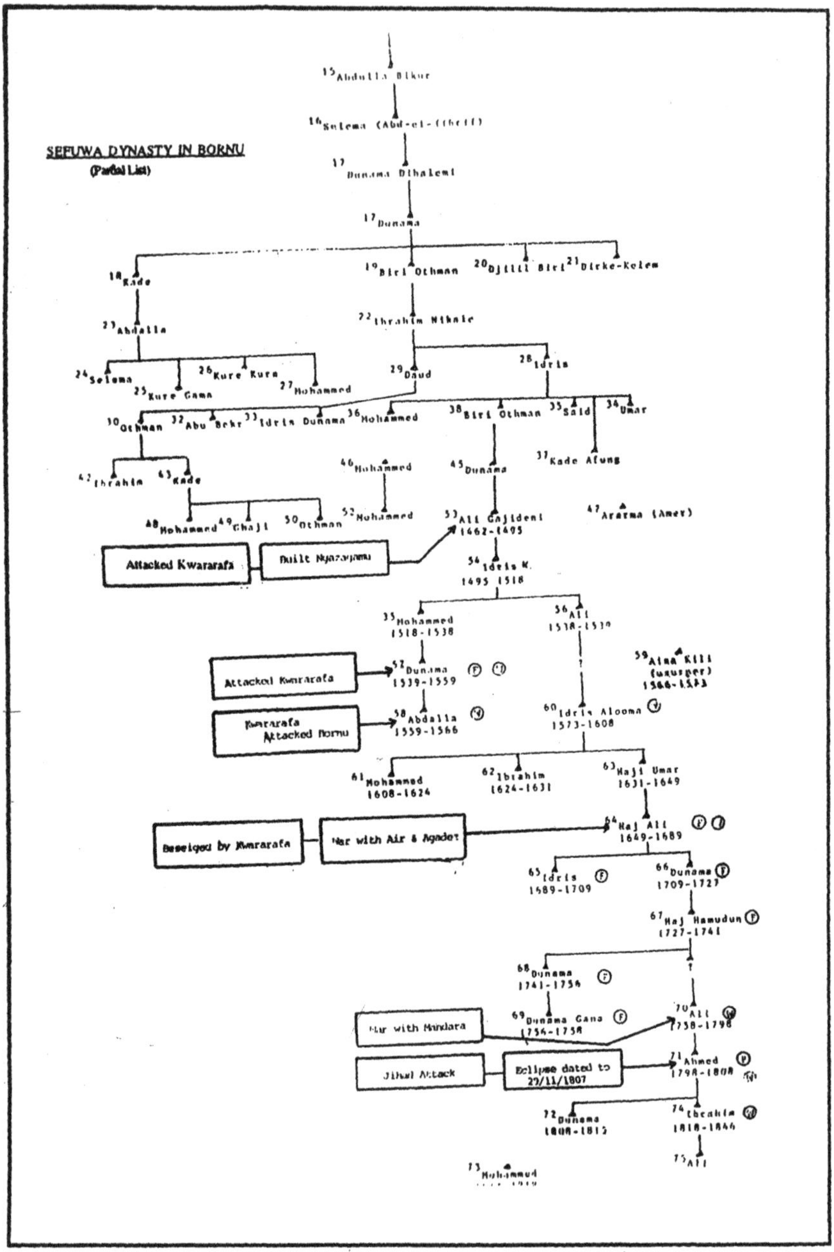

Chart X: Sefuwa Dynasty in Bornu

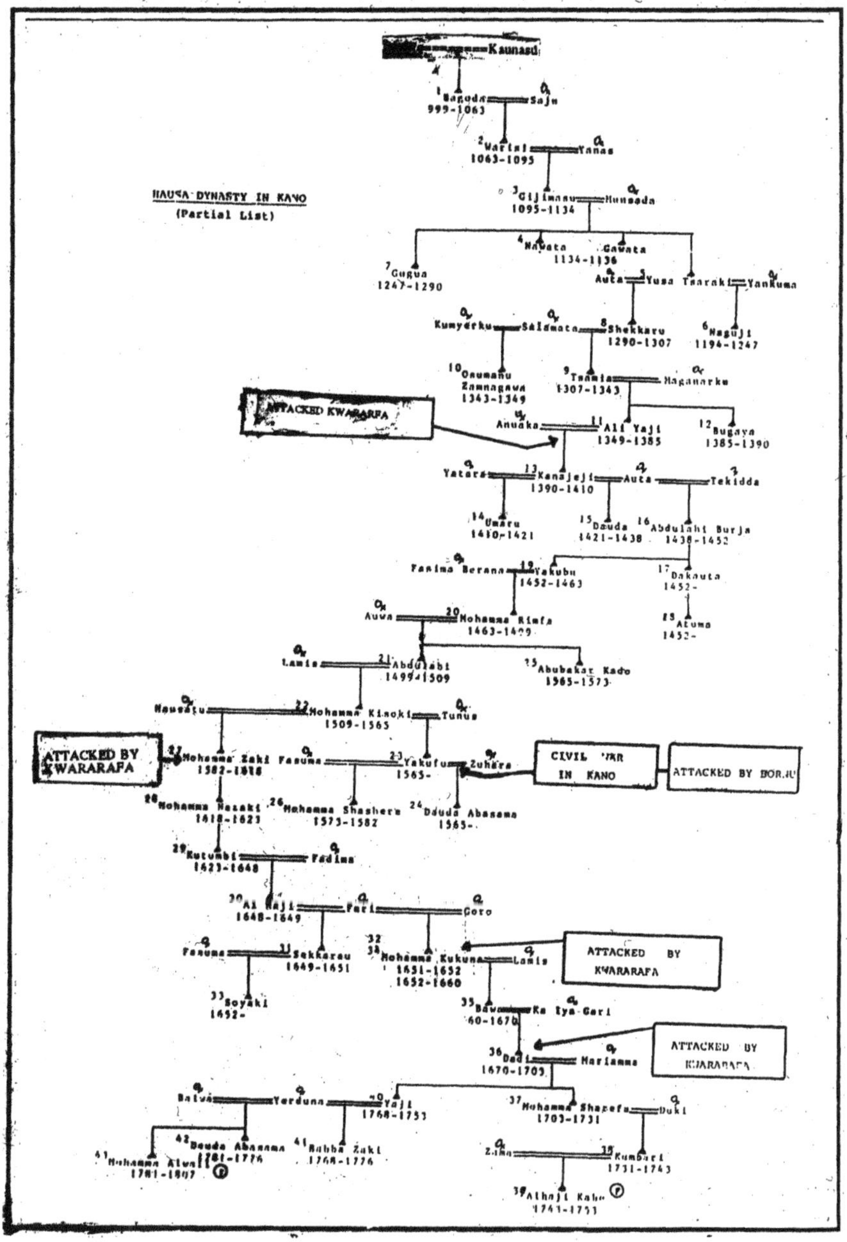

Chart XI: Hausa Dynasty in Kano

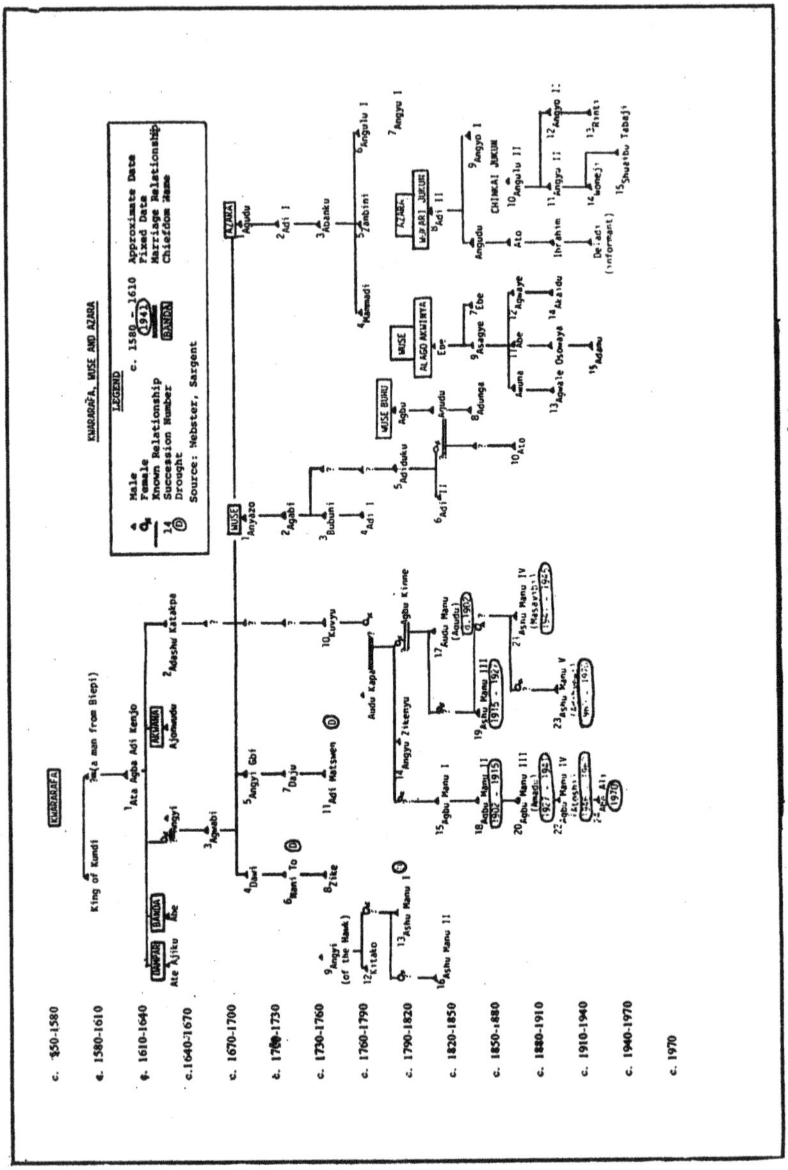

Chart XII: Kwararafa, Wuse and Azara

Chapter 7

Commerce And Politics In The Sudanic Zone And Middle Belt, c. 1300-1600

Kwararafa was a significant political and economic force in both the sudanic zone (pre-1500) and the middle belt (post 1500), and provides a crucial link between these two distinct sub- regions of the Benue Basin. Over three centuries Kwararafa progressively moved its capital south into the Benue Valley as it sought to effectively compete within the political and economic geography of the sudanic zone, and in the process suffered various military defeats by powerful and aggressive neighbours. This chapter examines that process, the continued strains on the multi-ethnic confederacy, and the slow collapse of the state which gave rise to a variety of successor states. The struggle for survival, and the competition for control of long distance trade, particularly with Kano and Bornu, lasted for over four hundred years and transformed Kwararafa from a sudanic state with limited access to the trans-Saharan commercial system,[1] to a troubled middle belt polity competing for Benue commerce and overland trade to Calabar in the south.

Kwararafa's peripatetic nature has been documented by J.B. Webster and will not be examined in detail here. However, an examination of the process of relocating the Kwararafa capital at Biepi (c. 1520-1550), and the ensuing internal political turmoil, is necessary to an understanding of Kwararafa's role in regional politics and economics.[2] The foundation of Biepi, and the series of emigrations which followed in subsequent generations, were the result of regional commercial and political change. The establishment of Beipi coincided, for example, with the emergence of the Atlantic coastal trade at the Rio del Rey,[3] and a drought induced famine in Bornu.[4] Also, Idah was emerging as a powerful political force at the confluence and was able to increasingly influence commercial developments along the Niger and in parts of the sudanic zone. The scope of economic change in the region imposed strains upon Kwararafa which the state was unable to withstand: it was forced to move and emerged as a middle belt trading formation, with a substantially altered population, economic focus and political organization. Encroachment into the middle belt imposed both demographic and economic changes on that region. Thus, while originally a sudanic state, Kwararafa became a major middle belt trading formation.

Kwararafa's political and economic history cannot be examined in the same depth as that of Benin and Idah because of a paucity of direct evidence.[5] Until a specific and comprehensive research program has been completed in the upper Benue and Gongola River Valleys, conclusions based upon existing evidence must be postulated cautiously. The data available, however, does provide some insights into the relationship of this multi-ethnic confederacy to sudanic zone and middle belt economics and politics. Furthermore, the evidence from the successor states which emerged after the collapse of the confederacy provides fairly detailed information about Kwararafa in the later stages of its history. This analysis endeavours to correlate the data from the successor states with the patterns of regional politics and economic change in the Benue Basin. It seeks also to relate the changes evident in Kwararafa and the states southward shift from Santolo to Tagara to Biepi with events, politics, economics, and personalities in both the sudanic zone and middle belt.

Any reconstruction of Kwararafa history must consider the relationship of this confederacy to Jukun political power and commercial presence in the Benue Basin. This reconstruction lays to rest the persistent although erroneous assumption developed and perpetuated by early writers that this state and Jukun authority were synonymous.[6] The Jukun Kingdom was one of the successor states which emerged during the declining years of Kwararafa (c. 1597-1717), and Jukun authority was not firmly established until the mid-eighteenth century. The Jukun claim to continuity with Kwararafa dates no further back in time than c. 1597-1627,[7] whereas Kwararafa's history extends back into the eleventh century. The Kingdom of Wukari might be considered the main successor state since it sought to absorb and perpetuate the central Kwararafan traditions, but Wukari was not established as a Jukun stronghold and capital until c. 1820-1850. Therefore, while Jukun traditions provide information on Kwararafa, they cannot be held as synonymous with Kwararafan historical traditions, and the perception that Kwararafa was a Jukun-dominated polity from as "far back as the thirteenth century" must be abandoned.[8] Early Kwararafan history shows no evidence of Jukun involvement, particularly when the capital was at Santolo, north of the Gongola River.

One of the earliest references to Kwararafa comes from the Kano Chronicle, during the reign of Sarkin Yaji (1349-1385) when Kano attacked Santolo. The Islamization which had started in the Habe city states and which proceeded under Sarkin Yaji, apparently contributed to this conflict. Large numbers of urban, pagan Hausa-speakers had fled the city states and re-settled in pagan strongholds, including the Kwararafan capital of Santolo. We can thus postulate a direct correlation between religion and commercial development. While northern commercial links through the trans-Saharan trade system were paramount, a primary focus of the state political and economic elite would be on Islam. However, the advantages of links to southern commerce could not totally be ignored and at certain stages in the economic history of the region the resurgence of southern commerce added impetus and power to the non-Islamic religious sects since they were the main actors in that trade. The invasion of Santolo, therefore, may have been caused by mounting commercial competition from this pagan city state, indicating a growth in southern commercial trends. Kano was a major trading centre within the trans-Saharan commercial network, and the Islamization process in this city state was directly related to the growth of international commerce with the Muslim world. Santolo also sought to extend its links to regional and international trade, and thus emerged as a competitor for control of commercial opportunities in the sudanic zone. Kano flourished, and Islam became a factor in the development of long distance trade. From this base Kano attempted to extend political and commercial hegemony across the Central Sudan, and Santolo was the "key to the south."[9] It was therefore a bastion of paganism against Islam, and a major strategic, and economic competitor.

The conquest of Santolo by Sarkin Yaji set in motion a southward migration of pagan-Hausa or Abakwariga who founded a new capital at Tagara, north of the Gongola-Hawal confluence. The rocky outcropping at "Atagara"[10] provided a strong defensible capital in which the Abakwariga could hold out against the military aggression of Kano. It also gave the Kwararafans an opportunity to revitalize their economic, political and military strengths through the incorporation of both Pabir, and Koro-Gwari populations.[11] The additions established a complex multi-ethnic state based upon the various internal alliances between factions. Thus the conquest of Santolo in 1349-1385 changed the demographic composition of Kwararafa, forced a change in the location of the capital, and contributed to the redefinition of regional politics and commerce.

The movement of Kwararafa to the south effectively weakened, but did not eliminate, Kwararafa's relations with the trans-Saharan international trading network, and imposed a new set of regional commercial interactions on the sudanic zone. Kano had clearly emerged as a prominent trading state with hegemonic power in the Central Sudan and commercial paramountcy in trans-Saharan trade. Kwararafa had been temporarily reduced as a political force in the region and declined as a trading state in the sudanic system. Over the next few generations Kwararafa re-oriented commercial production, and re-defined trade relations from its base at Tagara, and eventually re-emerged as a relatively powerful trading formation. The opportunities within the trans-Saharan trading system were still present, and Kwararafa thus once again became a competitor for access to that system. However, the geography of trade also meant that Kwararafa sought access to a different trans-Saharan trade network which operated to the north-east of Lake Chad, and direct competition with Kano was somewhat reduced.

From this re-vitalized base, trade and political relations with Kano took a turn for the better. Violent competition shifted to a process of reciprocal exchange where equivalent numbers of Kwararafan slaves were exchanged for Kano horses. This reciprocal exchange contributed to the flowering of the Habe city states and to the revitalization of Tagara as the Kwararafan capital. The Abakwariga commercial system seemed to flourished in the fifteenth century, and the Kwararafan army was remounted on horses acquired through the trade agreement with Kano, making Kwararafa better able to defend its position within the sudanic trading network.

By 1463-1493 the commercial stability and political harmony in the Central Sudan experienced a major upheaval when Mai Ali Gajideni relocated the capital of Bornu at Ngazargamu.[12] The encroachment of Bornu west of Lake Chad occurred when Kano was "probably at the height of its power," and when Kwararafa had fully recovered its military abilities.[13] It also coincided with the economic boom under the Songhai pax. The relocation of Bornu brought direct competition with Kwararafa, not only for control of trans-Saharan commerce, but for control of the salt deposits in the Hadejia River Valley. Kwararafa, therefore, represented one of the major obstacles to the development of Ngazargamu as a significant regional political and economic power, and Mai Ali Gajideni launched a successful military offensive to consolidate his capital. The campaign against both Kano and Kwararafa established Bornu's hegemony west of Lake Chad. The King of Kwararafa was captured, 17,000 people enslaved,[14] and Tagara was abandoned. Kwararafa had suffered another major military defeat and lost its advantageous position within the sudanic commercial system. Thus the southward retrenchment of Kwararafa continued after a period of approximately one hundred years on the rocky outcropping of Tagara.

It is interesting to note that the shift of Bornu to Ngazargamu coincided with the foundations of the Songhai pax over the southern perimeter of the trans-Saharan trade network. It is also interesting to note that these events fit well with the construction of the regional chronology and show how the intrusive effects of competition for commercial access and control affect regional political geography. The pacifying influence of Songhai established ideal conditions under which international commerce could flourish. Bornu, located to the north-east of Lake Chad would have thus experienced a decline in trade volumes along the routes reaching that locale. The relocation of the capital, therefore, reflects the concern in Bornu to participate effectively in trans-Saharan trade, and provided the opportunity to develop commerce indirectly under the umbrella of the Songhai pax. In order to consolidate the economic position, however, the Mai had to deal with competition from both Kano and Kwararafa. Kwararafa was the main loser, in one sense, in this competition as the state relinquished direct access to trans-Saharan commerce, but gained ultimately by relocating closer to a relatively new form of commercial opportunity to the south.

The defeat of both Kano and Kwararafa during the late fifteenth century substantially altered the economic focus of the sudanic region. Bornu replaced Kano as the major southern entrepot for trans-Saharan trade, and the reciprocal trade agreement between Kano and Kwararafa lapsed. Kwararafa's place in sudanic regional and trans-Saharan long distance trade was again reduced, for its direct access to trans-Saharan commerce was prevented by Bornu hegemony. Kwararafa was evidently unable to withstand the second crushing defeat in its history, and opted to relocate further south.

The people who migrated southward after the defeat of Tagara in 1463-1493 included a large contingent of Abakwariga and Pabir,[15] with smaller numbers of Koro and Gwari. Major segments of the Koro-Gwari population also migrated to the west and eventually crossed the Jos Plateau and settled in southern Zaria.16 The movement south concerns us most since this migration accounted for the establishment of the third Kwararafa capital at Biepi in c. 1520-1550. The resettlement in the Benue Valley altered the demographics of Kwararafa by introducing new populations of Idoma Nokwu and Jukun. In turn, new political arrangements were required in the central government to accommodate these groups.

Kwararafa's history is marked by the continuing struggle to carve out a place of prominence in the trading patterns of the region. The competition between Kwararafa, Kano and Bornu suggests that the Kwararafans had designs on direct access to trans-Saharan trade. Their efforts to secure a niche in the lucrative commercial system, and perhaps emerge as one of the major southern entrepots of this trade met with violent opposition from the other competing states. From its geographic position south of Kano and Bornu, Kwararafa was disadvantaged in this struggle, but the population within the multi-ethnic confederacy retained its northern focus and persisted despite the power of Kano or Bornu. This northern orientation reflected not only the economics of trans-Saharan trade, and the rewards which might accrue to the successful southern entrepot, but also the northern origins of the dominant sector in the multi-ethnic population.

As the advantages of northern supremacy settled directly on Kano and Bornu the delicate balance of power within the Kwararafan confederacy shifted away from the northerners. Thus the progressive movement southward by Kwararafa increasingly suggests that southern social, political and economic influences were growing to fill the vacuum created by the failure of the northern orientation. This suggestion is enhanced by the fact that southern economic conditions were improving dramatically. By c. 1540-1570 the sudanic zone experienced major drought and famine which would negatively impacted upon the trans-Saharan trading system. The drought and famine conditions persisted, and were reported in Bornu in c. 1570-1600. Furthermore, in 1591 the Songhai pax was brought to a dramatic end by the Moroccan invasion. Thus, within the Kwararafan confederacy the northern population would have seen their economic base reduced by events and climatic conditions to the north. Coincidently the southern populations would likely have experienced an increase in their economic opportunities as southern trade remained prosperous and in fact, expanded during this period.

Kwararafa's political structure was apparently based upon a constitutional internal balance of power, and a multiplicity of alliances within and between the various ethnic elements in the state. There is evidence to suggest, for example, that the centralized institutions of government were shared between the main ethnic components in the multi-ethnic population. This rather unusual political structure has been perpetuated in some of the successor states of this now defunct confederacy, and serves as reminder of the internal organizations of Kwararafan politics. As the state moved southward, with the capital settling successively at Santolo, Tangara, Biepi, Uka, Wuse, and finally Wukari in the nineteenth century, the balance within the state altered dramatically, and new alliances and political relationships were required as new ethnic groups were absorbed into the mainstream of Kwararafa's political and economic life. With the settlement at Biepi and the incorporation of the Idoma Nokwu and Jukun the character of Kwararafan alliances was changed forever. These new populations demanded a share in the confederal political system, and supported these political demands with sound economic reasons. The Jukun population, for example, had prosperous economic links to a vibrant southern trading network probably reaching as far as the Rio del Rey, and given this commercial influence sought to reorient Kwararafa's perspective from the north to the south. This reorientation required political authority, and such power could only be exercised through the internal confederal alliance system. By c. 1550, while northern aspirations had not been totally abandoned southern influences were beginning to encroach upon the internal political and economic structures of this multi-ethnic confederacy, and the delicate balance of power progressively shifted toward the new southern populations.

The political culture of Kwararafa had been built upon principles of a shared basis for political power. Each of the main ethno-linguistic populations recognized as legitimate within the constitution of the state offered candidates to the central throne in a rotating order. The administration was organized through female-side and male-side relationships, with the latter forming the royalists and nobility and the former the commoners. The female-side, related to the ruling house through marriage, could not aspire to hold the paramount position in the confederacy, but retained a powerful and effective voice in the organization and administration of the state. Inter-marriage by newly absorbed populations, such as the Idoma Nokwa and Jukun, provided the mechanism through which political legitimacy and ultimately political authority could be achieved. The Jukun, for example, began to integrate with the Kwararafan population and effectively utilized the marriage instrument to build their power-base in this social formation. Inter-marriage and access to female-side positions accelerated rapidly in the seventeenth century.

This period in Kwararafa's history represented the first occasion when Jukun actually appear in the state. While we have been able to document Kwararafan traditions in the Central Sudan, Jukun evidence clearly establishes their point of origin in the Cross River Basin far to the south.[17] The Jukun apparently expanded progressively northward from the Cross River and eventually entered the Benue Valley in the early sixteenth century. It was only after the fall of Tagara in c. 1463-1493 and the retrenchment of the Kwararafan monarchy southward that these two populations were joined, probably at Biepi. This conjunction occurred after Kwararafa had been in existence for over five hundred years, and the Jukun could hardly have been among the founding peoples of Santolo. Clearly it was only at Beipi that the Jukun became influential in Kwararafa.

The relocation at Biepi allowed Kwararafa once again to revive after a crushing military defeat. By c. 1550-1580, the recovery was sufficient to allow for a military intervention in sudanic zone affairs, and a concerted effort to reopen commercial links with the regional and long distance trading network associated with the trans-Saharan trade. Kwararafa attacked and defeated Bornu, but drought and famine prevented the military success from being translated into permanent economic advantage. Webster has shown that climate was a major factor in intra-state relations, and argued that a continent-wide "climatic deterioration occurred between the 1560's and 1620's."[18] Lovejoy has argued that "famines of these magnitudes must have seriously affected large parts, if not all, of the southern Sahara in the Central Sudan and set in motion major population shifts."[19] One of the results of the climatic degradation in the late sixteenth century was that the Kwararafan military remained south of the Benue and could not pursue its military advantage. Rainfall would have been more consistent in Biepi, and the middle belt climate contributed to the recovery of Kwararafa as a major commercial centre and significant political force.

The period following the "Sima Azadu" drought,[20] when Sarkin Mohamma Zaki ruled in Kano and Mai Idris Alooma governed Bornu, was a particularly dramatic time in Benue Basin history. The western section of the trans-Saharan trade collapsed with the conquest of Songhai (August 25, 1591),[21] and trade shifted toward Bornu and the Central Sudan. Mai Idris Alooma capitalized on this opportunity and extended his authority far to the north along the major trans-Saharan trade routes. Kano recovered from the impositions by Bornu and Songhai and carved out new commercial ties with the trans-Saharan commercial network.[22] Kwararafa, on the other hand, faced an economic decline, despite the climatic advantages of its location in the middle belt.

Commerce in the Benue Basin was in the process of dramatic change, and while Kwararafa retained ambitions of becoming a major sudanic zone trading state, and entered directly into violent competition with both Kano and Bornu, avenues to trans-Saharan trade had been effectively closed. The last resort for Kwararafan traders interested in northern commerce was in another military incursion into the sudanic zone in an effort to resuscitate commercial exchange. In c. 1582-1616, Kwararafa invaded Kano, despite the droughts, and "ate up the whole country."[23] This second military success did not rejuvenate northern trade, and Abakwariga commercial influences, which had been based upon northern trade links, continued to decline. This also forced Kwararafa to re-orient its economy and economic focus, because northern commercial links were either closed or produced little profit. However, to the south and along the River Benue very profitable economic potential could be realized if control of overland and riverine trade was imposed from Biepi. Kwararafa had, therefore, not only to reorient economic thinking, but enter into a new set of regional competitions for control of southern and riverine trade. The major beneficiaries of this economic reorientation would be the small number of local traders who were engaged in commercial activities along the Benue and the southern overland routes. The Abakwariga entrepreneurs who were losing economic and political influence, also energetically turned to southern commerce and thus expanded Kwararafa's penetration of riverine and overland trade.

This commercial reorientation, based upon the location of Biepi in the middle belt, brought Kwararafa into contact and competition with a new set of regional trading patterns, populations and polities, including the Bini dynasty at Idah and the Idoma Nokwu population of the Benue Valley. The upper Benue region was linked to the south through the Manatee/Bini-Idah dominated riverine trade on the Benue and Niger, and a Jukun-Igbo overland trade route to Calabar, while local production was dominated by the large Idoma Nokwu population around Biepi. Kwararafa chose to incorporate the Idoma Nokwu population, and thus added a third major ethno-linguistic component to the multi-ethnic confederacy. Within the state, thereafter, three distinct populations, the Abakwariga, Koro-Gwari, and Idoma Nokwu, were numerically significant, while the Bini, Pabir and Jukun were small in number, politically weak, but economically important. The introduction of the Idoma Nokwu - the progenitors of the Idoma linguistic group which includes the Idoma, Alago, Etulo, part of the Igala and Igbirra, and the Awka[23]- represented a major demographic change in Kwararafa. The disproportionate economic power of the small Bini and Jukun populations, imposed a realignment of political alliances within the Biepi administrative structures, which in turn created a polarization around ethnic-based political groups. The Bini, who had been in contact with the Idoma Nokwu near Ibi, Abinsi and Dampar for some generations, and who had experienced a number of generations of inter-marriage, now politically aligned with them.[25] The Jukun newcomers lined up with the Abakwariga-Pabir, also newcomers to the area, while the Koro-Gwari apparently remained unaligned and disaffected but interested observers. The Koro seemed to find that their political ambitions were ignored in the newly polarized circumstances and soon opted for dis-association and emigratior from Biepi.

The Abakwariga-Pabir-Jukun alliance appears initially to have been the dominant political force in the new Kwararafa. The Jukun began to establish female-side links within the constitutional framework to facilitate direct involvement in the state administration, and became an increasingly potent voice despite their small numbers. The Abakwariga, previously the principal merchant and entrepreneurial class when the northern focus held sway, had to explore alternatives in the new commercial nexus. Riverine trade required special skills and was thus closed to Abakwariga overland traders. The southern routes became the preferred option, and Abakwariga merchants joined with the Jukun and eventually settled as far south as the Atlantic coast. The political alliance between the Abakwariga, Pabir and Jukun apparently included an economic alliance which allowed them to dominate the southern overland routes.

The Idoma Nokwu and Bini alliance was established as the main opposition to the ruling Abakwariga-Pabir-Jukun group, and sought to develop a political base from their strong economic position in riverine trade. It would seem, however, that by c. 1580-1610, the Bini and Idoma Nokwu were excluded from the political mainstream. The Abakwariga were still concerned about their own northern connections, but, increasingly, southern overland trade was taking precedence. Clearly the opportunities in the overland trade through to the Rio del Rey were economically significant and provided sufficient support for the Jukun-Abakwariga alliance. The riverine trade was not, however, insignificant and retained sufficient influence and wealth-generating capabilities to maintained Bini-Idoma Nokwu pressures for political accommodation. Intermarriage and the development of female-side relationships, over time, provided the sense of political legitimacy which might be exploited as a basis for political authority. The Bini-Idoma Nokwu appear to have been influential enough to compete for political status, but the Abakwariga-Pabir-Jukun alliance maintained sufficient economic strength to retain political dominance, and even Bini-Idoma Nokwu marriages with the ruling group did not provide political integration in the administration of Biepi.

As the struggle for political power developed, and the Bini-Idoma Nokwu alliance repeatedly saw their political ambitions rejected by the ruling alliance, tension mounted. The Jukun were emerging as a potent political force, and enhanced their political power through the control and development of the salt deposits in the Benue Valley. In fact, Jukun settlement patterns north of the River Benue coincided to a remarkable degree of consistency with the location of the salt deposits in the region. From the economic base of overland traders, with connections to the Rio del Rey, and the monopolization of the Benue salt industry, the Jukun began to agitate for even more political power.

The internal political confrontation in Kwararafa was based upon the distinctions of ethnic alliances, economic orientation, trade, and the political aspirations of the various groups. Abutu Eje clearly represented the Bini-Idoma Nokwu alliance.[26] He was of the leopard totem of Bini origins, yet presumably Idoma Nokwu in language. The Bini colonists on the Benue had been associating through trade and intermarriage with the Idoma

Nokwu since the expansion from Idah in c. 1507-1537. Three generations of Bini-Idoma Nokwu intermarriage had cemented the social, economic and political ties. Abutu-Eje's major competitor was Adi Agba Kenjo, a Jukun of the female-side to the Abakwariga- Pabir royal house of Biepi.[27] If Abutu Eje was a serious competitor, he must also have had some claim to female-side kinship with this royal house. Actually, it would appear that by 1600 there were probably two royal houses in Biepi, one Abakwariga representing the ancient Santolo establishment, and the other, the new Pabir royal house from Tagara. There is no evidence to suggest that Kenjo was female-side to one royal house and Abutu Eje to the other, but it would seem likely. In that case Kenjo probably represented the Pabir, while Abutu Eje was linked to the ancient Abakwariga establishment. Kenjo was eventually recognized as the first monarch in the Jukun traditions of Kwararafa. The major significance of this succession dispute lies in the fact that it involved elements of northern origins allying with two distinct southern commercial competitors - the Bini dominating the Benue trade and the Jukun controlling the southern overland routes.

In c. 1580-1610 the political struggle in Biepi brought various competing factions into major confrontation. The Bini-Idoma Nokwu alliance endeavoured to promote Abutu Eje as the next candidate for the Biepi throne, but the Jukun nominee eventually emerged victorious. The emigrations from Kwararafa, that had begun with the migration of disaffected Koro groups in c. 1550-1580,[28] continued with the emigration of Bini and Idoma Nokwu in c. 1580-1610.[29] They responded to the disappointing political developments by disassociating from Kwararafa and migrating down the River Benue. The Idoma Nokwu abandoned their homelands up river and resettled in Agatu. This migration according to Igala sources, included Alago, Idoma, Igala, Igbirra, and some Hausa and Jukun.[30] Apparently the alliances established in Biepi were not mutually exclusive, and while some Jukun and Abakwariga left during this phase of the Kwararafa diaspora some Bini and Idoma

Nokwu stayed in Biepi. The Kwararafa diaspora in c. 1550-1610, occurred in waves and each wave incorporated a diverse ethnic mix, and involved a substantial number of people. This diaspora also contributed to the foundation of a number of successor states, and accelerated the decline of Kwararafa's economic and political power, particularly after the Benue riverine trade route was closed to Kwararafan trade by the refugees in Agatu.

Kenjo's tenure as a Kwararafan ruler was short-lived, and he was unable to consolidate political authority or effectively utilize Jukun domination of southern trade to reinforce political power. His reign ended in a revolt of Abakwariga from their major settlement at Uka. Kenjo was "murdered and his descendants excluded from the throne,"[31] and control of the central government was thus seized by Adashu Katakpa. As a martyr to Jukun political ambitions, Adi Agba Kenjo was deified as the god of war and became an important spirit in the Jukun collection of cults and ancestor worship.[32] Adashu Katakpa, representative of Abakwariga political ambitions, decided that Uka, with its substantial Abakwariga population, would be a more secure and suitable settlement for the Kwararafan palace. Katakpa may also have favoured Uka because it was closer to the emigrating Idoma Nokwu and possible economic links to the Benue riverine trading network.

Adashu Katakpa represented a resurgence of northern influences in Kwararafa. As an Abakwariga of the Santolo royal house, he was probably more acceptable to the majority of northern peoples in the state. The resurgence of northern orientation indicates that the Abakwariga retained aspirations to reintegrate with northern commerce, and maintained at least minimal northern commercial links. The strong Bini threat and the Jukun encroachment would have alienated both northern entrepreneurs and the population of northern origins, who apparently still recognized Santolo as their homeland. The emigration of the Koro, Gwari, Bini and Idoma Nokwu had changed the nature of the fragile confederacy and left only two opposing political factions to resolve the internal problems of the state. The Abakwariga emerged, at least temporarily, as victorious and solidified their domination of Kwararafa from the capital at Uka.

Uka was advantageously located for both regional and long distance trade, and became the northern terminus of the Rio del' Rey trade routes. As a consequence of the close commercial links to the south, Jukun migration into the region accelerated after c. 1610. The Jukun were no longer merely traders. They came in large numbers and settled as craftsmen, traders and salt producers until the entire region once dominated by the Idoma Nokwu became the centre of concentrated Jukun economic activity. Apa later became known as their homeland, and Uka grew to be an Abakwariga urban enclave in a predominantly Jukun region. Uka retained its status as a central place and maintained regional control over commercial activities, but was forced to recognize Jukun settlement and the Jukun contribution to the economy through overland trade, salt production, and regional marketing.

The reign of Adashu Katakpa (c. 1640-1670) in Uka saw the resurgence of Abakwariga influences in Kwararafa's political and economic affairs despite the growth of Jukun influence. This development may be directly linked to the move of European Atlantic trade from the Rio del Rey to Calabar. Certainly Calabar was reasonably close to the main overland routes that had been exploited by Abakwariga and Jukun traders since the founding of Beipi in c. 1520. To assure the longevity of Abakwariga political hegemony in the state, however, commercial strength had to be reasserted in the northern trading nexus. Therefore, Adashu Katakpa struck at Kano with the aim of developing a share in the commerce of the sudanic zone. He attacked and defeated Kano during the reign of Sarkin Mohamma Kukuna (1651-1660).[33]

> Sarkin Kwoararafa Adashu came to attack Kano. Sarkin Kano went to Dan Magadu where he stayed for seven days, and then to Auyo and Abewa, where he remained forty days. On his return he found that the Kwararafa had battered down the Kofan Kawayi [Kawayi Gate].[34]

The attack on Kano was also the result of broader economic factors, as ascendancy of Adashu Katakpa in Kwararafa corresponded with a brief period of economic recovery in the northern Benue Basin after the deprivations of drought and famine. The modest economic recovery between c. 1640 and 1670 allowed for a brief resurgence of Saharan commerce, and thus provided impetus to the Kwararafan invasion. It seems hardly coincidental that Adashu Katakpa would endeavour to develop Kwararafa's commercial links with the north, particularly given the history of economic growth during the boom period between 1490 and 1590. The recovery was brought to an abrupt end with the return of drought and famine at the end of the century. The reign of Sarkin Mohamma Kukuna in Kano was a time of severe drought, and the Senegambia region suffered, "the great famine of the seventeenth century."[35] Bornu traditions also indicate a massive drought and widespread famine that ravaged the Lake Chad region from the reign of Mai Haj Ali (1649-1689) to that of Mai Dunama Gana (1756-1758). With the northern sudanic states weakened by drought and persistent famine, Adashu Katakpa seems to have been determined to establish Kwararafan influences. These efforts to reassert Kwararafan power might be considered acts of political opportunism, but they were also logical responses to the need to resuscitate Abakwariga commercial dominance within Kwararafa.

Adashu Katakpa's invasion of the north coincided with a Tuareg attack on Mai Haj Ali's stronghold at Ngazargamu.[36] The conflict between the Kanuri of Bornu and the Tuareg on the desert side of the empire was exacerbated by the conditions of drought and famine, and Mai Haj Ali was forced to confront two violent aggressors.[37] To lift the seige of Ngazargamu, Mai Haj Ali temporarily negotiated with the Tuareg and allied his forces to concentrate upon meeting the threat from Adashu Katakpa. Bornu won a resounding victory, and Mai Haj Ali gained fame throughout the Hausa city states for his defeat of the powerful pagan invaders. Dan Marina, a Katsina poet and contemporary of Mai Haj Ali, expressed the euphoria that swept through Bornu and the Hausa states after the defeat of Kwararafa in a song composed in "praise of Amir ul Muminia `Ali Sultan of Bornu', and in censure of Kwararafa."[38]

> Ali has triumphed over the heathen, a matchless triumph in the path of God. No Sultan like him: A Laith among Laiths, ever stout of heart. Has he not brought us succour? Verily but for him our hearts had never ceased from dread of the unbelievers. Narrow had become to us the earth pressed by the foe. Till Ali saved our children and their children yet unborn. [39]

After the defeat by Bornu, Adashu Katakpa's son, Agwabi, the successor to the Kwararafan throne, endeavoured once again to secure a 'place in the northern sun' by renewing the attack on Kano.[40] He led the invasion in c. 1670-1700 which represented the last effort on the part of the Abakwariga to reassert their rights in northern commerce. After the war with Bornu, the two powers exchanged ambassadors and arranged an exchange of slaves for horses, like the earlier agreement with Kano. Thereafter, permanent peace was established. With Kano, it seemed that traders interested in the southern commercial focus favoured a similar agreement but devout Muslims objected because the horses sent to Kwararafa built up the power of its army. Thus Muslim kings broke the agreement and often provoked a Kwararafan military response while less devout rulers permitted or even encouraged the southern commerce and thus promoted peace. Unfortunately, Kwararafan had not broken through with direct access to trans-Saharan trade, and the lack of any lasting political and economic agreement points to a flaw in Kwararafan foreign policy. Their reliance on the military solution leading to victory in a single battle might temporarily weaken the vanquished and thus generate some commercial activity, but it did not necessarily establish longlasting stability, peace, and conditions in which trade might permanently develop.

Religious motives also seem to have encouraged the Abakwariga from Uka to attack the Habe and Kanuri states in the north. Traditions taken from the Kano Chronicle provide a clue to a possible explanation for the persistence of Kwararafan invasions.[41] With the failure of his father in the preceding generation, and given the power of both Kano and Bornu, it is surprising that King Agwabi continued to attack the north. As Kano traditions reveal, and Bornu traditions confirm, the military invasion of Kano in 1671 was partly motivated by Abakwariga desires to control the religious shrines of the pagan Hausa.

> The Sarki wished to go out and fight him [Agwabi] but the chiefs of Kano demurred and he remained in his house. The Kwoararafai entered Kano by the Kofan Gadon Kaia, slaughtered the men of Kano, and reached Bakinrua. The Galadima Kofankani said to the Sarkin Kano, who was in the Pugachin Kishi with his Jarumai: "Establish `Tchibiri' at Toji and 'Bundu' at Rimi Bundu." (Two pagan shrines) The Galadima said to the Sarki, "Rise up! The Kwoararafai have destroyed the best part of your town and have killed many men! They have penetrated to the Kurmi, and will attack the `palace'." The Sarki mounted his horse and went out, and came to the Kofan Fada with the Galadima... He went to Rimin Bundu, took the `Bundu' and gave it to Dan Durma Mazza Mazza, and thence hastened to Kafa Bai. He found the Kwoararafa had come near the `Tchibiri' but everyone of them who came close died at once. The Sarkin Kwoararafa told his people to take away the 'Tchibiri'. The Kwoararafa tried to charge, but they failed to seize it. The Sarki Kano came to the `Tchibiri', and took it. On his right hand he had a hundred warriors, in front of him ninety-five chiefs, all of them mallams, and on his left hand a hundred warriors. They were all slaughtered by the Kwoararafai; only a few were left alive. Sarkin Kano fled to Daura. The Kwoararafai followed him to Jelli and then returned (home).[42]

The 'Tchibiri cult' had been first practised in Kano during the reign of Sarkin Tsamia in c. 1307-1343, before the conquest of Santolo.[43] Although the Kano monarchy was converting to Islam, and originally endeavoured to suppress the cult, the Sarkin was eventually compelled to allow it to continue. He may also have been impressed with the cult's ability to develop commerce and organize trade.

> The Sarki returned to the tree, and destroyed the wall together with all else connected with 'Tchibiri' which was beneath the tree. All the pagans had in the meantime fled, except Makare, Dan Samagi, and

> Dunguzu Dan Dorini. The Sarki said to them. "Why do you not run away?" They said, "Where were we to run to?" "Praise be to God," said the Sarki. "Tell me the secret of your God." They told him. When he had heard, the Sarki said to Danguzu, "I make you Sarki Tchibiri."[44]

The traditions about the invasion of Kano in c. 1670-1700 establish a relationship between Kwararafan ambitions and the Bundu and Tchibiri cults. Further research in Kano might clarify this connection. However, it is possible to suggest that the Sarkins tolerance of Pagans, in Kano, and the acceptance of their cults, reduced the exodus of alienated Abakwariga into Pagan states such as Kwararafa. Clearly, the appointment of a Sarki Tchibiri in c. 1307-1343 established a connection between an Islamic monarchy and the Pagan population, a circumstance forced upon the King because, "all of the pagans had... fled," or deserted. Also, the willingness to defend Bundu and Tchibiri in 1670-1700 suggests that these cults had retained importance for the merchants, residents and monarchy of Kano. The fact that Islamic mallams gave up their life to protect the Tchibiri ritual object indicates the significance of this cult to Kano, and suggests that the battle was more than a simple political conflict, or religious quarrel between Pagans and Muslims.

The Kano traditions are quite clear that the invasion under Agwabi was related to the presence of the cult objects of "Bundu" and "Tchibiri." It would seems, therefore, that as the principal representative of Pagan Hausa in the Benue Basin, the leadership in Kwararafa was determined to control these cult objects. Apparently, Pagan ritual and spiritual pride were offended by the fact that Bundu and Tchibiri were in the hands of Islamized people like those in Kano. The force of the attack to liberate Bundu and Tchibiri also suggests that the Kwararafans related religion and economics, and thus saw these cult objects as their commercial salvation. The other religions in the Benue Basin-Oluokun, Ifa, Islam and Christianity - had all been oriented toward commerce, and Bundu and Tchibiri represented commerce and the power of the monarchy to control markets, labour and trade. Agwabi certainly seemed intent upon recapturing these cult objects, and the description of his attack on Kano reflects this singled-minded purpose. Perhaps, therefore, Abakwariga political and economic ambitions culminated in the invasion of Kano with the hope of liberating Bundu and Tchibiri and returning these cult objects to Kwararafan control and thus contribute to the development of Pagan Hausa trade.

Acquiring the ritual objects from Kano would have cemented Agwabi's internal position in Kwararafa. He had seen his power decline in the face of increasing Jukun authority and of a decreasing support from the Abakwariga. Abakwariga merchants and entrepreneurs, who had not achieved economic returns from their support of the invasion of Bornu and Kano would have been less likely to back an administration which was unable to resolve their problems. The Tchibiri cult, with its headquarters in Kwararafa, might have strengthened the state as a place of pagan Hausa refuge, and would certainly establish Uka as an important non-islamic spiritual centre. Thus the government which returned Tchibiri and Bundu to the Pagan Hausa in Kwararafa might expect to be recognized. supported and perhaps deified as the political and economic saviour of the long suffering Abakwariga. A spiritual rejuvenation of Abakwariga political and economic aspirations might consolidate the Abakwariga monarchy as the legitimate power, and thus implement centralized institutions of government which would support regional and long distance trade, and promote Abakwariga to the positions that they formerly held in Santolo.

Upon his return from the attempted conquest of Kano, Agwabi founded a related dynasty at Awe. Awe traditions claim that Agwabi arrived riding a roan antelope.[45] Possible this is a subtle indication that Kwararafa's military strength was reduced, and that it relied less on horse-mounted cavalry - perhaps only officers and titled officials were equipped with horses - and more upon foot soldiers with bows and arrows. The prevalence of the tsetse fly south of the Benue had presumably limited the number of horses available, and the recent invasion of Kano would have reduced the cavalry even more. Thus the Kwararafan cavalry strength, upon which they had depended so often for protection and penetration of the sudanic zone, was apparently becoming less of a factor.

The change in military capacity and political organization in Kwararafa would have favoured the Jukun segment of the population, since their experience would not have been with horses or cavalry. The Jukun were familiar with bows, arrows, and spears, and were foot soldiers more suited to the climate and environment of the middle belt and forest zone rather than the open plains of the Sudan. This newfound military advantage coupled with the Jukun domination of salt production and overland trade in the middle belt and forest zone enabled them to enhance their political status in Kwararafa. After c. 1670-1700, the prominence of the Jukun in Kwararafan affairs increased, and Jukun political authority grew. Agwabi's attack on Kano was thus the last Kwararafan invasion of the northern Islamic city states, not only because the distance was too great for foot soldiers, but also because the economic and political concerns of the Jukun had superseded the Abakwariga's northern interests.

In the generation c. 1680-1710 the Jukun were expanding north of the River Benue and actually penetrating sudanic zone markets. This economic and commercial organization gave the Jukun certain political advantages, and despite the struggles in Kwararafa between the Abakwariga and the Jukun for control of the throne, the Abakwariga rulers could not oust the Jukun from the state. By the eighteenth century the Jukun had seized political power, and came to look upon Kwararafa as their unique state. It was also in the eighteenth century that the Jukun language came to be spoken by all other peoples in Kwararafa, including the Abakwariga. Pressure to Jukunize, in the face of massive immigration, caused some migrations out of Kwararafa, including some Abakwariga who founded Katsina Ala in the eighteenth century. By 1820-1850 the Jukun had achieved exclusive political power, and the remaining Abakwariga clans had become the kingmakers, a complete reversal of the social and political hierarchy evident a century before.

By c. 1700-1730 Kwararafa had substantially changed, and the Abakwariga were slowly settling in to a secondary position in economic life, while their political power was progressively eroded. Kwararafa had thus changed from a sudanic multi-ethnic confederacy in which the Abakwariga played a prominent economic and political role, to a middle belt nation state in which the Jukun were emerging as the commercial, military and administrative leaders. The exodus of Pabir, Bini, Idoma Nokwu, Koro and Gwari contributed to the rise of Jukun authority. The alliances which had worked so well in previous generations had gone, and in the political vacuum the Jukun emerged as the dominant power. Corresponding to the rise of the Jukun in Kwararafa was the foundations of Jukun settlements at Wuse and Azara, two important commercial and administrative enclaves governed by female-side Jukun relations of the Kwararafa royal house. In c. 1700-1730 the Jukun also developed central responsibilities in Kwararafa, and began to assert their dominance in the administration of the state.

The change from Abakwariga to Jukun predominance was a slow process and contributed to the reorganization of Kwararafa as a middle belt trading formation. Various factors and pressures combined to force Kwararafa to reorient toward the middle belt, including overland trade, Jukun political power, foot soldiers, and the orientation of regional commerce to the south rather than the north. The eventual collapse of Kwararafa as a imperial trading formation, and its reconstitution as an eighteenth century Jukun national state, were rooted in the abandonment of the principles of a shared central government. Previously the administration of Kwararafa involved the various representatives of the multi-ethnic population. The rise of Jukun paramountcy consolidated political power in Jukun hands. This fundamental change in the organization and administration of Kwararafa was a result of the transformation of economic orientation, altered demographics, and the shift from cavalry to footmen. The replacement of the relatively egalitarian, multi-ethnic, confederal central administration with a Jukun monopoly dealt a final crucial blow to the confederation. Abakwariga, Idoma Nokwu, Bini, Koro, Pabir and Gwari were all dissatisfied with the political transformation, and opted to disassociate rather than accept imposed central authority by a single ethnic component. Clearly the Kwararafa polity in the Benue Valley at the end of the seventeenth century bore little resemblance to the powerful state which had dominated the Gongola Basin two centuries previously. The reorganization of the state during the slow retrenchment into the Benue Valley, the internal struggles for political and economic pre-eminence, the population shifts imposed by the Kwararafan diaspora, and the disassociation of large numbers of people, combined to shatter any remaining social, political, and economic cohesion.

This decline in state unity was most marked in the changes in the confederal structure of Kwararafa. The ability of the various segments to retain their distinct ethnic identity - symbolized most clearly by totemic representations such as crocodile, leopard, manatee and owuna bird - after a number of generations in Kwararafa, suggests that there was only a limited attempt at assimilation or acculturation. The development of a common, Kwararafan ideology or state social structure which would minimize ethnic separation might have engendered widespread acceptance of the state government. The war to regain Tchibiri, however, represented Abakwariga ambitions which had apparently survived almost three hundred years of association with Kwararafa. The Idoma Nokwu retained their distinctive symbols after the Kwararafa diaspora and the dispersal to the various successor states of the middle belt. The Jukun, as relatively late arrivals in Kwararafa, still held strongly to their own identity, and had not integrated with the Kwararafan state system. With this widespread tenacity in retaining separate ethnic, linguistic and cultural identification, the principle of political rotation or a shared succession to the central monarchy enabled the diverse groups in the state to retain relationships with the populations they represented rather than emphasize national symbols. Abandonment of this founding principle of a shared central government, and the introduction of a single national symbol, served to minimize the attachment of each group to the state and prompted further fragmentation.

Kwararafa had a brief period of glory when it had emerged as the dominant military and perhaps economic and political, power in the sudanic zone. It was during this period that attachments to the confederal structure might have been encouraged, and the various components of the multi-ethnic population aligned more firmly with central state policy. However, generations of violent commercial competition with aggressive neighbours, droughts, famines and internal political disputes undermined the central institutions and weakened the links between the distinctive segments in the population. The cumulative results of Kwararafa's inability to handle aggression, organize effective resistance, and develop consistent regional and long distance trade patterns was the slow movement of the capital into the Benue Valley. The moment of glory, which corresponded with the period of prosperity, quickly passed, and Kwararafa was forced into a prolonged struggle for survival in which the economic and political order was redefined. Throughout the seventeenth century, states tin the middle belt and southern sudanic zone were forced to recognize a changing balance of economic power which emphasized southern exchange patterns and minimized the old northern-oriented commercial links. The advent of Jukun paramount authority, in the abortive attempt to concentrate central political power in Jukun hands under Adi Agba Kenjo (c. 1610-1640), represented only the initial phase in this transformation of the Kwararafan confederacy.

The emergence of Aku (King) Dawi, first Monarch in a fairly long line of Jukun rulers, in c. 1700-1730, seems to support the conclusion that the Jukun had completely taken over Kwararafa by the eighteenth centurey.[46] Thus, it is also possible to conclude that in the early eighteenth century the multi-ethnic confederation of Kwararafa ceased to exist, and in its place was a Jukun national trading formation. With the ascendancy of Aku Dawi, the Abakwariga were reduced to the female-side and the kingmakers, but the Jukun were the rulers and provided the lingua franca of the reconstructed social formation. The capital of this successor state was moved from the Abakwariga town of Uka to the Jukun community of Wuse located north of the River Benue, and finally, in the nineteenth century, the capital was shifted to Wukari. The name "Wukari" relates to the Jukun settlement established in Kwararafa which developed close to the Abakwariga town of Chika, a major centre of weaving and dyeing.

This process of decline and change gave rise to a number of successor states, including various fragments and colonies in the middle belt. The region in which both Uka and Wukari were located was called Apa; and the rural areas of Apa had been populated by Idoma Nokwu. After the migration of the Idoma Nokwu, during the turmoil of the seventeenth century, they called their new region of settlement Apa in remembrance of their homelands in Kwararafa. To distinguish between the two "Apa" regions E.O. Erim referred to them as Apa I and Apa II.[47] The Kwararafa diaspora of the seventeenth century from Apa I, included Koro, Bini, Gwari, Idoma Nokwu and some Jukun and Abakwariga. This exodus gave rise to a number of distinctive successor states, and each polity reflected the ethnic origins of the founders which they had retained throughout their association with Kwararafa.

Jukun colonies were established throughout the Benue Valley and seem to have differed substantially in time of settlement. A few of the earlier colonies remain in the southern Gongola Basin, and Jukun are evident in the demographic mixture in Pindiga. Other successor states in the Benue Basin indicate Jukun connections, and in some cases have retained Jukun as the dominant language, including Awe, Wuse, Azara, and Akiri. The main upper Benue settlement for Bini colonists was Dampar; while in Rugwagu, Shabu, Giza and Kanje the Jukun and Abakwariga continue to share the throne. The Bini-Idoma Nokwu population founded successor states or new dynasties in Idah, Ankpa, Doma, Keana, Adoka, Ugboju, Oturkpo, and Etulo, to name but a few. The history of Kwararafa, therefore, seems to come to a fairly abrupt end during the seventeenth century dispersal, which accounted for the creation of a number of national social formations representing single ethnic groups, and a number of chiefdoms that retained more of the multi-ethnic flavour of the parent state and continued to recognize principals of a shared central administration.

This chapter has examined briefly the developments in Kwararafa as the changing fortunes of this sudanic zone state reflected the changing political and economic focus of the Benue Basin. The shift into the middle belt coincided with the demise of northern commerce and the rise of southern trade. The combination of factors which led to the decline and eventual collapse of this once powerful trading formation included internal dissension and external pressures. Some of the external factors were far beyond the ability of the state government to control or change, while others represented the impositions by violent, aggressive and imperialist-minded neighbours, such as Kano, Bornu and Idah. Internal inter-ethnic competition for paramount political and economic status in a state with no constitutional foundations for single ethnic domination was one of the significant factors in the demise of Kwararafa. Furthermore, the economic transformation wrought by the collapse of the Songhai pax and the expansion of Atlantic overseas trade created a new commercial pattern which directly affected political developments in many Benue Basin states, including Kwararafa. These purely regional political and economic conditions must also be correlated with the major climatic fluctuations which seriously affected political and economic decisions. Thus the expansion of southern forest zone trade and the vagaries of the sudanic zone environment can be directly related to the decline of Kwararafa, the Kwararafa diaspora of the seventeenth century, and the emergence of the various successor states in the middle belt.

Reference

1 J.B. Webster, "The Three Phases of Kwararafa: A Peripatetic State", in *Central Nigerian Perspectives*, edited by E. Isichei, forthcoming.

2. Relations between Kwararafa, Kano and Bornu were particularly close - physically, economically and culturally - prior to the sixteenth century. As the Kwararafan capital retrenched southward the physical relationships were weakened, and the economic and cultural attachments severed.

3. A.N. Nwauwa, 'The Aro Chiefdom: Chronology and State Formation c. 1690-1720', Dalhousie University MA., 1989, p. 78.

4. O.N. Njoku, 'A History of Iron Technology in Igboland, c. 1542-1900', Dalhousie University PhD., 1986, p. 82.

5. During the initial planning stages of the Benue Valley History Project in 1974 the importance of Kwararafa was clearly recognized, and a researcher was assigned the responsibility for collecting, recording and subsequently analyzing oral and documentary records for this state. Unfortunately this research was prematurely curtailed after the production of only a preliminary paper, based upon limited archival and published sources. See J. Sterkin, 'Some Reflections on Kwararafa', Amadu Bello University Seminar, Jos, 1974. This paper adds little to the general knowledge about Kwararafa, but it did emphasize the Abakwariga domination of the state during the early period.

6. Refer, for example, to C.K. Meek, *A Sudanese Kingdom*, New York, 1969 (reprint), and Sa'ad Abubakar, 'The Middle Benue Region Up to c. 1850', Amadu Bello University Seminar, Jos, 1974. Also see H.R. Palmer, *The Bornu, Sahara and Sudan*, London, 1936 (reprinted in 1970 by Negro Universities Press, New York), and H.R. Palmer, *Sudanese memoirs*, 3 Volumes, Lagos, 1922.

7. The chronology for Kwararafa was established by J.B. Webster, "To the Palace Gates", *History of Africa*, Vol. 11, 1984. Also refer to the Kwararafan regnal list.

8. Abubakar, 'The Middle Benue Region', p. 2. Also see H.R. Palmer's introduction to Meek, *A Sudanese Kingdom*, which suggests that the Jukun came from the east and subsequently migrated southward into the Benue Basin and the Lake Chad region. The southern origins for the Jukun, which completely oppose Palmer's view, have been expressed by Webster, "The Three Phases of Kwararafa", and 'Animals of the Kingdom', Benue Valley Project Paper No. 6, 1975, pp. 3-4. A great deal of supporting evidence can be marshalled to confirm Webster's conclusion, including linguistics, material culture, migration traditions, and settlement patterns. C. Hoffman, "The Languages of Nigeria by Language Family", in Studies in Nigerian Languages, Vol. 5, 1976, shows Jukunoid as a Cross River language, and thus cannot be northern sudanic in origins.

9. *The Kano Chronicle*, translated by H.R. Palmer, and reprinted in J.A. Burdon, *Northern Nigeria*, London, 1090, pp. 27-29. The description of the attack on Santolo suggests certain important characteristics about the "key to the south." When the Kanawa entered Santolo, they attacked the main religious centre and found "a bell, and two horns, a battle axe and leg irons", which they plundered. "Yaji stayed seven days.and destroyed the place of sacrifice, and after dismantling its walls and tree and important religious shrine returned to Kano."

This description leaves no doubt that Santolo was a pagan stronghold. The evidence also suggests that a connection between Santolo and the Koro-Migili, who have been described as the "people of the horns." Refer to J. Power, "Lafia: Layers of Settlement', Dalhousie University, Honours Essay, 1984. The Koro claim to have left Kwararafa at a very early stage, and probably came out in three distinct waves. The first wave came from Santolo, the second from Tagara, and the third from Biepi.

10. Abubakar, 'The Middle Benue Region', p. 5.
11. J.E. Miller, 'The Babur Dynasty of Biu', Dalhousie University, MA., 1984, and Power, 'Lafia'.
12. Palmer, *The Bornu, Sahara and Sudan*, p. 222.
13. *Gazetteers of the Northern Province of Nigeria*, Vol. 1, *The Hausa Emirates*, London, 1972. *The Gazetteer of Kano Province*, originally compiled by W.F. Gowers, published in London, 1921, p. 2.
14. Palmer, *The Bornu, Sahara, and Sudan*, p. 223.
15. Webster, "The Three Phases of Kwararafa", and Miller, 'The Babur Dynasty of Biu'.
16. Power, 'Lafia: Layers of Settlement'.
17. Refer to A.E. Afigbo, "The Aro of South-eastern Nigeria: A Socio-Historical Analysis of Their Origins", Part II, *African Notes*, VI, 2, 1971, pp. 91-106; G.I. Jones, "Who are the Aro?", *Nigerian Field*, No. 3, 1939, pp. 100-103; and F.I. Ekejuiba, "The Aro System of Trade in the Nineteenth Century", *Ikenga*, 1972.
18. J.B. Webster, 'Periodization in African History, c. 1050-1850', Dalhousie University Pre-Colonial Workshop, June 1983, p. 7.
19. P.E. Lovejoy and S. Baier, "The Desert-Side Economy of the Central Sudan", *The International Journal of African Historical Studies*, VIII, 4, 1975, p. 572.
20. D.J. Schove, "African Droughts and the Spectrum of Time", in *Droughts in Africa*, edited by D. Dalby and R.J.H. Church, London, 1973.
21. Palmer, *The Bornu, Sahara and Sudan*, p. 228.
22. Ibn Fartua, *History of the First Twelve Years of the Reign of Mai Idris Alooma*, translated by H.R. Palmer, Lagos, 1926.
23. *The Kano Chronicle*, p. 35.
24. Hoffman, "The Langues of Nigeria".
25. It would appear that the Bini expansion up the River Benue began as early as c. 1482-1537 during the major expansion of the Benin empire. The foundation of a Bini dynasty at Idah in c. 1507- 1537 added impetus to the organization of Bini trading colonies.
26. I.H.T. No. 5, Idah, January 8, 1977.
27. J.B. Webster, 'Spirits of the Kingdom', Benue Valley Project Paper No. 7, 1975.
28. The Koro-Gwari component had been greatly weakened by the migration from Tagara of a large segment of this population.
29. E.O. Erim, *Idoma Nationality, 1600-1900*, Enugu, 1981, pp. 2-30.
30. I.H.T. No. 5, Idah, January 8, 1977.
31. *Ibid.*, and repeated in a similar form in Meek, *Sudanese Kingdom*, p. 266.
32. Meek, *Sudanese Kingdom*, p. 266. Refer to the statements that "Kenjo is also the patron of war", and "the cult of Kenjo is a very ancient Jukun cult."
33. *The Kano Chronicle*, p. 38.
34. *Ibid.*

35. P.D. Curtin, *Economic Change in Precolonial Africa: Supplementary Evidence*, Madison, 1975, p. 5.
36. Palmer, *The Bornu, Sahara and Sudan*, p. 248.
37. Lovejoy and Baier, "The Desert-Side Economy", p. 572. This argument states that the "Tuareg trade network and commercial infrastructure not only formed a link between the economies of the desert and savanna, but also provided a safety valve for the desert during drought."
38. Palmer, *The Bornu, Sahara and Sudan*, p. 246.
39. *Ibid.*, pp. 246-247.
40. *The Kano Chronicle*, p. 38.
41. *Ibid.*, pp. 38-39. Also see S.J. Hogben and A. Kirk-Greene, *The Emirates of Northern Nigeria*, London, 1966, p. 195.
42. *The Kano Chronicle*, pp. 38-39.
43. *Ibid.*, p. 27.
44. *Ibid.*, p. 28.
45. Webster, "The Three Phases of Kwararafa".
46. *Ibid.*
47. Erim, *Idoma Nationality*, pp. 14-20. Also see E.O. Erim, 'The Pre-Colonial History of the Idoma of Central Nigeria', Dalhousie University, Ph.D., 1976.

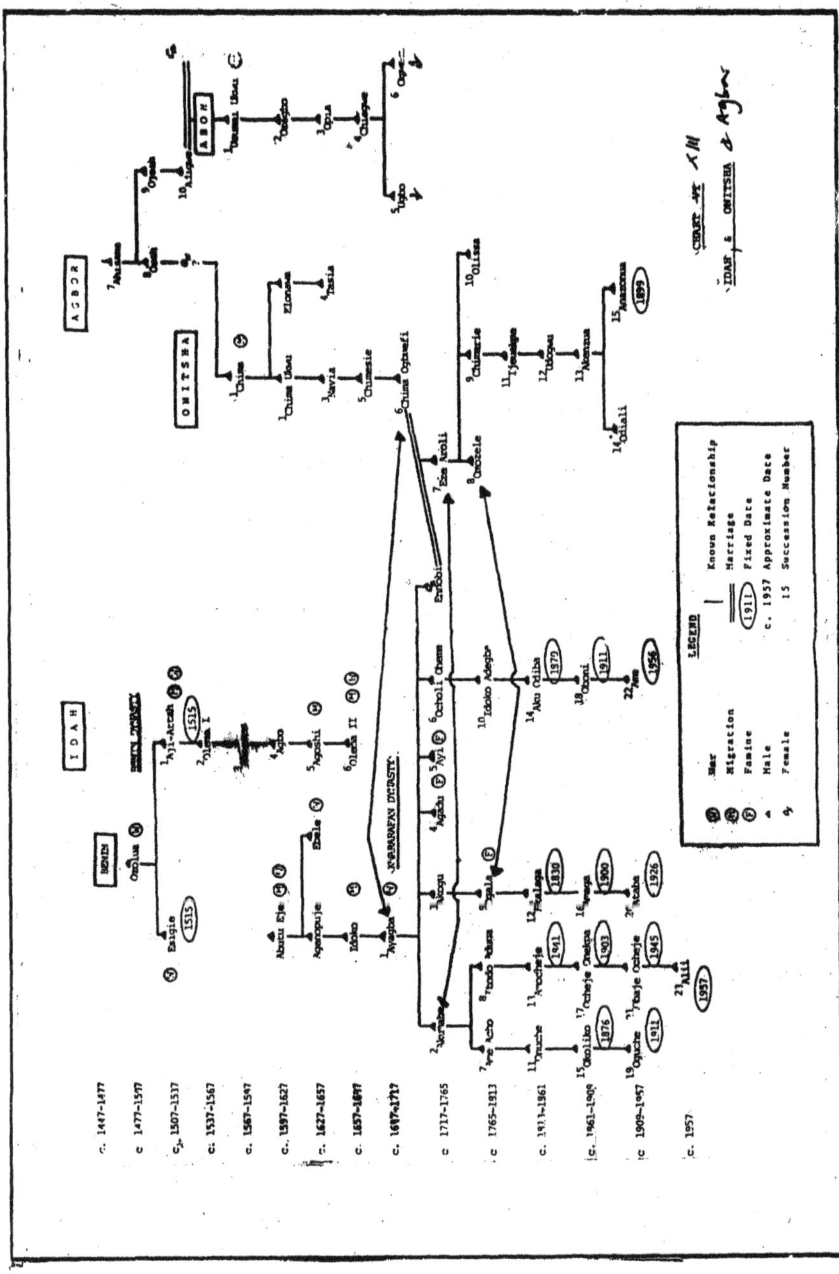

Chart XIII: Idah, Onisha and Agbor

Chapter 8

Demographics, Trade And Political Change Kwararafa And Idah c. 1600-1700

The decline of Kwararafan political and economic power in the northern sudanic zone and the corresponding slow retrenchment southward into the Benue Valley prompted waves of outward migration from that confederacy.[1] This Kwararafan diaspora contributed to the rise of a number of successor states in the middle belt and sudanic zone. Part of this much larger diaspora was the Bini-Idoma Nokwu migration from Kwararafa during the period c. 1597-1657.[2] This emigration was a response to the political, demographic, social and economic transformation of the upper Benue, and the rise of Jukun political and economic predominance which restricted Bini and Idoma Nokwu in both the commercial and political affairs. This chapter examines the changing demographic patterns and the rise of the successor states. Particularly attention has been focused upon the emergence of the third Idah dynasty which replaced the Bini monarchy in the confluence region. The Agatu diaspora, a second phase in the demographic shift of the seventeenth century, which fragmented the Idoma Nokwu into its component parts and the emergence of an Idoma Nokwu-Bini dynastic authority in the middle belt significantly altered Benue Basin political geography. For example, when Ayagba-om-Idoko replaced the Bini monarch at Idah the policy of accommodation followed by his administration gave rise to the Igala Kingdom and the development of an imperial trading formation that utilized Okpoto, Igbo and Idoma Nokwu in the government of a re-invigorated and imperially-minded state.[3]

The Idoma Nokwu or Greater Doma population disassociated from Kwararafa because of a decline in both its political and economic influence within the confederacy. The changing demographic features of Kwararafa, with a massive influx of Jukun after c. 1567-1597, contributed to this decline and resulted in a corresponding increase in Jukun power, influence and economic domination. The Bini community on the upper Benue suffered a similar fate, and joined with the Greater Doma in opposition to both the Abakwariga and Jukun. The seizure of political power by Adi Agba Kenjo in c. 1610-1640, not only elevated Jukun authority over that of the Greater Doma, but served to enhance Jukun commercial and economic progress at the expense of other ethnic groups.[4]

The eventual overthrow of Kenjo in c. 1640-1670 returned an Abakwariga to the throne, but did little to reassure Greater Doma or Bini political concerns. The majority of Greater Doma apparently opted to disassociate completely from Kwararafa, no matter the social or economic costs of leaving their homelands, and chose migration down the River Benue as the logical alternative to continued involvement in a state which catered little to their ambitions and needs. The first wave of the Greater Doma diaspora began in c. 1597-1627 and the exodus continued unabated for the next two generations.[5] The dominant element in Kwararafa, particularly the Abakwariga monarch, Adashu Katakpa, and his successor King Agwabi in c. 1640-1700,[6] endeavoured to retain some measure of solidarity in the confederacy by trying to force the Bini and Greater Doma to accept their authority and to pay tribute to Uka.[7] Katakpa and Agwabi dispatched the army to coerce the refugees to remain within the state, but the right of protest, and the option to disassociate through emigration, were vigorously defended. The hard-won autonomy resulted in the founding of a number of new settlements throughout the lower and middle Benue Valley; settlements which recreated much of the administrative ideology, social structures and political culture of the parent state. Agatu thus became the first major successor state which reflected the Kwararafan origins of its refugee population.

The political culture of Kwararafa was constructed upon a shared basis for political power. Each of the main populations had an effective voice, and could be represented in the central government as either male- or female-side segments of the royalists and commoners. The various groups in the Kwararafan diaspora of the seventeenth century transported elements of this culture during their emigration down the Benue. It is partly through the examination of these inherited political traits, and the comparison of material and political culture, social institutions and language that we can establish the links between so many of the middle belt populations and polities. The wide occurrence of similar political and social institutions, such as the shared political arrangement, or the common totems and taboos, are all testament to the pervasive influence of the Kwararafan heritage.

Information from the distinctive elements in the diaspora shows that the largest contingent, the Greater Doma, was made up of elements which went into the Idoma, the Alago, and the Igala.[8] The Etulo, Koro and Abakwariga traditions corroborate the date of departure at c. 1597-1627, and confirm that the system of government in Agatu was a reconstitution of the shared political authority evident in Kwararafa.[9] The political culture of Kwararafa was thus transported intact and recreated even in polities which were not directly involved in the original constitutional rotation. The Bini settlement at Dampar, for example, although it was not party to the migration down the Benue, retained the shared system in its administration. It would seem, therefore, that the settlement at Dampar had been directly altered by Kwararafan political culture and no longer displayed the centralized ideology of a dominant ruling elite common to Bini settlements elsewhere. This can be seen as a political accommodation probably based upon rational economic considerations. Through such accommodations a numerically small sector of the population may hold political power in a cooperative arrangement with other sectors. Retaining political power also seems to establish economic opportunities which can thus be exploited by the empowered sectors. A number of other smaller communities, including the Etulo,[10] adopted or retained the Kwararafan political culture and still share the monarchy between various ethnic groups.[11]

In part, the circumstances of successor state formation necessitated the transfer of the political culture. The successor states were, after all, separating from Kwararafa because of changes in the political structure of that parent state. They were thus objecting to centralization and violations of the constitutional structures. As the balance of power in Kwararafa shifted, the impetus for disassociation by disaffected sectors of the population increased. Furthermore, the central authorities in Kwararafa objected to the disassociation response. The exodus by the alienated Greater Doma-Bini population was not a peaceful departure in search of new and more stable settlements. Troops loyal to Adashu Katakpa and Agwabi repeatedly tried to force the refugees to comply with state policy, pay state tribute, and recognize the Abakwariga-Jukun government.[12] It was only after a decisive encounter in Agatu, where the Kwararafan forces where turned back by the emigrants, that these migrants achieved relative security. The circumstances of the Kwararafan diaspora, therefore, were hardly conducive to experimentation with new political forms or methods of administration. The situation in Agatu, where an immigrant refugee population was seriously threatened not only by the Kwararafan army, but also by the violent opposition of the Bini dynasty in Idah, demanded a strong government which could provide recognized, legitimate, stable authority and organize the defense of Agatu against the Kwararafan and Idah opponents.

The rotational principle of the central government of Agatu, reflecting the political culture of the multi-ethnic parent state, was not the only common custom or cultural trait inherited by the refugees. One of the main unifying features in the Greater Doma population was a linguistic affinity which linked the various sub-groups in a common language family. The Greater Doma form a sub-division of the Kwa language, and this linguistic classification (1.a.4.6.) includes the Alago, Idoma, Yala, Awka, Igede and Etulo.[13] As Kress and Hodges argued, "language.... is a key instrument in socialization, and the means whereby society forms (and).permeates the individual's consciousness."[14] In this respect, the mutually intelligible sub-group languages of the Greater Idoma suggests that they not only had similar backgrounds, but that this cultural affinity was maintained long after the Kwararafan diaspora of the seventeenth century.

Another of the important examples of common cultural heritage retained in the successor states was a strong taboo against menstrual blood.[15] This taboo, directed primarily against food prepared by menstruating women, was part of Igala, Idoma, Alago and Jukun culture.[16] It seems to have been commonly held by people from different communities within the same cultural complex and enabled these people to interact - socially, economically and politically according to a clearly defined set of rules. Intermarriage between groups who held the menstrual taboo was recognized and encouraged, whereas groups outside the taboo system were not acceptable as marriage partners. In economic terms the taboo enabled individuals in an exchange relationship to operate with known and mutually acceptable norms. Thus, when two traders met to discuss business they could operate confident in the knowledge that their interaction was based upon common cultural practices. Also, this taboo was related to the royal custom among the Greater Doma and of all Jukun of eating in relative seclusion, and the general avoidance of discussion concerning both food and drink.[17] The menstrual taboo and eating customs probably originated in Kwararafa and developed relatively early in its history. The taboo became a symbol of early associations with Kwararafa, and still defines the outer limits of social interaction and inter-marriage for ethnic groups which adhere to it today.

A third common cultural trait, not only displayed by the Greater Doma but popular among the other ethnic elements that originated in Kwararafa, was the piercing of the ear. As early as c. 1539-1559, the Mai of Bornu had noted that the Kwararafans had "holes in their ears."[18] The third Igala dynasty in Idah, descendant from the Greater Doma segment of the Kwararafan diaspora, perpetuated the custom, and the ear piercing ritual became an important part of the coronation ceremony.[19] The Osana (Chief) of Keana, one of the Alago polities in the Obasadoma (Alago homeland), also has his ear pierced during the installation ceremony.[20] A great many Jukun in the Benue

Basin still practice this custom and wear the earring associated with Kwararafa. This cultural symbolism is significant in the political arena as the earring carries particular messages about the status and authority of the wearer.

Perhaps the most significant cultural symbols of the former Kwararafan population scattered throughout the Benue Basin were totemic beliefs. The degree of totemic similarity throughout the middle belt indicates that these diverse populations were directly related genealogically or commonly affiliated politically within the Kwararafan confederacy. Kinship totems signify, symbolically at least, the relationship between an individual or group and his or its family and clan. Similarities in totemic belief systems facilitate social intercourse and inter-marriage relations among various ethnic groups and clans. Furthermore, similar totemic systems can reveal common (genetic) relationships among what might appear to be widely separated and distant groups. Not every population holds the same symbols; on the contrary there are some important distinctions between Igala, Idoma, Alago, Jukun and Abakwariga totems. But there is sufficient similarity to point to a common origin. As Ataba has noted,

> As [a] member of a large clan, a man is related to common and distant ancestors symbolized by sacred animals [totems and taboos], as a member of a lineage, to closer ancestors symbolized by totems."[21]

Totemic relationships might, in fact, prove to be one of the more concrete determinants of a common ancestory in disparate populations.[22] Totems are generally fairly stable indicators of an individual's relationships. The genealogical relations are perhaps the most stable of all as they indicate ties of kinship. Political totems are slightly more flexible as the individual may alter political affiliations in a changing political demography, and seek through political totemism to align with a new political authority.

The following list identifies totemic data for the Benue Valley and connects individual totems with groups and possible origins of the totemic symbol. This data indicates that the successor states, and the various Kwararafa refugee colonies in the middle belt, were related to the Greater Doma, Bini, Koro, Abakwariga or Jukun before the diaspora. The totemic data also suggests that while the exodus and re-settlement in the Agatu enclave may have been dominated by Bini and Great Doma clans there were remnants of the Koro, Abakwariga and Jukun in this diaspora. This totemic evidence thus indicates that the 1597-1657 diaspora distributed the Kwararafan ethnically-mixed population throughout the middle belt, and in the process preserved those symbols which served to identify or define the various components. The distribution of the manatee totemic group, for example, shows that this population, the major riverine transportation population in the Benue Basin, retained that special interest in waterborne trade. Crocodile and leopard groups also appear throughout the Benue Basin, and became the royal totems in a number of the successor states. Commoner totems in the diaspora include black monkey, agba fish, fox, and ground squirrel.

Totems in the Benue Basin

Totem	*Distribution*		*Possible Origins*
Leopard	Iyala	Nupe	**Benin**
	Alago	Idoma	
	Igala	Etulo	
	Benin	Egede	
	Koro		
Manatee	Etulo	Bura	**Jukun/Proto-Aro**
	Jukun	Pabir	(Cross River) ≥
	Igala	Kede	
	Ijaw	Banu	
	Koro	Aro	
	Efik		
Crocodile	Igala	doma	**Bura-Pabir**
	Alago	Abakwariga	
	Etulo	Koro	
	Jukun		
Civet Cat	Igala	yala	**Okpoto**
	Idoma	Egede	
	Etulo	Koro	
	Igbirra		
Monitor Lizard	Mada Eggon		**Eggon**
	Koro		
	Idoma		
Dog & Snail	Igala		**Igbo**
	Igbo		
Snake/Python	Abakwariga		**Abakwariga**
	Koro		

The exodus of leopard, crocodile, manatee, red monkey and other royal and commoner groups drastically altered the demographic and political balance throughout the middle belt. The movement of ambitious royalist sectors into the confluence region, for example, served to alter substantially the balance of political and economic power. Royalist who could acquire the backing of large commoner populations shifted the potential for political authority away from the entrenched ruling class. With the settlement at Agatu increasing through the influx of more and more Kwararafan refugees political, economic, social and cultural factors shifted in favour of the ruling elite within that Kwararafan population. The Agatu enclave, in particular, emerged as a prominent Benue trading centre endeavouring to exercise wide political authority at the expense of the Bini dynasty in Idah.

The leadership in Agatu had been considered by the refugee population as a legitimate contender for the Kwararafan throne.[23] But Abuto Eje (c. 1597-1627), the leader of the leopard community, had his candidacy swept aside in the Jukun seizure of power under Adi Agba Kenjo.[24] Abutu Eje and Adoga Oje,[25] the leader of the Idoma segment in the migration, responded to this alteration in the political constitution of Kwararafa by leaving their Apa settlements. These Greater Doma leaders thus sought alternative settlement outside the Kwararafan sphere of influence and hoped to sever the ties with the parent state. Abutu Eje and Adoga Oje led their supporters to Apa II and founded the Agatu enclave. The refugee population in Agatu endeavoured to establish a political order in which Kwararafan constitutional principles would be honoured and the shared monarchy recreated.

The Kwararafan military endeavoured to force the Agatu refugees to accept the paramount authority of the parent state but were vigorously repulsed. After the assassination of Adi Agba Kenjo, Adashu Katakpa tried to consolidate Kwararafan power and solidify the peripheral areas through the conquest of Agatu. An attack on the refugee enclave in c. 1640-1670 resulted in the death of Abutu Eje and the rise of Adoga Oje as the successor in the rotating system. The battles for Agatu did not encourage the refugees to accept Kwararafan authority, and Abutu Eje became the "martyr of Agatu" and a permanent symbol of their struggle for independence.[26] Abutu Eje was buried in a sacred grove at

Amagedde, in the Agatu enclave, and this spot is still considered an important shrine to the Igala, Idoma and Alago.

Adashu Katakpa's persistence in attempting to force Agatu to recognize his paramount authority probably stemmed from his perception of the regional economy and regional commerce. Agatu was in an advantageous position to control Benue riverine trade, and could effectively seal off this commercial link to the south, and thus prevent Kwararafan merchants from gaining access to the Niger. Also, Agatu managed to wrestle Loko, an important crossing point on the Benue from Idah's control, and came to dominate the north-south overland trade route. Kwararafa's primary concern was the competition for southern overland trade, and to exercise a regional monopoly in the distribution of goods imported from the Atlantic overseas trade into the sudanic zone it was necessary to control both Agatu and Loko. The Kwararafan diaspora thus established a three way competition for pre-eminence in middle belt commerce, and the role of middleman in the distribution of forest zone and Atlantic overseas products into the sudan was vigorously contested by Idah, Agatu and Kwararafa.

As the newcomer to middle belt political life and commercial development Agatu depended upon an ability to develop effective non-centralized, constitutional principles of government which might prove attractive to the other populations in the middle belt. The rotational, or shared pattern of succession in the Agatu enclave was dissimilar to the highly centralized authority of the government at Idah and proved to be an attractive alternative to both Igbo and Okpoto in the middle belt. They apparently could align with the Agatu leaders, and develop female-side relations to enhance their political status, while directly contributing to the commercial development in the Loko overland trading system. Thus Agatu became a regional competitor, and incorporated large segments of the indigenous Okpoto and Igbo into the operations of the state.

The following tradition rationalizes the eventual failure of Agatu as an independent, multi-ethnic middle belt polity, and accounts for the diaspora of Greater Doma across a much broader region. This tradition also traces the pattern of shared succession in the Agatu enclave, and emphasizes the problems associated with the collapse of the reconstructed constitutional process among the refugee population:

> The rule of succession was that it went between several ruling houses. Thus.the chieftaincy stool alternated between the Alago, Idoma and Igala families... The rotational principle was strictly adhered to by all. Soon trouble started to brew... After Igala and Idoma [Abutu Eje and Adoga Oje] had served their turn the Alago put forward Ogiri as the next king... It was at this time that the Igala raised a constitutional objection. The Alago left and moved eastward. In fact, they left at nightfall after refusing peaceinitiatives by the Igala and Idoma.[27]

The Igala and Idoma raised their constitutional objection because "Atah Ogiri died before he was fully installed as king, and this represented an official turn."[28] When the Alago tried to offer another candidate the Igala argued that after the death of Ogiri it was their turn in the rotation.[29] According to normal succession patterns the rotation went Igala, Idoma and Alago, and the Igala had the right to select the next candidate. The Alago maintained that Ogiri had not been a ruler and that they were entitled to name his successor.

This tradition clearly rationalizes the failure of Agatu politics, and accounts for the Agatu diaspora in terms of political differences. It does not, however, include the severe pressures maintained by the Kwararafa monarchy in the attempt to conquer Agatu, or the disruptive influence of the Idah monarchy in their attempt to undermine Agatu's stability. Yet the aggressive stance of the regional competitors must have contributed to the fragile nature of Agatu politics and the subsequent Agatu diaspora. The following schematic chart shows the relationships between the three parties in the Agatu dispute and the connections between the Alago component and the Bini monarchy in Idah. This alliance, in which the Idah rulers backed the Alago claim, exacerbated the divisions within the Agatu population,[30] and clearly contributed to the diaspora. King Agoshi of Idah endeavoured to influence this decision in favour of the Alago, but Igala and Idoma objections prevailed. The debate provided additional impetus for the dispersal of Greater Doma from Agatu, and with the threat or renewed Kwararafa violence, the population scattered throughout the middle Benue region. When the Alago component in Agatu opted to emigrate rather than see their political power overturned in a constitutional debate, they moved north to join King Agoshi in Doma. Agoshi, the former ruling Bini monarch in Idah, had been under considerable pressure from the combined Okpoto, Igbo and Greater Doma alliance in Agatu, and apparently considered his economic position in the riverine enclave untenable after the seizure of Loko and the re-direction of tribute to the Kwararafa leaders in Apa II. He "assumed that the reign of his son would be more acceptable" and that King Olema II would salvage Bini authority in the confluence region.[31] Agoshi, therefore, became a prominent figure in the political developments north of the River Benue and contributed to the foundations of new dynasties in Keana and Doma. The dynasty in Keana emerged as a particularly significant political power, and developed an important economic base through the major salt deposits in the region.[32] The centralized government of Doma and Keana thus reflected the Bini-Idah and Alago-Kwararafan alliance which had been unsuccessful in the constitutional debate in Agatu. Thus political intervention, constitutional breakdown, military aggression, and economic rivalry all contributed to the instability of Agatu and the collapse of social and political cohesion. The Idoma, Iyala and Egede segments of the Greater Doma expanded southward from Agatu and established a large number of independent polities in greater Idomaland.[33] The Igala component began to expand to the southwest, and aligned with the Okpoto and Igbo to accommodate their resettlement near the confluence. Both Idoma and Igala expansions were facilitated through their interactions with the Okpoto and Igbo, and the process of assimilation resulted in the cultural and linguistic domination of the Greater Doma over these 'indigenous' populations.

Schematic Chart of Agatu Politics

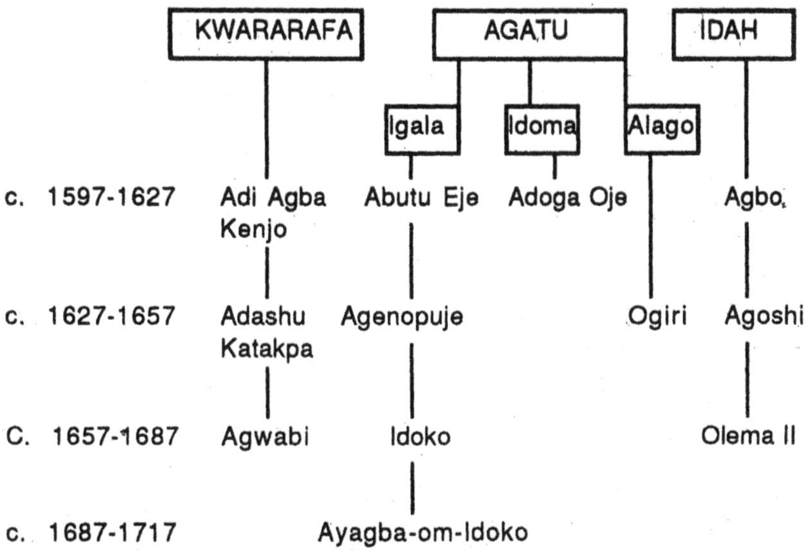

The Kwararafa diaspora, and the subsequent dispersal from Agatu, therefore, provided the impetus for the creation of a new political geography and the emergence of a number of re-formed polities in the middle belt.

The expansion of the Igala component of the Greater Doma population eventually served to isolate the Idah dynasty from a number of its vassal, tribute-paying chiefdoms on the eastern borders. The process of reducing the economic base for the Bini authority in Idah thus began with the redistribution of tribute, with its symbolic recognition of political authority. The highly polarized society in the Idah enclave thus sought to redefine its allegiance and provided an opportunity for the Igala-Kwararafan royalists to interact and eventually align with the subordinate Okpoto and Igbo.

Furthermore, this alliance between an incoming royal segment and the indigenous local population served to isolate the Bini further from important commercial contacts, and thus extended economic pressures on the Bini government. The trade route through Loko, for example, fell under Igala - Kwararafa control in c. 1627-1657,[34] and commercial organization in the middle Benue region gravitated toward Agatu rather than Idah. By c. 1657-1687, the Igala-Kwararafan expansion had severed Idah's contacts with Keana and Doma where the Bini under Agoshi were playing an influential role in the development of the salt industry, and thus further isolated King Olema II in the Idah enclave.

By c. 1657-1687 the combination of Okpoto, Igbo and Igala-Kwararafans had become a potent political force intent upon forcing dynastic change in Idah. The Igala-Kwararafans openly expressed their political ambitions, and received the economic support of the local chiefs and commoner population. The policy of inter-marriage with the indigenous population, something that the Bini dynasty in Idah had never encouraged, cemented the social and political association of Igala-Kwararafan, Okpoto and Igbo, and suggested to the latter groups that a formal alliance would result in their "involvement in decisions of state and governmental affairs."[35] The political choice was apparently not a difficult one for the suppressed and exploited Okpoto and Igbo in and around the Idah enclave. The depredations of the Bini dynasty for the past one hundred and fifty years had alienated its subjects, and the potential of the Kwararafan alliance "was plain for all to see."[36]

The first official act to cement the relationship between the indigenous population and the Kwararafan refugees was marriage between a Kwararafan princess and a prominent Igbo. Inter-marriage was an effective mechanism whereby political and social alliances could be established, and assimilation and acculturation might begin. The liaison between a daughter of the "martyr of Agatu" (Abutu Eji) and an Igbo representative called Ahaga Okpoluwa established an official connection between Kwararafan and Igbo aspirations.[37] The romantic traditions recalling this marriage between Princess Ebele and Ahage Okpoluwa are detailed:

> Ebele Jauna was a woman of the royal family of Wukari [Kwararafa], she was the daughter of Abutu Eje, and her brother was the great leader

> Agenopuje. She came with a great number of followers after the battle atAgatu in which her father was killed. One day a young man was captured by one of her hunting parties and brought to her as a slave. His name was Ahaga Okpoluwa, an Igbo. In the morning all the men went out hunting and the women said they wanted Ahaga to help them. He was called and put to work. The women observed his good looks and splendid figure and told Ebele about him, saying it was a pity he was a slave as he would make a fine husband. Ebele said for them to be quiet because he was a free person before being enslaved. She used words like ushadu (slave) and oma (son). Ebele ordered water to be brought so that Ahaga might wash, and she presented him with a very fine black robe to dress in. That night when Ebele retired she sent for Ahaga and he spent the night with her. In the morning Ebele told him not to go back among the other people, and then she called her people and announced that they should salute Ahaga as her husband.[38]

A second version of this tradition provides an interesting variation on the major theme of inter-marriage and cross-cultural alliance. This particular variation came from the Achadu lineage, which was the title created for the offspring of the marriage between Ebele and Ahaga after the Kwararafan royalists assumed power in Idah. It therefore reveals the Igbo bias toward this association, and indicates the relationship between Ahaga and Ebele from the Igbo perspective. The Achadu, or Prime Minister, became the second most powerful position in the Idah administrative hierarchy after c. 1687-1717 when Attah Ayagba-om-Idoko founded the third Idah dynasty.

> Ahaga, who had the title Ashadu among the Igbo, came on a hunting expedition to the Idah area, and settled nearwhat is now called Igalogwu. Ebele Junu arrived with her followers and because of her power and beauty Ahaga wanted to marry this princess. They were married and because of his respect for his wife he ordered all his followers to become her subjects, and he himself offered to act as her slave.
>
> As Ahaga had arrived in the area before Ebele and had a previous claim to the land, she asked him to give her a title. He enquired what she wished to be called. Ebele responded by saying call me "Attah Ita", that is, "Attah" (father) and "Ita" (ends), meaning, "a father is the greatest title of all and ends the power of all others". He bargained with her as to what price such a title should cost. They agreed upon the sum

> of nine slaves. These were given on the condition that the next Ashadu would have to pay the reigning "Attah Ita" nine slaves when the Ashadu received confirmation of his title.[39]

The relationship between Ahaga and Ebele established a female-side title system, and promoted the descendants of this union to the politically prominent and powerful Achadu office. The concept of female-side title holders was imported from Kwararafa where female-side lineage heads were members of the Kingmakers Council, and thus played a significant intercursive political role in the power relations in the multi-ethnic confederation.[40] As female-side, these lineage heads had no overt or legitimate claim to the throne, but were, nevertheless extremely powerful titled officials who controlled access to the highest office in the state. Also, as female-side title holders they were less able to disrupt normal or constitutional succession directly. Ahaga's descendants thus became the female-side Achadu lineage, and the Igala Mela clan heads - the leaders of the Okpoto clans in the Idah enclave - became the Kingmakers' Council.

The Igala Mela clan leaders were also connected to the Kwararafa royalists through inter-marriage and became part of the central, female-side administrative body in the emerging Agatu alliance. The eventual recognition of the Achadu as the head of the Kingmakers Council, with the leading representatives of the nine Igala Mela clans as councillors, established a positive relationship between the male-side dynastic group and a major segment of the indigenous population. This relationship served to isolate the Bini dynasty from the subordinate vassal population. The changing balance of power, and the redirection of tribute and allegiance toward the Kwararafans and their allies clearly weakened Bini domination of Idah. Therefore the politically astute inter-marriage with the Okpoto and Igbo, and the promise of increased participation in the administration, provided the basis for the Kwararafan claim to political prominence.

The policy of association and the process of inter-marriage not only included the distribution of Kwararafan wives to the main representatives of the indigenous population, but also the acceptance of wives from the Igbo and Okpoto. This reciprocal marriage relationship strengthened the association of the various ethnic elements and cemented the political alliance of Okpoto, Igbo and Kwararafan. One of the most famous liaisons resulted in the Kwararafan monarchy at Ankpa, a prominent sub-chiefdom under the third Idah dynasty, which was a female-side descent group of the former Okpoto chieftaincy clan. Ayagba-om-Idoko's brother married an Okpoto princess in Ankpa and established a lineage which provided the legitimate candidates for the Onu (Chief) title. Apparently the Okpoto were willing to "accept the Kwararafans as ruler", and recognized the female-side as legitimate successors.[41]

Schematic Chart of Kwararafan-Okpoto Allianc

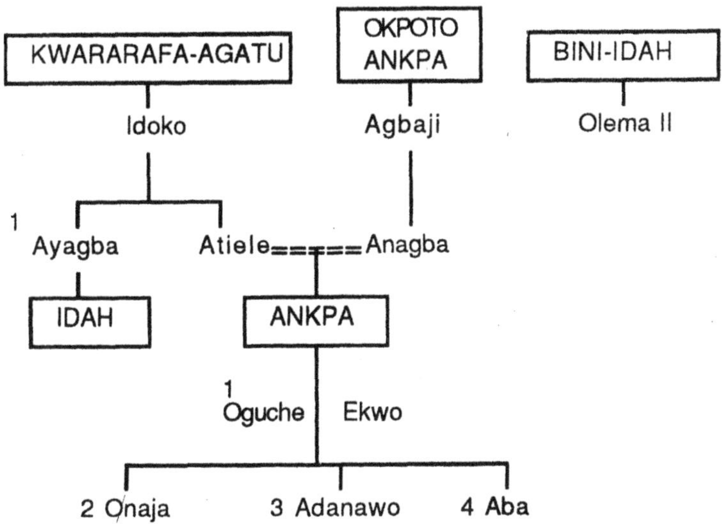

The foundation of a Kwararafan regime at Ankpa was only the first step in the development of the third dynastic era in Idah history. The marriage of Ahaga and Ebele, and Atiele and Anagba, contributed to the isolation of the Bini government in Idah, and may have struck the final blow to Bini political aspirations in the confluence region. Ayagba-om-Idoko, the heir to central leadership in the Kwararafan royal line, and the holder of Kwararafan royal regalia, continued to press for the removal of the Bini monarchy. Ayagba's claim to this title was supported by the Achadu Igbo, the Igala Mela Okpoto, and the new Ankpa regime which recognized him as the "legitimate power in the region".[42] This public recognition of the Kwararafan royal line was enhanced by the policy of association through intermarriage, Ayagba's own royal image, the success and popularity of the Ankpa regime, and the integration of Okpoto and Igbo in the central government. Contributing further to the foundation of Kwararafan political ambitions and their consolidation of political power was the royalist tradition imported from the Kwararafan confederacy. The leaders in the Agatu enclave had an impressive array of royal regalia, through which historic rights to rule and legitimate authority were embodied in symbolic objects. The use of the mask *Ejube-auilo* by the Bini dynasty, for example, is a classic case where a symbol of central government and political authority became a physical representation of that monarchy.[43] This kind of royal regalia is silent but eloquent testimony to the majesty of the past, the power of the present, and the potential for the future. *Ejube-auilo* became the symbol for the antagonism and hatred that characterized Bini rule over the Okpoto and Igbo. The Kwararafa royalists, on the other hand, managed not only to present an impressive monarch in full regalia, but coupled this imagery with policy designed to cement the relationships between central royal authority and commoner vassal subjects, and could use regalia as symbols of such positive associations.

One of the significant symbols of office brought from Kwararafa, and still held in high esteem in Idah, was a small brass bowl called *Ane*. The importance of this bowl lies in the cultural attributes associated with the Kwararafa population, and the manner in which the monarch had to eat and drink. The strict daily observances of special food taboos, ritual practices of eating in seclusion, and consuming only food prepared by virgins,[44] established an air of mystery around the Kwararafan leaders.

Schematic Chart of Kwararafan-Igbo Allianc

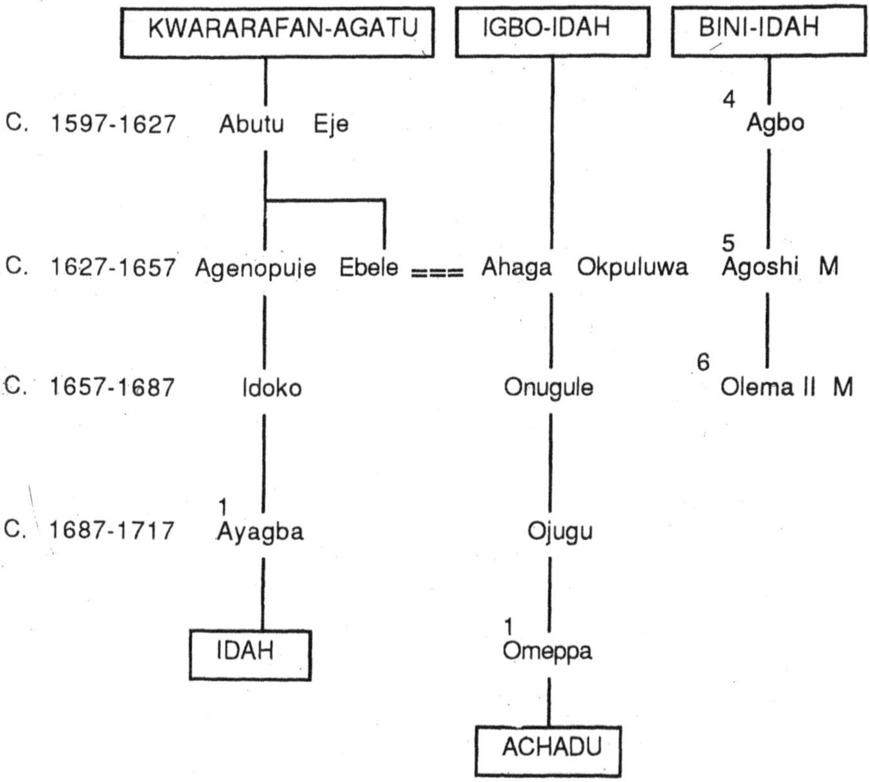

The Ane is part of this ritual, and is thus a spiritual reflection of the Kwararafan leadership. Furthermore, the *Ane* can be related to the paradox in Idah's social and political association, where the ruler is the recognized spiritual owner of the land (*ane*), while the Okpoto and Igbo are its physical owners. In this respect the "land bowl" serves to identify this relationship, and remind the central monarchy that the Okpoto and Igbo held prior claim to Igalaland and are an integral part of the state.[45] The description of the Ane also indicates the dual symbolism associated with this piece of Kwararafan royal regalia.

> *Ane* is.a small brass pot covered with cowries. it is believed to have been brought to Idah by the first Attah [Ayagba-om-Idoko]. A minute portion of whatever the Attah eats or drinks is placed in this. It is kept by the Okpoto.a eunuch takes charge of it on the death of the Attah. It is part of his duty to see that there is always water in it.[46]

The royal spurs were another important part of the Kwararafa royal regalia. The Igala claim that these "spurs came from Wukari, [sic. Biepi] and were brought to Idah by Abutu Eje."[47] According to Clifford these royal spurs are very similar to those worn by the Jukun, and they are probably remnants of the earlier cavalry traditions of Kwararafa.[48] The shrine of Adi Agba Kenjo, the famous warrior king of Kwararafa, contains a small carved wooden horse as a sacred relic, and the association of Kwararafa with horses and cavalry traditions dates back to the fourteen century.[49] The royal spurs in Idah, therefore, link the Greater Doma population in the confluence region with the Kwararafan military and political establishment, and establish a distinction between Bini and Kwararafa administrations.[50]

There were two other major items of royal regalia introduced by Ayagba-om-Idoko in c. 1687-1717. The first was a brass stool decorated with bells and relief figures. Only the ruler was allowed to sit on this stool. The second item was the ear decoration which was used to signify that the heir apparent was ready to mount the throne during his installation ceremony. The piercing of the ear was an important Kwararafan cultural symbol, and was recreated in many of the successor states. In Idah, the ceremony of piercing the ear was performed as a special ritual during the installation of each Kwararafan monarch in the third dynastic era.

> The Adu Kainya (Attah elect) must have his ear pierced like a woman. The actual ceremony of ear piercing is carried out by the Achadu's chief wife to whom is granted the title Achainya Anuku. Whilst performing the operation she is required to wear sandals and sit on a mat least through contact with her, the dynamism of the king elect be dissipated.[51]

The impressive regalia and the complex rituals surrounding the Kwararafan monarchy served to instill a sense of legitimacy and acceptance in the Okpoto and Igbo population. The mystery of kingship and the presence of the king in all his regalia clearly enhanced the image of royalty. Furthermore, Okpoto and Igbo segments of the commoner population were involved in this ritual process, and appointed to a variety of positions in the central bureaucracy. The development of the administrative structures, the delegation of responsibility, and the potent imagery associated with a semi-divine and mysterious monarch, all contributed to the legitimacy of the Kwararafan kings, and served to associate these rulers with the formal centralized government.

The increasing popularity of the Kwararafan administration was further enhanced by economic policies implemented to encourage widespread participation in commercial activities. The Kwararafan government in Agatu allowed free access to the markets, encouraged Igbo traders to pursue their professions, and lowered market taxes to encourage and expand trade. Tribute was also lowered, and thus the signs of loyalty to the administration were not only defined by economic support, but by inter-marriage and personal relationships. In these ways the association between Kwararafan royals and the commoner segments covered virtually every relevant aspect of social, political and economic affairs. With an active policy of integration and association it was not surprising that the Kwararafans became popular, and found a large support base for their political ambitions within the Okpoto and Igbo groups.

The growing power of the Kwararafan leaders, the popularity of their style of administration, and the abdication of King Agoshi in c. 1627-1657, served to weaken the Bini hold on the riverine capital of Idah and strengthen Kwararafan claims to paramount authority. Certainly by c. 1627-1657 the Bini authority in the hinterland had been undermined, and replaced with Kwararafan political administration. By c. 1657-1687 the pressures on the capital enclave were severe, and the Bini dynasty was at its weakest. Olema II clearly felt the economic pressures as he was powerless to halt the redirection of tribute to Kwararafan leaders. Furthermore, products from the hinterland no longer arrived in the capital. The ability of the Bini commercial agents, entrepreneurs and administrators was severely restricted, and commercial levies normally associated with the support of the central government in the trading formation were completely curtailed. Olema was thus cut off from most economic support and endeavoured to institute new policies designed to restore the power of his throne. He attempted to increase tribute from the few peripheral areas still under his authority, ordered compulsory military service, and imposed stringent control over the remaining trade routes.[52] However, a major exodus of Bini settlers from Idah in c. 1657-1687, in protest against the increase in taxes, negated any positive effects that might have been achieved by these decisions, and the Bini monarchy continued to weaken.

The emigration of Bini settlers down the River Niger in c. 1657-1687 was the result of the oppressive policies and increased tribute levies imposed by Olema II. The migrants eventually established a number of colonies south of Onitsha, which became significant outposts of the riverine trading network. Apparently the conditions in Idah had deteriorated to such an extent that these groups preferred to seek their fortune elsewhere, rather than remain under the exploitative administration of the Bini monarchy. It is significant, however, that they did not completely disassociate, and maintained the tradition that they were outposts of the Idah commercial system and thus represented Idah in the Niger informal alliance.

> According to tradition the eight groups that left Idah of Ika, Iteku, Inyaman, Iroma, Uje, Odekpe, Oko and Osomari originally lived in part of Idah, the capital of the Igala kingdom. Each group headed by its leader stopped in the course of their downward journey along the Niger and founded a community which today bears his name... Osomari was considered the most important and most powerful of the Igala colonies and traded not only with the Isuama Ibo of the hinterland but with the Igala to the north.[53]

The exodus down the Niger provided a crushing blow to Bini political ambitions in Idah, and Olema II found a large segment of his remaining supporters emigrating beyond his control. Other segments of the Bini population, particularly the Agaidoko clan, chose to support the Okpoto, Igbo and Kwararafan alliance, and openly opposed the imposition of increased tribute. The Agaidoko clan was one of the few Bini groups to develop any relationship with the Okpoto prior to c. 1657-1687, and their decision to align with the opposition may have been partially based upon this previous association.

By the late 17th century the severely weakened Bini monarchy and the increasingly powerful Kwararafan royalists seemed ready to exchange positions, and thereby create the third Idah dynasty under Ayagba-om-Idoko. The generation of Ayagba-om-Idoko and his brother Atiele (c. 1687-1717) witnessed the decimation of Olema's political and economic base. The Igbo, represented by the Achadu lineage, the Okpoto, under the Igala Mela clan heads, and a small number of Bini clans, such as the Agaidoko, severed their tributary relations with the Bini monarchy and offered their allegiance to Ayagba. Olema II was thus presented with a fait accompli, and found himself ruler of a restricted area and a tiny population, with few resources to back his claim to paramount authority. Achadu Omeppa approached this besieged monarch and offered him his life in exchange for the throne.[54] Olema II agreed and fled across the River Benue to join his father in exile.[55] The relatively peaceful coup[56] "provided the opportunity for Ayagba-om-Idoko to enter Idah as the first monarch in the third dynasty",[57] and supported by the Igbo (Achadu), Okpoto (Igala Mela) and Bini (Agaidoko), founded a popular and relatively egalitarian regime.

Between c. 1627-1657, there had been a concerted effort to develop relations with the indigenous population through inter-marriage, and this process resulted in political dividends for the Kwararafan royalists. It established the female-side supporters and titled officials who became influential in the eventual seizure of power. The connections between the royal aspirants and the Igbo and Okpoto were cemented not only through inter-marriage, but also through the development of an administration with an hereditary central bureaucracy which included representatives of every ethnic group in the state. Positions and rewards were widely distributed, and even before the ascendancy of the first Kwararafan monarch in the third dynasty almost every prominent Igbo or Okpoto had been appointed to an important position, or promised official status under the new regime. Attah Ayagba lived up to these promises and expanded the state bureaucracy through the incorporation of Igbo, Okpoto and Bini administrators, commercial managers, and ritual authorities.

The seizure of the reins of office was only the first step ir the creation of an effective and popular central administration. The Bini monarchy had failed to establish permanent links with the indigenous population, and provided no avenue through which support and allegiance to the government could be fostered. In contrast popular participation was a prominent feature of Kwararafan political structures, especially through the female-side title holders. Also, succession in Kwararafa had been an extremely effective mechanism for involving large numbers in the actual administration of the state. The new monarchy in Idah sought to recreate much of the Kwararafan system, and establish a bond between the royal house and the commoner population. The bonding system involved patronage titles, appointments, marriage gifts to prominent individuals, and the incorporation of almost every segment of the society in the political, cultural, social and economic well-being of the state. Ayagba-om-Idoko made a large number of appointments, and installed a number of clan chiefs as heads of specific craft organizations, specialized services, ritual institutions, and official government agencies.[58]

The concept of political and economic patronage, as a mechanism for the promotion of loyalty and devotion to the state and for legitimizing the administration, apparently served the Kwararafan monarchy well. Within a very short period Ayagba-om- Idoko appointed a large number of bureaucrats, and established a number of hereditary positions. The Attah also appointed a number of clans as purveyors to the royal house, including the Eguola and Adokpulu clans who were responsible for the royal burial grounds,[59] and the Adenyi who supplied the royal shoes.[60] The Atebo clan were made guardians of the royal staff, called Otutubatu, while the Idokoliko were appointed as custodians of the shrine dedicated to the nature spirits,[61] and the Ohina clan provided the royal diviners.

Three of the most important positions founded by Ayagba-om-Idoko were the waterside chieftaincies. These were primarily economic appointments designed to provide direction and organization to riverine commercial traffic. The duties of the three economic chiefs were essentially similar, and their jurisdictions slightly overlapped.[62] The Agaidoko clan head was appointed as the Downstream Chief to oversee matters on the Niger from Idah downriver. Another clan head - Abokko - was made Upstream Chief and controlled matters upriver from the capital, including the Benue. The third clan head from Omogbaje controlled the waterside area in the capital enclave, and was known as the Waterside Chief. The responsibilities of these appointed hereditary officials included the control and taxation of all movements of goods on the river and remittance of revenues to the Attah, the safeguarding of peace and commercial traffic along the Niger and Benue, the provision of canoes for the Attah's own commercial transactions, and the transportation of the Attah's produce to suitable markets on the Niger, the ordering of contacts between the central monarchy and foreigners on the river desiring an audience, and the provision of economic support for the palace, organization of markets, and the general good conduct of commerce and commercial agents.

The success of the third Idah dynasty can be measured not only in the policy of social, cultural and political integration which linked nearly every major segment of the diverse population into a centralized structure, but also in the development of the social formation as a unified whole. The fragmentation and decline of the Bini dynasty had reduced the Idah enclave to the status of a redistributive social formation dominated by a highly coercive and exploitative central administration. The third dynasty re-established a national trading formation, and managed to incorporate tribute payments as part of the economic support for the central elite without seeming to employ coercive and exploitative tactics. Apparently the resurgence of long distance trade, organized through the riverine chiefs and a number of hinterland commercial agents, provided the primary support for the state elite. The ascendancy of the third Idah dynasty, therefore, coincided with the development of riverine trade and an economic expansion which has been described as the 'golden age' of the Igala.[63] The expansion of coastal trade, and European commercial demands, clearly affected the political and economic status of the hinterland trading states. Just as the economic boom of the trans-Saharan trade between 1490-1590 had contributed to the development of Zaria, Oyo, Nupe and Kwararafa as major trading formations, the expansion of overseas trade through the coastal ports made the eighteenth century an important period in the economic development of Idah. The organization of Idah as the capital of a national trading formation, which included the sub-chiefdoms of Ankpa and Dekina, which were under genealogically related chiefs, established the Kwararafan monarchy as the most important commercial authority on the Niger.

The foundation of the third dynasty was accomplished, as we have seen, through a formal alliance with the indigenous population. This alliance, perpetuated through the creation of hereditary titles, including the Achadu and Igala Mela Kingmakers Council, established the central administrative structures of the national trading formation. The egalitarian principles of Kwararafa politics apparently served the central administration of the Igala Kingdom in good stead, and created a stable and efficient power relationship which was acceptable to the majority of the population.

> The balance of power between the major segments of the royal clan is maintained ultimately by the group that controls the succession to their principle corporate offices. The king exercises this control over appointments to the headship of the provincial royal subclans, but his own office is subject in this respect to the authority of the kingmakers at Idah, who control the election of the new king and umpire the rotation of authority amongst the four maximal lineages of the ruling house ...
>
> Igala oral tradition explains the role of the kingmakers in the state system by postulating a transfer of political sovereignty from the

> original landowners at Idah to the immigrant founder of the royal clan (Ayagba-om-Idoko).this transfer creates a contractual relationship between the one group of clans and the royal descent group.[64]

The distinction that might be made between the political organization of Idah under the third dynasty and other centralized political structures in other states - Benin, Idah under the second dynasty, and Kwararafa - lies in the relationship of the monarchy to the indigenous population. In Benin the palace had established a centralized Otu system which provided an avenue for upward social and economic mobility although it was clearly controlled by the palace hierarchy. The Kingmakers Council had been appointed from the indigenous nobility when the Eweka dynasty achieved paramount authority in c. 1320-1347. The Bini dynasty in Idah, on the other hand, failed to establish any form of relationship with the indigenous population, except to the extent of exploiting production and viewing their subjects as vassals. In Kwararafa the central administration provided for a wide range of social and political connections through the creation of the female-side title holders. This system was adopted and adapted by the third Idah dynasty and established close reciprocal relations between various segments of the population. The Kingmakers Council was appointed from the existing lineage or clan leadership, and cemented through intermarriage with the royal house - female- side relations. The establishment of the Achadu as a female- side hereditary nobility added a new dimension to central political structures under the third dynasty. Neither Benin, Idah under the Bini dynasty, nor the Kwararafa administration seems to have had a Prime Minister, which makes the Achadu unique in the political system of the middle belt. Neither the Achadu title nor his position is evident in any of the other successor states to Kwararafa. It may, therefore, have been an expedient innovation adopted to reinforce Kwararafan claims to paramount authority in the confluence region.

On another level the political changes introduced by Ayagba-om-Idoko wrought significant social changes in the Idah population. The subordinate role which had been endured by Okpoto and Igbo under the Bini dynasty was, theoretically at least, abolished. In fact, the class structures evident under the Bini administration which distinguished a citizen of the enclave by his ethnic origins, and dominated the economic and political life of the exploited subordinate vassal stratum, were severely modified if not totally abolished. There was a much more equitable social system fostered by the positive policy of the third dynasty. Some of the changes can be attributed to the experience in Kwararafa where interaction, and inter-marriage with other ethnic groups, created a powerful political structure. Unlike Kwararafa, however, where ethnic identities remained a factor in social and political life, and eventually defined the divisions into which the social formation would fragment after c. 1600-1630, the Kwararafan monarchy in Idah advocated acculturation and assimilation to minimize ethnic cleavages. Henceforth social, political and economic development and the internal relations in the national trading formation contributed to the development of the Igala language, culture and nationalism.

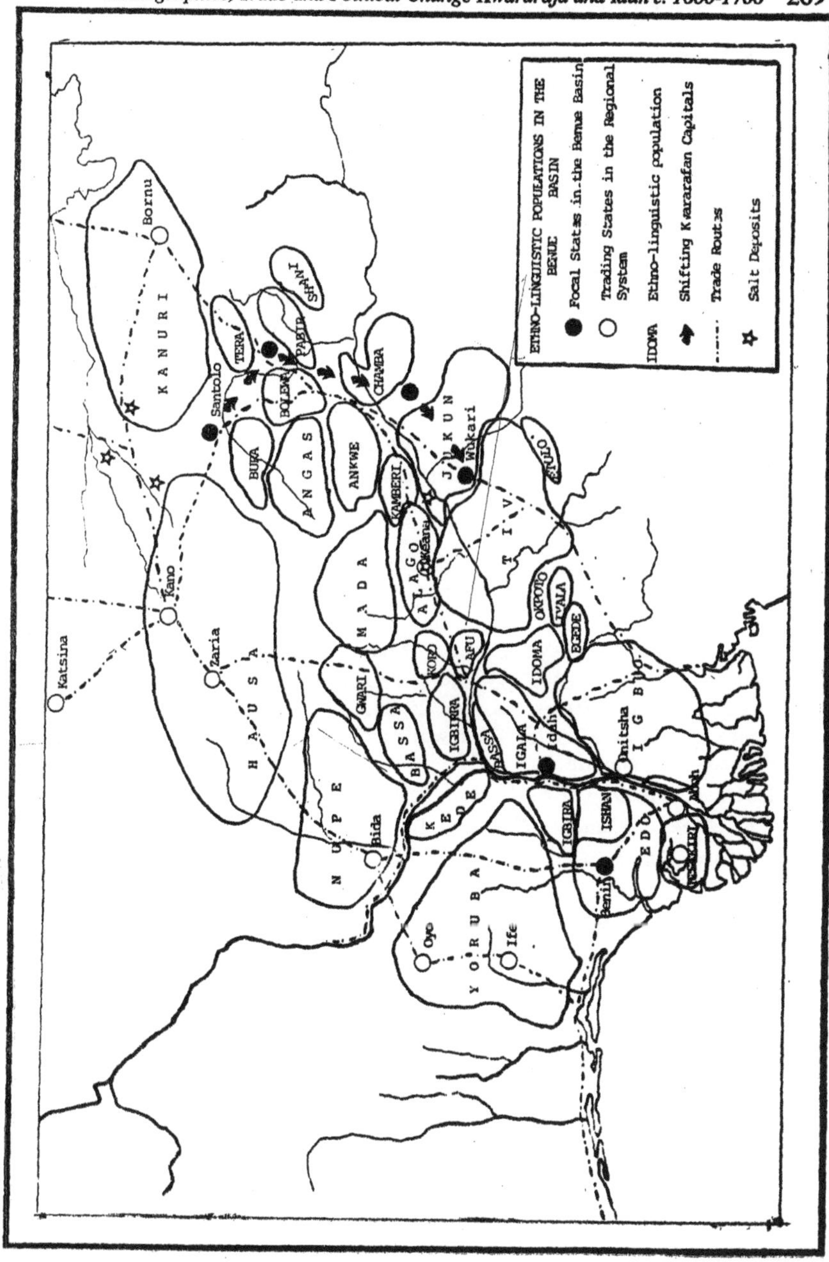

Map Nine: Ethno-linguistic Populations in the Benue Basin

References

1. E.O. Erim, *Idoma Nationality, 1600-1900*, Enugu, 1981, pp.1-35, discusses three waves of emigration between 1567 and1657. J. Power. 'Lafia: Layers of Settlement', paper presented to the Johns Hopkins University African History Workshop, Baltimore, 1984, documents Koro emigrations from Tagara in 1463-1493. J.B. Webster, "The Three Phases ofKwararafa: A Peripatetic State", Benue Valley Project Paper No. 7 ,1983.
2. The chronology of this discussion has been developed in R.A. Sargent, "A Benue Basin Regional Chronology", Benue Valley Project Paper, No. 27, 1984, and R.A. Sargent, "A Methodology of Chronology: The Igala Core Dating Progression", *History in Africa*, Vol. 11, 1984.
3. The concept of political accommodation and cooperation can be clearly seen in the developing relations between the Okpoto, Igbo, and Idoma Nokwu after c. 1687-1717.
4. I.H.T. No. 24, Asukako, Idah, February 16, 1977.
5. Webster, "The Three Phases of Kwararafa".
6. *Ibid.*
7. I.H.T. No. 24.
8. Keana Historical Text No. 100, June 24, 1974, Alhaji Adu, Alhaji Adamu and Egwu, Keana, collected by E.O. Erim. Also see Agwatashi Historical Text No. 101, June 27, 1974, Osho's palace, Agwatashi, collected by E.O. Erim. I.H.T. No. 53, Ayaga, Ankpa, March 15, 1977.
9. Erim, *Idoma Nationality*, pp. 53-77. Power, 'Lafia', and K.M. Tortema, *In Search of Etulo History*, nd., pp. 20-35. Also, a personal communication from G. Barkow after his field work among the Koro of Lafia Division, Plateau State, Nigeria, in 1977.
10. Tortema, *In Search of Etulo History*, pp. 30-45.
11. C.K. Meek, *A Sudanese Kingdom*, London, 1931, pp. 48-49.
12. I.H.T. No. 24.
13. C. Hoffman, "The Languages of Nigeria by Language Families," Department of Linguistics, University of Ibadan, 1972.
14. G. Kress and R. Hodges, *Language as Ideology*, London, 1979, p. 1.
15. This particular taboo holds extremely wide social currency and appears in a number of pre-colonial social formations, but the unique quality of the Kwararafan taboo serves as identification of the proponents of this convention and links them in a recognized and acceptable social system.
16. I.H.T. No. 143, Angwa, Okaku, August 20, 1977, and I.H.T. No. 186, Agrame Aheme, Ojadola, September 21, 1977.
17. I.H.T. No. 143. The Igala have a number of other associated rituals dealing with the observances about food and drink. One of the most common rituals in the Benue Basin is that the monarch's food must be served by either a male or by a young girl. Both rituals avoid the problem of menstrual blood.
18. H.R. Palmer, *The Bornu, Sahara and Sudan*, London, 1936, p. 246.

19. I.H.T. No. 24, and R.S. Seton, "Installation of the Attah of Idah", *Journal of the Royal Anthropological Institute*, LVIII, 1928, p. 261.
20. Personal observation in Keana, July 1974, and confirmed during a private conversation with the Osana (chief) of Keana.
21. Refer to F.B. Ataba, 'Recent Developments in the Use of Non-Documentary Evidence in African Historiography, With Special Reference to Totemism and Regional Chronology', Dalhousie University, M.A., 1976. Also see Webster and Sargent, "Totemism", in *Practical Oral Methods.*
22. J.B. Webster and R.A. Sargent, *Practical Oral Methods: Historical Data Collection in Africa*, Dalhousie Series in African Studies, forthcoming.
23. I.H.T. No. 89, Alhaji Mallam, Dekina, July 4, 1977.
24. J.B. Webster, 'Spirits of the Kingdom', Benue Valley Project Paper No. 7, 1975. Also see I.H.T. No. 35, Onu Ankpa, Ankpa, February 28, 1977, and M. Clifford, "A Nigerian Chiefdom", *Journal of the Royal Anthropological Institute*, LXVIII, 1936, p. 396.
25. Idoma Historical Text, Agatu No. 6, and Idoma Historical Text. No. 42, collected by E.O. Erim, 1977-78.
26. I.H.T. No. 224, Aku and Ada Odiyu, Adoru, January 4, 1978.
27. Keana Historical Text No. 100, and also repeated in substantially the same context in I.H.T. No. 143.
28. I.H.T. No. 161, Akoja of Idah, September 6, 1977, and I.H.T. No. 201, Ache Achebu, Aiyamgba, September 30, 1977. Also refer to Idoma Historical Text, Agatu No. 6.
29. I.H.T. No. 53, I.H.T. No. 161, and I.H.T. No. 190.
30. I.H.T. No. 190, Umeta, Agwado, September 23, 1977.
31. I.H.T. No. 3, Anacho, Idah, January 8, 1977. The informant provided a detailed historical narrative about the removal of Agoshi and the ascendancy of his son Olema II, but he did not know what happened to Agoshi. O. Temple, *Notes on the Tribes, Provinces, Emirates and States of Northern Nigeria*, edited by C.L. Temple, London, 1919, p. 516 states that "Agoshi, King of Ida" founded the Alago chiefdom of Keana. This would explain the presence of the Bini leopard totem in Keana.
32. Keana Historical Text No. 100, also refer to "Keana Salt Camps", *Nigeria Magazine*, anonymous, 1954.
33. Greater Idomaland would include the related group areas settled by the Iyala and Egede to the south of Idomaland proper.
34. I.H.T. No. 113, Igala Mela clan heads, group interview, July 27, 1977.
35. I.H.T. No. 113, and I.H.T. No. 18, the Achadu, and the leaders of the Achadu clans, group interview, February 5, 1977.
36. I.H.T. No. 119, Igala Mela clan heads, group interview, July 28, 1977.
37. I.H.T. No. 101, Onu Ankpa, Ada, July 16, 1977.
38. I.H.T. No. 3, and Seton, "Installation of the Attah", pp. 269-270.
39. I.H.T. No. 18.
40. I.H.T. No. 5, the Attah, Idah, January 9, 1977.

41. I.H.T. No. 29, Onu Ankpa, Ankpa, February 19, 1977.
42. I.H.T. No. 3.
43. For more information on the role of cultural artifacts and royal regalia refer to R.A. Sargent, "Igala Masks and Masquerades: Dynastic History and the Face of the Nation", in *West African Masking*, edited by S.L. Kasfir, in *Africa-Tervuren*, special edition, November, 1985.
44. I.H.T. No. 5.
45. I.H.T. No. 126, Igbacha, Ayangba, August 1, 1977.
46. I.H.T. No. 20, Okwoli, Idah, February 6, 1977, also refer to Clifford, "A Nigerian Chiefdom", p. 410.
47. I.H.T. No. 5, I.H.T. No. 20, and I.H.T. No. 113.
48. Clifford, "A Nigerian Chiefdom", p. 423. Clifford notes that the "Emir of Katsina had one or more of this pattern which are said to have been taken from the bodies of Jukun warriors in his territory in the 17th century".
49. Personal communication from J.B. Webster who had done the preliminary research on Adi Agba Kenjo. Also see Webster, 'Spirits of the Kingdom'.
50. I.H.T. No. 20.
51. Clifford, "A Nigerian Chiefdom", p. 421.
52. I.H.T. No. 115, Igala Mela clan heads, group interview, July 27, 1977.
53. I. Nzimiro, *Studies in Ibo Political System*, London, 1972, p. 17.
54. I.H.T. No. 18.
55. I.H.T. No. 19, the Attah, Achadu, and council, Idah, February 6, 1977.
56. I.H.T. No. 58, Imami, Ankpa, May 30, 1977 reported that therewere occasional outbreaks of violence, and a number of people were killed, however, this number was "quite small".
57. I.H.T. No. 20.
58. R.A. Sargent, 'The Ocho Festival: New Yams and Historical Reconstruction', paper presented to the Centre for African Studies Seminar, Dalhousie University, October 1982.
59. I.H.T. No. 59, Ogala, Ankpa, June 1, 1977.
60. I.H.T. No. 63, Agbani, Onede, June 16, 1977.
61. I.H.T. No. 61, Okwoli, Idah, June 3, 1977.
62. I.H.T. No. 185, Atembu, Biraidu, September 19, 1977, I.H.T. No. 81, Gabi, Shintaku, June 28, 1977, I.H.T. No. 83, Gabi, Omagba, and Toki Ateme, Shintaku, June 29, 1977, and I.H.T. No. 107, Aguda, Idah, June 24, 1977.
63. This 'golden age' was a second period of prosperity for the central monarchy, and coincided with the return of favourable climatic conditions, a factor which would prompt a fairly general economic recovery.
64. J.S. Boston, *The Igala Kingdom*, Ibadan, 1968, pp. 82-83.

Chapter 9

Conclusion: The Benue Basin In Retrospect

This study of the Benue Basin has interpreted the region's past, not from the perspective of a narrow, limited examination of a single polity or ethnic group, but through a complex set of regional relationships. These relationships have been viewed through the activities of the focal states of Benin, Idah and Kwararafa. By cutting across regional sub-divisions based on ethnicity, geography, culture, language, climate or political organization, these states afford the historian the maximum possible contact with the great variety of social formations in the Benue Basin. They were the principal actors in regional affairs, and hardly a state or population remained unaffected by developments within them. Commercial growth in one centre, for example, dictated production patterns in neighbouring regions, led often to imperial expansion in support of trade, and consequently altered political and social institutions across the entire region. At another level individual ethnic groups had to choose between migration and assimilation, or perhaps between cultural emasculation and adaptation as the focal states and various other polities expanded and contracted in the shifting set of regional interactions.

Yet if the focal states provide the historian with the best prism through which to view regional history in the Benue Basin, they are not in themselves the be all and end all of that history. They reflect and represent change in the region, but are by no means the only manifestation of it. They are the historian's tool, not his product. Focal states were as much affected by developments within the region as they were the prime movers; indeed the two processes are frequently impossible to distinguish. It is possible, therefore, to point to a unity in the Niger-Benue past that transcends the rise and fall of great imperial powers, or the social and political isolation of individual groups or states. That unity was manifested in a number of different ways. At one level we can point to common political cultures, shared religious systems, ethnic intermixture as a result of migration and re-settlement, and an integrated regional commercial network, all of which downplay the importance of state borders, linguistic divisions, and cultural differences. At another level unity can be seen in the vulnerability of all social formations in the Benue Basin to larger, external events, such as climatic change. Most importantly, unity existed simply because of the interdependence of the various communities in the Benue Basin. For the historian, as for its inhabitants, the Niger-Benue is and was a unified entity because any event or process had ramifications across a wide spectrum of time and place. Just as this study began with an examination of the Benin and Lower Niger diversity, so should it end with an assertion of its unity. The Benue Basin was a regional agglomeration of peoples, not a collection of isolated and unrelated ethnic groups, and it is this unity which provides the key to an understanding of the rich and complex past of a major region of West Africa before 1700.

Political unity is evident through both genealogically related dynasties and the association of states in a co-ordinated administrative system. Genealogical links existed between Benin, Idah, Warri, Lagos and Nupe, while Idah was itself also related to Keana and at a different time had links to Oturkpo, Osomari, Panda and Kwararafa. Kwararafa was related to the dynasties at Keana, Doma, Wuse and Wukari. Moreover, the states of Ondo, Akure, Owo, Ishan, Dampar and Keana, although not directly related to Benin, adopted Bini political culture and perpetuated regional political unity through this common administrative system. The informal Niger alliance perhaps best illustrates the efficacy of political associations in the region: genealogical links through their common Bini heritage fostered commercial exchange between the riverain trading states of Nupe, Idah, Onitsha, Aboh and Warri.

Extensive and extended regional relations between states were thus a common, indeed a constant, feature in regional politics.

Unity in the Benue Basin can also be seen in the social relations and interactions between various segments of the diverse and highly mobile population. Enclaves of merchants and specialists settled throughout the region, regardless of political affiliations or ethnic origins. Bini trading colonies were established along the upper Benue, Idah weavers and dyers operated far beyond the confines of their homeland, and Jukun entrepreneurs were settled in Pindiga, on the Jos plateau, throughout the middle belt, and as far south as Calabar. Intermarriage became a mechanism whereby an entrepreneur could penetrate an alien market and establish legitimacy in business relations in a distinctive population. Through the continuing process of migration, association and intermarriage many of these dispersed settlements were absorbed by the host population. In most cases few indications remain to identify the origins of these acculturated and assimilated groups, and often only totemic symbols can be used to reconstruct the process of social integration in the Benue Basin. It is difficult to find a single ethno-linguistic population that does not contain trace elements of other cultures and ethnic groups. It is even more difficult to find a population in the Benue Basin that has not been affected, politically, economically or socially, by other Benue Basin peoples or states. The Idoma Nokwu or Greater Doma, for example, were affected by the Bini, Abakwariga, Jukun, Koro and Pabir, and in their turn they influenced the development of the Igbirra, Iyala, Idoma, Igala, Etulo, Aro, Igbo, Okpoto and Alago. This extensive network of social relations, based upon intermarriage, migration and acculturation, established a region-wide pattern of links between the distinctive peoples of the Benue Basin and profoundly affected its demography and political geography.

Political and ethnic connections contributed to the development of an integrated trading network which in turn fostered greater intra-regional connections as the entire Benue Basin became part of and dependent upon the maintenance of that economic and commercial unity. Demands for ecologically specialized products provided regional commercial incentives, and trade progressed with relative ease through the broad set of inter-related or linked communities and populations. Productivity was maintained, market forces translated into production incentives, and local, regional and long distance exchange became a significant factor in the life of virtually every individual in the region. This regional economic structure was dominated by the main trading formations, particularly Benin, Idah and Kwararafa, which utilized commercial management to establish regional order for the exchange of commercial goods.

In some way or another every individual in the Benue Basin was involved in commercial activities or was affected by the commercial system. Individuals in this extensive economy, whether they were producers, consumers or entrepreneurs, may not have been aware of the distinctive features of the others in the system. Muslim-Hausa merchants might sell goods through the linked commercial chain to satisfy consumer demands in pagan-non-Hausa markets. Many women were actively involved in commercial production and, in some cases, dominated local markets. Children tended crops, assisted with the harvests, and became apprentices to the region's craftsmen and artisans. Men were engaged in craft production, agriculture, and regional and long distance trade. Goods were produced, exchanged and transported between different ethno-linguistic populations; and markets reflected the cosmopolitan nature of Benue Basin commercial relations. Basic differences in language, culture and politics were not barriers to the smooth flow of regional and long distance trade, and commercial incentives transcended the various political, ethnic and social distinctions. The Niger alliance illustrates the regional nature of economic relations, as the various populations and states combined to form a sophisticated trading network which tapped Benue Basin commercial production and organized exchange from Raba to the sea.

Regional unity is further exampled by the extent to which all states and populations were affected by external forces beyond the power of any individual state or group of states to control. Droughts, famines, and economic depressions, influenced the entire region and touched upon every individual in this area. States that were relatively immune to drought and drought-related famine maintained commercial production in spite of economic changes imposed by climatic degradation, but were nevertheless forced to alter their exports to the affected region, and perhaps to look away from these areas as their major trading partners. Once conditions returned to normal, trade was re-opened and commercial links re-established. Regional commercial patterns were thus altered to suit imposed conditions, but remained intact and functional despite restrictions imposed from extra-territorial, supernational or natural forces. At another level the impositions of external commercial pressures, from the trans-Saharan trade or the Atlantic overseas system, forced change on the Benue Basin and gave impetus to the rise of some imperial trading formations, the decline of others and an increase in violence and competition in the regional commercial network. These imposed conditions created higher levels of social mobility as dislocated populations sought to escape the ravages of drought, or to redefine their relationship to the altered economic patterns, and became refugees or settlers in immune, unaffected or booming areas. This mobility enhanced social, political and economic interaction, and thus fostered greater unity in the region as refugees joined the growing numbers of acculturated and assimilated people in the Benue Basin.

Finally, the unity of the region can be seen clearly in the interdependence and mutual interactions of its component parts. The process of political consolidation and centralization in one state inevitably affected others as political systems and regional controls evolved, commercial networks and economic relations were extended, and production demands and market forces increased. As one state embarked on a process of imperial expansion, and in the process imposed regional economic controls, other states were not only affected, but may have been forced to contract, move or realign their political and economic network. Imperial formations could thus subvert distinct social and political groupings and remove these independent populations and polities from the political geography and economic network of the region. Political or military actions to solve social and economic problems resulted in migrations, wars and the redefinition of regional relationships. In each case, changes in one state could affect the regional commercial nexus, alter the political status quo, or impose new, and perhaps unacceptable, social, political or economic constraints upon neighbouring populations. These changes gave rise to migrations away from the offending states, or impelled rebellions against the imposed conditions.

Violent competition occurred because of the regional nature of political, economic and social interactions, not in spite of them. Thus competition reflected the extensive quality of regional commerce and the quest for political prominence. As the various segments of the Benue Basin population responded to changing circumstances, or endeavoured to redefine their relationship to regional trade, certain links were temporarily broken while new ones were forged. While the process of re-orientation seems to reflect a disunity in the region, the mobility of various polities and populations was related to internal structures and connections to the regional political and economic pattern. Therefore, when Kwararafa fought against Bornu and Kano the state actually defined its position in Benue Basin regional affairs, and emerged as a middle belt social formation with a broad set of relationship to other Benue Basin states and populations. Thus while regional unity was pervasive it was not necessarily a complementary or a co- operative effort, and Benue Basin political, economic and social relations survived and grew through both acculturation and competition.

The Benue Basin was less a mixture of different competing states or peoples and more an integrated entity in which various polities and populations enjoyed multiple connections and experienced jointly, if in different ways and at different times, the effects of each other's actions. The lines of demarcation between ethnic groups, states, economic activities, districts, religions and languages were softened over time. Such distinctions were, in fact, minimized through the process of regional competition, integration and interaction which was crucial to the understanding of regional history and the reconstruction of the past of an extensive area like the Benue Basin.

Bibliographic Note

The source material for this reconstruction of Benue Basin history between 1300 and 1700 includes a vast collection of both primary and secondary evidence. The primary materials, including oral traditions and oral histories recorded by a number of different researchers in the middle belt of Nigeria, have been collected in the Benue Valley History Project Series at the Killam Library, Dalhousie University, Halifax, Nova Scotia, Canada. Included in this mass of primary evidence are traditions collected among the Jukun, Tiv, Hausa, Koro, Alago, Idoma, Igbirra, Igbo, and Igala. The work of recording and classifying oral traditions is still going on, and this new material will eventually be added to this collection.

My own field research included extensive field trips among the Igala, Igbirra and Tiv populations of the middle belt. I was fortunate enough to be able to refer to the work of other researchers in the region and supplied them with questions which might illuminate particular concerns and relationships revealed in my own interviews. In this way the variety of historical evidence was correlated and compared across a broad regional spectrum. The co-operative nature of the Benue Valley History Project, which was originally conceived by Dr. J.B. Webster in 1974, greatly assisted in the development of this regional perspective. The large number of Canadian and Nigerian historians involved in this project maintained close working relationships and continue to exchange ideas and information. The Benue Valley History Project Series is the focal point of that co-operative venture.

Out of this accumulated mass of primary evidence a large number of master's and doctoral dissertations have been produced. The relevant works have been cited in this bibliography. However, what is not evident is the close interaction that developed between project members and the opportunity that this provided to compare, contrast and debate specific points of information, interpretation of ideas, and conclusions about the past.

The organization and classification of all materials in the Benue Valley History collection follows the same format. Each interview has been identified with a specific number, which indicates the ethnic origins of the informant(s) and the relationship of that interview to the series of interviews in that group. For example, Igala HIstorical Text No. 122, would be the one hundred and twenty-second interview in that sub-series. The reference has been abbreviated to I.H.T. No. 122. The full citation of an interview includes reference to the date and place of interview, the informants name, and any relevant associations or relationships which might affect the interpretation of the information provided. This mechanism establishes a logical standard through which information collected in literally thousands of interviews can be accessed. There are, for example, five hundred and thirty-six Igala Historical Texts, and the Idoma collection consists of over three hundred interviews.

Thus the material for a Benue Basin historical reconstruction was not a single researchers responsibility. It called extensively upon the field work of J.B. Webster, A.C. Unomah, A.I. Adefuye, J. Sterkin, J. Morrison, E.O. Erim, J.N. Orkar, and R. Shain. Many other individuals also provided insights into the development of regional relationships in the Benue Basin from their own experiences as researchers in this area of West Africa. I am, therefore, indebted to R.G. Armstrong, O. Ikime, S. Kasfir, M. Mason, F.B. Ataba, J. Power, J.O. Ijomah, J.E. Miller, T.M. Mkar, and P. Dike.

While recognizing the extensive nature of the source material it is equally important to briefly describe the nature and value of oral sources as they influence the interpretation of the historical record. Clearly the mass of data independently collected by different researchers in different ethno-linguistic populations, provided the basis for an extensive comparative analysis. Both types and styles of information were thus contrasted, and the reliability of various forms of information about the past checked. The results of this comparative study, which involved both factual and textual correlations, established a remarkable degree of consistency between various pieces and forms of information. For example, data collected by E.O. Erim in 1974 among the Idoma was compared with information provided by Igala-speaking informants collected in 1979. The level of coherence between such dissimilar pieces of evidence were, at first incomprehensible. It seemed unlikely that these informants could have conspired to present compatible information which confirmed the collective memories of each group. However, as the range and scope of this comparative analysis expanded, including information collected beyond the borders of what had become known as the Benue Basin, the levels of agreement and thus confirmation continued to reinforce the emerging regional reconstruction.

Thus despite cultural and linguistic differences, and the separation by great distances, many of the informants were apparently identifying a common experience preserved within the corpus of their own oral traditions. For example, Idoma, Alago and Igala informants provided a perspective on their common past as former citizens of the now defunct Kwararafan Empire. Similarly, Benin colonists in the middle belt region provided a coherent body of information about the Benin Empire as they knew it. Their information compared favourably with evidence collected in Ontisha, Agbor, and Benin itself.

Once thousands of pieces of information had been compared the richness of the historical record suggested a regional approach to the reconstruction of the past. It was not an artificial imposition of a regional perspective, but a view of regional interactions that had been defined by the records themselves. Benue Basin history has, therefore, been defined by the informants who have stored traditions about the past of that region.

As a general rule no single reference within oral accounts can be taken as fact. Levels of agreement and disagreement between all forms of evidence must be taken into account. Data must be checked and cross-checked. Eventually ideas and interpretations of accumulated evidence can generally be confirmed or denied by the wide range of historical evidence that is so richly available even in pre-literate societies. This general rules applies not only to oral evidence, but must include the detailed comparison of linguistic, archaeological, cultural, documentary, and all other forms of evidence. No decision to accept ideas can thus be taken lightly. All interpretations must be informed by the evidence itself, and the factual and textual comparisons that are so necessary when depending upon orally preserved evidence as the primary source for the historical reconstruction. No historian accepts evidence unquestioningly. No oral historian should accept and record evidence for a subsequent literal interpretation. There is always the possibility that the informant has selected metaphor or allegory. Evidence is always tested. But once it begins to withstand the rigors of analysis and comparison and retains its internal coherence it is much harder to reject.

I have been accused of adopting a rather too literal approach to the interpretation of oral evidence. Such an accusation fails to consider the strenuous tests applied to each and every piece of information. I certainly believe that oral evidence is a source for the reconstruction of the past, but I also maintain that any source must be confirmed and corroborated by as many other sources as possible. The reader must, therefore, be aware that oral information has inherant problems, but they can be overcome. Also, such evidence is not necessarily taken literally, but always must be seen in the context of all other forms of historical evidence which serve to corroborate the interpretations.

Finally, while many of the sources for this reconstruction are orally preserved it should be noted that the sequence of events related here was not based upon a single account. Literally hundreds of accounts have been compiled and compared, and thus a relative framework of those events was established. There is no doubt in my mind, based upon the massive weight of evidence, that we can sequence events in a regional framework in an orderly chain. This could not be accomplished if I depended solely upon Igala informants. I also recognize that the sequence applied here is an interpretation of the past, and that it might require restructuring should new evidence come to light. This is why qualifying terms such as 'probably', or 'most likely' appear throughout the text. I do not, however, accept the view that these events did not occur. They are, after all, part of the past experiences of the people whose forefathers occupied the Benue Basin. Thus while we record that Tsoede attacked Oyo it is not only Robert Smith's account in the contemporary record that affirms this, but evidence from a variety of sources including oral tradtions.

Once all available evidence - and this reconstruction has by no means exhauted all potential evidence - has been checked by the image of the past takes on a new clarity. Seemingly unrelated experiences, recorded in one set of traditions, appear to have causal relationships not explicitly stated in the evidence, with events in other bodies of recorded information. Thus, the evidence for the interactions between religion and politics or dynastic struggle in Benin are based upon the interpretation of data which shows competing candidates espousing different religious philosophies. Do we actually require evidence that says that the political struggle was based upon religious differences to suggest that religion was a factor in the dynastic disputs? It was clear that there was a perceived distinction between the candidates based upon a social understanding of their religious affiliations. We can interpret, but do not change, the historical record.

Space precludes a full listing of all recorded interviews in the Benue Basin. Such listings are available in the Benue Valley History Project Series, and verbatim transcripts are also available on microfiche. The attached bibliography represents the remaining secondary literature relevant for this regional reconstruction. It is a select bibliography in that many other sources refer to this region, but they were either not directly relevant for this time period, or dealt with matters beyond the immediate scope of this study. This listing has been arranged in three categories: books, articles and unpublished papers. I have, rightly or wrongly omitted any reference to the extensive archival collections that were informative for this study. A great deal of time was spent in the Nigerian National Archives in Kaduna, Enugu and Ibadan, and if required a full listing of these files can be found in R.A. Sergent, 'Politics and Economics in the Benue Basin, c. 1300-1700' Dalhousie University Ph. D dissertation, 1984.

Bibliography

Books

Alagoa, E.J., *A History of the Niger Delta*, Ibadan, 1972.

Asabia, D.D., and J.O. Adesbesan, *Idoani Past and Present*, Ibadan, 1970.

Bascom, W., *Ifa Divination*, Bloomington, 1969.

Bascom, W., *The Yoruba of Southwestern Nigeria*, New York, 1969.

Belasco, B.I., *The Entrepreneur as Culture Hero*, New York, 1980.

Ben-Amos, P. *The Art of Benin*, London, 1980.

Boahen, A.A., *Britain, The Sahara and the Western Sudan, 1788-1861*, Oxford, 1964.

Boston, J.S., *The Igala Kingdom*, Ibadan, 1968.

Bovill, E.W., *The Golden Trade of the Moors*, London, 1958.

Bovill, E.W., *Caravans of the Old Sahara*, London, 1933.

Bradbury, R.E., *Benin Studies*, edited by P. Morton- Williams, Oxford, 1973.

Bradbury, R.E., *The Benin Kingdom and the Edo-speaking Peoples of Southwestern Nigeria*, in the Ethnographic Survey of Africa, edited by D. Forde, London, 1959.

Burdon, J.A., *Northern Nigeria, Historical Notes on Certain Emirates*, London, 1909.

Connah, G., *The Archaeology of Benin*, Oxford, 1975.

Crowther, S., and J.F. Schon, *Expedition Up the Niger in 1841*, London, 1842.

Crowther, S., *Journal of an Expedition Up the Niger and Tshadda in 1854*, London, 1855.

Curtin P.D., *Economic Changes in Precolonial Africa, Supplementary Evidence*, Madison, 1975.

Darling, P.J., *Archaeology and History in Southern Nigeria: the ancient linear earthworks of Benin and Ishan*, Parts i and ii, Cambridge Monographs in African Archaeology 11, BAR Int. 215, Cambridge, 1984.

Egharevba, J.U., *Some Stories of Ancient Benin*, Lagos, 1950.

Egharevba, J.U., *A Short History of Benin* (third edition), Ibadan, 1960, (fourth edition published Ibadan, 1968).

Egharevba, J.U., *The Concise Lives of Famous Iyase*, Lagos, 1946/47.

Egharevba, J.U., *The Murder of Imaguero and the Tragedy of the Idah War*, Sapele, 1949.

Egharevba, J.U., *Bini Titles*, Benin, 1946.

Egharevba, J.U., *Benin Laws and Customs*, Lagos, 1947.

Einzig, P., *Primitive Money*, London, 1946.

Erim, E.O., *Idoma Nationality 1600-1900: Problems in Studying the Origins and Development of Ethnicity*, Enugu, 1981.

Forde, D., and P. Brown, with R.G. Armstrong, *People of the Niger-Benue Confluence*, in the Ethnographic Survey of Africa, edited by D. Forde, London, 1955.

Fyfe, C. and M. McMaster (Eds.), *African Historical Demography*, Vol. 11, Edinburgh, 1981.

Gowers, W.P., *Gazetteer of Kano Province*, London, 1921.

Hassan, F.A., *Demographic Archaeology*, London, 1981.

Henderson, R.N., *The King in Every Man*, New Haven, 1972.

Henige, D.P., and A.H.M. Kirk-Greene, *The Emirates of Northern Nigeria*, London, 1966.

Hubbard, J.W., *The Sobo of the Niger Delta*, Zaria, 1948.

Hutchinson, T.J., *Narrative of the Niger, Tshadda and Benue Explorations*, London, 1855.

Isichei, E., *The Ibo People and the Europeans*, London, 1973.

Isichei, E., *A History of the Igbo People*, London, 1976.

Isichei, E., (ed.), *Studies in the History of Plateau State, Nigeria*, London, 1982.

Isichei, E., *A History of Nigeria*, London, 1983.

Johnson, S., *A History of the Yorubas*, Lagos, 1921.

Jungwirth, M., *Benin in den Jahren 1485-1700*, Wein, 1968.

Kea, R., *Settlement, Trade and Polities in the 17th Century Gold Coast*, Baltimore, 1982.

Latham, A.J.H., *Old Calabar, 16000-1981*, Oxford, 1973.

Law, P., *The Oyo Empire, c. 1600-1836*, Oxford, 1977.

Manoukian, M., *Akan and Ga-Adangme*, in the Ethnographic Survey of Africa, edited by D. Forde, London, 1950.

Meek, C.K., *The Northern Tribes of Nigeria*, (2 volumes), New York, 1936.

Meek, C.K., *Tribal Studies in Northern Nigeria*, (2 volumes), London, 1931.

Meek, C.K., *Law and Authority in a Nigerian Tribe*, New York, 1947.

Meek, C.K., *A Sudanese Kingdom*, New York, 1969, (reprint).

Moore, W.A., *History of Itsekiri*, London, 1936.

Nadel, S.F., *A Black Byzantium*, London, 1942.

Northrup, D., *Trade Without Rulers*, London, 1978.

Ochidi, G., *The Original History of Anoma and Achadu*, Enugu, 1956.

Okojie, G.C., *Ishan Native Laws and Customs*, Yaba, 1960.

Omwuejeogwu, M.A., *An Igbo Civilization: Nri Kingdom and Hegemony*, London, 1981.

Palmer, H.R., *Sudanese Memoirs*, Lagos, 1928.

Palmer, H.R., *The Bornu, Sahara and Sudan*, London, 1936.

Ryder, A.F.C., *Benin and the Europeans*, 1485-1897, Ibadan, 1969.

Sanceau, E., *The Reign of the Fortunate King*, New York, 1969.

Schultze, A., *The Sultante of Bornu*, (translated by P.A. Benton), London, 1972.

Shaw, T., (ed.), *Lecturers on Nigerian Prehistory and Archaeology*, Ibadan, 1969.

Shaw, T., *Igbo-Ukwu*, (2 volumes), London, 1972.

Shaw, T., *Nigeria, Its Archaeology and Early History*, London, 1973.

Sowande, F., *Ifa*, Yaba, n.d.

Talbot, P.A., *The Peoples of Southern Nigeria*, (4 volumes), London, 1926.

Temple, C.L., *Notes on the Tribes, Provinces, Emirates and States of Northern Nigeria*, Cape Town, 1919.

Thomas, N.W., *Anthropological Report on the Edo- Speaking Peoples*, (2 volumes), London, 1910.

Tortema, J.K., *In Search of Etulo History*, n.d.

Ughulu, J., *Short History of (Esan) Ishan-Benin*, Lagos, 1950.

Urvoy, Y., *Historie de l'Empire du Bornu*, Memoires de l'Institut Francais d'Afrique Noire No. 7, Paris, 1949.

Articles

Adefuye, A.I., "The Alago Kingdoms: A Political History", in *Studies in the History of Plateau State*, Nigeria, edited by E. Isichei, London, 1982.

Adeleye, R.A., "Hausaland and Bornu, 1600-1800", in *The History of West Africa*, edited by J.F.A. Ajayi and M. Crowder, 2nd. ed., Vol. 1, New York, 1976.

Afigbo, A.E.,"Trade and Trade Routes in Nineteenth Century Nsukka," *Journal of the Historical Society of Nigeria*, VII, I, 1973.

Agbola, S.A.,"The Middle Belt of Nigeria - The Basis of its unity", *Nigerian Geographical Journal*, 4, (1), August, 1961.

Akintoye, S.A., "The Southeastern Yoruba Districts and the Benin Kingdom", *Journal of the Historical Society of Nigeria*, IV, 4, 1969.

Alagoa, E.J., "Long Distance Trade and States in the Niger Delta", *Journal of African History*, XI, 3, 1970.

Armstrong, R.G., "The Igala", in Peoples of the Niger-Benue Confluence, in the *Ethnographic Survey of Africa*, edited by D. Forde, London, 1955.

Armstrong, R.G., "The Use of Linguistic and Ethnographic Data in the Study of Idoma and Yoruba History", in *The Historian in Tropical Africa*, edited by J. Vansina, R. Mauny and L. Thomas, London, 1965.

Armstrong, R.G., "Comparative Word List of Two Dialects of Yoruba with Igala", *Journal of West AFrican Languages*, 2, 2, 1965.

Ballard, J.A., "Historical Inferences from the Linguistic Geography of the Middle Belt of Nigeria", *Africa*, 1971.

Boahen, A.A., "Caravan Trade in the 19th Century", *Journal of African History*, III,'2, 1962.

Boston, J.S., "Notes on the Origins of Igala Kingship", *Journal of the Historical Society of Nigeria*, 2, 1962.

Boston, J.S., "Oral Tradition and the History of the Igala", *Journal of African History*, X, I, 1969.

Boston, J.S., "Notes on Contacts Between the Igala and Ibo", *Journal of the Historical Society of Nigeria*, 2, 1960.

Boston, J.S., "Ifa Divination in Igala", *Africa*, XVIV, 4, 1974.

Bradbury, R.E., "Chronological Problems in the Study of Benin", *Journal of the Historical Society of Nigeria*, 1, 1959.

Bradbury, R.E., "Divine Kingship in Benin", *Nigeria Magazine*, 62, 1959.

Butcher, H.L.M., "Some Aspects of the Otu System of the Isa subtribe of the Edo People of Southern Nigeria", *Africa*, 8, 1935.

Byng-Hall, F.F.W., "Notes on the Okpoto and Igara Tribes", *Journal of the African Society*, 7, 1907.

Clifford, M., "A Nigerian Chiefdom", *Journal of the Royal Anthropological Institute*, LXVI, 1936.

Cohen, R., "The Bornu Kinglists", *Boston University Papers on Africa*, Vol. II, 1966.

Cohen, R., "The Kingship in Bornu", in *West African Chiefs*, edited by O. Ikime and M. Crowder, New York, 1970.

Connah, G., "Benin", in *Lecturers on Nigerian Pre-history and Archaeology*, edited by T. Shaw, Ibadan, 1967.

Connah, G., "New Light on the Benin City Walls", Journal of the *Historical Society of Nigeria*, III, 4, 1967.

Conquery-Vidrovitch, C., "The Political Economy of the African Peasantry and Modes of Production", in *The Political Economy of Contemporary Africa*, edited by P.C.W. Gutkind and I. Wallerstein, Beverly Hills, 1976.

Coquery-Vidrovitch, C., "Research on an African Mode of Production", in *African Social Studies: A Radical Reader*, edited by P.C.W. Gutkind and P. Waterman, New York, 1977.

Dark, P.J.C., "Benin Bronze Heads: Styles and Chronology", in *African Images*, edited by D.F. McCall and E.G. Bay, New York, 1975.

Darling, P.J., "The Ancient Canoe Port of Benin," *Nigerian Field*, 46, 1981.

Darling, P.J., "A Change in Territory: attempts to trace more than a thousand years of population movements in the Benin and Ishan peoples in southern Nigeria," in *African Historical Demography*, edited by C. Fyfe and M. McMaster, Vol. 11, Edinburgh, 1981.

Darling, P.J., "Notes on the Earthworks of the Benin Empire," *West African Journal of Archaeology*, 6, 1976.

Dike, K.O., and F.I. Ekejiuba, "The Aro State: A Case Study of State Formation in Southeastern Nigeria", *Journal of African Studies*, 5, 3, 1978.

Ekejiuba, F.I., "The Aro Trade System in the Nineteenth Century", *Ikenga*, 1, 1, 1972.

Fagan, B.M., "Radiocarbon Dates for Sub-Saharan Africa", *Journal of African History*, VIII, 3, 1967.

Fage, J.D., "Some Remarks on Beads and Trade on Lower Guinea in the Sixteenth and Seventeenth Centuries", *Journal of African History*, 3, 1962.

Gray, R., "Eclipse Maps", *Journal of African History*, IX, 1, 1969.

Gray, R., "Annular Eclipse Maps", *Journal of African History*, IX, 1, 1969.

Griffeth, R., "The Hausa City-States from 1450 to 1804", in *The City-State in Five Cultures*, Santa Barbara, 1981.

Hiskett, E.M., "Materials Relating to the Cowry Currency of the Western Sudan", *Bulletin of the School of Oriental and African Studies*, 19, 1966.

Hunwick, J.O., "Songhay, Bornu and Hausaland During the Sixteenth Century", in *The History of West Africa*, edited by J.F.A. Ajayi and M. Crowder, 2nd ed., Vol. 1, New York, 1976.

Hutchinson, W.F., "A Seventeenth Century Slaver's Diary," Elder *Dempster Magazine*, 4, 1925.

Igbafe, P.A., "Benin in the Pre-colonial Period", *Tarikh*, 5, 1, 1974.

Johnson, M., "The Cowrie Currencies of West Africa", *Journal of African History*, II, 1970.

Jones, G.I., "Who are the Aro?", *The Nigerian Field*, 1939.

Kalous,M.,"Ifa Divination", *New Orient*, VI, 4, 1967.

Kalous, M., "A Contribution to Some Problems of Benin Chronology", *Archiv Orientalni*, XXXVIII, 4, 1970.

Law, R.C.C., "The Dynastic Chronology of Lagos", *Lagos Notes and Records*, II, 1, 1968.

Lloyd, P.C., "The Itsekiri", in R.E. Bradbury's *The Benin Kingdom and the Edo-speaking Peoples of South-western Nigeria*, in the Ethnographic Survey of Africa, edited by D. Forde, London, 1957.

Lovejoy, P.E., "The Borno Salt Industry", *The International Journal of African History*, XI 4, 1978.

Maliphant, G.K., A.R. Rees and P.M. Rise, "Defense Systems of the Benin Empire - Uwan," *West African Journal of Archaeology*, 6, 1976.

Mason, M., "The Tsoede Myth and the Nupe Kinglist: More Political Propaganda", *History in Africa*, 2, 1975.

Mauny, R., "A Possible Source of Copper for the Oldest Brass Heads of Ife", *Journal of the Historical Society of Nigeria*, II, 3, 1962.

Meulemeester, J. de and J. Nenquin, "Voorlopig bericht over twee seizoenen protohistorich onderzock in het gebied van de Midden-Benue (Nigeria)", *Africa Tervuren*, 18, 1972 (translated by Ms. R. Krut).

Meulemeester, J. de, "De Jukan. Een Status Questionis van hun Geschiedensis", *Africa Tervuren*, 16, 1970.

Monckton, J.C., "Burial Ceremonies of the Attah of Idah", *Journal of the African Society*, XXVI, 1922- 1923.

Morton-Williams, P., "The Oyo Yoruba and the Atlantic Trade, 1690-1830", *Journal of the Historical Society of Nigeria*, 3, 1964.

Morton-Williams, P., "The Influence of Habitat and Trade on the Politics of Oyo and Ashanti", in *Man in Africa*, edited by M. Douglas and P.M. Kayberry, London, 1969.

Nadel, S.F., "Nupe State and Community", *Africa*, VIII, 3, 1935.

Nadel, S.F., "The Kede: A Riverain State in Northern Nigeria", in *African Political Systems*, edited by M. Fortes and E.E. Evans-Pritchard, London, 1940.

Neumark, S.D., "Trans Saharan Trade in the Middle Ages", in *An Economic History of Tropical Africa*, Vol. 1, edited by Z.A. Konczaski and J.M. Konczaski, London, 1967.

Nicholson, S., "Climatic Variations in the Sahel and Other African Regions During the Past Five Centuries", *Journal of Arid Environments*, Vol. 1, 1978.

Northrup, D., "The Growth of Trade Among the Igbo Before 1800", *Journal of African History*, 2, 1972.

Nwauwa, A.O. "The Dating of the Aro Chiefdom: A Synthesis of Corrleated Genealogies", *History in Africa*, Vol. 17, 1990.

Nzekwu, D., "Keana Salt Camp", *Nigeria Magazine*, 88, 1964.

Omwuegeogwu, M.A. and Omwuegeogwu, "The search for the missing link in dating and interpreting the Igbo-Ukwu finds," *Occassional Publication of Odinawu*, 3, 1970.

Palmer, H.R., "The Kano Chronicle", *Journal of the Royal Anthropological Institute*, 38, 1908.

Pardo, A.W., "The Songhay Empire Under Sonni Ali and Askia Muhammed: A Study in Comparison and Contrast", *Boston University Papers on Africa*, Vol. V, 1971.

Patridge, C., "Burial of the Ata of Igaraland and the Coronation of His Successor", *Blackwoods Magazine*, 1904.

Philpot, W.A.S., "Notes on the Igala Language", Bulletin of the *School of Oriental and African Studies*, 1935.

Ryder, A.F.C., "A Reconsideration of the Ife-Benin Relationship", *Journal of African History*, VI, 1, 1965.

Ryder, A.F.C., "Dutch Trade on the Nigerian Coast During the Seventeenth Century", *Journal of Historical Society* of Nigeria, III, 2, 1965.

Ryder, A.F.C., "The Rise of the Benin Kingdom", in *The Middle Age of African History*, edited by R. Oliver, London, 1967.

Ryder, A.F.C., "An Early Portuguese Trading Voyage to the Forcados River", *Journal of the Historical Society of Nigeria*, 1, 1954.

Ryder, A.F.C., "The Re-establishment of Portuguese Factories On the Costa de Mina to the Mid-Eighteenth Century", *Journal of the Historical Society of Nigeria*, 1, 1958.

Sargent, R.A., "On the Methodology of Chronology: The Igala Core Regnal List", *History in Africa*, Vol. 11, 1984.

Sargent, R.A., "Igala Masks" Dynastic History and the Face of the Nation", in *West African Masks and Cultural Systems*, edited by S.L. Kasfir, Musee Royale de l'Afrique Centrale Tervuren, Belgium Vol 126, 1989.

Sargent, R.A., "A Benue Basin Regional Chronology", *Journal of of General Studies*, (Kano), Vols. 4 and 5, No. 1, 1984/5.

Sargent, R.A., "From a Redistributive to an Imperial Formation, Benin, c. 1293-1536", *Canadian Journal of African Studies*, Vol. XX, No. 3, 1986.

Schove, D.J., "Eclipse, Comet and the Spectrum of Time in Africa", *Journal of the British Astronomical Association*, 1968.

Schove, D.J., "African Droughts and the Spectrum of Time", in *Drought in Africa*, Vol. 2, edited by D. Dalby and R.J. Harrison-Church, London, 1980.

Seton, R.S., "Installation of the Attah of Idah", *Journal of the Royal Anthropological Institute*, LVIII, 1928.

Smith, M.G., "The Beginnings of Hausa Society - 1000- 1500 A.D.", in *The Historian in Tropical Africa*, edited by J. Vansina, R. Mauny, and L.V. Thomas, London, 1964.

Smith, R., "The Alafin in Exile: A Study of the Igboho Period in Oyo History", *Journal of African History*, VI, 1, 1965.

Smith, R., "List of Alafin of Oyo", *The African Historian*, 1, 3, 1965.

Struck, B., "Chronologifder Benin - Alterturner", *Zeitschrift fur Ethnologie*, Vierund Furtziester Jahrgany, 1922.

Sweetman, D., "Amina of Hausaland", in *Women Leaders in African History*, London, 1984.

Thomas, N.W., "Totemism in Southern Nigeria", *Anthropos*, 10-11, 1915-1916.

Thornton, J.K., "Traditions, Documents and the Ife-Benin Relationship", *History in Africa*, Vol. 15, 1988.

Ukwu, U.I., "The Development of Trade and Marketing in Iboland", *Journal of the Historical Society of Nigeria*, 3, 1967.

Unomah, A.C., "The Low Land Salt Industries", in *Studies in the History of Plateau State*, Nigeria, edited by E. Isichei, London, 1981.

Urvoy, Y., "Chronologie du Bornou", *Journal de la Societie des Africanistes*, XI, 1941 and XII, 1942.

Wallerstein, I., "Three Stages of African Involvement in the World Economy", in *The Political Economy of Contemporary Africa*, edited by P.C.W. Gutkind and I. Wallerstein, Beverly Hills, 1976.

Webster, J.B., "The Three Phases of Kwararafa: A Peripatetic State", *Studies in the History of Plateau State*, edited by E. Isichei, London, 1984.

Webster, J.B., "Periodization in African History, c. 1050-1840, *The Journal of General Studies*, (Kano), Vol.4, No. 1, 1983.

Unpublished Papers:

Documents, Manuscripts And Disserations

Abubakar, S., `The Middle Benue Region up to c.1950', A.B.U. Niger-Benue Seminar, Jos, 1974.

Adefuye, A.I., `Keana, The Gift of Salt', B.V.P.P. No. 11, Lagos, 1975.

Adefuye, A.I., `Historical Development of Social and Political Institutions in Doma', University of Lagos, History Staff Seminar, March, 1977.

Afigbo, A.E., `Pre-Colonial Links between South-eastern Nigeria and the Benue Valley', A.B.U. Niger-Benue Seminar, Jos, 1974.

Akinola, G.A., `The Origins of the Eweka Dynasty of Benin: A Study in the Use and Abuse of Oral Tradition', University of Ibadan Seminar, April, 1976.

Aruwa, I.M., `History of Idah Town From the Earliest Times Up to 1960', B.A. dissertation, Dept. of History, University of Jos, June 1983.

Ataba, F.B., `The Concept of Totemism and its Relevance to African History', B.V.P.P. No. 17, 1976.

Ataba, F.B., 'Recent Developments in the Use of Non-documentary Evidence in African Historiography, with Special Reference to Totemism and Regional Chronology,' Dalhousie University, M.A., 1976.

Hoffman, C., `The Languages of Nigeria by Language Family', Development of Linguistics, University of Ibadan, 1972.

Ijomah, J.O., `The Evolution of Kingship Among the West Niger Igbo Chiefdom', Benue Valley Project Paper No. 24, 1981.

Jeffries, M.D.W., `The Divine Umundri Kings of Iboland', University of London, Ph.D., 1934.

Jones, D.H., `The Northern Nigerian Emirates', Niger-Benue Seminar, A.B.U., Jos, 1974.

MacLeod, T.M., `Ethnological Report on the Okpoto, Egedde of Idomaland', 1925, Kaduna National Archives.

Mason, M., `The Nupe Kingdom in the Nineteenth Century: A Political History', University of Birmingham, Ph.D., 1970.

Miller, J.E., `Ishan-Benin Relations, c.1455-1504', Dalhousie University, Honours Essay, 1983.

Miller, J.E., `A Pre-Colonial History of Biu, Northern Nigeria', Dalhousie University, M.A., 1984.

Mkar, T.M., `Tiv Society at the Turn of the Eighteenth and Nineteenth Centuries', A.B.U., Ph.D., 1972.

Morrison, J.M., `Jos Plateau Societies: Internal Change and External Influences, 1800-1935', University of Ibadan, Ph.D., 1976.

Njoku, O.N., `A History of Iron Technology in Igboland, c. 1542- 1900,' Dalhousie University, Ph.D., 1986.

Nwauwa, A.O. `The Aro Chiefdom: Chronology and State Formation, c. 1690-1720,' Dalhousie Univeristy, M.A., 1989.

Omwuejeogwu, M.A., 'The Political Organization of Nri, Southeastern Nigeria', University of London, M.Phil., 1974.

Roberts, R., `Multiplier Effects on the Ecologically Specialized Trade of Precolonial West AFrica', African Seminar, Dalhousie University, February 1980.

Sargent, R.A., `Politics and Economics in the Benue Basin, c. 1300 - 1900', Dalhousie University, Ph.D., 1984

Silverstein, R., Igala Historical Phonology', Ph.D., University of California, 1973.

Webster, J.B., 'Chiefs and Chronology: Jukun Colonies in the Benue Valley, B.V.P.P. No. 4, 1975.

Webster, J.B., 'The Manatee', B.V.P.P. No. 20, 1975.

Webster, J.B., 'Animals of the Kingdom', B.V.P.P. No. 6, 1975.

Webster, J.B., 'Spirits of the Kingdom', B.V.P.P. No. 7, 1975.

Webster, J.B., 'A Critical Analysis of the Royal Chronicle of Agbor', B.V.P.P. No. 13, 1972.

Webster, J.B., 'Periodization in African History, c. 1050-1850', History Seminar, Dalhousie University, 1982.

Williamson, K., `Lexicostatistical Comparison of Itsekiri, Standard Yoruba and Igala, Department of Linguistics, University of Ibadan, 1972.

Young, M.W., 'The Divine Kingships of the Jukun', University of Wisconsin, Ph.D., 1972.

Map Ten: Population Movements in the Benue Basin, c. 1300-1700

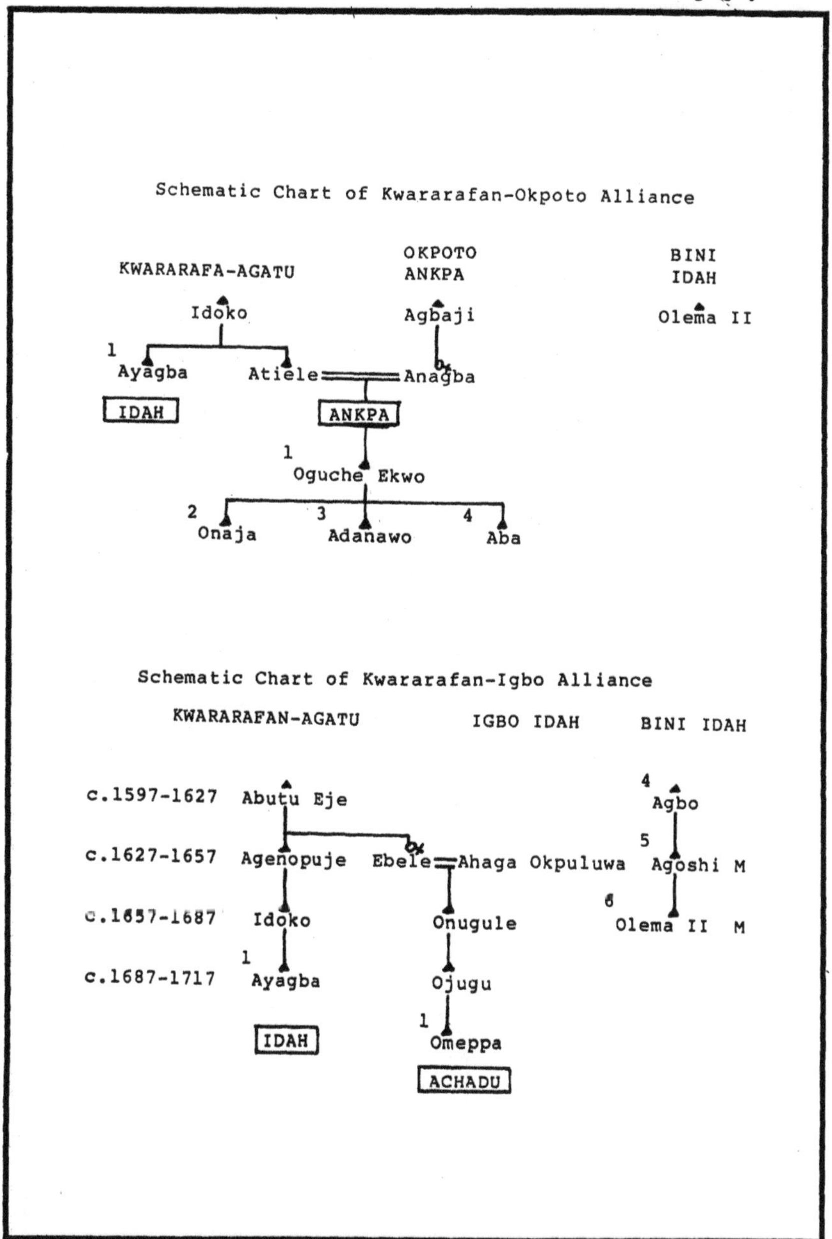

Map Eleven: Schematic Chart of Kwararafan-Okpoto Alliance

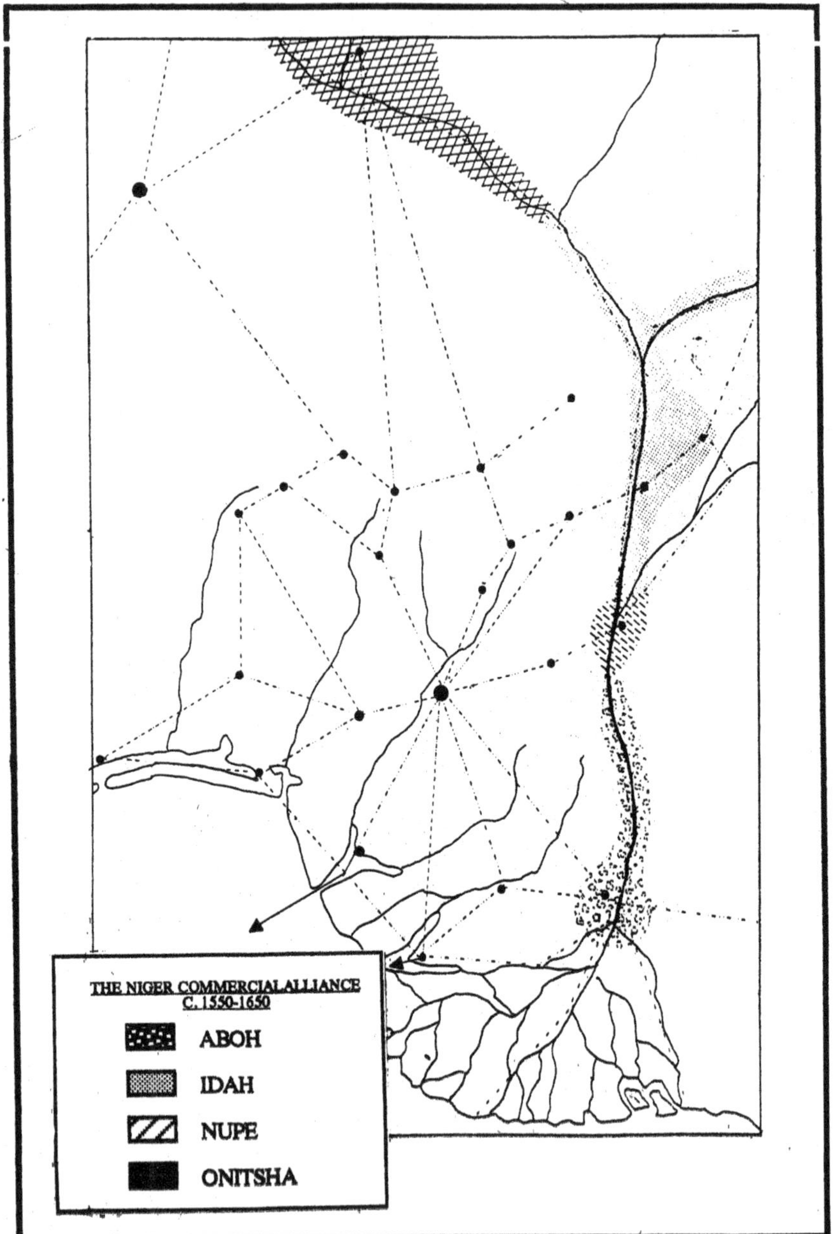

Map Twelve: The Niger Commercial Alliance c. 1550-1650

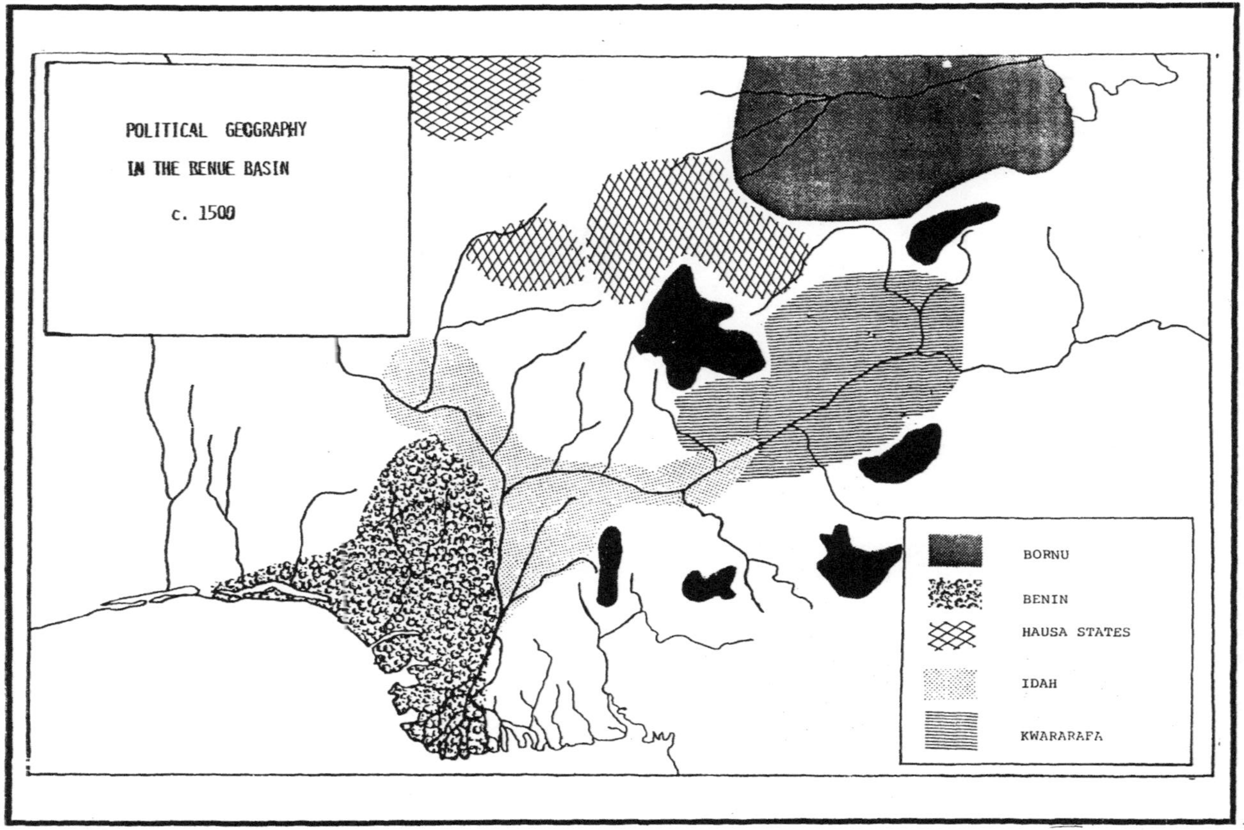

Map Thirteen: Political Geography in the Benue Basin c. 1500

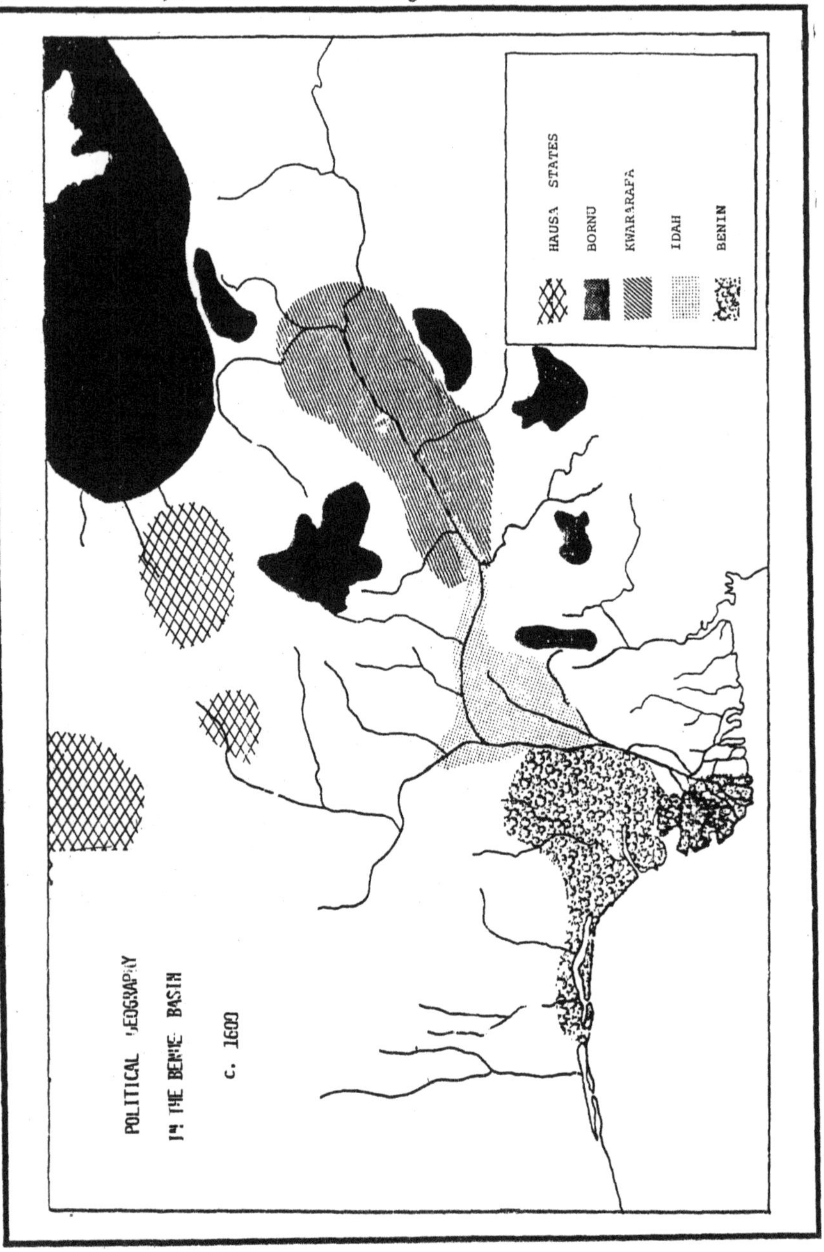

Map Fourteen: Political Geography in the Benue Basin c. 1600

Map Fifteen: Political Geography in the Benue Basin c. 1700

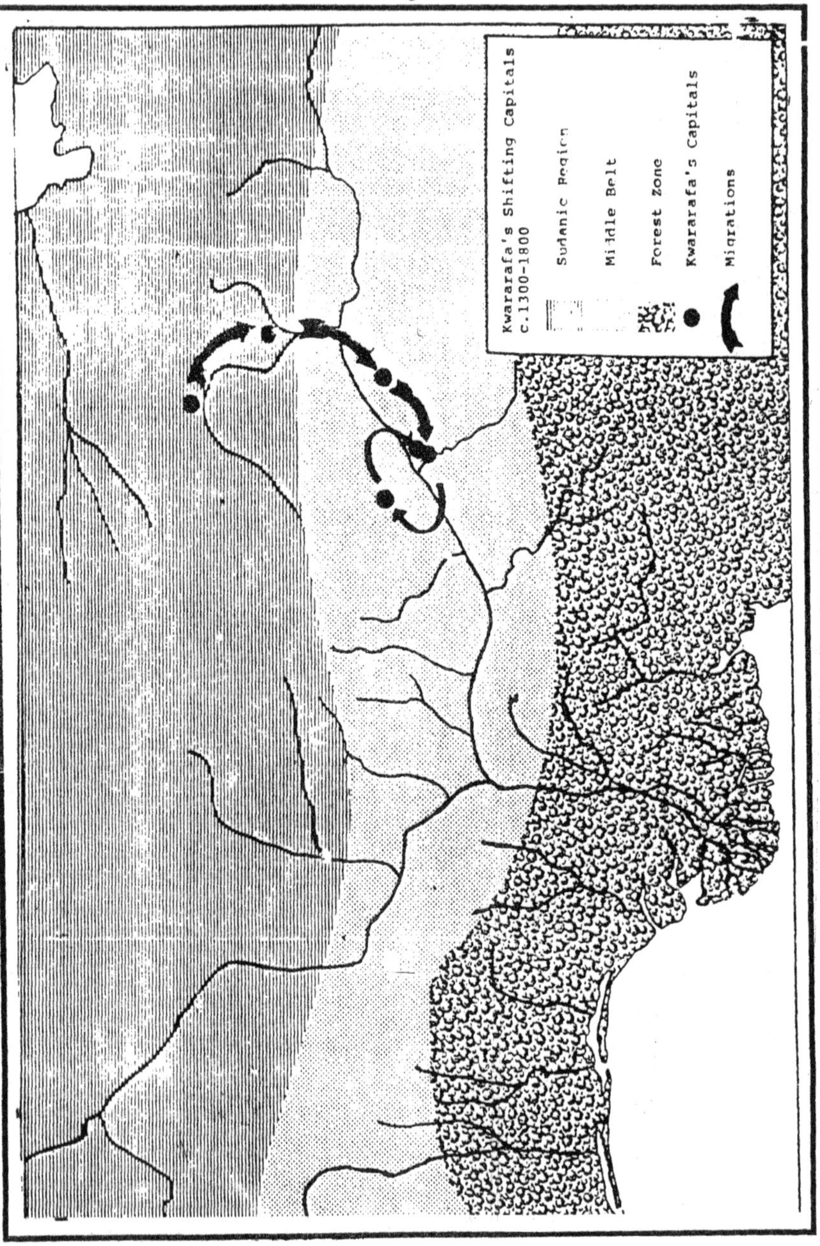

Map Sixteen: Kwararafa's Shifting Capitals c. 1300-1800

Index

www.ingramcontent.com/pod-product-compliance
Ingram Content Group UK Ltd.
Pitfield, Milton Keynes, MK11 3LW, UK
UKHW040226290926
15471UKWH00001B/22

9 789781 564154